IN THE NAME OF ALLAH, MOST GRACIOUS, MOST MERCIFUL

Muhammad Nejatullah Siddiqi

A *Mujaddid* and Pioneer of Islamic Economics and Finance

Muhammad Nejatullah Siddiqi

A *Mujaddid* and Pioneer of Islamic Economics and Finance

Foreword by
Anwar Ibrahim

Edited by
Mohammad Ahmadullah Siddiqi & Imtiyaz Yusuf

CENTER FOR ISLAM IN THE CONTEMPORARY WORLD
at Shenandoah University

IBT
Islamic Book Trust
Kuala Lumpur

Published by
Center for Islam in the Contemporary World (CICW)
at Shenandoah University
44160 Scholar Plaza Suite 100
Leesburg, Virginia 20176
USA

In collaboration with
Islamic Book Trust
607 Mutiara Majestic, Jalan Othman
46000 Petaling Jaya, Selangor, Malaysia
www.ibtbooks.com

Islamic Book Trust is affiliated with The Other Press.

ISBN: 978-1-955653-08-4

Copyediting: Dr. David Warren

Printed by
Vinlin Press Sdn. Bhd.
No. 2, Jalan Meranti Permai 1
Meranti Permai Industrial Park
Batu 15, Jalan Puchong
47100 Puchong, Selangor D.E.

Contents

APPENDIX

Foreword

Anwar Ibrahim
10th Prime Minister of Malaysia

Growing up in *Angkatan Belia Islam Malaysia* (ABIM—Muslim Youth Movement of Malaysia), many of us immersed ourselves in Nejatullah Siddiqi's works and were profoundly impressed by his, for then, enigmatic thinking. He was a steadfast critic of the prevailing capitalist system and its banks and was deeply engaged in investigating its shortcomings. His thought in fact shaped many of our perspectives.

He once invited me, as an ABIM representative, to visit Aligarh Muslim University in India. We had an exceedingly pleasant meeting during which, in my youthful eagerness to make an intellectual contribution, I suggested that he read the works of socialists to uncover the faults of capitalism. I said the idea was to examine the arguments of both sides to offer a more viable alternative system. He didn't say much in response until three decades later, when we bumped into each other in Jeddah and he exclaimed, "Yes, you are right, young man."

When I became the Minister of Education in the 1990s, we sought to raise the level of intellectual discourse in Malaysia by asking prominent Muslim scholars from across the globe to bring their wisdom to teaching posts in Kuala Lumpur. Nejatullah was one of these figures, but it was only in 2006 that he finally came to fill up the post of Distinguished Professor at the International Islamic University of Malaysia.

Nejatullah agrees with many other economists on the urgent need for a structural and axiological rectification of the current economic system, which is largely defined by the concentration of wealth in the hands of a few and the widening gap of inequality. The 2008 financial crisis—originating in the US financial system, mortgage markets and subprime lending—compelled Washington to create a $700 billion bailout package whereby the state salvaged giant corporations but was unforgivably slow in rescuing the thousands who lost their jobs in layoffs. The enthusiasm once showed by elites proclaiming the capitalist system as the only way to progress following the collapse of communist regimes has proved temporary. And now the world is again flabbergasted by profound disparity and inequality, underscored by new scholarly findings on the subject, such as those by Thomas Piketty[1] and Joseph Stiglitz.[2]

---

[1] Thomas Piketty, *A Brief History of Equality*, trans. Steven Rendall (Harvard University Press London: Belknap Press: An Imprint of Harvard University Press, 2024); Thomas Piketty, *Capital in the Twenty First Century*, trans. Arthur Goldhammer (Cambridge, Massachusetts London: Belknap Press: An Imprint of Harvard University Press, 2017); Thomas Piketty, *Capital and Ideology*, trans. Arthur Goldhammer (Cambridge, Massachusetts ; London, England: Belknap Press: An Imprint of Harvard University Press, 2020).

[2] Joseph E. Stiglitz, *Globalization and Its Discontents Revisited: Anti-Globalization in the Era of Trump* (New York: W. W. Norton & Company, 2018); Joseph E. Stiglitz, *Globalization and Its Discontents* (New York: W. W. Norton & Company, 2002); Joseph E. Stiglitz, *The Road to Freedom: Economics and the Good Society* (New York: W. W. Norton & Company, 2024); Joseph E. Stiglitz, *The Origins of Inequality and Policies to Contain It* (New York: Oxford University Press, 2024); Joseph E. Stiglitz, *The Price of Inequality: How Today's Divided Society Endangers Our Future* (New York:

But communism was never a viable alternative to capitalism. It is prone to dictatorship as it concentrates power in the hands of a bureaucracy, transforming the economic structure into one of military control and regulated markets.

Against this backdrop, it is my conviction that Islamic economics bears an immense responsibility as a viable alternative. I implore our scholars and economists to swiftly develop pathways toward a just and more equitable society, one whose foundations rest upon core ethical principles, to achieve universal need-fulfilment, human dignity with basic freedoms for all and a distribution of income and wealth that maintains balance by keeping inequality in check. Within the national framework of Malaysia MADANI, we have stressed time and again that our notion of Prosperity must consider a state of complete and holistic wellbeing, drawing upon the enduring tradition embodied in the Islamic concept of *falah*—success, happiness and wellbeing coming from the spiritual fulfilment of following the commands of God. We must pursue *falah* by ensuring sustainable economic growth and empowerment and inclusivity of the citizenry with due regard for the spiritual, holistic wellbeing of individuals, communities and the nation.[3]

The Qur'an heavily emphasizes defense of the oppressed, the weak and the downtrodden, and this resonates with most religious and philosophical teachings. The hallmark of such a humane economy is justice and equity, alongside the elimination of corruption and oppression while ensuring sustainability.

W. W. Norton & Company, 2013).

[3] Ibrahim, A. (2023). *SCRIPT: For a Better Malaysia—An Empowering Vision and Policy Framework for Action.* Institut Darul Ehsan and The Centre for Postnormal Policy and Future Studies. http://www.popularonline.com.my/default/catalog/product/view/id/204664/s/9789672066415/

Prohibiting monopolistic practices, oppression of the working class, corruption, extortion and all forms of abuse of power is essential to upholding and imparting justice across all strata of society. These Islamic ideals have been systematically codified and meticulously expanded within the corpus known as *Maqasid al-Shari'ah*, the higher objectives of Islamic law.

During one discussion with Nejatullah, I raised the issues and complexities involved in bridging ideals with practice. He was acutely aware of the gaps between idealism and reality and between policies found in the *turath* (tradition) and those associated with modern practices. And he was sharply critical of the focus on market rather than family and of the overstatement of selected history divorced from the sociology of populations. In his analysis of the universal economic trajectory, he consistently emphasized the role of *Maqasid al-Shari'ah* in realizing ideals for the general populace within a contemporary setting. However, notably absent from these arguments is the state structure within which economic policies operate. I contend that Islamic economics and finance cannot function without good governance. How does one administer an economic system capable of propelling growth and progress? Will any economic model flourish in trust-deficit environments and in the absence of an appropriate legal framework? There must be clarity in both policy and governance, by which we mean preventing leakage and corruption. Countries of the Global South, like many Muslim-majority nations, are not inherently poor; rather, poverty prevails due to endemic corruption, the condoning of power and privilege and the resultant squandering of wealth. However effective Islamic instruments may be, operating within a system of poor governance will hinder the fulfilment of *Maqasid al-Shari'ah*. I believe we must therefore address the fundamentals to establish a correct premise. Good governance is essential. Through it, the economic framework, policies, instruments and institutions may proceed with a far greater prospect of efficiency and success.

Upon this sound foundation, we can then advance into the more practical dimensions of Islamic economics and finance. *Alhamdulillah*, owing to the *idée-force* of enlightened scholars such as Nejatullah Siddiqi, Umar Chapra, Zubair Hasan, Monzer Kahf and Khurshid Ahmad, and paired with robust political will, we did succeed in establishing an Islamic bank, an independent institution with its own financial infrastructure and products.[4] The noble intention was to transcend interest-based transactions that have been rooted in the money economy since the Crusades, a system that has fostered the incestuous creation of money from money, further enriching the wealthy and impoverishing the poor.

We recognize the success of Islamic banking, but it has become clear to us that it constitutes little more than a stunted, minor reform, particularly within the broader framework of *Maqasid al-Shari'ah*. In a session at Harvard University in the presence of the governors of Islamic banks, I said we must move beyond interest-

---

[4] Muhammad U. Chapra, *Islam and the Economic Challenge* (Herndon, VA: Amana Publications, 1992); Muhammad Umar Chapra, *The Islamic Welfare State and Its Role in the Economy* (Leicester: The Islamic Foundation, 1979); Muhammad Umer Chapra, *Objectives of the Islamic Economic Order* (Leicester: The Islamic Foundation, 2007); M. Umer Chapra, *The Future of Economics: An Islamic Perspective* (Leicester: Kube Publishing Ltd, 2016); M. Umer Chapra, *Muslim Civilization: The Causes of Decline and the Need for Reform* (Kube Publishing Ltd, 2015); Muhammad Umer Chapra, *The Islamic Vision of Development in the Light of Maqasid Al-Shari'ah* (Herndon, VA: International Institute of Islamic Thought (IIIT), 2008); Zubair Hasan, *Leading Issues in Islamic Economics and Finance: Critical Evaluations* (Singapore: Palgrave Macmillan, 2020); Dr Monzer Kahf, *Islamic Finance Contracts* (S.I: CreateSpace Independent Publishing Platform, 2015); Khurshid Ahmad, *Studies in Islamic Economics* (Leicester: Islamic Foundation, 1981); "Life and Works of Prof. Khurshid Ahmad," Islamic Economics Project, April 14, 2025, https://islamiceconomicsproject.com/2025/04/14/prof-khurshid-ahmad/.

free banking. Islamic banks are now understood as merely conventional banks without usury, augmented by profit-sharing arrangements. This limited reform of the conventional model has failed to fulfil its developmental promise, owing to inherent weaknesses in its practical application. At the same time, we remain mindful that this does not represent the entire *Maqasid* of Islamic economics. It is a critical beginning, but it must evolve through *islah mastata'tu,* reform to the best of one's ability.

Four decades of experience now call for a thorough post-mortem to unravel the complexities and contradictions arising in part because we were unknowingly subdued by a capitalist worldview and by policies filtered through a lens of profit when we should instead pursue ideals such as honesty, justice and social welfare. The current ecosystem of Islamic banking has paid scant attention to the welfare of the poor and downtrodden. In *A Vision for the Future of Islamic Economics*, Nejatullah laments the failure of Islamic financial institutions to emphasize the problems of inequality and poverty.[5] Islamic finance, in his view, is now being led by "the greedy whims of the free market, like its conventional counterpart." If Islamic finance were truly to live up to its spirit of poverty alleviation, it should have incorporated microfinance and cooperatives from the outset as these institutions are fundamental to serving small enterprises and self-employment, the mainstay of Muslim economies. He advocates liberation from the capitalist worldview and stresses that commercial banks should not be the sole vehicle for financial intermediation in Islamic finance.

There is a deeper problem involving the agents of Islamic finance. To my mind, this can be managed only by cultivating

---

[5] Mohammad Nejatullah Siddiq, "A Vision for the Future of Islamic Economics," September 9, 2013,
http://www.siddiqi.com/mns/AVisionForTheFutureOfIslamicEconomics.ht
m.

laudable attitudes and the fear of God. The issue stems from lucrative Shariah advisory allowances, which may induce a conflict of interest in a *quid pro quo*. The players often resort to legal stratagems to circumvent the Shariah, tilting toward the interests of capital. Products are designed or endorsed to satisfy client demand—such as *bay' al-'inah*, commodity *murabahah* and *tawarruq*—whereby complex contracts are tailored by the *fuqaha'* of Islamic finance to accommodate investors' risk appetites, producing results similar to interest-based contracts in conventional banking without technically violating the prohibition of usury.

Nevertheless, some *fuqaha'* remain faithful to the Shariah; they have not budged before investors' demands for leniency and a compromise of the sacred law. But few have been bold enough to question the industry's prevailing practices and to propose radical solutions. Therefore, more than Islamizing instruments, we need to Islamize the self. We require not only knowledgeable experts and *fuqaha'* within the Islamic economic ecosystem—of whom we are also in dire need—but also sincere ones devoted to the cause of Islam and its values.

Cynicism will grow if these Islamic institutions fail to stand out as authoritative institutions. Many lament the shortcomings of Islamic banks precisely because they differ so little from their conventional counterparts. There is also truth in the perception that Islamic finance has evolved from a strategic decision into opportunistic behavior. Eventually, any institution bearing the Islamic label—be it a bank, a zakat agency, or a Hajj management body—risks falling into the same trap of fraudulent practice. For example, in the case of zakat and, by extension, *awqaf*, a persistent floating sentiment remains over whether funds are being distributed effectively to rescue poor families out of poverty. Nejatullah rightly argues that the principles of accountability, transparency and efficiency must govern both the collection and distribution of zakat, as it holds the potential to be a true gamechanger in addressing poverty and inequality. In addition to that, zakat also requires adequate data and workable models grounded in rigorous analysis to eradicate poverty effectively. Yet Muslim economists and policymakers alike have paid little attention to improving the efficiency of its delivery. The underlying harmony between cultivating the earth (*'imarat al-dunya*) and striving for the hereafter (*ibtigha' al-akhirah*) has always been the defining element of the Islamic worldview. If every Muslim were to calculate and disburse their zakat accurately and faithfully, we could conceivably eliminate poverty from the world.

However, it has not been all gloom and doom in the world of Islamic economics and finance. It has proven to be the most formidable force in dethroning unbridled capitalism, a system which even Keynesian economics struggles to grapple with. But this dialectic must be grounded in the principles of the Shariah as we strive for continuous recalibration and refinement. Nejatullah's call to return to humanity's natural predisposition based on the perfection of ethics (*li utammima makarim al-akhlaq*) in charting the Shariah-based economy underscores the severe unnaturalness of the current global system. The drive for profit must be balanced out by a commitment to welfare; both businesses and individuals thus bear a responsibility to contribute to the prosperity of society. While corporate social responsibility offers a pragmatic policy model based on tax exemptions to encourage generosity among the wealthy, the atmosphere of Islamic economics allows for the natural cultivation of empathy and care for the downtrodden. We should be able to see the strength of the Islamic economic system as a viable and credible alternative and showcase it to the world.

Putrajaya
21st April 2026

References

Ahmad, Khurshid. *Studies in Islamic Economics.* Leicester: Islamic Foundation, 1981.

Chapra, M. Umer. Muslim Civilization: The Causes of Decline and the Need for Reform. Kube Publishing Ltd, 2015.

_____, The Future of Economics: An Islamic Perspective. Leicester: Kube Publishing Ltd, 2016.

Chapra, Muhammad U. *Islam and the Economic Challenge.* Herndon, VA: Amana Publications, 1992.

Chapra, Muhammad Umar. *The Islamic Welfare State and Its Role in the Economy.* Leicester: The Islamic Foundation, 1979.

Chapra, Muhammad Umer. *Objectives of the Islamic Economic Order.* Leicester: The Islamic Foundation, 2007.

_____, *The Islamic Vision of Development in the Light of Maqasid Al-Shari'ah.* Herndon, VA: International Institute of Islamic Thought (IIIT), 2008.

Hasan, Zubair. Leading Issues in Islamic Economics and Finance: Critical Evaluations. Singapore: Palgrave Macmillan, 2020.

Ibrahim, A. (2023). *SCRIPT: For a Better Malaysia—An Empowering Vision and Policy Framework for Action.* Institut Darul Ehsan and The Centre for Postnormal Policy and Future Studies. http://www.popularonline.com.my/default/catalog/product/view/id/204664/s/9789672066415/

Kahf, Dr Monzer. *Islamic Finance Contracts.* S.I: CreateSpace Independent Publishing Platform, 2015.

"Life and Works of Prof. Khurshid Ahmad." *Islamic Economics Project*, April 14, 2025. https://islamiceconomicsproject.com/2025/04/14/prof-khurshid-ahmad/.

Piketty, Thomas. *A Brief History of Equality.* Translated by Steven

Rendall. Harvard University Press London: Belknap Press: An Imprint of Harvard University Press, 2024.

_____, *Capital and Ideology*. Translated by Arthur Goldhammer. Cambridge, Massachusetts; London, England: Belknap Press: An Imprint of Harvard University Press, 2020.

_____, *Capital in the Twenty First Century*. Translated by Arthur Goldhammer. Cambridge, Massachusetts London: Belknap Press: An Imprint of Harvard University Press, 2017.

Siddiqi, Muhammad Nejatullah. "A Vision for the Future of Islamic Economics." September 9, 2013. http://www.siddiqi.com /mns/AVisionForTheFutureOfIslamicEconomics.htm.

Stiglitz, Joseph E. *Globalization and Its Discontents*. New York: W. W. Norton & Company, 2002.

_____, Globalization and Its Discontents Revisited: Anti-Globalization in the Era of Trump. New York: W. W. Norton & Company, 2018.

_____, The Origins of Inequality and Policies to Contain It. New York: Oxford University Press, 2024.

_____, The Price of Inequality: How Today's Divided Society Endangers Our Future. New York: W. W. Norton & Company, 2013.

_____, The Road to Freedom: Economics and the Good Society. New York: W. W. Norton & Company, 2024.

Muhammad Nejatullah Siddiqi— A *Mujaddid* Reformer and Pioneer of Islamic Economics and Finance

Mohammad Ahmadullah Siddiqi & Imtiyaz Yusuf

1. The Socio-Religious *Tajdidi* Thought of Professor Nejatullah Siddiqi

This *festschrift* to honor of Professor Muhammad Nejatullah Siddiqi (1931-2022) is the produced out of the suggestion by Dr. Yaqub Mirza, (1946-2025) the founder and President of the Center for Islam in the Contemporary World (CICW) at the Shenandoah University. This volume comprises of articles by prominent scholars in Islamic Economics, Banking and Finance and Islamic thought from around the world.

Professor. Dr. Nejatullah Siddiqi was born in Gorakhpur, India. After obtaining his initial Islamic education from Rampur and Azamgarh, Professor Siddiqi was educated at Aligarh Muslim University in India from where he received his Bachelor's (1956), Master's (1960) and Ph.D. degree in 1965. He was first appointed as lecturer and went to become an Associate Professor of Economics at the Aligarh Muslim University.

Professor Nejatullah Siddiqi's role as a teacher of Islamic economics first at the department of Economics at the Aligarh Muslim University and his innovative and creative approach to Islam and the social science of economics caught the attention of the then vice-chancellor of the Aligarh Muslim University Professor A.M. Khusro, (1974-79) a distinguished economist himself. In 1977, Professor Khusro appointed Professor Nejatullah Siddiqi concurrently as a professor of economics and also the chairman of the Department of Islamic Studies at the Institute of Islamic Studies of the Aligarh Muslim University. This was first interdisciplinary appointment in the long history of the Aligarh Muslim University and probably for the first time in the Indian academia.[1]

Professor Siddiqi's contribution to Islamic thought along with economics has been applauded globally. He is famously known for his pioneering contribution of Islamic theory of economics and finance for which he was awarded King Faisal International Prize for Islamic Studies in 1982. For his contributions to Islamic Economics, he received the American Finance House Award in 1993 and the Shah Waliullah Award from the Institute of Objective Studies (IOS) in New Delhi in 2003, respectively. In 2010, he was appointed as Emeritus Professor of Management Studies at the Aligarh Muslim University in India.

Professor Nejatullah had pioneered the thinking, planning ad of the discipline of Islamic Economics, Banking and Finance in the modern age. Apart from his contribution to the field of Islamic Economics, Banking and Finance, he was also an original thinker and scholar in Islamic Thought, Islamic Studies and

---

[1] Kamta Prasad, "Obituary: Professor A. M Khusro (1925-2003)," *The Indian Economic Journal* 50, nos. 3-4 (March 2003): 144-46, https://doi.org/10.1177/0019466220030317.

Maqāṣid al-Sharī'at.[2]

Professor Siddiqi was not an ivory tower thinker alienated from understanding the dire and grinding socio-economic conditions of the Ummah. As a Muslim thinker and activist, he was effected by social, political and economic changes at the national and global levels. The main purpose behind developing the contemporary Islamic economic thought is to address a myriad of challenges faced by the Muslims and humanity at large from the materialist social sciences and the related theories borne out of capitalism and communism the two dominant worldviews shaping public policies globally.[3]

As a Muslim thinker of the post-colonial era during which the capitalist and socialist-communist economic thought challenged the Ummah intellectually and practically in the forms of anthropocentric modernity and a desacralized worldview, Professor Siddiqi embarked on a new venture. He stated that, "Our mission was to introduce Islamic ideas to economics. These were at three levels: A background provided by Islam's worldview places economic matters in a holistic framework, a set of goals for

---

[2] *Shari'ah* is referred to as "*Sharī'at*" in Urdu language, it is employed by Professor Siddiqi in the title of his main work in Urdu language titled, *Maqasid-e-Shari'at.*

[3] The eighteenth-century Enlightenment marks the beginning of the modern age, when the scientific method and belief in reason and progress came to hold sway over the Western world. In the twentieth century, however, the Enlightenment has often been judged harshly for its apparently simplistic optimism see. Peter Gay, *The Enlightenment: The Rise of Modern Paganism* (New York: W. W. Norton & Company, 1995); Peter Gay, *The Enlighten-ment: The Science of Freedom* (New York: W. W. Norton & Company, 1996); Anthony D. Smith, *The Ethnic Origins of Nations* (Oxford: Wiley-Blackwell, 1991); Anthony D. Smith, *Nationalism: Theory, Ideology, History* (Cambridge, UK ; Malden, MA: Polity Press, 2010).

individual behavior and monetary policy, [and] norms and values should lead to appropriate institutions."[4] Professor Siddiqi was not intellectually nor socio-theologically alienated from the dire social and economic conditions of the Ummah. He critiqued the underachievements and lesser impact of Islamic Economics, Banking and Finance in alleviating the economic condition of the downtrodden sections of the Muslim Ummah and humanity at large.

Professor Nejatullah Siddiqi was a born researcher, scholar and an original systematic thinker or *Mujaddid*—a reviver or a religious reformer who engaged in revitalizing Islamic thought in general and Muslim socio-economic practice of the Qur'an and Sunnah (practice of Prophet Muḥammad) as dynamic sources for rejuvenating Islamic way of life and thought. Professor Siddiqi delved on the question of revitalizing Muslim way of life and thought in the face of postcolonial era challenges of humanist ideologies and challenges of globalization on the world stage.[5]

Professor Siddiqi's most widely read book which inspired the movement for the growth of Islamic economics and finance as a scientific development is "*Banking Without Interest*," it has been published in 30+ editions between 1973 and 2022. It was first published in Urdu in 1969 by the Markazi Maktaba Jama'at Islami Hind, Delhi. India. Its English translation was published by the Islamic Publications Ltd., Lahore, in 1973; it was reprinted in a third (unchanged) edition in 1980. The Islamic Foundation, Leicester, UK published a substantially improved English

---

[4] "Dr. Nejatullah Siddiqi's Accomplishments," Issu, accessed November 2, 2023, https://issuu.com/isnacreative/docs/ih_january-february_23/s/177925 38.

[5] C. Cahen, "*Dhimma*", in *Encyclopaedia of Islam New Edition Online (EI-2 English)*, ed. P. Bearman (2012), https://doi-org.proxy.library.georgetown.edu/10.1163/1573-3912_islam_SIM_1823.

translation without any revisions or updating of its substance and content in 1983.The book has been translated into numerous languages due to its global reach. Commenting on the popularity of the book, Professor Siddiqi said:

> Thus, the author has to concede in his preface (written in 1981): "The readers' expectations from a book on interest-free banking published in the eighties will most likely be more than this translation can satisfy". So why the re-issue of this book? The main reason given by the author in his preface and by Khurshid Ahmad in his Foreword is that Banking without Interest has a historical value as the first book-length treatment of this subject. And since the subsequent development has "not drastically modified the basic model incorporated in this book it deserves preservation". (Preface). The historical value of Professor Siddiqi's model is beyond all doubt, but for the ordinary reader it should also have an actual value, i.e. should give him something that he cannot find in the same or even better presentation somewhere else.[6]

Apart from his numerous Urdu books, Professor Nejatullah's English-language works include *Islam's View on Property* (1969), *Recent Theories of Profit: A Critical Examination* (1971), *Economic Enterprise in Islam* (1972), *Muslim Economic Thinking* (1981), *Issues in Islamic Banking: Selected Papers* (1983), *Partnership and Profit-sharing in Islamic Law* (1985), *Insurance in an Islamic Economy* (1985), *Teaching Economics in Islamic Perspective* (1996), *Role of State in Islamic Economy* (1996) and *Dialogue in Islamic Economics* (2002). A full bibliography of the writings of Professor Siddiq to Islamic thought including Islamic Economics

---

[6] Volker Nienhaus, "Book Review: Banking Without Interest: The Islamic Foundation," *Journal of King Abdulaziz University: Islamic Economics* 1, no. 2 (1984): 85-90.

in English and Urdu appears at the end of this book. Professor Siddiqi authored 63 significant books, published hundreds of articles and gave thousands of lectures worldwide.

As mentioned earlier, this *festschrift* in honor of Professor Muhammad Nejatullah Siddiqi is produced out of the recommendation of the late Dr. Yaqub Mirza.

Dr. Yaqub Mirza, a longtime friend and admirer of Professor Nejatullah Siddiqi as both of them were engaged in the world of Islamic scholarship, finance and institution-building. Dr. Mirza was a man of few words who would rather build, establish, support and strengthen scholarship and academic centers. Dr. Yaqub himself an expert practitioner of faith-based entrepreneurship sourced in Islamic principles of management style which led to business success in corporate social responsibility. Through his successful business management enterprises, he was instrumental in proving that faith and business ethics are not contradictory rather mutually reinforce societal good.[7]

Dr. Yaqub's legacy challenges us to pursue success not just in creating wealth accumulation but in building systems and organizations that reflect deep religio-ethical commitments.[8]

I, Imtiyaz Yusuf, remember vividly that after the death of Professor Nejatullah Siddiqi in California, USA in November

---

[7] M. Mirza and Miles Davis, "Faith-Based Entrepreneurship," *New England Journal of Entrepreneurship* 13, no. 1 (January 2010): 1-7; M. Yaqub Mirza, *Five Pillars of Prosperity: Essentials of Faith-Based Wealth Building* (Ashland: White Cloud Press, 2014); M. Yaqub Mirza and Gary Moore, *Heavenly Returns: What the Abrahamic Faiths Teach Us about Financial & Spiritual Well-Being* (Center for Islam in the Contemporary World, 2022).

[8] "Dr. Yaqub Mirza, Pioneer of Faith-Based Finance and Philanthropy," Iqra.Ca, December 4, 2025, https://www.iqra.ca/2025/dr-yaqub-mirza-pioneer-of-faith-based-finance-and-philanthropy/.

Decoloniality actively seeks to dismantle ongoing colonial structures and Western-centric thinking, often starting earlier historically (15th century Americas). It emphasizes on political action, linking to indigenous knowledge to break with modernity itself.[12]

In the case of Islam, the postcolonial and decoloniality is aimed at building a Pan-Islamic or Pax-Islamic world. It appeared at with the ending of the Ottoman Caliphate (c. 1299-1922) by Kemal Atatürk (1881-1938) and the emergence of secular nation of Turkey in 1923 and also non-secular Muslim states.[13]

The 1920 Treaty of Sèvres dismantled the Ottoman Empire and divided its territories among the Allies. The following 1923

---

[12] Gurminder K. Bhambra, "Postcolonial and Decolonial Dialogues," *Postcolonial Studies* 17, no. 2 (April 2014): 115-21, https://doi.org/10.1080/13688790.2014.966414; Walter D. Mignolo, "The Geopolitics of Knowledge and the Colonial Difference," *South Atlantic Quarterly* 101, no. 1 (January 2002): 57-96, https://doi.org/10.1215/00382876-101-1-57; Walter D. Mignolo, *The Idea of Latin America* (Malden, MA; Oxford: Blackwell Publishing, 2005); Gayatri Chakravorty Spivak, "Can the Subaltern Speak?" in *Marxism and the Interpretation of Culture* (Champaign, IL: The University of Illinois Press, 1988), 271-316.

[13] David Fromkin, *A Peace to End All Peace: The Fall of the Ottoman Empire and the Creation of the Modern Middle East*, 2 Reprint edition (New York: Holt Paperbacks, 2009); Niyazi Berkes, *The Development of Secularism in Turkey* (New York: Routledge, 1998); Cemil Aydin, *The Idea of the Muslim World: A Global Intellectual History* (Cambridge, Massachusetts: Harvard University Press, 2017); Ismail R. Al-Faruqi, *Islam: Religion, Practice, Culture & World Order*, ed. Imtiyaz Yusuf (London: International Institute of Islamic Thought, 2012); Elie Kedourie, *Afghani and 'Abduh* (London: Routledge, 2014); Jacob M. Landau, *The Politics of Pan-Islam: Ideology and Organization* (Oxford: Oxford University Press, 1994); James Barr, *A Line in the Sand: The Anglo-French Struggle for the Middle East, 1914-1948* (New York: W. W. Norton & Company, 2013).

Treaty of Lausanne established the modern secular Turkish Republic and its borders. The 1920 Treaty of Sèvres carved up Anatolia, creating mandates for France (Syria, Lebanon, Iraq) and Britain (Palestine, Jordan), granting land to Greece, and promising autonomy for Armenians and Kurds, but Turkish nationalists rejected it, leading to war and its supersession by Lausanne, which recognized a sovereign Turkish state.[14]

The postcolonial era also witnessed the creation of 57 Muslim countries who are the members of the Conference of Islamic Organizations as states based on the identities of tribes, races and ethnicities and not as Muslim nations.[15]

Islamic history is replete with references to hundreds of persons who have engaged in the activity of *tajdid*—Islamic revivalism.[16]

The term *mujadid* derived from the Arabic term *tajdid* means "renewal." The term refers to conscious efforts to bring about the renewal of religious faith and practice, emphasizing strict adherence to the prescriptions of the Qur'an and Sunnah—the example of the practice of prophet Muḥammad. A *hadith*—report which is accepted widely is reported to have said that "Allah ﷻ will send to this *Umma* [the post-Hijrah world] at the head of each century those who will renew its faith for it." Narrated by Abu Dawood (4291)

Throughout the twentieth and the twenty first centuries,

[14] Orçun Can Okan, "Treaty of Lausanne and the Construction of the Arab Middle East," *Journal of the Ottoman and Turkish Studies Association* 8, no. 1 (2021): 457-61.

[15] Abdullah Al Ahsan, *OIC: The Organization of the Islamic Conference* (Herndon, Va., U.S.A: Intl Inst of Islamic Thought, 1988); "Organization of Islamic Cooperation," accessed January 12, 2026, https://www.oic-oci.org/.

[16] Sayyid Abul A'la Maududi, *A Short History of the Revivalist Movement in Islam* (Lahore: Islamic Publications Limited, 1963).

the Muslim world witnessed the rise of the movements of monothetic-rationalist renewal of Islam and reform of Muslim countries geared towards their development on the world stage.

The three prominent Muslim movements advocating broader programs of *tajdid* are the الإخوان المسلمون, *al-Ikhwān al-Muslimūn* or the Muslim Brotherhood established in Egypt by Hasan al-Banna in 1928; Jamaat-e Islami in the Indian sub-continent founded by Sayyid Abul Ala Maududi in 1941 and the Ennahda Movement (حركة النهضة, *Ḥarakatu n-Nahḍah* or the *Mouvement Ennahdha* also known as the Renaissance Party of Tunisia, founded in 1981 by Rached Ghannouchi and Abdelfattah Mourou. All of them represent examples of modern-style renewal movements. These movements presented programs for creating Islamic states and societies in the modern world amidst the secular nationalist and radical leftist movements.

The four prominent *mujaddids*—as intellectuals who emerged from these movements are Yusuf al-Qaradawi (1927-2022) as a *mufti*—a jurist and Hasan al-Turabi (1932-1916)—a political theorist for the Muslim Brotherhood of Sudan, Rached Ghannouchi of the Ennahda as a political activist and Mohammed Nejatullah Siddiqi (1931-2022) of Jamaat-e-Islami Hind in India. All four of them viewed *tajdid* as a necessity for rethinking and restructuring the fundamentals of economic, political, social, and legal structures in the Muslim world.[17]

[17] John Voll, "*Tajdid*" in Muḥammad al-Hāshimī. Ḥāmidī and Ḥasan Turābī, *The Making of an Islamic Political Leader: Conversations with Hasan al-Turabi* (Boulder, Colo.: Westview Press, 1998), http://catdir.loc.gov /catdir/enhancements/fy0833/98005352-b.html; Richard C. Martin et al., eds., *Encyclopedia of Islam & the Muslim World* (New York: Macmillan Reference USA, 2004), 675-76; Seyyed Vali Reza Nasr, *Mawdudi and the Making of Islamic Revivalism* (New York: Oxford University Press, 1996); Seyyed Vali Reza Nasr, *The Vanguard of the Islamic Revolution: The*

3. Professor Nejatullah Siddiqi's Life Journey as an Islamic Economist and a *Mujaddid*

Professor Nejatullah Siddiqi was born during the colonial era. He had witnessed the devastation of the Muslim world in the postcolonial age in whose aftermath the Muslims were left with the option to manage their way of life through the ideologies of capitalism posing itself as the world of freedom and godless communism. Both the ideologies subjugated the life, thought and practice of a Muslim both as an individual and as a member of larger society and the world. The postcolonial age offered little option for Muslims to live and practice their way of life independent of dominant ideologies.

His life journey in the development of the theory of Islamic

Jama'at-i Islami of Pakistan (Berkeley, Calif.: University of California Press, 1994); Richard P. Mitchell, *The Society of the Muslim Brothers* (New York: Oxford University Press, 1993); Usaama al-Azami, *Islam and the Arab Revolutions: The Ulama Between Democracy and Autocracy* (London: C Hurst & Co Publishers Ltd, 2021); Sagi Polka, *Shaykh Yusuf Al-Qaradawi: Spiritual Mentor of Wasati Salafism* (Syracuse, New York: Syracuse University Press, 2019); Ron Shaham, *Rethinking Islamic Legal Modernism: The Teaching of Yusuf al-Qaradawi* (Leiden: Brill, 2018); Bettina Gräf and Jakob Skovgaard-Petersen, *Global Mufti: The Phenomenon of Yūsuf al-Qaraḍāwi*—(New York: Columbia University Press, 2009); Azzam S. Tamimi, *Rachid Ghannouchi: A Democrat within Islamism* (Oxford ; New York: Oxford University Press, 2001); Abdelwahab El-Affendi, "The Long March from Lahore to Khartoum: Beyond the 'Muslim Reformation,'" *Bulletin (British Society for Middle Eastern Studies)* 17, no. 2 (1990): 137-51; Ahmad Dallal, "The Origins and Objectives of Islamic Revivalist Thought, 1750-1850," *Journal of the American Oriental Society* 113, no. 3 (1993): 341-59, https://doi.org/10.2307/605385; Ahmad S. Dallal, *Islam without Europe: Traditions of Reform in Eighteenth-Century Islamic Thought* (Chapel Hill: The University of North Carolina Press, 2018); Ahmad Dallal, "Appropriating the Past: Twentieth-Century Reconstruction of Pre-Modern Islamic Thought," *Islamic Law and Society* 7, no. 3 (2000): 325-58.

economics and finance is described in detail in his 2015 article titled, "My Life in Islamic Economics" published in the journal *Critical Muslim.*[18] He starts by describing his educational formation that after finishing his primary school with focus on the study of the natural sciences he joined the Aligarh Muslim University (AMU) in 1949 for his bachelor's degree in economics, Arabic and English literature.

> The decision was influenced by my reading habit. I was devoted to *al-Hilal* and *al-Balagh* magazine, published under the guidance of Maulana Abul Kalam Azad (1888-1958), poet, critic, thinker and one of the great leaders of the Independence Movement. I also read *al-Tableegh*, and was influenced by the Deobandi scholar Maulana Ashraf Ali Thanawi (1863-1943), the author of the famous book on belief and correct conduct (for women), *Heavenly Ornaments.* And, as most young people of my age and time, I studied the works of Maulana Abul Ala Maududi (1903-1979). Two of Maududi's works had a deep impact on me: lectures he gave at Nadwatul Ulama, Lucknow, and a scheme he proposed to Aligarh Muslim University, both in mid-1940s, later published in a collection titled *Taleemat.* Under the influence of these *ulamas*—religious scholars—I abandoned science and the engineering career I had planned. What I wanted now was to learn Arabic, gain direct access to Islamic sources, and discover how modern life and Islamic teachings interacted. I stuck to this mission, even though I had to take a number of detours stretching over six years—to *Sanwi Darsgah e Jamaat e Islami*, Rampur and *Madrasatul Islah* in Saraimir

[18] Muhammad Nejatullah Siddiqi, "My Life in Islamic Economics," *Critical Muslim* (London) 15 (September 2015), 143-158 also available at https://criticalmuslim.com/explore/issues/educational-reform/my-life-islamic-economics.

> before I arrived (again) eventually at Aligarh to earn a PhD in economics.[19]

The years of study at Rampur and Saraimir were distinguished by lively interaction with Ulama discoursing on the Qur'an and Hadith—the traditions of the Prophet, commentaries on the Qur'an, *fiqh* (jurisprudence) and *usul-e-fiqh*—principles of jurisprudence. With such intellectual formation, Siddiqi along with some of his young friends were fired by the same zeal to study modern disciplines of political science, philosophy, economics—with the intention to acquire an understanding of the modern life and thought.

The overall goal was to combine the modern-secular knowledge with traditional religious learning to produce something that would make right what was wrong with the postcolonial world. Their noble intention was welcomed warmly by Dr. Zakir Hussain the then Vice-Chancellor of Aligarh Muslim University (November 1948 – September 1956) and also his colleagues like Professor Mohammad Aaqil Saheb—a professor at Economics and also eminent professors at the Jamia Milliah Islamia, Delhi and at Osmania University in Hyderabad. Dr. Zakir Hussain went to become the President of India (1967-1969).

The mission of the young Siddiqi and friends was to introduce Islamic ideas in economics at three levels: **a)** by introducing the background of economic matters provided by Islam's worldview in a holistic framework; **b)** setting up of goals to be achieved by individual behavior and economic policy; **c)** and a set of norms and values, resulting in appropriate institutions.

The devastating impact of three centuries of colonization on the Muslim communities which had resulted in their stagnation

---

[19] Siddiqi, "My Life in Islamic Economics", 143.

and intellectual deterioration amidst the dark side of capitalism and the Soviet sponsored communism. The young Nejatullah Siddiqi, commented:

> "In Aligarh, I attended lectures by the eminent Marxian economist, D P Mukherji. Those were heady days for socialists in India. Islam and everything Islamic was perceived as anti-socialist, even pro-capitalist. That was what the Mukerji thought. The student body was predominantly pro-Islamic. That provided a lively environment for discussion in the class room and at the campus. The Department of economics had eminent visitors like the British economist J R Hicks and post-Keynesian economist Joan Robinson. Their talks were inevitably followed by discussions along the ideological divide of that time: socialist planning versus unregulated markets. One of my earlier books, *Economic Enterprise in Islam* (1972) was influenced by this controversy. What we learn and discuss is dictated by what we feel is needed and relevant at the time. With that age gone and new challenges emerging, our focus changes and emphases shift. There must be something more enduring in the book as despite its simple language and elementary approach *Economic Enterprise in Islam* continues to inspire students. The reason: it tries to build an Islamic behavioral model and provide a framework for Islamic economic policy in the light of the Qur'an and Sunnah. Unlike other similar publications it is not focused on critiquing capitalism and socialism. It aspires to highlight divine guidance relevant for economic behavior and policy. The book appears incomplete and a little naïve in hindsight as it seems unaware of the problems a cooperative approach would pose with respect to information. As we pass from an agricultural to industrial to service to a knowledge-

> based economy, the information needed for meaningful cooperation among economic agents changes in nature and quantity. It is only during the last two decades that the economics profession has made meaningful progress on that front."[20]

In view of the enormous encyclopedic and comprehensive contributions of Professor Nejatullah Siddiqi in Urdu and English languages. It is very difficult to encapsulate his contribution in a few pages. There is the need to write and analyze his contributions in different areas of knowledge in a deep and comprehensive manner. While he wrote largely in the areas of Islamic economics and banking, his contributions to topics in Islamic thought, Islamization of Knowledge and socio *Maqāṣid-e-Shariat* in the modern age are not of lesser importance, hence our attribution to him the title of a *mujaddid* of the modern era.

In this introduction, we cover the following four themes in the thought of Professor Nejatullah Siddiqi, viz.,

1. *Tawḥīdic* Epistemology—As the Foundation of Islamic Worldview of Life, Thought and Practice;
2. Islamic Economics and Finance;
3. Islamization of Knowledge;
4. *Maqāṣid-e-Shariat*

In the following sections we will delve upon Professor Siddiqi's views on the above-mentioned topics. Hopefully, they will propel further research on Professor Siddiqi's *tajdidi* contributions and its relevance to the contemporary Islamic world.

4. *Tawḥīdic* Epistemology—As the Foundation of Islamic

[20] Siddiqi, "My Life in Islamic Economics", 144-145.

Worldview of Life, Thought and Practice.

Religious epistemology or epistemology of religion aims at providing "an epistemic status (such as knowledge, justification, warrant, and rationality to religious beliefs). The current debate is focused on how religious believers justify belief in God (whether God exists, what attributes God has, what God is doing, etc.)."[21]

Religious epistemology affirms, "Belief in in God. Some form of transcend. Real, has been assumed in virtually every culture throughout human history. The issue of the reasonableness or rationality of belief in God or particular beliefs about God typically arises when a religion is confronted with religious competitors or the rise of atheism or agnosticism. In the West, belief in God was assumed in the dominant Jewish, Christian and Islamic religions. God, in these traditions, is the omnipotent, omniscient, perfectly good and all-loving Creator of the universe (such a doctrine is sometimes called 'bare theism').[22]

Islam is founded on the Qur'anic basis of *Tawḥīdic* epistemology. According to Professor Osman Bakar, the current Rector of the International Islamic University of Malaysia, "*tawḥīdic* epistemology or monotheistic epistemology is the foundation of knowledge. He explained that it is the way of acquiring and understanding knowledge rooted in the oneness of God (*Tawḥīd*). The second (is the) layer, the *tawḥīdic* mind, refers to individual awareness and the application of *tawḥīdic* principles in one's life. The third layer, (is) the *ummatic* mind, (it) focuses on collective consciousness and societal well-being, fostering a sense of shared responsibility. Finally, the outermost layer, *ummatic* excellence, represents the highest standards of ethical, intellectual,

---

[21] Trent Dougherty and Chris Tweedt, "Religious Epistemology," *Philosophy Compass* 10, no. 8 (2015): 547-59, https://doi.org/10.1111/phc3.12185.

[22] Kelly James Clark, *Religious Epistemology* in *Internet Encyclopedia of Philosophy*, n.d., accessed January 25, 2026, https://inep.utm.edu/relig-ep/.

and professional excellence, aiming to serve the broader Muslim community, or the *Ummah*. *Tawḥīdic* epistemology is essential for achieving *ummatic* excellence. He explained that it should guide us towards developing a *Tawḥīdic*—mind, distinguishing it from a non-*tawḥīdic* or anti-*tawḥīdic* ways of thinking. He pointed out that when individuals adopt *tawḥīdic* mind, they align their actions with the oneness of God, fostering unity, compassion, and ethical behavior.[23]

In terms of interreligious relations between the three monotheistic religions of Judaism, Christianity and Islam the Qur'an confirms:

> The Prophet of Islam, and his followers, believe in what has been bestowed upon him from on high by his Sustainer: they all believe in God, and His angels, and His revelations, and His apostles, making no distinction between any of His apostles; and they say: "*We have heard, and we pay heed. Grant us Thy forgiveness, O our Sustainer, for with Thee is all journeys' end!*"—Qur'an 2:285

There is also another Qur'anic acknowledgment of the commonalities between these traditions:

> *Lo! those who believe (in that which is revealed unto thee, Muḥammad), and those who are Jews, and Christians, and Sabaeans whoever believeth in Allah and the Last Day and doeth right surely their reward is with their Lord, and there shall no fear come upon them neither shall they grieve.—*

---

[23] Nur Maisarah Mustafa, "'*Tawhidic* Epistemology Is the Root of *Ummatic* Excellence'—Prof. Emeritus Datuk Dr. Osman Bakar," *IIUM Today*, March 17, 2025, https://news.iium.edu.my/?p=183273; Osman Bakar, *Islamic Civilisation and the Modern World: Thematic Essays* (Brunei Darussalam: UBP Press, 2018).

Qur'an 2:62

Belief in *tawḥīd* involves value of commitment in form of an individual or a societal action and mission as exemplified in the practice of Prophet Muḥammad's ﷺ establishing of an inclusive *ummah.*[24] The *ummah* or the inclusive Muslim community as established during the time of Prophet Muḥammad and later Muslim history embraces all members of humanity.[25] It functions on the Qur'anic principle of promoting the value of *maruf* (good) and prohibiting the *munkar* (bad and evil). (Qur'an 3:11; 2:143)

Professor Nejatullah's emphasis that *tawḥīd*—monotheism as the fundamental belief entails value of commitment in form of an individual or a societal action and mission are absent or not practiced by the contemporary Muslim societies. The Muslims of today are "unemancipated" rather are in bondage; age-degeneration; lacking in proper consciousness of commitment to Allah ﷻ and have instead adopted the non-prescriptive practice of "following in the footsteps of their forefathers" mentioned above.[26]

For Nejatullah, to make *tawḥīd* a process requires: a) emancipatory educational training which will enable, "(wo)men who think for themselves, exercise their judgment and make their own choice. They must be emancipated from the menial slavery and cultural imitation of other human beings by allowing for empiricism and the use of the faculties of observation, inference

---

[24] Muhammad Nejatullah Siddiqi, "*Tawhid*: The Concept and the Process," in *Islamic Perspectives: Studies in Honour of Mawlana Sayyid Abul a'la Mawdudi* (Leicester: Islamic Foundation, 1979), 22; Muhammad Hamidullah, *The First Written Constitution in the World: An Important Document of the Time of the Holy Prophet*, Third revised edition (Lahore: Sh. Muhammad Ashraī, 1975).

[25] Siddiqi, "*Tawhid*: The Concept and the Process," 22.

[26] Siddiqi, "*Tawhid*: The Concept and the Process," 27.

and reasoning which generally hardly have any place in the mind of the contemporary Muslim. Creativity hardly has any role and knowledge is reduced to the learning of the already known. Religious behavior has become synonymous with behavior regulated by authority; b) transforming of religious life from inward to outward looking—value-oriented intellect of man and c) removal of human intermediaries who have become blockages in direct contact between the human and Allah ﷻ.[27]

> The consequences of this loss of freedom, fall from the status of being human, and lack of commitment to the will of Allah ﷻ and the un-mindfulness of the concomitant Mission are many. Economic backwardness, political disintegration, social chaos, moral degeneration, intellectual stagnation and spiritual decay, all are the results of the distorted religion that prevails in the name of Islam. Islam in the first place is not a list of "dos" and "do nots" to which one is nowadays urged to conform. It is the live man-God relationship depicted above that is based on *tawḥīd*, the concept as well as the process. Islam is not a static system of rules and rituals. It is rather a dynamic process in which man himself actively participates. It involves knowing, thinking and creating. It involves learning, inventing and constructing.[28]

Therefore, the contemporary Islamic movement should standup for the task of not only working for the establishing of Islam among the Muslims but the whole of humanity. It should not remain, "preoccupied with the revival of traditional religiosity in Muslim countries and involved in political struggle with their westernized elite, both the Muslims and other people in general will have to wait for a fresh attempt for the regeneration of

[27] Siddiqi, "*Tawhid*: The Concept and the Process," 28-29.

[28] Siddiqi, "*Tawhid*: The Concept and the Process," 29.

humanity on the basis of *tawḥīd*."[29] In other words, liberation through *tawḥīd* otherwise the contemporary Muslims will have wasted their life energies.

Herein lies the evidence of the role of Professor Nejatullah Siddiqi as *mujaddid* of the modern era in both thought and action.

It is on the basis of the above described *Tawḥīdic* epistemology that Professor Nejatullah Siddiqi made his important contributions to Islamic thought and movement until his last breath.

5. Islamic Economics and Finance

There is much written on the formation of a new discipline of Islamic economics and finance by Professor Nejatullah Siddiqi. His pioneering contribution continues to influence this field until today. Islamic economics and finance as well as banking have grown into a worldwide phenomenon today. Professor Siddiq's contribution to it both in terms of similarities and differences and divergence from conventional economics and finance is well described as follows:

> Mohammed Nejatullah Siddiqi, a prominent Islamic economist of the recent decades, to the subject of economics. Siddiqi, renowned for his substantial contributions to the reexamination of Islamic economics within a contemporary context and its relevance in the current global economic system, is also celebrated for his innovative solutions to the challenges of its practical implementation. Central to his research, particularly in the analysis of practice, is the notion that the principles of Islamic economics are harmonious with contemporary economics. In several of his works, he contends that the Islamic economic philosophy aligns with classical liberal

[29] Siddiqi, "*Tawhid*: The Concept and the Process," 33.

> economic concepts, including rationality, individual freedom, private property, and market economy, thereby substantiating this approach. However, Islamic economics diverges from conventional economic theory in its treatment of interest, *riba*, and ethical concerns, despite sharing significant parallels in certain aspects. Its solution to these difficulties makes it a notable and environmentally friendly model. Siddiqi's formulation of a systematic framework for Islamic economics is a significant contribution he has made to the discipline. By integrating the fundamental scriptures of Islam and traditional *fiqh* sources with contemporary economic analysis, this approach facilitates the advancement of Islamic economics as a scholarly field and its active participation in current economic discussions. Furthermore, his proposed remedies for practical issues actively contribute to the advancement of Islamic finance, which he asserts is harmonious with the contemporary financial system. Consequently, he is regarded as one of the trailblazers who established the fundamental principles of Islamic finance.[30]

Professor Nejatullah also recognized that merely Islamic critiquing of the capitalist and communist economic philosophies and models are not enough. There was a need for a new approach in identifying economic agents. Instead of placing them in the market as buyers-consumers and sellers-producers, why not focus on the family or the household from where they come? One advantage of doing so would be downgrading self-interest as the motive force behind economic behavior. We are born into a

[30] Murat Ustaoğlu and Cenap Çakmak, eds., *The Palgrave Encyclopedia of Islamic Finance and Economics* (Cham: Springer Nature Switzerland, 2024), 1-10, https://doi.org/10.1007/978-3-030-93703-4.

family and benefit from loving care of the mother and other members of the household. We experiences gift relationship before self-interest enters the picture. Reciprocity precedes exchange relationships:

> "because by projecting the market as the premier economic institution and obliterating the roles of family and community, conventional economics wrongly projected competition as the engine of progress, relegating cooperation to the margins ... I think we, those working on Islamic economics, were duped by the ruling ethos of the mid-twentieth century. We neglected the rich Islamic literature on *tadbeer e manzil* (management of the household) and missed a potential pad for launching an alternative to conventional economics, eschewing the scarcity-selfishness-competition-maximization route, which inevitably leads to aggression and is responsible for the mess in which humanity currently finds itself."[31]

In 1968, Professor Nejatullah published *Islam's View on Ownership* (1968) with quotations from the Qur'an and Sunnah and precedents from early Islamic history. He emphasized on the limits within which ownership rights had to be exercised and the obligations the owner had towards others. He also called for the intervention by the authorities to ensure that such goals as meeting basic universal needs and keeping disparities in the distribution of income and wealth were kept in check. His argument was based on Islam and not socialism or communism.[32]

As a budding Islamic Economist—an unimaginable theorist of the Cold War era in other words "a world without Islam" when being a Muslim was a private and personal affair according to the

---

[31] Siddiqi, "My Life in Islamic Economics", 145.

[32] Siddiqi, "My Life in Islamic Economics", 146.

philosophy of secular Enlightenment.[33] The young Nejatullah wished to write his, "doctoral dissertation on interest-free banking but was persuaded to opt instead for 'a critical examination of the recent theories of profit' to avoid a tiff with the examiners."[34] The academics at the Department of Economics at AMU had serious reservation about mixing Islam with economics ... only few in the department fully endorsed the idea of applying Islam to economics, yet, the idea caught on.[35] He graduated with a Ph.D. in Economics with a doctoral thesis titled, "A Critical Examination of the Recent Theories of Profit" from the AMU in 1966.

As an awakened decolonized young mind, Nejatullah Siddiqi along with his friends launched a quarterly journal aptly titled *Islamic Thought* (1954-1971)—an indication of the formation of Nejatullah Siddiqi not only as Muslim economist but also a Muslim thinker of the postcolonial age. The journal drew inspiration from the thought of the pioneers of Islamic revivalism.[36] He continued pursuing his dream of developing the theory of Islamic Economics and Finance as integral part of the discipline of Economics. "It all culminated with the First International Conference on Islamic Economics, held in Mecca in 1976. It was attended by vice chancellors from several universities. Among them was the Vice Chancellor of Aligarh, the eminent economist A M Khusro (1925-2003), who returning back home suggested the Department of Economics should take initiative in teaching Islamic economics. Encouraged, I moved a resolution at the Board of Studies that an optional course on economic thinking in Islam should be introduced at the Master's level. I lost the

[33] Margaret Jacob, *The Secular Enlightenment*, p. 145. (Princeton (N.J.) Oxford (GB): Princeton University Press, 2019); Hugh McLeod, *Religious Crisis of the 1960s* (Oxford; New York: Oxford University Press, 2010).

[34] Siddiqi, "My Life in Islamic Economics", 146.

[35] Siddiqi, "My Life in Islamic Economics", 146.

[36] Ali Rahnema, ed., *Pioneers of Islamic Revival* (London: Zed Books, 2006).

motion by one vote as the chairman, supported by some senior lecturers, thought adopting it would make the department of economics look like the department of theology or Islamic studies. The course was introduced two decades later. Another decade would pass before the Academic Council of AMU would adopt a resolution to establish a post-graduate Diploma in Islamic Banking and Finance in the department of Business Administration leading to a full-fledged department of Islamic Finance."[37] By 1980s, "Many universities were now teaching Islamic economics and doctoral dissertations and the subject proliferated even in western universities. Besides the International Centre for Research in Islamic Economics at the King Abdulaziz University, Jeddah, which publishes the *Journal of Islamic Economics*, there were now half a dozen others focusing on research and publications. I joined the Jeddah Centre in early 1980s. It seemed that Islamic economics and Islamic Banking had come of age."[38]

The initiation of Islamic Economics and Finance began at the Aligarh Muslim University, India. This was before the advent of the intellectual movement of Islamization of Knowledge led by Professor Ismail al-Faruqi and others at the 1977 First World Conference on Muslim Education (WCME) held in Mecca, a landmark event aiming to revitalize Islamic civilization by reorganizing education on Islamic concepts, integrating faith with modern learning, and addressing secular influences.[39]

Professor Nejatullah's Siddiqi's books *Banking Without Interest* and its companion volume, *Banking Without Interest and Partnership and Profit-Sharing in Islamic Law,* came out in late

---

[37] Siddiqi, "My Life in Islamic Economics", 147.

[38] Siddiqi, "My Life in Islamic Economics", 147.

[39] Ismail R. Al-Faruqi, *Islamization of Knowledge: General Principles and Workplan* (Wyncote, PA: International Institute of Islamic Thought, 1982).

1960s. The book produced practitioners as well as new ventures in Islamic economics and finance. For example, the Malaysian, Tabung Haji, pilgrim fund board, was established in 1963 and survives up to now as does the Philippine Amanah Bank, established in 1973, with a changed name. The Mit Ghamr Savings Bank, established in Egypt in 1963 by Dr. Ahmad Elnaggar, is widely regarded as the first modern, successful implementation of interest-free Islamic banking. It focused on profit-sharing for local investments instead of interest-based loans. The project thrived before being absorbed into the state banking system by 1967. While the Islamic bank established in Karachi by Ahmad Irshad is almost forgotten."[40]

During 1970s Islamic banking and finance movement got a boost with establishment of the Dubai Islamic Bank in the private sector and the Islamic Development Bank in Saudi Arabia as an inter-governmental joint venture, both materialized in 1975.

Political changes in Iran, Pakistan and Sudan during the 1970s favored Islamic initiatives; and global banks and financial giants like Citi, Standard Chartered, ABN Amro, and HSBC, etc., also started engaging in Islamic banking. The idea of Islamic economics and finance is not restricted to banking activities but is also part of the social welfare movements in both Muslim majority and minority countries around the world. "This continued through the 1980s till the first audible voices began to be heard wondering how Islamic could be an 'Islamic finance' which operated within the comfort zone of capitalism with its consumerism, greed and increasing concentration of wealth."[41]

Professor Nejatullah has also elaborated on the problems in the Muslim aspirations for Islamic economics and finance by pointing out new and emerging challenges. He forewarned that:

---

[40] Siddiqi, "My Life in Islamic Economics", 147.
[41] Siddiqi, "My Life in Islamic Economics", 147.

1. "A main problem is that Muslim aspiration is totally out of sync with contemporary reality. Muslim aspiration to teach the world the compassionate economics preached by the Prophet Muḥammad ﷺ requires serious research as well as viable institution building.[42]

2. Islamic economics is not merely a part of religious or traditional form approaches to the study of Islam because of the, "Apathy towards empirical studies seems embedded in religious scholarship ... No one seems to be interested in empirical field work, or learn from ground reality or pays heed to how and why behavior is changing.[43]

3. The resistance on the part of the Ulama—religious who live by the dictum that, "It is enough for us to learn what the great *fuqaha* (jurists) among the *salaf* (first three generations of Muslims) have said and to transmit their opinions faithfully to posterity and in "the challenges we are facing, and are likely to face in the future, will the methodology ... Our current methods of teaching crush all independent thinking, extinguish any flicker of curiosity and kill all creativity. Absence of empirical work makes our researches hollow. We are entirely focused on texts to the total neglect of observing ground realities and learning lessons history can teach. The young minds under the tutelage of our professors and researcher are denied the benefits of a larger conversation encompassing intuition, dialogue and pragmatic considerations in dealing with their subjects of study."[44]

4. Even the way we examine history is seriously flawed. A

---

[42] Siddiqi, "My Life in Islamic Economics", 149.

[43] Siddiqi, "My Life in Islamic Economics", 150.

[44] Siddiqi, "My Life in Islamic Economics", 150-151.

selective approach is the norm. Modern historians find serious gaps between theory and practice in the Islamic past. Muslim scholars paint an idealized picture of history where everything was rosy. Truth suffers in both cases depriving us from the real benefits of history ... We have to assume that all Muslims in history were sincere, decent and shining beacons of humanity! Variety of interpretations as well as the compulsion of circumstances cannot be recognized."[45]

5. Opting for a, "selective view of Islamic history combined with little attention to the reality around us often results in mass depression or acute frustration, which could lead to violence ... Whatever I know about the leadership of Islamic parties in the Arab world, the Indian subcontinent and South-East Asia this is a common malaise. There is very little tolerance of dissent. Nobody invites criticism. There is no tradition of democratic decision making. Both naivety and intolerance are wicked, but their combination has been fatal. As a result the theory and practice of Islamic economics and banking is flawed, full of anomalies, and have basically failed as projects. All we can do is to congratulate ourselves on having re-invented capitalism by using Islamic jurisprudence!"[46]

6. I realized some years back that Muslims in general and the *ulema* in particular had no idea how banks functioned. The role of credit and the process of money creation in a fractional reserve system were beyond their comprehension. They could understand some institution that took people's money with the promise of doing profitable business for a share in the returns. My works,

[45] Siddiqi, "My Life in Islamic Economics", 151.
[46] Siddiqi, "My Life in Islamic Economics", 151.

building on the idea of *al-mudarib yudarib* (the working partner obtaining people's money to use it profitably entering into a similar relationship with another person), argued that banking was possible by replacing fixed interest payment by a share in profit. In other words, it projected profit-sharing as a possible basis of financial intermediation. Meanwhile some scholars think it will be better to do away with banks and switch over to some other institution having roots in Islamic history, like *baitulmal*, the financial institution responsible for the administration of taxes in an 'Islamic state'. The debate continues. But I am not impressed by this trend of returning back to Islamic history literally. Our Prophet ﷺ retained business practices that were honest and fair. He rejected only what was harmful, like gambling and interest on loans. After all, institutions are means for realizing certain goals and operationalization of certain values. Banking itself is not without precedents in early Islamic history.[47]

7. The recent financial crisis has exposed the inequities and inefficiencies of the current system of money and finance initiating a world-wide rethink. Instead of promoting human felicity on a universal scale, it is enriching the top one percent and relegating most of humanity to the margins of poverty. But the discussion is focused around the mechanics of banking and finance at the expanse of the core issue: who are we creating wealth for and how can it reach them. Once again there are calls for separating investment banking from managing medium of exchange and doing away with fractional reserve in favor of hundred percent reserves. But the real issue is how risk is

[47] Siddiqi, "My Life in Islamic Economics", 154.

treated. I think no reform of the financial system would be effective until money and monetary policy are also radically changed. Debts carrying interest should not serve as money. Risks and uncertainties attending upon the human situation should be fairly distributed and shared.[48]

8. Modern money is all debts. I think it is this point which, above all, needs to be argued clearly and convincingly. Money is created at the central bank level and injected into the economy in exchange for bonds (promises to pay later). This 'high powered money' enables commercial banks to create more money (demand deposits) as debts owed to them. All debts carry interest. Since mere passage of time is no guarantee for growth to take place and not all money is used for productive purposes, default is built into the system and so is increasing inequality. More and more of the new wealth resulting from using money flows to the owners of money. A system that rewards enterprise more than it rewards mere ownership would be more efficient as well as more equitable. Such a system requires money that is not debt and debts that carry no interest.

   So how do we move forward in this new and rapidly changing context?[49]

9. There is a need for new text books. "It is clear that the current system has passed it 'sell by' date. Teaching current textbooks in modern economics prepares the students for endorsement of capitalism. Continuing with traditional curriculum is guaranteed to alienate the student from their environment. The confused products of our economic departments cannot make any progress towards a just and equitable society.

[48] Siddiqi, "My Life in Islamic Economics", 154.

[49] Siddiqi, "My Life in Islamic Economics", 155.

Economic management, especially monetary and financial arrangements, need to be put in an appropriate perspective. We have to create an environment that sustains and enhances the quality of life ... Growth alone does not ensure that the basic and universal needs of all are fulfilled. Indeed, growth may fuel inequality, increase deprivation and foster conflict. Capitalism's failure lies in its exclusive focus on growth without any commitment to sustenance with dignity for all.[50]

10. Focus on *Maqāṣid* approach can avoid this by focusing on *Maqāṣid* (purpose, intent and higher objectives) of Islam that are multi-faceted.

    Maqāṣid impacts the human situation on a number of levels. First, every rule serves some purpose; Islamic rules are neither arbitrary nor random. Second, should a rule cease to serve its purpose due to changed conditions it has to be replaced by one designed to serve the original purpose. Third, a situation not covered by existing rules is to be handled by devising a new rule rooted in the relevant *Maqāṣid*. Fourth, if implementation of a rule results in a perverse or an undesirable outcome, that rule has to be abandoned in favor of one suited to the relevant *Maqāṣid*. These points are well argued in the literature on *Maqāṣid*.

    Unfortunately, the current approaches to economic management, especially in money and finance, fail to take cognizance of them. They remain beholden to conventional ideals and try to operate within the framework of *fiqh* or jurisprudence codified a thousand years ago under different circumstances. Classical jurists gave due weight to *manfi* (interests), *masalih 'aammah*

[50] Siddiqi, "My Life in Islamic Economics", 156.

(public interest) and *ma'alat* (consequences), but the current generation of jurists advising decision-makers do not have the courage to do so. They are endorsing financial products that flood the market with debt documents which they allow to be traded. A commitment to *Maqāṣid* would have prevented such anomalies and given us Islamic models worth emulation by rest of the world.

Maqāṣid are clearly stated in the Qur'an. Sustenance has to be universally ensured based on God-given provisions (7:10). A share for the have-nots is appointed in the wealth of the haves (70:24-25). Ensuring justice and fairness in all relationships is the very purpose of God's Law (57:25 and 4:58). Chaos and disorder have to be prevented and felicity (*salah*) instituted (28:71; 30:41).

Traditional Shariah experts are suspicious of the idea of replacing old rules by rules designed to serve *Maqāṣid* in changed situation ... But this is not supported by the Prophetic precedents, who adopted different strategies in different circumstances, the focus being the *Maqāṣid*: communicating God's message, protecting those from harm who accepted the message, and being merciful to humanity in general.[51]

11. Whither Islamic economics? Professor Nejatullah comments, "The future of Islamic economics and finance is tied to our efforts to rethink the entire economic system as well as in promoting criticism and self-criticism and generate new ideas. The decline of the West and the shifts in power to the East provides us with an opportunity—it may be accompanied by rejection of capitalism or at the

---

[51] Siddiqi, "My Life in Islamic Economics", 157.

least its radical modification. The most pernicious product that Western Capitalism is leaving behind is inequality and the indignity that it has visited on the bulk of humanity. Islam with its emphasis on equality, human brotherhood and sharing may well succeed in building an economy that is different. But we need new ideas suited to our time. Ideas change behavior, give birth to institutions and change the reality on the ground. Unfortunately, our record is generating new ideas is not encouraging. But I am still hopeful. Waiting and watching for the formulation and popularization of the new and innovative ideas to emerge from Islam and Muslims.[52]

5. Islamization of Knowledge

The postcolonial and the era of Muslim nationalism in its variety of forms and models witnessed the emergence of the Islamic educational movement the Islamization of Knowledge.

Professor Ismail al-Faruqi and the scholars of the International Institute of Islamic Thought (IIIT) are identified as the founders of this movement. Professor Faruqi was the philosopher-activist of this movement. As a scholar-activist, Isma'il al Faruqi was very much concerned with the state of education in the Muslim world in the post-colonial era of the 1960s to the 1980s when Western secular, capitalist, Orientalist, and Marxist approaches towards knowledge were presented to Muslim and third world academia as the only valid approaches to knowledge. This trend was causing a heavy toll on the state of the Muslim mind and approach to knowledge, especially in the area of religion and politics, and also in agricultural practices and economics. These influences were sapping at the very roots of the Islamic worldview, way of life, thought, practice, and civilization.

---

[52] Siddiqi, "My Life in Islamic Economics", 158.

The prevalence of such an intellectual environment demanded an educational reform in the Muslim world. This led to the call for the First World Conference on Muslim Education, which was held in Makkah, Saudi Arabia, between 31 March and 8 April 1977. It was attended by 313 Muslim Scholars from various parts of the world and different areas of discipline.

The conference resulted in the establishment of the international Islamic universities in Islamabad, Pakistan (1980); Kuala Lumpur, Malaysia (1983); Say, Niger (1986) and Mbale, Uganda (1988) which were recognized by the Organization of Islamic Cooperation (OIC). The Makka conference on Muslim Education resulted in the initiation of Islamization of Knowledge in different disciplines.[53]

The conference addressed the issue of the theoretical and methodological dichotomy and dualism in the educational system of secular vs Islamic; secular humanistic basis of modern education; the disenchantment of nature, the desacralization of politics and the deconsecration of values.

Reflecting on the history, achievements and the status of the Islamization of Knowledge project in 2011 i.e. thirty-four years since the 1977 Makkah conference, Professor Nejatullah Siddiqi

---

[53] Syed Sajjad Husain and Syed Ali Ashraf, *Crisis in Muslim Education*, Islamic Education Series (Sevenoaks [England], Jeddah [Saudi Arabia]: Hodder and Stoughton ; King Abdulaziz University, 1979); Muhammad Naguib Al-Attas, *Aims and Objectives of Islamic Education*, Islamic Education Series (Sevenoaks [England], Jeddah: Hodder and Stoughton ; King Abdulaziz University, 1979); Mohammad Wasiullah Khan, *Education and Society in the Muslim World*, Islamic Education Series (Sevenoaks, Kent, Jeddah [Saudi Arabia]: Hodder and Stoughton ; King Abdulaziz University, 1981); Isma`il R. Al-Faruqi and Abdullah Omar Nasseef, eds., *Social and Natural Sciences: The Islamic Perspective*, Islamic Education Series (Sevenoaks, Kent: Hodder and Stoughton : King Abdulaziz University, Jeddah, 1981); Al-Faruqi, *Islamization of Knowledge*.

made the following remarks:

1. The assumptions on which the Islamization of knowledge project was linked to the movement for restoration of Islam to a position of leader-ship and dominance in contemporary society may not have all been correct.
2. Knowledge creation and beneficial use of new knowledge are two distinct though complementary processes. Each has its own requirement.
3. Morality rooted in spirituality is decisive in ensuring that new knowledge is used beneficially.
4. Creation of new knowledge requires freedoms of thought and discussion, encouragement of creativity and innovation, and toleration of dissent and diversity.
5. It requires a mindset that can entertain ambiguity, one that does not hasten to discard potential spoilers of legacies long established as sacred requirements which the sponsors of the Islamization of knowledge project might have failed to give due weight.
6. The project can be revived only by recognizing the primacy of expanding knowledge over the necessity of ensuring proper use of knowledge. It is in the nature of the first, expansion of knowledge (by creating new knowledge) that is universal.
7. Differences of faith or moral vision, so important in the context of the second stage (putting knowledge to good use) need not stand in the way of cooperation and collaboration in the first stage.
8. Have the sponsors of the Islamization project neglected this truth?
9. What could be worse: have they abdicated the first step in

their eagerness to do justice to the second?

10. Professor Siddiqi called for the expansion of the Islamization of knowledge project saying that for it become a universal movement the enthusiasts of Islamization should not consider it as an exclusively Muslim project. Rather it should invite the rest of humanity to join in expanding knowledge, while simultaneously working for creating universal awareness of what makes use of knowledge beneficial and prevents the fatal error of allowing *laissez-faire* in the use of knowledge.
11. I also argue that conceiving of knowledge as a tool for power and hegemony can be frustrating if not outright destructive.
12. Last but not the least, we cannot know all that needs be known and, no less important, not everything is known with the same degree of certainty.
13. Humility requires that we recognize our limits. Ambiguity and a degree of uncertainty is built into the human situation. It cannot be wished away.
14. Having adopted a humble stance, the way forward is to share the quest of knowledge and its proper use with all and everyone.
15. Delinking Islamization of knowledge from a quest for world leadership and political power; changing the focus from Ummah to humanity at large; expanding the search for solutions involving all rather than ʿulama only; encouraging Muslims to think, speak up, listen, discuss, tolerate dissent, and accept decisions made through mutual consultation ... all these steps are necessary but not sufficient conditions for realizing our objectives:

knowledge responding to the changing needs of the time that is used in a beneficial way, and guided by a moral vision rooted in spirituality.

This moral vision, and the spirituality needed to sustain it, is fortunately available to us in Qur'an and Sunnah. What is needed is reaching out to humanity to build a consensus around this vision.

16. Islamization-of-knowledge teams continue working at the fringe of institutions of modern learning in Muslim countries and communities, if not outside them. This keeps them starved of manpower and financial resources and severely restricts the reach of Islamization ideas among Muslims while decreasing their credibility among others.

    This situation must be remedied by bringing these teams in the mainstream. This can happen if we sympathize with the objectives of modernizers and they see in the objectives of Islamization something not hostile to what they do but likely to add value to what they are doing. It is easier to navigate the globalized scenario around us if we emphasized similarities rather than the differences. The change of stance is a must if we want to avoid marginalization leading to irrelevance.

17. Islamization of Knowledge project should by identifying a few basic values shared by almost everybody, by the entire humanity. These would include justice and fairness (*'adl*), compassion and benevolence (*ihsan*) and mutual accommodation and cooperation (*samaha, ta'awun*).

18. The emphasis should be on expanding knowledge as well as on preserving knowledge accumulated so far. And also translating values into institutions and behaviors

appropriate for our time and place.

19. In view of differences in terms of time and space of the earlier generations there is the need to use scientific knowledge under the guidance of values such as truth, justice, beauty, and goodness.

20. Research in revealed knowledge as well as in social and natural sciences should be directed more and more toward problems facing all peoples. Ecological imbalances, global warming, water shortage, world peace, weapons of mass destruction, terrorism, poverty alleviation, increasing inequalities, failing states, corrupt democracies, crumbling families, insecure neighborhoods, increasing levels of anxiety, new epidemics, etc.

21. While specialization is absolutely necessary, every Muslim should be encouraged to approach Qur'an and Sunnah directly for personal as well public matters.

22. Power relations should be left to be shaped by convenience, local traditions, and popular aspirations. Knowledge, its acquisition, importation, and use should not be seen as a means to political power and domination.

23. The teaching of Islamic sciences should be updated to include later development, rather than being frozen in fifth century ah. Latest thinking on social economic and political issues, informed by the bitter experiences of recent decades, should guide the teaching of social sciences. The inspirations Muslim scholars derive from divine guidance could also be utilized at that stage.

24. Muslim intellectuals and educationists should reach out to non-Muslim intellectuals and educationists, including men of faith, for meaningful dialogue and cooperation. It is high time we came out of our narrow shells and

breathed freely, exploring the vast possibilities of global cooperation.[54]

6. *Maqāṣid-e-Shariat*

Professor Nejatullah Siddiq's last book in Urdu titled, *Maqāṣid-e-Shariat* (Objectives of the Shariah) is a *magnum opus* in terms of his unique contribution to both the advancement and expansion of the Islamic revivalist thought. Professor Siddiqi's *Maqāṣid-e Shari'at* was published in two editions. The first edition published in 2009 comprised of eight chapters.[55] The second edition published in 2017 comprises of 12 chapters; he added 4 new chapters to it.[56] The chapters no. 6 and 12 are translated by Professor Muhammad Ahmadullah Siddiqi, they appear as appendix to this book.

Professor Siddiqi's *Maqāṣid-e Shari'at* raises pertinent issues concerning the restrictions placed on the discourse of *Maqāṣid* and the role the *ulama/fuqaha* jurist-class who consider this subject as their own preserve which is limited to offering *fatwas*—legal opinions. Such restrictions and limitations placed on the discourse of *Maqāṣid-e Shari'at* does not lead to the higher exercise of doing *ijtihad*—systematic original thinking based on the objectives of the Shariah principles in the Qur'an and the Sunnah of Prophet Muḥammad. Professor Nejatullah opines that the need of the hour is to expand the exercise of *ijtihad* based on Shariah objectives to different areas of *ilm*—addressing the new

---

[54] Mohammad Nejatullah Siddiqi, "Islamization of Knowledge: Reflections on Priorities," *American Journal of Islam and Society* 28, no. 3 (July 2011): 15-34, https://doi.org/10.35632/ajis.v28i3.335.

[55] Muhammad Nejatullah Siddiqi, *Maqāṣid-e-Shari'at* (New Delhi: Markazi Maktabah-e-Islami Publishers, 2009).

[56] Mohammad Nejatullah Siddiqi, *Maqāṣid-e-Shari'at* (New Delhi: Markazi Maktabah-e-Islami, 2017).

and future theological-sociological-political-economic and other challenges facing the Muslims and the humanity at large.

Dr. Siddiqi was not only an economist but also a native Islamic thinker who had for several decades held that envisioning Islamic economy in twenty-first century is better done by addressing the issue of poverty and inequality in Muslim countries and the world at large. He had come to a conclusion that implementation of Islamic economics and finance has become an elitist enterprise. It has not yet achieved its main objective of bridging the gap between the rich and the poor who still grinding in poverty, illiteracy, malnutrition and poor health conditions.

He was of the view that there is a need to separate between Islam as a way of life and the objectives of Islamic jurisprudence through innovative methodology addressing serious issues facing humanity.[57] While it important to discuss the known rules of *fiqh* as done routinely, it is also important to expand the discussion to a wider topic such as what does *Sharia* have to offer for the building a better future for all humanity. He opined that Muslims can play a crucial role in this endeavor both as individuals and also as members of humanity. Professor Siddiqi held an inclusive definition of the term Ummah as defined in the Qur'an which addresses the entire humanity. The Qur'an is not only an exclusivist revelation for the Muslim only. The problems faced by the entire humanity are also the problems of the Muslims. The Qur'an calls upon the Muslims to play to their role of being the best of people,

> *"You are the best community ever raised for humanity—you encourage good, forbid evil, and believe in Allah."—Qur'an 3:110*

---

[57] Abdul Azim Islahi, "Book Review: *Maqāṣid-e Sharīʿat* (Objectives of the Shariah)," *Journal of King Abdulaziz University: Islamic Economics.* (Jeddah) 23, no. 2 (2010): 238, 224, https://doi.org/10.4197/islec.23-2.9.

For Professor Nejatullah, the issues to be addressed by the *Maqāṣid-e Shari'at* do not only concern *Usul al-Din* (the roots or fundamental beliefs) and *Furu'* the practical, derivative laws and obligations of Islam but also the problems that concern the entire humankind, which cannot be solved unless collective efforts of the whole population of the world are exerted to solve them. For example, problems of global warming, environmental pollution, prevention of epidemics, weapons of mass destruction, and maintenance of global peace and security.[58]

> According to Dr. Siddiqi, the teachings of the Qur'an and the Sunnah which enjoin goodness toward the whole mankind, require us to exert our efforts to solve the problems faced by the entire humankind. The need to remain fully informed about the various aspects of the efforts being made all over the world to solve these problems cannot be overemphasized. It is also necessary that we should have well thought out and clear stand on these issues and make it fully known to the world. To make his point clear the author presents the case of weapons of mass destruction as an example. He says that there is no doubt that use of those weapons does not distinguish between fighter and peace lover, between men and women, between old aged and children, etc. Rather its effects extend to even the future generation. There could be no doubt that it comes under the definition of *fasad fi'l-ard*. Thus, there is no doubt about the need to get rid of them, and therefore it will come within the purview of the objectives of Shariah. Therefore, in the opinion of the author, it is religiously prohibited without any reservation or hesitation to manufacture, trade or use them, as *fasad fi'l-ard* is never permitted in any condition. In this respect

[58] Islahi, "Book Review," 243-44.

he notes hypocrisy and hidden attempts on the part of big nations to acquire such weapons. However, he emphasizes that Islamic stand should not be based on the stands of others as this is a question of principle and value. He supports his stand by the story of the two sons of Adam (the Qur'an 5: 27-32) and by the Qur'anic verse "*Repel evil with that which is better ...*" (Qur'an 41: 34-35). He claims that the context of these two verses shows that the issue is not related to individual problem. It was a principle-based issue that wins hearts in the long-term. To him, non-possession of such weapons by Muslim countries will not finish Islam or Muslim Ummah from the world at the hand of big powers having such weapons. Here it may be said that the real issue is not their elimination from the face of the earth but aims at keeping them weak, dependent and subordinate, depriving them from justice, and interference in their affairs. In fact, as he notes, in one of his meetings, audience opposed his views in the light of the Qur'anic verse "*waa'iddu lahum maistata'tm min quwwah* ... (Qur'an 8: 6) in which the word *quwwah* is common for all kind of power with the aim of deterrence. Dr. Siddiqi's response was "there is need to compare between merits and demerits, advantages and disadvantages of acquisition of such mass destruction weapons". In his own opinion harms of possessing weapons of mass destruction are much more than theirs benefits. Apparently, he seems to think that majority of people would not agree with his opinion. Therefore, he invites for further dialogue on the issue.[59]

As per Professor Siddiqi, there is the need to adopt a method that should attract the attention of people and prepare minds and

[59] Islahi, "Book Review," 243-44.

hearts to Islam. Methods which lead to human flourishing.[60] He called for respect and toleration for diversity of opinions for cooperation between humans. He was critical of the exclusivism practiced by the *fiqh* seminaries and *ulama* who arrogate for themselves the statues of the being the sole advisors in addressing the problems faced by the common Muslims through issuing *fatwas*—non-binding legalistic opinions while avoiding the exercise of *ijtihad* on the pretext the doors of *ijtihad* were closed from the late eighteenth century to the present day.[61] Professor Siddiqi disagrees with such interpretation. He is of the opinion that differences of opinion among the Muslims are boon and not a bane. Rather, it strengthens the movement of Islamic thought therefore:

1. … he expands the scope of the *ijtihad* saying it is not limited to matters of conventional wisdom; *ijtihad* covers the general affairs of life, such as education, health, tourism, dealing with the neighbors and friends, bringing up children, marital relations, calling to Allah ﷻ, training

---

[60] Miroslav Volf, *Flourishing: Why We Need Religion in a Globalized World* (New Haven London: Yale University Press, 2017).

[61] Knut S. Vikør, "Development of Ijtihad," The third Nordic conference on Middle Eastern Studies: Ethnic encounter and culture change, The Development of Ijtihad and Islamic Reform, 1750-1850, Joensuu, Finland: Nordic Society for Middle Eastern Studies, June 19, 1995, ttp://www.hf-fak.uib.no/Institutter/smi/paj/Vikor.html; W. Montgomery Watt, "The Closing of the Door of *Ijtihād*," in *Orientalia Hispanica Sive Studia Pareja Octogenario Dicata* (Leiden, The Netherlands: Brill, 1974), 675-78, https://doi.org/10.1163/9789004661219_052; Joseph Schacht, *An Introduction to Islamic Law* (Oxford: Clarendon Press, 2012), 72; Wael Hallaq, "Was the Gate of Ijtihad Closed?," *International Journal of Middle East Studies,* (Cambridge) 16, no. 1 (March 1984): 3-41; Shaista P. Ali-Karamali and Fiona Dunne, "The Ijtihad Controversy," *Arab Law Quarterly* (Leiden, The Netherlands) 9, no. 3 (1994): 238-57, https://doi.org/10.1163/157302594X00031.

of callers, organization of parties and financing them, interaction with the national system and participation in it, dealing with the other communities, international relations, etc. which do not fall under the sphere of conventional jurisprudence. It is possible for one who is expert of these fields to exercise *ijtihad* in the sphere of his expertise…

2. To prepare oneself to meet those challenges one needs to have knowledge of contemporary sciences, and experience of practical life, in addition to traditional sciences. The present problems cannot be solved in purely traditional way.
3. … we need the same methodology that was used during the times of the Prophet's companions.
4. Dr. Siddiqi makes clear that the world after fifty or eighty years will be entirely different from the world that existed fifty years or a century ago in terms of economy, geography and politics. Thus, the tools and strategies used by Islamic movements to cope with problems in the past century, will not work in the coming years … This needs a critical evaluation of our present situation and readiness for dialogue and discussion without any reservation.[62]

The length and the depth of Professor Siddiqi's discussion in *Maqāṣid-e Shariʿat* clearly makes him a *Mujaddid* of postcolonial era along with scholars who share similar interpretations concerning *ijtihad* from both the Sunni and Shiʿi schools of Islamic thought which includes jurists, social scientists, natural scientists, etc.

Another important feature of Professor Nejatullah Siddiqi is his discussion on new issues and challenges of the postcolonial

[62] Islahi, "Book Review," 244-245.

and postmodern era such as Islamic theory of citizenship in the age of nation-state, Muslims serving in the armed forces of non-Muslim majority democratic countries and the use of Weapons of Mass Destruction (WMDs) and other issues. And Muslim specific issues such as:

> *Shari'ah* rules about paper money, *tawarruq* (a person who buys a commodity at a deferred price in order to sell it for cash at a lower price), women travelling without a close relative/cognizant (مَحْرَمْ —*mahram*), fixing fasting and prayer times at the North and South poles, the probability and permissibility of women marrying Jews or Christians, the leadership of women and their social roles and responsibilities, non-Muslim citizens in a Muslim country, and universal human issues.[63]

While being well informed about the contemporary worldwide discourse on *Maqāṣid-e Shari'at* and this theme becoming fashionable as evident in unlimited usage:

> ...in his opinion, most of the scholars and writers have not gone beyond traditional *fiqh* despite the pressing need to benefit from the *maqāṣid* in other matters like preaching, training, and reforming society. Siddiqi maintains that reconstructing Islamic thought, reforming the global Muslim community, and restoring Islamic civilization's former honor and dignity requires recognition of the *maqāṣid*, ascertaining the differences in their understanding and application, and discussing and deliberating upon them.

[63] Tauseef Ahmad Parray, "Exploring Nejatullah Siddiqi's Contribution to the *Maqāṣid al-Sharī'ah* in Urdu Literature," *American Journal of Islam and Society* 34, no. 1 (January 2017): 80-103, https://doi.org/10.35632/ajis.v34i1.275.

> He never insists upon his own stand, but always invites his readers to a dialogue and exchange of ideas so that Muslims, especially experts and specialists, can advance this initiative, examine the issues, become more involved, and utilize their skills and experiences about complex matters that are of concern to humanity as a whole. They should come forward and offer an ethical contribution, more soul and positive creativity, to societies, the sciences, and human progress for the sake of maintaining and advancing humanity through peace, progress, and prosperity. In this, he sees the success and realization of his efforts and contributions.[64]

7. Conclusion

Professor Nejatullah Siddiqi qualifies as a *Mujaddid* of the Postcolonial Era for several reasons. He was not only a trained economist but also an Islamic thinker of the modern age. His thought, contributions and recommendations for the practical application of his ideas made him a Muslim polymath or a walking encyclopedia of the contemporary age. Being a product of combined modern disciplines and traditional religious educational systems, his thought contribution were not restricted to Islamic economics and finance but are interdisciplinary to the core.

The main distinctive features of the contributions of Professor Nejatullah Siddiqi are his emphasis on *tawḥīd*—monotheism; *tajdid*—renewal and revival of Islamic thought and civilization in the postcolonial era where Islam as a way of life and a force of civilization has been put on the back burner or shelved to the traditional تقليد —*taqlid*—blind imitation of the past while living a

[64] Parray, "Exploring Nejatullah Siddiqi's Contribution to the *Maqāṣid al-Sharī'ah* in Urdu Literature," 97.

life marked by rapid social change and development in all the dimensions of life or worldviews.

Professor Siddiqi as a member of the Jamaat-e-Islami Hind positioned himself into realm of academic and Islamic thought where he made significant contributions to the renewal of Islamic way of life and thought. without entering into realm of political leadership of Jamaat-e-Islami Hind. His primary emphasis was as discussed in this introduction on topics of *tawḥīdic* epistemology; *tajdid*, postcolonial and decolonization of Muslim mind and pedagogy; Islamic economics and finance; Islamization of Knowledge and *maqāṣid al-shari'ah.* All these topics are of contemporary relevance to Muslim life and thought as well as Muslim and inter-human relations at large.

This *festschrift* to honor the lifetime achievements of Professor Nejatullah Siddiqi to the world of knowledge and life in the postcolonial and postmodern age of great disruption in which humanity stands at the abyss of self-destruction through ecological and other crises. It is hoped that this *festschrift* will keep alight the flame of *tawḥīd* and *tajdid* for the betterment of the present and future generation and contribute towards the reconstruction of knowledge, peace and harmony in face of the global weaponization of religions being witnessed around the world in the forms of religious nationalisms, racism and majoritarian oppression of the minorities as being the other or not qualified to deserve the state of human dignity which lies at the foundation of all religions—well described in the following verse of the Qur'an.

وَلَقَدْ كَرَّمْنَا بَنِيٓ ءَادَمَ وَحَمَلْنَٰهُمْ فِي ٱلْبَرِّ وَٱلْبَحْرِ وَرَزَقْنَٰهُم مِّنَ ٱلطَّيِّبَٰتِ وَفَضَّلْنَٰهُمْ عَلَىٰ كَثِيرٍ مِّمَّنْ خَلَقْنَا تَفْضِيلًا

Now, indeed, We have conferred dignity on the children of

Adam, and borne them over land and sea, and provided for them sustenance out of the good things of life, and favored them far above most of Our creation.—Qur'an 17:70

And finally, the editors express their immense gratitude to all the contributors who made this *festschrift* a valuable addition to the celebration of the life and legacy of Professor Nejatullah Siddiqi.

We also want to remember our friend and mentor, the late Dr. Yaqub Mirza for initiating this work and assigning us the difficult task of editing and producing this volume. It is indeed a *Sadaq-e-Jariyah* for Dr. Yaqub. Last, but not the least, we thank the Center for Islam in the Contemporary World (CICW) at the Shenandoah University for agreeing to finance and publish this project. We take responsibility for any error and hope to correct it in subsequent editions. Our hope is that the young generation of the Ummah will take note of a daring intellectual—a *Mujaddid* such as Muhammad Nejatullah Siddiqi and his scholarly guidance to elevate our status of *Khair-e-Ummah*. So that we can break the entangled deadlock and move forward as an integral part of the human civilization in this digital era of the Artificial Intelligence (AI). Which is referred to as the **fourth industrial revolution**, moving from academic research to become a ubiquitous tool in healthcare, finance, transportation, and entertainment. AI is characterized by the rapid integration of intelligent technologies into everyday life, transforming industries, enhancing human capabilities, and redefining the boundaries of machine functionality as a present-day reality.[65]

References

[65] "What Is the History of Artificial Intelligence (AI)?," *Tableau*, accessed March 25, 2026, https://www.tableau.com/data-insights/ai/history.

Abdullah, Aslam. "Muhammad Nejatullah Siddiqi." *Islamic Horizons*, January 4, 2023. https://islamichorizons.net/mohammad-nejatullah-siddiqi/.

Ahsan, Abdullah Al. *OIC: The Organization of the Islamic Conference*. Herndon, Va., U.S.A: Intl Inst of Islamic Thought, 1988.

Al-Attas, Muhammad Naguib. *Aims and Objectives of Islamic Education*. Islamic Education Series. Sevenoaks [England], Jeddah: Hodder and Stoughton; King Abdulaziz University, 1979.

Al-Faruqi, Isma`il R., and Abdullah Omar Nasseef, eds. *Social and Natural Sciences: The Islamic Perspective*. Islamic Education Series. Sevenoaks, Kent: Hodder and Stoughton: King Abdulaziz University, Jeddah, 1981.

Al-Faruqi, Ismail R. *Islam: Religion, Practice, Culture & World Order*. Edited by Imtiyaz Yusuf. London: International Institute of Islamic Thought, 2012.

Al-Faruqi, Ismail R. *Islamization of Knowledge: General Principles and Workplan*. Wyncote, PA: International Institute of Islamic Thought, 1982.

Ali-Karamali, Shaista P., and Fiona Dunne. "The Ijtihad Controversy." *Arab Law Quarterly* (Leiden, The Netherlands) 9, no. 3 (1994): 238-57. https://doi.org/10.1163/157302594X00031.

Aydin, Cemil. *The Idea of the Muslim World: A Global Intellectual History*. Cambridge, Massachusetts: Harvard University Press, 2017.

Azami, Usaama al-. Islam and the Arab Revolutions: The Ulama Between Democracy and Autocracy. London: C Hurst & Co Publishers Ltd, 2021.

Bakar, Osman. Islamic Civilization and the Modern World: Thematic

Essays. Brunei Darussalam: UBP Press, 2018.

Barr, James. A Line in the Sand: The Anglo-French Struggle for the Middle East, 1914-1948. New York: W. W. Norton & Company, 2013.

Bell, P. M. H., and Mark Gilbert. *The World Since 1945: An International History*. London; New York: Bloomsbury Academic, 2017.

_____, *The World Since 1945: An International History*. London Oxford New York New Delhi Sydney: Bloomsbury Academic, 2017.

Berkes, Niyazi. *The Development of Secularism in Turkey*. New York: Routledge, 1998.

Bhabha, Homi K. *The Location of Culture*. London ; New York: Routledge, 2004.

Bhambra, Gurminder K. "Postcolonial and Decolonial Dialogues." *Postcolonial Studies* 17, no. 2 (April 2014): 115-21. https://doi.org/10.1080/13688790.2014.966414.

Cahen, C. "*Dhimma*." In *Encyclopaedia of Islam New Edition Online (EI-2 English)*, edited by P. Bearman. 2012. https://doi-org.proxy.library.georgetown.edu/10.1163/157 3-3912_islam_SIM_1823.

Clark, Kelly James. *Religious Epistemology | Internet Encyclopedia of Philosophy*. n.d. Accessed January 25, 2026. https://iep.utm .edu/relig-ep/.

Dallal, Ahmad. "Appropriating the Past: Twentieth-Century Reconstruction of Pre-Modern Islamic Thought." *Islamic Law and Society* 7, no. 3 (2000): 325-58.

_____, "The Origins and Objectives of Islamic Revivalist Thought, 1750-1850." *Journal of the American Oriental Society* 113, no. 3 (1993): 341-59. https://doi.org/10.2307/605385.

Dallal, Ahmad S. Islam without Europe: Traditions of Reform in Eighteenth-Century Islamic Thought. Chapel Hill: The University of North Carolina Press, 2018.

Dougherty, Trent, and Chris Tweedt. "Religious Epistemology." *Philosophy Compass* 10, no. 8 (2015): 547-59. https://doi.org/10.1111/phc3.12185.

El-Affendi, Abdelwahab. "The Long March from Lahore to Khartoum: Beyond the 'Muslim Reformation.'" *Bulletin (British Society for Middle Eastern Studies)* 17, no. 2 (1990): 137-51.

Fromkin, David. A Peace to End All Peace: The Fall of the Ottoman Empire and the Creation of the Modern Middle East. 2 Reprint edition. New York: Holt Paperbacks, 2009.

Gay, Peter. *The Enlightenment: The Rise of Modern Paganism.* New York: W. W. Norton & Company, 1995.

_____, *The Enlightenment: The Science of Freedom.* New York: W. W. Norton & Company, 1996.

Gräf, Bettina, and Jakob Skovgaard-Petersen. *Global Mufti: The Phenomenon of Yūsuf al-Qaraḍāwi.* New York: Columbia University Press, 2009.

Hallaq, Wael. "Was the Gate of Ijtihad Closed?" *International Journal of Middle East Studies,* (Cambridge) 16, no. 1 (March 1984): 3-41.

Ḥāmidī, Muḥammad al-Hāshimī., and Ḥasan Turābī. *The Making of an Islamic Political Leader: Conversations with Hasan al-Turabi.* Boulder, Colo.: Westview Press, 1998. http://catdir.loc.gov/catdir/enhancements/fy0833/98005352-b.html.

Hamidullah, Muhammad. The First Written Constitution in the World: An Important Document of the Time of the Holy Prophet. Third revised edition. Lahore: Sh. Muhammad Ashraī, 1975.

Husain, Syed Sajjad, and Syed Ali Ashraf. *Crisis in Muslim Education.* Islamic Education Series. Sevenoaks [England], Jeddah [Saudi Arabia]: Hodder and Stoughton; King Abdulaziz University, 1979.

Iqra.Ca. "Dr. Yaqub Mirza, Pioneer of Faith-Based Finance and Philanthropy." December 4, 2025. https://www.iqra.ca/2025/dr-yaqub-mirza-pioneer-of-faith-based-finance-and-philanthropy/.

Islahi, Abdul Azim. "Book Review: Maqasid-e Shariʿat (Objectives of the Shariah)," *Journal of King Abdulaziz University: Islamic Economics.* (Jeddah) 23, no. 2 (2010): 224. https://doi.org/10.4197/islec.23-2.9.

Issuu. "Dr. Nejatullah Siddiqi's Accomplishments." Accessed November 2, 2023. https://issuu.com/isnacreative/docs/ih_january-february_23/s/17792538.

Jacob, Margaret. *The Secular Enlightenment.* Princeton (N.J.) Oxford (GB): Princeton University Press, 2019.

Kedourie, Elie. *Afghani and 'Abduh.* London: Routledge, 2014.

Landau, Jacob M. *The Politics of Pan-Islam: Ideology and Organization.* Oxford: Oxford University Press, 1994.

"Life and Works of Prof. Khurshid Ahmad." *Islamic Economics Project,* April 14, 2025. https://islamiceconomicsproject.com/2025/04/14/prof-khurshid-ahmad/.

Martin, Richard C., Said Amir Arjomand, Marcia Hermansen, Abdulkader Tayob, Rochelle Davis, and John Obert Voll, eds. *Encyclopedia of Islam & the Muslim World.* New York: Macmillan Reference USA, 2004.

Maududi, Sayyid Abul A'la. *A Short History of the Revivalist Movement in Islam.* Lahore: Islamic Publications Limited, 1963.

McLeod, Hugh. *Religious Crisis of the 1960s.* Oxford; New York:

Oxford University Press, 2010.

Mignolo, Walter D. "The Geopolitics of Knowledge and the Colonial Difference." *South Atlantic Quarterly* 101, no. 1 (January 2002): 57-96. https://doi.org/10.1215/00382876-101-1-57.

_____, *The Idea of Latin America.* Malden, MA; Oxford: Blackwell Publishing, 2005.

Mirza, M., and Miles Davis. "Faith-Based Entrepreneurship." *New England Journal of Entrepreneurship* 13, no. 1 (January 2010): 1-7.

Mirza, M. Yaqub. Five Pillars of Prosperity: Essentials of Faith-Based Wealth Building. Ashland: White Cloud Press, 2014.

Mirza, M. Yaqub, and Gary Moore. Heavenly Returns: What the Abrahamic Faiths Teach Us about Financial & Spiritual Well-Being. Center for Islam in the Contemporary World, 2022.

Mitchell, Richard P. *The Society of the Muslim Brothers.* New York: Oxford University Press, 1993.

Mustafa, Nur Maisarah. "'Tawhidic Epistemology Is the Root of Ummatic Excellence'—Prof. Emeritus Datuk Dr. Osman Bakar." *IIUM Today*, March 17, 2025. https://news.iium.edu.my/?p=183273.

Nasr, Seyyed Vali Reza. *Mawdudi and the Making of Islamic Revivalism.* New York: Oxford University Press, 1996.

_____, The Vanguard of the Islamic Revolution: The Jama'at-i Islami of Pakistan. Berkeley, Calif.: University of California Press, 1994.

Nienhaus, Volker. "Book Review: Banking Without Interest: The Islamic Foundation." *Journal of King Abdulaziz University: Islamic Economics* 1, no. 2 (1984): 85-90.

Okan, Orçun Can. "Treaty of Lausanne and the Construction of the

Arab Middle East." *Journal of the Ottoman and Turkish Studies Association* 8, no. 1 (2021): 457-61.

"Organisation of Islamic Cooperation." Accessed January 12, 2026. https://www.oic-oci.org/.

Orhan, Zeyneb. "Mit Ghamr Savings Bank: A Role Model or an Irreplicable Utopia?" *Journal of Humanity and Society (Insan & Toplum)* 8 (June 2018): 85-102. https://doi.org/10.12658/M0263.

Parray, Tauseef Ahmad. "Exploring Nejatullah Siddiqi's Contribution to the Maqāṣid al-*Sharī'ah* in Urdu Literature." *American Journal of Islam and Society* 34, no. 1 (January 2017): 80-103. https://doi.org/10.35632/ajis. v34i1.275.

Polka, Sagi. *Shaykh Yusuf Al-Qaradawi: Spiritual Mentor of Wasati Salafism*. Syracuse, New York: Syracuse University Press, 2019.

Prasad, Kamta. "Obituary: Professor A.M Khusro (1925-2003)." *The Indian Economic Journal* 50, nos. 3-4 (March 2003): 144-46. https://doi.org/10.1177/0019466220030317.

Rahnema, Ali, ed. *Pioneers of Islamic Revival*. London: Zed Books, 2006.

Said, Edward W. Covering Islam: How the Media and the Experts Determine How We See the Rest of the World. Revised edition. New York: Vintage, 1997.

_____, *Orientalism*. 1st Vintage Books ed edition. New York: Vintage, 1979.

Schacht, Joseph. *An Introduction to Islamic Law*. Oxford: Clarendon Press, 2012.

Shaham, Ron. Rethinking Islamic Legal Modernism: The Teaching of Yusuf al-Qaradawi. Leiden: Brill, 2018.

Siddiqi, Muhammad Nejatullah. "Islamization of Knowledge:

Reflections on Priorities." *American Journal of Islam and Society* 28, no. 3 (July 2011): 15-34. https://doi.org/10.35632/ajis.v28i3.335.

_____, *Maqasid-e-Shariat.* New Delhi: Markazi Maktabah-e-Islami, 2017.

Siddiqi, Muhammad Nejatullah. *Maqasid-e-Shari'at.* New Delhi: Markazi Maktabah-e-Islami Publishers, 2009.

_____, "My Life in Islamic Economics." *Critical Muslim* (London) 15 (September 2015). https://criticalmuslim.com/explore/issues/educational-reform/my-life-islamic-economics.

_____, "Tawhid: The Concept and the Process." In *Islamic Perspectives: Studies in Honour of Mawlana Sayyid Abul a'la Mawdudi.* Leicester: Islamic Foundation, 1979.

Smith, Anthony D. *Nationalism: Theory, Ideology, History.* Cambridge, UK; Malden, MA: Polity Press, 2010.

_____, *The Ethnic Origins of Nations.* Oxford: Wiley-Blackwell, 1991.

Spivak, Gayatri Chakravorty. "'Can the Subaltern Speak?" In *Marxism and the Interpretation of Culture*, 271-316. Champaign, IL: The University of Illinois Press, 1988.

Tableau. "What Is the History of Artificial Intelligence (AI)?" Accessed March 25, 2026. https://www.tableau.com/data-insights/ai/history.

Tamimi, Azzam S. *Rachid Ghannouchi: A Democrat within Islamism.* Oxford; New York: Oxford University Press, 2001.

Ustaoğlu, Murat, and Cenap Çakmak, eds. *The Palgrave Encyclopedia of Islamic Finance and Economics.* Cham: Springer Nature Switzerland, 2024. https://doi.org/10. 1007/978-3-030-93703-4.

Vikør, Knut S. "Development of Ijtihad." The third Nordic conference on Middle Eastern Studies: Ethnic encounter and culture change. The Development of Ijtihad and Islamic Reform, 1750-1850, Joensuu, Finland: Nordic Society for Middle Eastern Studies, June 19, 1995. ttp:// www.hf-fak.uib.no/Institutter/smi/paj/Vikor.html.

Volf, Miroslav. *Flourishing: Why We Need Religion in a Globalized World*. New Haven London: Yale University Press, 2017.

Wasiullah Khan, Mohammad. *Education and Society in the Muslim World*. Islamic Education Series. Sevenoaks, Kent, Jeddah [Saudi Arabia]: Hodder and Stoughton; King Abdulaziz University, 1981.

Watt, W. Montgomery. "The Closing of the Door of *Ijtihād*." In *Orientalia Hispanica Sive Studia Pareja Octogenario Dicata*, 675-78. Leiden, The Netherlands: Brill, 1974. https://doi.org/10.1163/9789004661219_052.

ONE

A Message from Prof. Khurshid Ahmad

Prof. Khurshid Ahmad

Dr. Nejatullah Siddiqi was a colleague and friend whose long association I value as prize of my life. While Mawlana Mawdudi and Baqar as-Sadr were the real founders of Islamic Economics. Dr. Nejatullah was a key figure in the promotion of Islamic Economics and its application in the contemporary world. He not only developed the ideas of the founders, he made many original contributions particularly in the field of the concept of property in Islam and in respect of the possibilities of future development and expansion of *Maqasid-e-Shariah.*

His thought and writing would remain a source of light and guidance for researchers in Islamic Economics and for those involved in the application of the values and principles of Islam towards the establishment of a Just Social Order.

Because of my health I have not been able to contribute an article to this volume but through this message I associate myself to paying tribute to the contribution of Dr. Nejatullah Siddiqi.

17th September 2023

TWO

We All Miss Professor M. Nejatullah Siddiqi

M. Yaqub Mirza

I, first met Professor M. Nejatullah Siddiqi in the mid-70s when he was a professor at King Abdul Aziz University, Jeddah, Saudi Arabia. Then I met him several times at various conferences around the world. He was very kind to me. He was a unique person with unique qualities and intellect. He was humble and soft-spoken. He authored many books and articles. He was one of the pioneers of Islamic finance. One may call him the "Father of Islamic Finance." We were very delighted and celebrated when he received the Faisal Award, which I consider a Noble Prize. He was very impressed with the Amana Mutual Fund, which we created in 1986. This fund has become the change the world's largest Islamic fund, with over $8 billion in assets. He told me to write down all these experiences; otherwise, these accomplishments would be lost! This gave me the inspiration and encouragement to write my first book, *Five Pillars of Prosperity* (Mirza 2014).

Success Is Not a Success Without a Successor

During one of my conversations with Anwar Ibrahim, the Prime Minister of Malaysia, I requested that he write a foreword to this book. Although I know he is a busy person, Anwar Ibrahim was delighted that the Center for Islam in the Contemporary World at Shenandoah University (CICW) is producing a book about him. Anwar Ibrahim mentioned to me that when he went to India for an academic sojourn, Dr Siddiqi was his host, and they had many sessions of mutual discussions. Anwar Ibrahim spoke of benefiting from those conceptual discussions about Islamic banking and finance after he returned to Malaysia in the context of the practical dimension of the Malaysian economy.

Professor Nejatullah used to visit his son who lives in San Jose, CA. Then, during one of my visits with him in San Jose, CA, I requested him to write foreword for my book, which he did. I was very elated that a scholar of his stature had honored me by writing the foreword. I visited with him several times. During one trip my wife had accompanied me and had the opportunity to visit with him in San Jose, CA. I have benefited greatly from his knowledge, vision, encouragement, and mentorship.

We pray Allah ﷻ will grant him *Jannah*.

References

Mirza, M. Yaqub. 2014. *Five Pillars of Prosperity: Essentials of Faith-Based Wealth Building*. Ashland: White Cloud Press.

THREE

The Meta-Economics of Crises and the Islamic Worldview

Muhammad Anas Zarka

Introduction

The scholar we are honoring, Professor M.N. Siddiqi, clearly recognized the need to think beyond the confines of conventional economics. For instance, in 2017, he wrote, "*'Tyranny of Discounting' versus the 'Tyranny of Growth': Need to Go beyond Economics to Attain a Just Society*" (Siddiqi 2017). Building on the spirit of Professor Siddiqi's legacy and his call to transcend traditional economics, this paper explores the potential effects of Islam's worldview during crises. I observe that economic crises impact not only economic life but also:

A. The individual's mind and emotions, influencing personal behavior.

B. Social relations and responses.

C. Both (A) and (B) are influenced by and influence public policy responses to crises. If a policy is perceived as just, it is less likely to generate negative incentives or evasive behavior, resulting in lower enforcement costs.

Element (A) is strongly shaped by an individual's worldview. Similarly, elements (B) and (C) are influenced by the prevailing worldview within a society, along with its rules and institutions. This paper highlights key concepts and principles of the Islamic worldview and tentatively explores their potential impact on individuals and societies during times of crisis.[1]

The Islamic Worldview

Below is a concise summary of key elements of the Islamic worldview, as derived from its two primary sources: the Holy Qur'an and the authentic traditions (Hadith) of the Prophet Muḥammad ﷺ. The fundamental principles of all true religions are encapsulated in God's first address to Prophet Musa ﵇, as stated in the Qur'an 20:14.

> *Verily, I—I alone—am God; there is no deity save Me. Hence, worship Me alone, and be constant in prayer, so as to remember Me! (20:15) Behold, [although] I have willed to keep it hidden, the Last Hour is bound to come, so that every human being may be recompensed in accordance with what he strove for [in life].*

The Qur'an repeatedly asserts that the drama of human life is, in effect, a play with two acts and an intermission.

Act One: Life is brief and unfolds in the present moment. A moral code has been revealed by God through His prophets for humanity. Every adult with a sound mind and body has the ability to embrace this code and live by it, or to reject it and act irresponsibly.

---

[1] Methodological note: Meta-economics, by definition, is not economics. Therefore, an economist is merely an educated layperson in this field, which applies to me. I view this short paper as a layperson's invitation to psychologists and sociologists to professionally address the issues raised.

[It is He] who has created death and life that He may test you which of you is best in deeds ... And He is the All-Mighty, the Oft-Forgiving.—Qur'an 67:2

The intermission for every person is the period between death and resurrection. Act Two is eternal life, beginning with the Day of Judgment. All humans will be resurrected and individually face their Creator for final judgment, ultimately destined for either eternal bliss (Paradise) or eternal torment (Hell).

Act One serves as a test of one's beliefs, intentions, and actions, all of which are fully known and precisely recorded by God. Unlike standardized educational tests where the same questions are given to all students, God assigns a unique test to each individual. Some face much harder trials (e.g., being blind, sick, or poor), while others encounter easier circumstances (e.g., being healthy, wealthy, or well-connected). People also experience vastly different social and personal realities during their lifetimes. All these stark differences are fully, accurately, and justly accounted for in the Hereafter by the All-Knowing, All-Just Judge.

And it is He who has made you generations coming after generations, replacing each other on the earth. And He has raised you in ranks, some above others that He may try you in that which He has bestowed on you.—Qur'an 6:165

Receiving a difficult test in this life is not a sign of God's disapproval, nor does an easy test indicate divine favor. Hardships and calamities can affect anyone, even the most pious and the prophets. Conversely, those who reject their Creator and act unjustly may still enjoy a comfortable life on earth. In both cases, these are worldly tests that will be fully and justly accounted for in the Hereafter.

A Major Tenet

The Qur'an states that nothing occurs in the natural universe or human society without God's permission. Whatever happens is allowed by God to occur. Even if humans cannot comprehend the wisdom or justice behind a particular event or circumstance, they can trust that it is the deliberate decision of their Creator—the All-Merciful, All-Wise, All-Knowing, and Just God. God has given humans the free will to obey or disobey His commandments during their earthly lives, though He desires their obedience. Those who disobey will face punishment in the Hereafter."

> *If you disbelieve, then verily, Allah is not in need of you; He likes not disbelief for His slaves. And if you are grateful (by being believers), He is pleased therewith for you.—Qur'an 39:7*

The Mighty Recompense

God promises great rewards and abundant compensation in the Hereafter to believers who patiently endure the trials He sends them in this life. The only requirement is to have faith in Him, follow His commandments, and remain steadfast in the face of adversity.

> *We shall certainly test you by afflicting some fear, hunger, loss of properties and lives and fruits upon you. Give glad tidings, then, to those who remain patient.—Qur'an 2:156*

> *And when an affliction smites them, they say: Verily to Allah do we belong, and it is to Him that we are destined to return.—Qur'an 2:157*

> *Upon them will be the blessings and mercy of their Lord, and it is they who are rightly guided.—Qur'an 2: 155*

The Prophet Muḥammad ﷺ said in two hadiths, both related

by Imam Muslim:

> Wondrous indeed is the situation of a believer. If good fortune comes to him, he is thankful to God, with goodly [reward]. If misfortune befalls him, he is patient, with a goodly [reward]. And none but a believer [is so fortunate].
>
> [Even for a small misfortune] such as a thorn, God grants a believer a reward, and also an expiation of a sin.

Unacceptable Attitudes

The Islamic worldview firmly rejects certain misguided attitudes. One might wrongly assume that since God allowed a misfortune to occur, efforts to change or minimize its harm are unnecessary. For example: **(a)** a sick person refuses to seek treatment; **(b)** a poor person makes no effort to improve their situation; or **(c)** others refuse to help them. These attitudes are unequivocally rejected in the Islamic worldview. The Prophet ﷺ said in an authentic hadith:

> God created the disease and the cure; [so] seek cures, but avoid unlawful things.

And in the Qur'an we find:

> *And when it is said to them: Spend of that with which Allah has provided you, those who disbelieve say to those who believe: Shall we feed those whom, if Allah willed, He (Himself) would have fed? You are only in a plain error.— Qur'an 3:47*

And:

> *Then when the (Jumu'ah) prayer is ended, you may disperse through the land, and seek the Bounty of Allah (by working, etc.), and remember Allah that you may be successful.— Qur'an 62:10*

The Islamic versus the Atheistic Worldview

The Islamic worldview offers humanity hope and resilience in the face of adversity, regardless of its form. In contrast, an atheistic worldview, which denies the existence of God and the Hereafter, attributes everything to blind, arbitrary forces. When adversity strikes, the inevitable question arises: Why me? Within an atheistic framework, no satisfying answer is possible, creating fertile ground for despair, depression, and suicidal thoughts. Unsurprisingly, suicide may appear as a solution to misfortunes perceived as the result of random, meaningless forces.

Suicide Rates According to Religion

Figure 4. Suicide rates (per 100,000) according to religion.

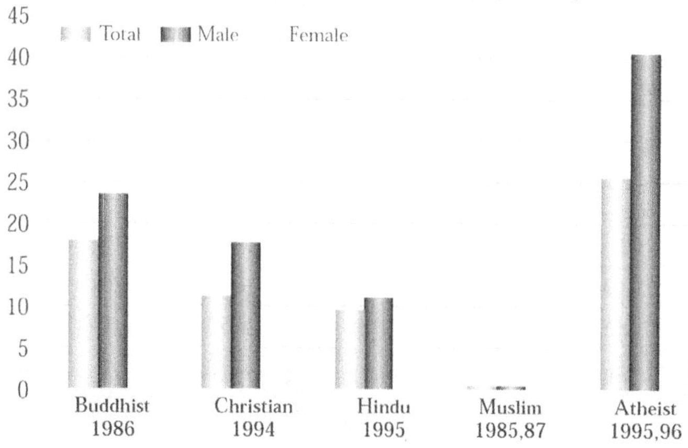

Source: J. M. Bertolote and A. Fleischman: "A global perspective in the epidemiology of suicide," in *Suicidology* 2002, arg. 7, nr. 2.

The Potential Social Impact of Economic Crises

All crises disrupt society and demand an examination of their causes and appropriate policy responses. When adversity is perceived as unjust, it creates a volatile and combustible mix that can lead to antisocial behavior. To preserve social harmony and peace, it is crucial to develop fair and effective policies to address crises.

A Historical Policy Example

A notable example of an effective policy response to a crisis within the Islamic framework was provided by the second Caliph, Umar, during a famine that occurred around the year 18 AH / 640 AD due to extreme drought.

Key aspects of his response include:

A. The Caliph Umar personally reduced his food consumption and urged his family members to do the same.

B. He requested urgent food supplies from the governors of Iraq and Egypt and closely supervised their distribution.

C. He continually prayed for relief and designated a specific date for people across various provinces to join in special prayers for rain.

D. For a long-term solution, he facilitated the rapid transport of food to Makkah, al-Madinah, and surrounding areas by ordering the restoration of an ancient canal (the River of Trajan) that had silted up. This costly project reopened the canal to ships, connecting the Nile to the Red Sea."

Reference

Siddiqi, Muhammad N. 2017. "'Tyranny of Discounting' versus the 'Tyranny of Growth': Need to Go Beyond Economics to Attain a Just Society," *Journal of King Abdulaziz University: Islamic Economics*, 73-74, 30(1). https://papers.ssrn.com/abstract=3179368.

FOUR

M. Nejatullah Siddiqi: Harbinger of a Paradigm Shift in Contemporary Islamic Thought

M. Zaki Kirmani

Civilizational Crisis and Diverging Responses

In the first half of the twentieth century, as Muslim political power rapidly collapsed against the West, Muslims faced economic threats and intellectual upheaval that had severe consequences on their self-assurance and confidence. Amidst their growing civilizational distrust, two major opinions emerged among the community of scholars, which they believed could remedy the situation the Ummah was facing. One perspective was the recognition that the achievements of the West were commendable, and that Islam did not hinder but rather supported and encouraged Muslims in such endeavors. This viewpoint was represented by figures like Sir Syed Ahmad Khan, Allama Mashriqui, and Jamaluddin Afghani from the subcontinent, as well as several others from Turkey and Tunisia (Akyol 2013; Ansari 2010). According to them, Islam as a religion supported and acknowledged these achievements and developments. However, it soon became apparent that beneath these accomplishments was an undercurrent of ideas and viewpoints with ideological overtones that did not necessarily fit into the Islamic framework. Awestruck as they were, these thinkers initially chose to overlook this, possibly believing that Islam's moral and ideological strength would be sufficient to address it.

Others believed that the main reason for this deterioration was rooted in Muslims' detachment from a vibrant and dynamic Islam. They argued that in order to change their conditions, it was essential to not only cultivate a deep and practical relationship with Islam, but to also be intellectually and creatively engaged with it. This viewpoint is, to some extent, represented by Islamic movements which held that the Muslim Ummah could only improve its situation when Islam became politically powerful and capable of making effective decisions in every aspect of life. This perspective was presented in such a way that Muslims began to believe that striving for political power was their religious destiny and that once achieved, many of their problems would be resolved. In the Indian subcontinent, the most prominent voice of this opinion was Syed Abu al-A'la al-Maududi. His writings had a profound impact on the intellectual landscape of 20th-century Muslims. He was instrumental in inspiring a new generation that was intellectually and practically committed to Islam and courageous enough to confront Western wisdom and intellect.

The Rise of *Jamaat-e-Islami* and Siddiqi's Early Intellectual Journey

The Jamaat-e-Islami, the Islamic movement of the subcontinent, was founded on the principles of dynamic intellectualism and the belief that Islam should be politically empowered. The establishment and growth of this organization, along with its multidimensional activities, is a phenomenon worth examining. It demonstrates how a small group of powerless individuals, with no resources or desire for personal gain, succeeded in building a strong organization and writing tales of unprecedented sacrifice solely on the basis of intellectual strength and commitment. Professor Nejatullah Siddiqi, at a relatively young age, came into contact with the Jamaat-e-Islami. Realizing the intellectual demands and commitments required by the Jamaat's objectives, he prioritized his educational career in economics. The frequent references in the Qur'an to economic guidance must have inspired him to delve deeper into the subject. Consequently, after learning Arabic and studying the Qur'an as a textbook through a specially designed curriculum, he became seriously involved in the discipline. His commitment to the belief that Islam was a comprehensive system of life and that making it politically powerful was an Islamic duty posed significant challenges. However, incorporating Islamic values into economics, economic institutions, and economic activities must have been an even greater challenge.

From the very beginning, he sought to understand the nature of these challenges. In fact, his writings can be divided into two categories of ideas:

1. A fresh understanding of Islamic thought and its reshaping according to the temporal context.

2. An Islamic critique of modern economics and the development of economic institutions in the light of Islamic values.

In his intellectual quest, he also became interested in Urdu literature and advocated for Islamic values in Urdu creative writings. His commitment to Maududi's thought, which promoted Islam as a driving force for a comprehensive struggle to rejuvenate Islam to its pristine condition, and reinstate Muslims' role in national and international affairs, as well as in intellectual and civilizational domains of individual and collective life, was evident. Despite his dedication to Maududi's ideas, he maintained his independent thinking and often adopted his own line of thought, which sometimes differed from Maududi's and the official stance of the Jamaat. This independence is evident from an early age. In 2000, he published a collection of his letters (Siddiqi, 2000) addressed to his colleague in the Jamaat-e-Islami and other eminent Islamic scholars in India and abroad, many of whom were not associated with the Jamaat. These letters clearly indicate how creatively he developed his opinions on various issues, departing from the commonly held approaches of contemporary scholars and colleagues.

The commitment to developing an economic system within an Islamic framework led him to approach new issues with fresh and independent thinking, particularly in areas where Islamic history offered no guidance. Islamic economic thinking provided him with a platform for innovative approaches to various issues related to the revival of Islam. Although he shared similarities with Maududi, Siddiqi distinguished himself as a first-rate scholar. While both aimed for the revival of Islam, Maududi viewed Islamic political revival as a crucial step. In contrast, Siddiqi believed that Islamic revival was closely tied to intellectual revival and knowledge generation, emphasizing research and specialization as essential for empowering Islamic thinkers.

Between Scholarship and Activism

It is important to address an interesting issue before exploring the intellectual dimensions of Siddiqi's thinking. Intellectuals and scholars within an organizational framework often face the challenge of balancing their scholarly pursuits with their activist responsibilities. These roles are inherently different: as an activist, one may need to prioritize the organization's human resource agenda, which might not align with the intellectual focus of a scholar. This creates a tension within the organization. Nejatullah Siddiqi experienced this tension and often had to clarify his position to critics. His letters clearly reflect his approach to such issues, especially during his academic tenure at Aligarh. He maintained his academic composure even when faced with provocative questions about his sincerity and commitment, particularly when he was planning to leave Aligarh.

During the era of King Faisal (1964-1975) of Saudi Arabia, a numerous intellectual conferences on Islam and contemporary issues were held, and Siddiqi played an active role in their organization. This involvement marked a pivotal moment, propelling him from a thinker rooted in the subcontinent to one with a global perspective. His ideas evolved from localized thinking to a more universal outlook. When he left Aligarh to join the Jeddah-based International Centre for Islamic Economics, his seminal contributions to Islamic Economics garnered significant attention in Western academia. Additionally, his views on Islamic activism, particularly *Iqamat-e-Deen*, underwent a notable transformation—shifting from an emphasis on political revival to a more realistic focus on the civilizational reformation of society.

Siddiqi's Emphasis on Human Intellect and Sense-Based Knowledge

Nejatullah Siddiqi introduced an Islamic worldview in which not only *wahy* (revelation) was significant, but human intellect, observation, and experiments were given due emphasis. In fact, knowledge based on sense perception assumed greater significance. Indeed, the Qur'an assigns the status of *ayat* (signs) even to sense-based intellectual and physical products (Qur'an, 42: 32-35). Siddiqi's ideas are evident in his talks, comments, articles, and books, where he compellingly presented and advocated for the human achievements of his time—largely the result of

Western efforts—to Muslim youth. He valued not only the products but also the methods and ethos, such as freedom of thought and action, and critical thinking, which were central to Western accomplishments. While these values are rooted in Islamic history, they were revitalized by the West to the extent that they became emblematic of Western culture. This was particularly evident in the twentieth century, where the Islamic knowledge tradition was characterized by strict adherence to tradition, making it challenging for modernists to gain acceptance among the *'ulama'* (scholarly elite). Siddiqi, however, earned widespread respect even among traditional scholars. His approach, for which he passionately advocated, is reflected in his three key writings that form the foundation of this article.

1. Islamization of Knowledge: Reflection and Priorities
2. My Life in Islamic Economics
3. *Maqasid-e-Shariat*

On Faruqi's project of Islamization of Knowledge, which quickly gained global recognition, Nejatullah Siddiqi (2011) had the opportunity to evaluate its objectives and methods when invited to contribute an article to the *American Journal of Islam and Society* (then known as the *American Journal of Islamic Social Sciences*, AJISS). He firmly believed that Islamization, or the acquisition of knowledge, should not be pursued for the sake of gaining power and authority. The connection between Islamization and authority was highlighted in the basic objectives of the project outlined in Ismail Faruqi's (1984) introductory document. Differing on this crucial point, Siddiqi argued that while knowledge and authority are deeply intertwined, Islam and authority are not inherently reciprocal. From this perspective, he concluded that the Islamization of Knowledge and authority do not have an inherent relationship. However, he acknowledged that the question of how Islam shapes behavior and governance when in power is a separate matter. Siddiqi maintained that authority is not the ultimate goal. Rather, the goal is to clarify and explain Islamic teachings that guide rulers to uphold the true objectives of authority. In a constantly changing world, knowledge must be continually refreshed and refined to remain relevant and aligned with the expanding objectives and scope of authority. This, he suggested, is the essence of the Islamization of Knowledge. In Islam, knowledge (*'ilm*) is a core value, making the concept of its Islamization somewhat redundant. What is truly needed, Siddiqi argued, is the integration of these values with contemporary knowledge. This integration process would involve varying degrees of editing, depending on the understanding of the situation. Siddiqi believed that in the modern era, power is achieved not through political struggle but through the acquisition of knowledge.

Along with *wahy* (revelation), Siddiqi includes the created universe as a source of knowledge (Qur'an 53:41). However, he seems less clear on how the knowledge of *wahy*, which has limited acceptability, can have the same universal status as knowledge understood today. This point is to be further discussed later. Siddiqi is nevertheless very clear when he states that acquiring knowledge, its creation, and its use are all for the betterment of humanity and not for Muslims' universal domination but for the welfare of humanity as a whole.

Rethinking Dominance: Power, Mission, and Purpose

Siddiqi raises an important and interesting question that has the potential to be viewed disapprovingly, particularly in movement-oriented Islamic circles today:

- Are Muslims duty-bound to be in a position to lead the world, to be dominant, and to redesign the world based on Islamic principles?

- Or is their real mission to present Islam to people, both verbally and intellectually, and invite them towards it?
- Should the end result of these efforts be the worldwide acceptance or domination of Islam?

The idea of a dominant Islam and its potential for dominance is so deeply ingrained today that it has become almost impossible to imagine otherwise. This is especially true after the emergence of Islamic movements in the 19th and 20th centuries. Siddiqi believes that the idea of the Islamization of Knowledge has its roots in the colonial environment of subjugation, where Muslims faced threats of all kinds. For the objective of freedom and independence, Islam was naturally the best and most plausible force to inspire Muslims to resist. However, it soon became clear that Western domination was rooted in their greater access to knowledge and their ability to use this knowledge for dominance. Ironically, it was repeatedly observed that despite the commitment of its thought followers, the Islamic movement was not in a position to challenge the domination of the secular local powers collaborating with the West and serving their interests in Muslim countries. Whenever the Islamic movements tried to challenge this dominance, they were ruthlessly suppressed and suffered greatly. Although this tyrannical treatment failed to destroy the Islamic movements, it did succeed in creating space for critical analysis and reflection upon what had been achieved and the costs paid. This introspection led to two major additions to the Islamic movement's vision: one related to the civilizational reinforcement of the Muslim Ummah and the other to the Islamization of Knowledge programs. Siddiqi contributed significantly to both.

It is interesting to note that gradually the discourse on political empowerment faded even in the public discourses of the Islamic movement, while the significance of activities related to civilizational reinforcement increased. Siddiqi's talks and discussions reflect this change. Although his academic involvement in economics already had civilizational overtones, his interest in interest-free microfinancing was more of an effort toward the civilizational empowerment of Muslims.

As to the Islamization of Knowledge, Siddiqi's concern about its roots in political empowerment is quite apparent. Unfortunately, however, Siddiqi does not go beyond this and falls short in addressing at least three important questions:

1. How do Qur'an-driven values, which construct the core of Islamic civilization, deal with other civilizations and their products? In the interactive phase, which involves the process of conscious and unconscious acceptance and rejection, what is the criterion?
2. How does the Qur'an view acts and thoughts generally described as worldly and secular, which apparently have nothing to do with religion but are significantly regarded by all human beings?
3. While commanding believers to think and reflect on nature and natural phenomena, the Qur'an imbibes and unites the metaphysical realm with the physical. The entire debate on the Islamization of Knowledge, including Siddiqi's criticism, seems unconcerned with this issue. Interestingly, this has been the most manifest aspect of the growth of knowledge during the Islamic era.

The discourse on the Islamization of Knowledge was rightly expected to clarify the need and rationale for such Islamization. Had the above three questions been reflected upon, the debate might have been more rational. Not only did the initiators of the debate neglect these issues, but even its later critics, including Siddiqi, failed to address them. Had they done so, two important domains might have opened for a lively and rich debate:

1. The role of worldview in shaping and directing the growth of knowledge.
2. The crisis of knowledge that the Western world is facing and the need and scope for interaction with Islamic knowledge traditions.

This interaction has great potential for a healthy exchange with Western knowledge, opening new windows for both the Islamic tradition, which is currently lacking in dynamism, and the Western tradition, which faces a value crisis despite its dynamism. Therefore, rather than focusing on Islamization, the time calls for the integration of knowledge. This depth seems to be missing in Siddiqi's musings on the Islamization of Knowledge debate.

Relevance of Freedom and Fresh Thinking in Islamic Knowledge

Genuine research and the advancement of knowledge require an environment of freedom. Society or the system must generously provide and protect individual freedom in both political and intellectual domains. In principle, humans cannot be deprived of this freedom (Qur'an 42:21, 12:40). Siddiqi (2014, 22-27) critically examined the mindset of superiority among Muslims, particularly within the Islamic movement. He challenges the widespread belief among Muslims that they are destined to dominate and dismisses the idea of a future where Islam will rule the world under a single leadership, labeling these notions as myths with no reasonable basis. Siddiqi argues that such views, rooted more in longing than reasoned opinion, fail to account for the changes brought about by time and space. This emphasis on outcomes rather than methods fosters hopelessness and despair when expectations are not met. Repeated failures have led to intolerance among enthusiasts and stagnation among the general populace. A significant aspect of this stagnation is the belief that only the *'ulama'* have the right to independent thinking and leadership. According to this belief, only the *'ulama'* are qualified to lead, direct, and provide opinions on methods for such struggles. Siddiqi rejects these ideas, emphasizing that the scope and nature of *'ilm* (knowledge) have changed so drastically that seeking solutions to contemporary issues through outdated knowledge is akin to living in a bygone era. Indeed, it is clear that such an approach is destined to fail.

The nature of today's issues and problems has drastically changed, and are well beyond the grasp of the traditional *'ulama'*. Given the complexity of these challenges, interactions with experts are essential for understanding contemporary issues. Problems arising from global actions and their impacts require global interactions among stakeholders, concerned groups, and communities. The *'ulama'* must broaden their thinking and acknowledge that many others have a better understanding of the modern world. They should embrace differences of opinion, listen to others, and engage in discussions. Among Muslims, the tradition of consultation with various sects and schools of thought has been strong and should be revitalized. Siddiqi advocates for a change in mindset, achievable through fresh interaction with the Qur'an and the Prophet's Sunnah. Additionally, there is a need to seek knowledge that addresses the evolving conditions of time and space. This knowledge should be inherently beneficial, infused with spiritual values, and grounded in a moral vision developed within the framework of the Islamic worldview. However, a crucial aspect of this endeavor is that knowledge should not converge on the Qur'an but rather diverge from it. Furthermore, the Sunnah should be seen more as a source of wisdom than a rigid set of rules and instructions.

Integrating Tradition with Modern Realities

The growth and development of the required knowledge will only be possible when the Qur'an and Sunnah are studied in an environment of independence and freedom. For instance, to understand the Qur'an's view on a particular issue, one should consider the related *ayat*, formulate all possible meanings, propositions, and instructions, and ensure that everyone involved works to understand independently and individually, giving equal weight to the opinions of all participants. In this process, history should not be idealized; rather, an attempt should be made to understand the actual context in which an opinion was formulated at a particular time and place. History provides lessons and indicates gaps between theory and practice. Without realizing these gaps, we will be unable to benefit from history and may be held accountable for obscuring the truth. A mindset based on the study of selected history suffers from great frustration and disbelief.

Expressing his opinion on the impact of social changes on intellectual development, Siddiqi notes that human society, having passed through periods of agriculture, industry, and services, is now entering a period of knowledge. Information sources have enormously expanded, increasing the potential for meaningful inter-cultural interaction. Unfortunately, the Islamic tradition has remained stagnant, failing to reap the benefits of this change. Referring to the economy, he says that in the period of a knowledge-based economy, the information explosion has challenged the long-held view that market forces and competition lead to growth and development. Now, we understand that the family structure and a passion for mutual cooperation, which played significant roles in the past, are still needed today. Ignoring these factors has rendered us subservient to the West. This is quite apparent in the Islamic economic evolution. This situation has been exacerbated by the movement for the Islamization of

Knowledge, which suggests that merely patching modern knowledge with classical knowledge is sufficient. Under this premise, it is believed that classical knowledge does not need to be rethought and redesigned. Referring to Islamic economics and Islamic banking, Siddiqi laments.,

> There is little tolerance of dissent. Nobody invites criticism. There is no tradition of democratic decision-making. Both naivety and intolerance are wicked, but their combination has been fatal. As a result, the theory and practice of Islamic economics and banking is flawed, full of anomalies, and have basically failed as project. All we can do is to congratulate ourselves on having re-invented capitalism by using Islamic jurisprudence! This is a far cry from the innovative creativity of jurists in the early centuries of Islam and more in line with the frozen attitudes during colonial era (Siddiqi 2015, 153).

Siddiqi firmly believes and confidently declares that the capitalism model has failed, as it does not give importance to fostering and rearing, support, and individual dignity. Progress alone is insufficient to meet human needs. Instead, we need an environment that sustains a high standard of living and enhance it. Life's necessities, freedom of choice, and other rights need to be taken care of, the absence of which renders life meaningless. Protection from exploitation and tyranny and peace and justice are of the utmost necessity. Progress often leads to inequality, deprivation, discord, and disturbance.

Siddiqi's Landmark Contribution: *Maqasid-e-Shariat*

This discussion finally leads us to Siddiqi's (2017) last academic venture, *Maqasid-e-Shariat* (The Objectives of the Shariah), the first edition of which appeared in 2009. Delving into the contents reveals that his lifelong passion for Islamic economics led him to the classical debates around the *Maqasid-e-Shariat*. To protect and provide food is a Qur'anic instruction (Qur'an 7:10). The poor in a society have a share in the wealth of the rich (Qur'an 70:24-25). Divine instructions are intended to restore human relations based on justice and honesty (Qur'an 57:25). Allah ﷻ wants to protect society from disturbance and chaos, and also to allow for people's abilities and capabilities to grow and flourish (Qur'an 28:71, 37:41). All these are parts of the objectives of the *din* (religion). Achieving, restoring, and protecting them is an Islamic act. Siddiqi emphasizes that modern Islamic economics should pursue these objectives. His *maqasid* initiative has opened a new avenue for intellectual discourse, extending beyond the economy to profoundly influence modern Islamic thought. In the revised edition (2017), he added two significant chapters: the ninth, on the "Objectives of Shariah and the Objective of Creation," and the tenth, discussing the "Islamic movement." These chapters showcase his creativity at its peak. This work solidifies his reputation as a leading Islamic intellectual rather than merely an Islamic economist. Siddiqi is fundamentally a thinker who has used Islamic economics as a testing ground for his ideas, achieving remarkable success in this endeavor.

The experiment of the Islamic movement in politics has not succeeded and has instead highlighted our shortcomings while raising questions about our preconceived notions. In contrast, Siddiqi's experiment in economics has fostered greater confidence and hope. In the ninth chapter, he introduces a profound principle: the objectives of Shariah should align with the objectives of creation. He asserts that Islam views life as a test, with humans held accountable for their actions. The purpose of creation is to guide humanity toward success in this test and ultimately to eternal bliss. For the test to be meaningful, it requires an environment that upholds freedom of thought and action. Without such freedom, that is, where individuals are coerced to practice Shariah, denied the ability to accept or reject, and stripped of choice, the test loses its validity. Therefore, any act that restricts human freedom conflicts with the objective of creation. This principle applies to all actions undertaken with the intention of achieving success and reward in the hereafter. From this perspective, Siddiqi even suggests that Islamic movements should not adopt or favor any policy that violates this principle and coerces people to act on the *din*.

Siddiqi's Unique Take on the Prophet's Strategy

In his study of the Prophet's life (the *sirah*), Siddiqi has drawn some unique conclusions. For example, when the Prophet ﷺ was returning unsuccessful from Taif, he accepted the protection offered by a non-Muslim. Similarly, he never hesitated to enjoy the benefits of positive tribal traditions and the benevolence of kings for the protection and benefit of his followers. The protection provided by the merciful king of Ethiopia to the Prophet's Companions is well known. This suggests that neither a system nor an individual is entirely illegitimate or devoid of merit. Many of their principles, regulations, or inclinations may be based on justice and humanity, which should not only be acknowledged but also taken advantage of. This approach is part of the Islamic strategy.

Gaps in Siddiqi's Framework: Knowledge and Universality

At this stage of discussion, it seems appropriate to mention some issues that, in the author's opinion, stand wanting in Siddiqi's thoughts. These are important issues that need to be addressed. The first important question relates to Siddiqi's assertion that, along with the universe, *wahy* (revelation) is also a source of knowledge. However, he does not elaborate on the fact that the methods of these two sources of knowledge are different, raising the question of how the universality of knowledge can be maintained. Universality is a defining characteristic of knowledge, and thus the knowledge from *wahy* can at best be considered potentially universal. As a result, the entire narrative of Islam becomes Muslim-oriented, which Siddiqi does not favor. Siddiqi's analysis reveals a nuanced understanding of how Islamic principles can integrate with modern realities and how the wisdom found in the *sirah* can be applied in contemporary contexts. Yet, his lack of elaboration on the methods of deriving knowledge from the *wahy* versus the universe leaves a significant gap. This gap points to the need for a more robust framework to harmonize these different sources of knowledge while maintaining their universality.

Siddiqi's emphasis on civilizational reinforcement over political empowerment and his critical stance on the Islamization of Knowledge movement reflect a forward-thinking approach. However, the absence of a concern about methodology for integrating knowledge from revelation and empirical sources indicates that his vision requires further development. Addressing this gap could lead to a richer, more inclusive Islamic intellectual tradition that embraces modern complexities while staying true to its foundational principles. Siddiqi raises a very important point related to the use of *fiqh* in Islamic economics and Islamic banking. He asserts that by relying on *fiqh* alone, Islamic finance has reinvented capitalism, albeit under an Islamic guise. This is a hard-hitting but honest critique of some aspects of his own contributions. Siddiqi seems to suggest that what is needed is not merely traditional *fiqh*, but a fresh and direct approach to the Qur'an and Sunnah. He advocates creating novel modes of interaction with the Qur'an to address contemporary economic and other disciplinary issues that were not encountered in earlier times. Siddiqi believes that the products derived from this creative interaction with the Qur'an, when incorporated into modern economic institutions, can prevent the mere re-invention of capitalism disguised as Islamic finance. He also observes that general human experiences and institutions should not be rejected because their intents are non-Islamic. For instance, he has sought to infuse Islamic values into the existing banking system rather than dismissing it outright.

Learning from the Flexibility of Islamic History

In the journal *Critical Muslim*, Siddiqi (2015) provides two historical examples that illustrate innovative approaches in early Islamic history, which he believes warrant extensive research. One example is related to a Companion of the Prophet ﷺ who converted things or property deposited with him as *amanah* (trust) into a business loan, promising the depositor a share of the profit he would earn. Another example from the Abbasid period involved an agreement where a loan could be repaid using income generated from new sources of revenue created on a particular piece of land. These examples may raise *fiqhi* issues but also open several new and positive possibilities. They demonstrate that historical Islamic practices were more flexible and innovative than often assumed. By revisiting these practices with a modern perspective, Siddiqi suggests that it is possible to develop genuinely Islamic economic systems that are not mere imitations of capitalist structures.

Similarly, his intervention in the supposedly juridical domain of *maqasid-e-shariat* is not without meaning. Although jurisprudence was not his field, he wrote a book on this topic and faced criticism from traditional *'ulama'*. He tolerated this criticism, which sometimes crossed the limits of civility, for a reason. In fact, he was in search of new avenues in Islamic economics and Islamic banking to protect this emerging system from capitalism. While *fiqh* failed to provide a comprehensive solution, the *maqasid-e-shariat* paved the way and opened up a vast field for intellectual maneuvering and new experiments. Siddiqi expanded this discussion further, extending it to Islamic movements. By developing a correlation between the objective of creation and the objectives of the Shariah, as discussed earlier, he succeeded in articulating a principle with the potential to make Islam and the Islamic movement a contemporary struggle. The core idea is that if the objective of creation is a test, then maintaining a proper environment for the test—i.e., freedom of thought and freedom of actions—is essential. The Islamic movement cannot fulfill the responsibility of *Iqamat-e-Deen* (establishing the religion) if these freedoms are sacrificed. Islam cannot be established if these freedoms are compromised.

This important aspect of the Shariah's objectives with reference to the Islamic movement remains incomplete because the tasks of accomplishing the *maqasid* are neither part of the Islamic movement's activities nor have they been given significant attention in Siddiqi's discussion. In fact, the Islamic movement, which tends to focus on educational reforms, judicial activism, and social improvement, often remains indifferent to basic human needs such as food, shelter, and health. It also struggles to collaborate with secular organizations that prioritize these basic needs but may not address social changes as robustly. Islamic movements need to reconsider their stance towards secular organizations, as these entities address objectives that are significant from a Shariah perspective. Emerging Islamic literature now includes environmental and ecological issues, as well as concern for the safety of flora and fauna, in the rich list of the *maqasid-e-shariat*. This shift has the potential to transform the traditional image of Islamic movements from being primarily theological and politically motivated to a more comprehensive socio-intellectual movement operating within an Islamic worldview. These views can be found in Siddiqi's writings and lectures and have necessary wherewithal to introduce a paradigm shift in contemporary Islamic thought and activities.

Towards a New Paradigm

Siddiqi's views gradually evolved from Maududi's deeply influential thoughts on total Islamic change. While both valued a dynamic Islamic worldview, Siddiqi believed that this change would remain elusive until the strength of the Islamic worldview was demonstrated both in the realms of knowledge and intellectual domains and began to show its potential in solving global human problems. In the Islamic worldview, thoughts and actions, experimentation and observation are highly important. Thinking, contemplation, and intellect are considered crucial tools, and the practice of these intellectual acts is regarded as purely religious, no less significant than prostration or genuflection (Qur'an 3:191). In Siddiqi's perspective, thinking and contemplation of natural phenomena, coupled with worship rituals, represent two sides of the same coin. Neither aspect alone can fully represent the human that the Qur'an aims to develop.

References

Akyol, Mustafa. *Islam without Extremes*. India: Viva Books, 2013.

Ansary, Tamim. *Destiny Disrupted*. USA: Public Affairs, 2010.

Faruqi, Ismail. Islamization of Knowledge: General Principles and Work Plan. USA: IIIT, 1989.

Siddiqi, Nejatullah. *Islami Maashiyat aur Adab* (in Urdu). India: Educational Book House, 2000.

Siddiqi, Nejatullah. "Islamization of Knowledge: Reflections on Priorities." *American Journal of Islamic Social Sciences* 28, no. 3 (2011): 15-34. Siddiqi, Nejatullah. "My Life in Islamic Economics." *Critical Muslim*, no. 25 (2015)

Siddiqi, Nejatullah. *Maqasid-e-Shariat* (in Urdu). Revised edition. India: MMI Publishers, 2017.

FIVE

The Legacy of Dr. Muhammad Nejatullah Siddiqi: Islamic Economics and Finance in India

Mohammad Manzoor Alam

My Time with Dr. Muhammad Nejatullah Siddiqi

I was fortunate to work under the guidance of Dr. Muhammad Nejatullah Siddiqi during my time as a research scholar in the early 1970s. Indeed, it was a privilege to spend those formative years with Dr. Siddiqi and his colleague Dr. Fazlur Rahman Faridi, who later became my Ph.D. advisor. They played a key role in teaching me how to integrate Islamic values into the social sciences. I spent almost five years completing my M.A., and a Ph.D. in Economics. I can still vividly remember how I was nurtured by these two great scholars. Dr. Siddiqi was not only my mentor but also a friend from the early 1970s, the days of my post-graduate and Ph.D. journeys in the Department of Economics at the Aligarh Muslim University (AMU). I always felt privileged to be closely associated with Dr. Siddiqi.

Over sixty years ago, Dr. Siddiqi, along with his colleagues, laid the foundation for Islamic economics as a new discipline in the social sciences. He entrusted me with managing the academic journal *Islamic Thought*, where I handled the selection of theme-based articles and communication with authors. I was responsible for all arrangements before the journal went to press. He gave me complete freedom in my work, and while we occasionally disagreed, he respected my perspective. His opinions on Islamic economics and finance were well-balanced, and his clarity of thought made his ideas easy to understand and communicate.

The Evolution of Dr. M. Nejatullah Siddiqi's Thought

Dr. Siddiqi served as an Associate Professor in the Department of Economics at AMU until 1975. He later became Professor of Islamic Studies at AMU before moving to the International Centre for Research in Islamic Economics at King Abdul Aziz University, Jeddah, Saudi Arabia. In 2006, he joined the International Islamic University Malaysia as Visiting Professor. During his time at AMU as a Ph.D. scholar, Dr. Siddiqi's most notable work was integrating Shariah principles with modern economic theories, which evolved into the concept of Islamic economics and finance. His Ph.D. thesis, *A Critical Examination of the Recent Theories of Profit*, was published by Asia Publishing House in 1971. Dr. Siddiqi then authored *Banking Without Interest* during a time when Islamic banking faced criticism, including from Muslim intellectuals and his own colleagues in the Department of Economics at AMU. In this work, he explained the rationale for Islamic finance and compared it with debt and equity financing, which were common in both Islamic and non-Islamic societies.

Dr. Siddiqi received his early training in a madrasa during the 1950s, under the guidance of distinguished scholars of the time. This education significantly enhanced his understanding of the Qur'an, Hadith, and Fiqh, which later proved instrumental in his grasp of Islamic principles of economics and finance. During his teenage years, Dr. Siddiqi developed a keen interest in the works of Maulana Syed Abul A'la Maududi, regularly reading publications such as *al-Hilal, al-Balagh*, and *Tarjuman-al Qur'an* after completing his higher secondary education. Although he joined Jamaat-e-Islami Hind at a young age, he maintained a distinct and independent perspective in his economic ideas, separate from his association with the organization. His translation of Sayyid Qutb's *Social Justice in Islam* into Urdu further motivated him to refine his concept of Islamic economics. Subsequently, he dedicated himself to developing a model of interest-free banking, incorporating *mudarabah* and *musharakah* financing into its framework. Dr. Siddiqi's *Banking Without Interest* stood out for its authoritative and practical application of *mudarabah* (profit and loss sharing) financing, surpassing previous research on the subject. The book garnered significant attention from both scholars and finance professionals. His early work on insurance within an Islamic framework remains a notable contribution, now recognized as a vital component of the global Islamic financial industry. In the 1970s and 1980s, Dr. Siddiqi also explored the subject of the *maqasid al-shari'ah*, producing a treatise that showcased the theoretical evolution of his ideas on Islam, society, and economics.

At the age of twenty-five, Dr. Siddiqi established a journal titled *Islamic Thought*, dedicated to exploring contemporary social sciences through an Islamic lens. This initiative, launched on the campus of Aligarh Muslim University (AMU), offered an alternative perspective to both traditional and modern interpretations of economy and society, attracting scholars and intellectuals alike. Dr. Siddiqi's writings on social and economic justice, interest, money, profit-sharing, the Islamic concept of ownership, and the economics of insurance were characterized by a clear historical perspective and a rational analysis of the challenges faced by Muslims in post-independence India. The International Mecca Conference on Islamic Economics, held in

Saudi Arabia in 1976, provided a significant platform for scholarly engagement. While Prof. Mohammad Shabbir, then Head of the Department of Economics at AMU, was also invited, Dr. Siddiqi emerged as the central figure among the scholars. His comprehensive survey of Muslim Economic Thinking received widespread acclaim and was later published by The Islamic Foundation, Leicester, United Kingdom, in 1981. It is important to note that Dr. Siddiqi's conception of Islamic economics and banking was not framed as a critique of capitalism or socialism. His academic works gained global recognition, particularly in the Muslim world. For instance, the Muslim discourse on *riba* (usury) took on a more theoretical and rational dimension as Islamic banking emerged as an alternative to conventional commercial banking. Furthermore, the idea that Islamic finance offered solutions to contemporary economic challenges resonated with many adherents of Islam, presenting a distinct approach to economic systems prevalent in the country.

Dr. Siddiqi has inspired economists for over five decades, convincingly demonstrating how Islamic economic philosophy and history can be analyzed within the context of the contemporary global economy. His economic thinking, however, evolved over time, adhering to the rigorous scientific framework of conventional economics while emphasizing the viability of Islamic economics as an alternative to both capitalism and socialism. Dr. Siddiqi further refined, developed, and organized his ideas within the framework of a secular global environment. He exemplified a mission-driven individual endowed with a value-oriented intellect. Dr. Siddiqi was one of the founders of the Institute of Objective Studies (IOS) and served as a member of its Governing Council, the executive body headquartered in New Delhi. In recognition of his contributions to the field of Islamic economics, he was honored with the Third IOS Shah Waliullah Award in 2003. Additionally, he received the prestigious King

Faisal International Prize for Islamic Studies in 1982.

Dr. Siddiqi authored several books for the Institute of Objective Studies (IOS), including *Jihad, Ijtihad aur Mujahid-e-Nafs* and *Tashaddud, Islam aur Tahreek-e-Islami*, and contributed numerous articles to IOS publications. He was instrumental in organizing and participating in several key conferences and seminars on banking and finance, as listed below:

1. Prospects for Islamic Venture Capital Fund in the Indian Economy (2011)
2. Emergence of Ethical Investment in India: Issues and Practices (2008)
3. Participatory Banking for All: A Business Proposition (2007)
4. Islamic Economics and the Economy of Indian Muslims (1989)

In the mid-1980s, establishing a think tank to address the social and economic challenges faced by Indian Muslims was a formidable task, both in conception and execution. Dr. Siddiqi's visionary suggestions and efforts, however, laid the foundation for the IOS to gain international recognition and collaboration with global research institutions. The IOS successfully persuaded the Islamic Development Bank (IsDB) to provide scholarships for talented Indian students to pursue research in social sciences from an Islamic perspective.

Concern for the Economic Upliftment of the Indian Muslims

The economic thinking of Dr. Siddiqi evolved over time, developing within the framework of conventional economics and focusing on the feasibility of Islamic economics and finance as an alternative to capitalism and socialism. Through his extensive writings in both Urdu and English, Dr. Siddiqi consistently demonstrated original and insightful thinking on the viability of Islamic economic principles. Although modest and humble about his contributions, he credited his senior, Dr. Uzair Ahmad of Allahabad University, for his influential *mudarabah*-based interest-free model of banking. Unlike traditional Muslim critiques of capitalism, *riba*, and their consequences, Dr. Siddiqi vigorously argued for the possibility of profit and loss sharing as the essence of Islamic finance. During his time at the Centre for Research in Islamic Economics in Jeddah, his analysis of equity financing in contrast to debt financing became more refined, with a particular focus on risk management techniques. As early as the mid-1960s, Dr. Siddiqi theorized convincingly that equity-based banking and investment banking without interest were viable alternatives. His seminal work, *Banking Without Interest*, published in 1967, marked a significant milestone in the understanding of Islamic finance in modern times. This work provided authoritative and practical insights into the application of *mudarabah* (profit and loss sharing) as an alternative to conventional interest-based commercial banking, emphasizing the feasibility of financial intermediation in contrast to the prevailing interest-based systems in the global market.

In the mid-1960s, during the peak of Western capitalism, Dr. Siddiqi presented a rigorous theoretical argument for financial intermediation based on *mudarabah* and *shirkah*, concepts akin to modern-day equity-based finance. This theory, later termed "Islamic banking," proposed a unique approach to financial systems. In the Islamic banking model, he argued, when money is borrowed from a bank, the bank becomes a financial partner in the project. Theoretically, this partnership-based model would result in zero non-performing assets, setting it apart from conventional commercial banks. Unlike traditional banks, Islamic banks do not create money; instead, they operate through contractual agreements with depositors, challenging the conventional understanding of money. Dr. Siddiqi, however, did not focus on justifying or discussing the concept of *riba* as mentioned in the Qur'an in his writings. Since the financial liberalization of the early 1990s, personal finance has evolved significantly, with equity funds and participatory finance in the stock market expanding rapidly. This shift prompted Muslim scholars to explore the potential of Islamic participatory finance in India. Dr. Siddiqi was not in favor of presenting Islamic economics and finance as a force of domination by Islam. Instead, he advocated for "seeking guidance directly from whatever is recognizably divine in human heritage, in the full glare of reason and intellect, aided by intuition, imagination, and knowledge."

Conclusion

Dr. Siddiqi was one of the most distinguished Indian scholars of Islamic economics and finance. In the mid-1960s, he presented a compelling theoretical argument that equity-based banking and investment banking without interest were feasible. His seminal work, *Banking Without Interest*, carried authoritative insights into the application of *mudarabah* as an alternative to modern commercial banking. Dr. Siddiqi's original thinking is evident in his views on interest-bearing instruments, his analysis of money, interest, and profits, and his critiques of debt and equity in Islamic finance. His critical evaluations of *murabahah* financing, contemporary experiments in Islamic banking, money creation, and his perspectives on *sukuk*, *takaful*, and *tawarruq* are widely recognized. His initiatives to promote Islamic economics and finance in India, particularly for the economic upliftment of Indian Muslims, are well documented.

The legacy of Dr. Siddiqi's contributions to Islamic economics and finance extends to his teaching and research in academic institutions across India and the Muslim World. A humble and devoted teacher, he was a creative and original thinker who engaged with his critics at the Centre for Research in Islamic Economics in Jeddah with an open mind, responding to them with clarity and rationality. He inspired young scholars and researchers to explore Islamic economics and finance within the context of contemporary economic challenges. His vision of *maqasid al-shari'ah* reflects twenty-first-century concerns, including justice, equity, human rights, economic liberties, poverty alleviation, equitable wealth distribution, and environmental protection. In the aftermath of the 2008 global financial crisis, Dr. Siddiqi's contributions remain highly relevant, inviting researchers to revisit his work and its influence on the development of Islamic economics and finance since the mid-twentieth century. His website, www.siddiqi.com, showcases his diverse interests in social sciences and humanities. As a pioneer in reconstructing the Islamic economics paradigm, Dr. Siddiqi distinguished himself among his peers in both the Arab and Asian academic communities.

SIX

A Tribute to Dr. Muhammad Nejatullah Siddiqi Visionary of Islamic Economics and Finance

Syed Nazim Ali

Introduction

Aligarh Muslim University (AMU) has played a pivotal role in shaping my professional journey, even though I am not an alumnus. From the beginning of my career at King Faisal University in 1976 to my subsequent roles at the University of Bahrain, Harvard University for twenty years, and now Hamad Bin Khalifa University for over a decade, I have been influenced by AMU graduates and faculty. My close interactions with AMU affiliates have maintained my strong connection to the university's rich heritage and have profoundly impacted my professional development.

One of the most influential figures from AMU who has significantly shaped my journey is Dr. Muhammad Nejatullah Siddiqi. His dual expertise as both a distinguished academic and a religious scholar sparked my interest in Islamic finance. Dr. Siddiqi's pioneering work in merging economic principles with Islamic teachings has made substantial contributions to the field of Islamic banking and finance. His seminal book, *Banking Without Interest*, exemplifies his innovative approach and deep understanding of both economics and Islamic jurisprudence.

I first encountered Dr. Siddiqi's work in 1967 as a student in Hyderabad attending a conference where he was a speaker, which ignited my interest in his ideas. Our paths crossed once more in 1976 at King Fahd University of Petroleum and Minerals in Dhahran. Dr. Siddiqi was returning from the First International Conference on Islamic Economics in Makkah, organized by King Abdulaziz University. This serendipitous meeting rekindled my fascination with his work and propelled me into a deeper engagement with the field of Islamic finance.

The impact of Aligarh Muslim University on my professional journey has been both profound and pervasive. My interactions with its distinguished alumni and faculty have consistently highlighted AMU's rich academic tradition and commitment to excellence. This enduring connection has not only inspired and guided me but also underscores the university's significant role in shaping the field of Islamic finance and beyond.

Dr. Nejatullah Siddiqi's Journey at Aligarh Muslim University

Dr. Siddiqi's tenure at AMU is a testament to his resilience and the profound impact of his work. Appointed as Professor of Islamic Studies, he demonstrated a deep understanding of both Islamic principles and modern economic theory. His interdisciplinary approach established him as a pivotal figure in integrating Islamic finance into academic discourse, leaving a lasting legacy in both academic and religious spheres. Dr. A. M. Khusro, the AMU Vice Chancellor from 1974 to 1979, played a crucial role in recognizing Dr. Siddiqi's interdisciplinary expertise. Khusro's decision to appoint Siddiqi as Professor of Islamic Studies was widely applauded and led to the establishment of separate departments of Islamic Economics and Finance at universities worldwide. This forward-thinking move inspired the creation of institutions dedicated to Islamic finance globally. Many Islamic economic scholars, such as Dr. Mohamed Ali Elgari, Dr. Mohd Daud Bakr, Dr Abbas Mirakhor, and Engku Rabiah Adawiah bt Engku Ali, have since become leading Shariah scholars as well.

Dr. Siddiqi's influence extends beyond academia into religious scholarship. His innovative thinking and commitment to integrating Islamic principles with economic practices have inspired many, including myself, to explore Islamic finance deeply. Prior to his contributions, the field often overlooked the crucial role of Shariah scholars, resulting in financial products and practices that did not fully adhere to Islamic principles, such as the prohibition of interest (*riba*) and the necessity of risk-sharing. Dr. Siddiqi's interdisciplinary approach, combining expertise in economics with deep Islamic knowledge, brought much-needed scholarly rigor to the field. His background in economics underscored his unique ability to bridge these disciplines, highlighting the importance of a scholarly foundation in both areas for developing robust Islamic financial systems.

One key change brought about by Dr. Siddiqi's work was the increased involvement of Shariah scholars in the development and approval of financial products. His emphasis on ensuring that all financial activities were backed by real assets and free from speculative risks aligned with core Islamic principles, leading to more robust and Shariah-compliant financial products. An illustrative anecdote of this shift is the growing frequency of conferences and workshops where economists and Shariah scholars collaborated. Dr. Siddiqi often facilitated these discussions, ensuring that both perspectives were considered. For example, during his tenure at Harvard University, many events underscored the need for Shariah scholars' input, a practice that became more common across the industry. Dr. Siddiqi's influence also extended to validating projects within the Islamic finance sector. His endorsement of initiatives like the Islamic Finance Information Program at Harvard University not only provided credibility but also encouraged Shariah scholars' involvement in similar projects. This validation was crucial for gaining support and funding, as evidenced by Mr. Iqbal Ahmed Khan's support for the Harvard project.

Dr. Siddiqi Instigates My Interest in Islamic Finance

Reflecting on my journey and the profound impact of AMU and its distinguished figures like Dr. Siddiqi, I am reminded of the enduring power of intellectual legacy and interdisciplinary scholarship. These influences have been instrumental in my professional and personal growth, continually inspiring me to explore and contribute to the field of Islamic finance. Growing up in India, I witnessed firsthand the pervasive nature of interest-bearing microloans, especially among impoverished communities. While these loans appeared to offer relief, they often trapped borrowers in a cycle of debt due to exorbitant interest rates. This observation fostered a deep aversion to interest-based lending and a strong desire to understand why those in need should be burdened with oppressive interest rates that worsened their financial struggles.

My engagement with Islamic banking was revitalized in the early 1980s. Upon joining the University of Bahrain in 1984, I was intrigued by the rapid growth of the offshore Islamic banking sector. This sector, with its focus on shared risk and the absence of fixed income, presented a stark contrast to traditional banking systems. Dr. Siddiqi's book, *Banking Without Interest* (1983), and my meetings with him continually inspired me to apply my expertise to Islamic finance. My move to Bahrain marked the beginning of my professional journey in this field, where I encountered its multidisciplinary nature. Islamic finance is not just a financial or economic concept but an integrated approach combining Islamic teachings, Shariah law, business practices, marketing, and legal frameworks. This realization resonated with my academic interests in information science and underscored the need to understand Islamic finance from multiple perspectives.

In response, I dedicated myself to the academic exploration of Islamic finance. I engaged in extensive online research, exploring secondary sources and databases across diverse fields such as sociology, psychology, business, religion, and economics. This comprehensive exploration revealed the vast and fragmented nature of information on Islamic banking and finance. Identifying key sources and understanding the intersections between various fields proved to be a challenging yet rewarding endeavor. This journey has been deeply fulfilling, merging my personal values with professional curiosity. It has allowed me to engage with a financial system that promotes fairness and equity, aligning with the ethical and moral principles I cherish. My involvement in Islamic finance has been a continuous process of learning, exploration, and contribution, driven by a commitment to fostering a more just and compassionate financial system.

Islamic Economic and Finance as a Field of Academic Interest

In 1984, I moved to Bahrain and immersed myself in the emerging offshore Islamic banking industry, which deepened my understanding of Shariah-compliant finance. My background in information science highlighted the interdisciplinary nature of Islamic finance. It is not merely a subset of economics or finance but an intricate field that integrates Islamic teachings, Shariah law, business practices, marketing, and legal frameworks. This complexity necessitates a holistic approach that combines diverse disciplines to build a financial system grounded in ethical and moral principles.

During my research, I came across Dr. Siddiqi's (1978) bibliography of "Contemporary Literature on Islamic Economics." This work was intriguing as it underscored the importance of a comprehensive bibliography for understanding the field. Inspired by Dr. Siddiqi's approach, I decided to explore the bibliometric aspects of Islamic finance, recognizing its potential to enrich my academic career. Building on my understanding of the discipline's interdisciplinary nature and Dr. Siddiqi's bibliography, I conducted extensive research across various online databases. I examined secondary sources from fields such as sociology, psychology, business, religion, and economics. This exploration of over thirty databases revealed numerous primary sources on Islamic banking and finance, highlighting the challenges researchers face in navigating this wealth of information. I realized the importance of identifying secondary sources that summarize key information and understanding the overlaps between different databases.

To address this need, I undertook a study using keywords like "Islamic finance," "Islamic economics," and "Islamic banking." The results, published in the *International Journal of Information Management*, attracted significant attention from economists. Building on this success, I compiled a comprehensive bibliography on Islamic finance and banking. This bibliography became a vital resource, mapping out the research landscape, identifying key players, and offering unique insights into the field. Following the publication of my article on the coverage of Islamic finance in online databases, I focused on compiling a bibliography specifically on Islamic finance. This was a crucial step in formally introducing myself to Dr. Siddiqi and presenting a fresh perspective by combining information science with Islamic finance. My compilation, titled "Information Sources on Islamic

Banking and Economics (1994), provided a detailed overview of the field, including key individuals and institutions, their geographical distribution, and more. This work proved instrumental in organizing conferences and identifying speakers, contributing significantly to the success of the Harvard University Forum. Currently, as Director of Research at Hamad Bin Khalifa University, I emphasize the importance of bibliometric studies in our Ph.D. program. We encourage students to conduct these studies to fully understand their research fields. Compiling my own bibliography offered invaluable insights and introduced me to key scholars across various disciplines related to Islamic finance. This comprehensive approach has been crucial in grasping the multifaceted nature of the field.

Dr. Siddiqi's Standpoint from Babri Mosque Demolition

As mentioned above, Dr. Siddiqi and I first met briefly at King Fahd University in 1976. However, it was after the demolition of the Babri Mosque in India on December 6, 1992, that I had a more substantial encounter with him. This tragic event sparked widespread anger and unrest among Muslims both in India and globally. Shortly after the mosque's demolition, Dr. Siddiqi visited Bahrain for reasons I no longer recall. Learning of his visit, I was delighted to host him at my home. Hosting Dr. Siddiqi was a significant honor for me, given his profound influence on my work in compiling a bibliography on Islamic banking and finance. I extended the invitation to several close friends, and news of his visit spread quickly. As a result, my home was filled beyond capacity, with over a hundred people seated on the floor while Dr. Siddiqi took a seat on the sofa.

The gathering was eager to hear Dr. Siddiqi's views on the mosque's demolition and its political implications. However, he began by stating that he was not there to discuss the mosque's destruction. Instead, he presented the crisis as an opportunity to foster understanding. Dr. Siddiqi encouraged us to engage with our non-Muslim acquaintances, friends, and neighbors in India through informal conversations. He believed that sharing our personal feelings about the demolition could help build empathy and understanding, particularly among Hindus. Dr. Siddiqi advocated for a constructive approach over anger and retaliation. He suggested that personal engagement and dialogue could influence many people more effectively than formal resolutions or acts of defiance. His positive and proactive stance resonated deeply with the audience, who had expected a more confrontational response. Dr. Siddiqi expressed his gratitude for the opportunity to speak and thanked me for hosting the gathering. He believed our meeting could encourage unity and understanding during times of crisis, leaving a lasting impact.

Dr. Siddiqi and My Meetings in Jeddah

After completing my article on Islamic finance coverage in online databases for the *Information Management Journal* (1993), I immersed myself in developing a bibliography of Islamic finance. It decided to meet Dr. Siddiqi and present my perspective, leveraging my background in information science to advance the field of Islamic banking and finance. When I visited Jeddah to meet him, I was both eager and a bit nervous. Dr. Siddiqi's response was highly encouraging. He was intrigued by my approach to applying information science in a structured and scientific manner to promote Islamic finance. I presented various graphs demonstrating the interdisciplinary nature of Islamic finance. Dr. Siddiqi was pleased to see the field being explored from multiple perspectives and recognized its broad, fragmented coverage.

During our discussion, Dr. Siddiqi introduced me to his

senior colleague, Dr. Anas Zarqa, an Islamic economist from Syria. Meeting these scholars was a pivotal moment for me. They were genuinely interested in the interdisciplinary approach to Islamic finance and supported my future plans. I shared my vision of creating an institutionalized information clearinghouse for Islamic economics and finance, a comprehensive electronic database to collect and disseminate information to researchers globally. They were enthusiastic about the idea and suggested that King Abdulaziz University could be a potential host for this project. This meeting was impactful. The endorsement and encouragement from Dr. Siddiqi and Dr. Zarqa were incredibly motivating and gave me the confidence to pursue my vision. Although Dr. Siddiqi has since passed away, I continue to stay in touch with Dr. Zarqa and value the mentorship and friendship I received from both. Their support has been invaluable throughout my journey in Islamic finance.

Dr. Siddiqi's Contributions to Harvard University Initiatives

In the early 1990s, I proposed establishing a dedicated Islamic finance information program at Harvard University. With Dr. Siddiqi's support and generous funding from Prince Mohammed Al-Faisal Al Saud, we launched this pioneering initiative at Harvard. Dr. Siddiqi was a key advisor from 1995 to 2014, significantly contributing to the program's success and the advancement of Islamic finance studies. The funding was secured through the efforts of Mr. Iqbal Ahmad Khan, a distinguished AMU alum and mentee of Dr. Siddiqi. I first met Mr. Khan in the early 1990s when he was General Manager at the International Islamic Investment Company of the Gulf (IICG), the investment arm of Dar Al Maal Islami Group. Our collaboration continues, as Mr. Khan is now the CEO of Fajr Capital in Dubai. Mr. Khan was particularly impressed by my proposal to institutionalize an Islamic finance program at Harvard, especially after learning of my discussions with Dr. Siddiqi. Dr. Siddiqi's endorsement played a crucial role in securing Mr. Khan's support and the necessary funding from the Dar Al Maal Islami Group.

The Harvard Islamic Finance Information Program (HIFIP) was established in 1995 in Cambridge, Massachusetts. Harvard was an ideal location, as the university had already shown interest in Islamic investment through a 1993 study administered by the Center for Middle Eastern Studies (CMES), with Harvard Law School (HLS) and Harvard Business School (HBS) as partners. This prior work set the stage for our program's successful launch. In 1997, we inaugurated the Harvard University Forum on Islamic Finance, which ran annually until 2002. Although the 2001 conference was postponed due to the September 11 attacks, it resumed in 2002 and became a biennial event. The forum continues today, with the 27th conference scheduled for November 8-10, 2024.

The forum quickly gained popularity among various stakeholders. Academics presented foundational theories of Islamic banking, Shariah scholars and legal professionals contributed to product development and regulatory frameworks, and financial professionals and policymakers facilitated market implementation. This diverse participation established the Harvard Conference as a renowned platform in the field. In 1999, Dr. Siddiqi attended the third annual conference, where HRH Prince Mohammed al-Faisal al-Saud, who had provided the seed funding, was also present. Dr. Siddiqi presented a paper titled "Islamic Finance and Beyond: Premises and Promises of Islamic Economics," discussing how Islamic finance can reduce financial market instability and improve productivity compared to conventional finance.

That year, the Islamic Society of North America (ISNA) held a conference concurrently with the Harvard Forum, allowing attendees to benefit from both events. This collaboration included a memorable banquet in Boston Harbor, where I had the opportunity to meet Dr. Siddiqi and his family in a social setting. Dr. Siddiqi also participated in the 2002 Harvard Forum, where he presented a paper on the comparative advantage of Islamic banking and finance. He highlighted three factors contributing to Islamic finance's progress: deficiencies in conventional systems, the resurgence of Islamic societies, and the strong moral orientation of Islamic finance.

In 2004, the sixth Harvard Forum featured a keynote address by John Taylor, Undersecretary for International Affairs at the U.S. Department of Treasury. The theme was "Current Legal and Regulatory Issues in Islamic Finance," and Dr. Siddiqi presented a paper on regulatory challenges. He explored the tension between the *maqasid al-shari'ah* (the higher purposes of the Shariah) and *Fiqh al-Mu'amalat* (Islamic jurisprudence of interpersonal transactions), arguing that involving economists and social scientists could enhance the resolution of these issues. The 2006 forum featured Anwar Ibrahim as the keynote speaker, and addressed the debate between form and substance in Islamic finance. To facilitate discussion between Shariah scholars and economists, we organized a pre-conference workshop titled "Select Ethical and Methodological Issues in Shariah Compliant Finance." The main conference focused on regulation, standardization, and transparency.

Dr. Siddiqi's paper, "Shariah Economics and the Progress of Islamic Finance: The Role of Shariah Experts," emphasized the role of Shariah experts in Islamic finance and its development. He argued for a broader understanding of economics and Shariah, noting that while traditional economics focuses on efficiency and equity, the Shariah's emphasis is on objectives over specific rules. At the 9th Harvard Forum in March 2010, a panel titled "From Islamic Finance to Multifaith Finance," Chaired by Noah

Feldman, Bemis Professor of Law at Harvard Law School, examined the role of faith in finance through two key papers: Seamus Finn's (2022) "Faith and Finance: A Catholic Consideration," and Dr. Siddiqi's (2022) "Faith and Finance: Value-Guided Pursuit of Interests." Dr. Siddiqi emphasized the significance of the relationships between individuals, the environment, and God, arguing that faith provides universal values that guide these connections. In contrast, Seamus Finn, Director of Justice, Peace & Integrity of Creation for the Missionary Oblates, focused on the universal values derived from Catholic social teachings. Both papers challenged Islamic finance to reconcile broad ethical values with specific legal constraints. The panelists provided critiques and suggestions on these guiding papers.

Yusuf DeLorenzo supported the integration of these ideals into Islamic finance, highlighting the need for community engagement, consumer education, standardization, and effective Shariah governance. He proposed including younger scholars on Shariah boards to bring fresh perspectives. Jay Harris, Harry Austryn Wolfson Professor of Jewish Studies, and the late Shahab Ahmed, Assistant Professor of Islamic Studies at Harvard, explored the broader implications of emphasizing universal values, noting potential challenges in investment and politics. Harris cautioned against universalistic faith values, suggesting that distinct moral and legal traditions create in-group versus out-group dynamics. Shahab Ahmed advocated for incorporating faith into the discourse on Islamic finance, framing it as a moral economy. Feldman synthesized the panel's discussions, framing the challenge of integrating universal values with the complexities highlighted by Harris and Ahmed, while considering DeLorenzo's recommendations for balancing ethical ideals with legal constraints.

Dr. Siddiqi's dedication to the Harvard Islamic Finance

initiatives is exemplary. Since our initial discussions about launching the Islamic Finance Information Program and the Islamic Finance Forum at Harvard, he devoted substantial time to advising, supporting, and participating in these events. His consistent involvement in Harvard and London School of Economics conferences and workshops underscores his deep commitment to our program and its growth.

Dr. Siddiqi engaged in conversation. Seated next to him is Jay M. Harris, Noah Feldman, and Yusuf DeLorenzo.

The HIFIP Relocation Drive

Initially based within the Center for Middle Eastern Studies (CMES), the Harvard Islamic Finance Information Program (HIFIP) thrived but soon faced the challenge of aligning with CMES's broader focus. Recognizing that HIFIP's specialized focus on Islamic finance might be better served by another department, I explored potential new homes within Harvard, such as the Kennedy School, the Law School, and the Business School, as well as external options at prestigious institutions like Oxford, Cambridge, and Yale. During this transitional period, I sought the advice of Dr. Siddiqi, whose guidance proved invaluable. He acknowledged the benefits of external support but strongly advocated for keeping the program at Harvard. He used the analogy of planting a tree by the seashore, illustrating that while it's challenging to establish roots in such conditions, once the tree has begun to flourish, it should not be uprooted. This metaphor highlighted the importance of preserving our achievements at Harvard despite the obstacles. Dr. Siddiqi's counsel was clear: maintaining the program at Harvard, even if it required downsizing or restructuring, was crucial. He believed that continuing to promote Islamic finance discourse within Harvard was essential. His perspective led me to forgo plans for relocating the program externally and to concentrate on securing its future within the university. Dr. Siddiqi's guidance during this pivotal time was instrumental in sustaining and advancing Islamic finance studies at Harvard, solidifying the program's role as a leading center for scholarly inquiry and dialogue in the field.

Dr. Siddiqi's Participation in Specialized Academic Workshops

The Harvard University Islamic Finance Forum had established itself as a distinctive intellectual platform, fostering dynamic and open discussions among scholars and practitioners. Since its inception in 1997, the forum had hosted seven iterations, engaging in robust debates on critical issues in Islamic finance. A recurring theme of these debates has been the "form vs. substance" discussion, which often contrasts the perspectives of economists with those of Shariah scholars. Economists generally approach the subject through an academic lens, while Shariah scholars bring deep religious training and often advanced Western education to their analysis. This divergence in foundational training contributes to their differing viewpoints, with Dr. Siddiqi played a prominent role in these discussions.

In response to the sector's evolving complexities, we launched a specialized pre-conference workshop in 2006. This workshop aimed to explore the nuanced relationship between Islamic law (Shariah) and finance. Supported by both Shariah scholars and Islamic economists, the workshop facilitated critical dialogue on key ethical and methodological issues, such as the use of legal stratagems by Shariah experts, the integration of the *maqasid al-shari'ah* into economic practices, and potential conflicts of interest among Shariah advisors. The goal was to strengthen collaboration between economists and Shariah scholars, thereby enhancing the foundation of Shariah-compliant finance.

Held under the Chatham House Rule to ensure open and candid discussion, the workshop was invitation-only and differed from traditional academic conferences in that no individual papers were presented. Instead, it featured a day-long dialogue where participants freely expressed their views, with only a written report produced and no attribution of comments to individuals. Co-moderated by Dr. Siddiqi and Dr. Frank E. Vogel, Founding Director of the Islamic Legal Studies Program at Harvard Law School, the workshop attracted prominent figures from the Islamic finance industry. Notable attendees included Shaykh Nizam Yaquby, Professor Baber Johansen, Dr. Mohammed Elgari, Professor Monzer Kahf, Mufti Barkatullah, Dr. Humayun Dar, Dr. M. Adam El-Sheikh, Professor M. Kabir Hassan, Professor Samuel L. Hayes III, Dr. Mohammad Iqbal Nadvi, Dr. M. Imran Usmani, and Shaykh Taha Abdul-Basser, among others.

Building on the success of this workshop, we decided to hold the next session in London in February 2007. This move aimed to facilitate easier attendance for Shariah scholars and other key industry players and regulators. Sir Howard Davies, Director of the London School of Economics, graciously hosted the event. The 2007 workshop focused on *tawarruq*—an economic practice in which a person buys something on credit and then immediately sells it for cash to a third party in a separate transaction. Dr. Siddiqi and Dr. Elgari presenting foundational papers on the topic: "Current Practices of *Tawarruq*" and "The Economics of *Tawarruq*."

Moderated by Dr. Vogel, the London workshop assembled distinguished figures in Islamic finance, including Professor Khurshid Ahmad, Professor Mabid Al-Jarhi, Sir William Blair, Sir Ross Cranston, Mr. Michael Hanlon, Professor Baber Johansen, Dr. Imran Usmani, Professor Rodney Wilson, Professor Anas Zarqa, Mr. Iqbal Khan, Shaykh Essam Ishaq, Mr. Husam El Khatib, and other prominent experts. Since 2007, this workshop has been held annually, initially at the London School of Economics until 2017, and subsequently at SOAS, University of London. These workshops have become a crucial platform for fostering critical discourse and collaboration within the field of Shariah-compliant finance. These events have significantly contributed to the advancement of discussions on the ethical and methodological underpinnings of Islamic finance.

One notable outcome of these workshops is the forthcoming book, *The Tawarruq Debate in Islamic Finance*, edited by Dr. Frank Vogel. This volume, which includes a contribution from Dr. Siddiqi, is set to be published by Edward Elgar Publishing. Dr. Siddiqi's involvement with the Harvard-LSE Workshop was profound, as reflected in this excerpt from one of his emails dated December 12, 2008 that stated:

> These days I am thinking only about the subject of LSE 2009. My reading finished for the time being, my greatest problem which I wanted to share with someone really engaged with the subject is: How far it is possible to MEASURE default risk of a particular party in a particular deal based on his track record of previous deals? Even if we deny any big role to loans, we have a huge mass of *MURABAHAH* RECEIVABLES—as good as accumulated debts.

In the 2009 Harvard-LSE Workshop, which focused on the theme of "Risk Management," Dr. Siddiqi outlined several key sub-themes for discussion. The workshop featured an opening remark by renowned economist Willem H. Buiter on "Current Financial and Economic Crises within Conventional Markets" (see Buiter & Rahbari 2015). Dr. Siddiqi's proposed sub-themes included:

- **Definition and Classification of Risks:** Exploring how risks in contemporary markets differ from those discussed in Islamic sources from the first five centuries.
- **Islamic Prohibitions and Goals in Risk Management:** Addressing the avoidance of *gharar* (excessive uncertainty), gambling-like speculation, and interest; ensuring fair dealings and increasing efficiency.
- **The Modern Context:** Examining what these Islamic principles mean in today's risk management practices.
- **Critical Survey of Islamic Literature:** Reviewing existing literature on Islamic approaches to risk management.
- **Conventional vs. Islamic Risk Management:** Evaluating what aspects of conventional risk management are acceptable and what are not, from an Islamic perspective.
- **The Contemporary Islamic Financial Industry:** Providing a critical evaluation of risk management practices within the industry.

In the 2011 LSE workshop, themed "Reappraising the Islamic Financial Industry after the Downturn," Dr. Siddiqi contributed a commentary titled "The Preacher and the Banker: Reappraising the Progress of the Islamic Finance Industry." He noted that while Islamic finance performed robustly during the 2007-09 financial crisis, it is essential to address the limitations of capitalism, which often overlooks spiritual and social incentives in favor of material ones. This oversight can lead to inequalities, poverty, and global instability. Dr. Siddiqi argued that Islam and other world religions emphasize the importance of spiritual and social incentives to foster cooperation and shared prosperity.

Dr. Siddiqi's interdisciplinary approach to Islamic finance underscored the need to integrate Shariah scholars into financial development, ensuring that products are asset-backed and free from speculative risks. His work has promoted collaboration between economists and Shariah scholars, as seen in various conferences and workshops. However, for the industry to thrive, it must balance material and spiritual incentives. The financial crisis exposed capitalism's shortcomings in offering a holistic approach to wealth creation. Islamic finance seeks to address this by emphasizing risk-sharing, ethical practices, and community welfare.

Reappraising Islamic finance involves understanding its unique incentive structure and addressing information deficits, psychological behaviors, and misaligned interests. Establishing institutions rooted in Islamic values can help restore balance and support a humane society where wealth serves as a means to a good life for all. During the 2011 workshop in London, Dr. Siddiqi faced some unexpected medical issues. Despite the concern from Dr. Frank Vogel and I, who were worried about his well-being given his long journey from California and advancing age, Dr. Siddiqi received a checkup that fortunately revealed no serious problems. He mentioned that, moving forward, he would travel with his wife to avoid any potential issues when traveling alone. This incident was challenging for both Dr. Vogel and me, and I thought it would be valuable for readers to be aware of it.

A Mentor Beyond Measure: The Personal and Professional Legacy of Dr. Siddiqi

In reflecting on Dr. Siddiqi's remarkable journey, it is crucial to recognize not only his professional impact, but also the personal connections he nurtured. Throughout my academic career—spanning institutions from Saudi Arabia to Bahrain, Harvard, and now Doha—I have had the pleasure of meeting many individuals from Aligarh Muslim University. These professional interactions are well-documented in my work. However, the bond between Dr. Siddiqi and me extended beyond professional realms. Our families developed a close relationship over the years. Our conversations over the phone, coupled with family meetings at conferences and other events, created a deep connection. During his illness, I frequently checked on him, speaking with both his son and wife, who always welcomed my calls with warmth and kindness.

Our last face-to-face meeting was at an LSE workshop in 2014. After that, my relocation to Doha to work with the Qatar Foundation unfortunately meant that our paths did not cross again. Dr. Siddiqi's presence in my life remained profoundly significant. He was more than a mentor. He was like an elder brother, offering invaluable support, guidance, and wisdom. His influence on my thinking and his heartfelt advice are treasures I deeply cherish. Dr. Siddiqi's passing has left a considerable void in my life, one that is hard to fill. His impact was profound and far-reaching, touching many lives. As I conclude my reflections on Dr. Siddiqi, I am filled with gratitude for having known him and for the lasting imprint he made on my journey. Dr. Siddiqi's work epitomizes a revival of traditional Islamic economic principles, skillfully integrating them with contemporary financial practices. His approach to "rooted revivalism" draws deeply from the rich heritage and cultural foundations of Islamic economics, applying these timeless values to modern contexts. This philosophy highlights the importance of a culturally anchored revival, rejuvenating centuries-old principles to invigorate Islamic economic thought in today's financial landscape.

References

Ali, S. Nazim, and Naseem N. Ali. 1994. Information Sources on Islamic Banking and Economics: 1980-1990. London: Routledge.

Ali, S. Nazim. 1993. "Information on Islamic banking and economics as represented by selected databases," *International journal of information management* 13(3): 205-219.

Buiter, Willem H. and Rahbari, Ebrahim. 2015. "Why Economists (and Economies) Should Love Islamic Finance," *JKAU: Islamic Econ.* 28(1): 139-162.

Finn, Seamus P. 2022. "Faith and Finance: A Catholic Consideration." In S. Nazim Ali (ed.), Building Bridges Across Financial Communities: The Global Financial Crisis, Social Responsibility, and Faith-Based Finance (263-279). Cambridge, MA: Islamic Finance Project.

Siddiqi, M.N. "Faith and Finance: Faith and Finance: Value-Guided Pursuit of Interests." In S. Nazim Ali (ed.), Building Bridges Across Financial Communities: The Global Financial Crisis, Social Responsibility, and Faith-Based Finance (280-290). Cambridge, MA: Islamic Finance Project.

Siddiqi, M.N. 1983. *Banking without Interest.* Leicester: Islamic Foundation.

Siddiqi, M.N. 1978. "Contemporary Literature on Islamic Economics: A Select Classified Bibliography of Works in English, Arabic, and Urdu up to 1975." Leicester. The Islamic Foundation.

SEVEN

Islamic Economics and the Alleviation of Poverty: Concepts and Challenges

Salman Syed Ali

Introduction

Dr. Nejatullah Siddiqi, in a reflection on his life and work, shared that he initially studied science subjects in school with the intention of pursuing a career in science and engineering. However, his avid reading of Islamic literature addressing contemporary issues, authored by prominent scholars of his time, inspired him to change his academic focus. He ultimately chose to study Economics, Arabic, and English for his BA. He wrote:

> I abandoned science and the engineering career I had planned. What I wanted now was to learn Arabic, gain direct access to Islamic sources, and discover how modern life and Islamic teachings interacted (Siddiqi 2015).

My earliest introduction to Dr. Nejatullah Siddiqi was through his three books, Economic Enterprise in Islam, Insurance *Islami Maishet* Main (Insurance in an Islamic Economy), and *Shirkat aur Mudarabat kay Sharai Usul* (Partnership and Profit-Sharing in Islamic Law), originally in Urdu. This was around the same time I was inspired by Islam and its economic ideas through several small books by scholars such as Abul A'la al-Maududi, Mufti Shafi, and Manazir Ahsan Gilani. It was some time before I formally started my own study of economics. It shows the lucid style of Dr. Nejatullah that a novice like me was inspired and understood the broad contours of his arguments. However, his other book on Islamic banking, Banking Without Interest, originally published in Urdu was difficult enough for me without any formal training in economics, so I left it and read it later when I had switched my studies to economics and Islamic economics at the School of Economics, International Islamic University Islamabad (SE-IIUI).[1]

I was fortunate to study at SE-IIUI alongside several motivated peers, in a unique B.Sc. program that combined economics, its related quantitative subjects, and Islamic jurisprudence, under the guidance of highly competent teachers who were dedicated to transforming the field of Economics in both theory and practice. Our instructors included renowned scholars such as Dr. Fahim Khan, Dr. Munawar Iqbal, Dr. Sayyid Tahir, Dr. Ramzan Akhtar, Mr. Hafiz Masood, Dr. Tariqullah Khan, and later Dr. Ziauddin Ahmed, among others. The faculty and student body at IIUI were truly international, representing diverse fields within Islamic sciences and hailing from various countries. The timing was ideal for we were full of energy and free from career or future concerns. The serene and secluded campus at Faisal Masjid, Islamabad, provided the perfect setting. Our commitment was unwavering, as our days were devoted to attending classes, engaging in meaningful discussions, writing term papers, playing sports, participating in dawah activities, and supporting each other academically. This environment fostered a

[1] It was elevated and renamed the International Institute of Islamic Economics IIIE at IIUI in 1983.

rich and immersive learning experience, during which I had the opportunity to explore several works by Dr. Nejatullah Siddiqi.

My first in-person encounter with Dr. Nejatullah Siddiqi occurred during his visit to Islamabad, Pakistan, for the Second International Conference on Islamic Economics in March 1983. As second-year Economics students, we were eager to meet him on the very first day of the five-day event. However, none of us had seen his photograph or knew him by face, which led to several mistaken identifications before we finally located him. To my surprise, he did not match the image I had envisioned. I had imagined him as a traditional religious scholar from India or Saudi Arabia, with a long beard and a cap. Instead, he appeared in a safari suit, sporting a short beard and no cap. At the conference, he presented his paper titled "Guarantee of a Minimum Level of Living in an Islamic State," which later became a chapter in his book Role of the State in the Economy: An Islamic Perspective (1996). At the conclusion of the conference, he was invited to the School of Economics at IIUI to speak and interact with the students. I was fortunate to help organize this session and recorded his talk on my cassette recorder. His inspirational speech focused on his journey into Islamic economics. Later, I transcribed the recording with the intention of publishing it in a student magazine we planned to launch, though the project never came to fruition. Years later, as I prepared to leave for Ph.D. studies in the USA, I entrusted the transcription to Dr. Sayyid Tahir, our teacher at IIUI, for potential use.

In his motivational talk to students at the School of Economics, IIUI, Dr. Siddiqi emphasized the importance of integrating Islamic sciences with economics and encouraged the students to dedicate themselves to this pursuit. He shared his personal journey of shifting from pure sciences and engineering to Economics during his youth. Together with several friends, he pursued studies in Economics, Arabic, and English to develop an economics framework rooted in Islamic principles—a goal that became their lifelong mission. Dr. Siddiqi recounted his transition from conventional schooling to madrasa education in Rampur and Azamgarh, and later back to mainstream education at Aligarh Muslim University. To us, he highlighted the unique opportunity provided by the establishment of IIUI, which integrates Islamic and conventional knowledge to nurture scholars capable of making a global impact. His words deeply resonated with us.

My second in-person meeting with Dr. Nejatullah Siddiqi took place in 1997, years after our first encounter. By then, I had completed my Ph.D. in economics at the University of Pennsylvania and was visiting Jeddah. A seminar on one of my Ph.D. papers on game theory was organized at the Centre for Research in Islamic Economics at King Abdulaziz University. Upon my arrival, I was warmly greeted by Dr. Nejatullah Siddiqi and several other scholars who had gathered for the event. Dr. Siddiqi expressed his appreciation for my paper and requested a copy of my dissertation for the Centre, which I was more than happy to provide. After the lecture, we sat in his office, where he enthusiastically discussed various potential research areas. I proposed a topic on the evolution of money and the rationale for the prohibition of *riba al-fadal* (excess in barter) and sought his opinion. He shared numerous valuable insights, reflecting his generosity in supporting students with his time, ideas, and guidance. I also recall an incident from several years earlier, during the final stages of my Ph.D. research, when I faced a shortage of funds. To address this, I applied for supplemental grants from various foundations and organizations, including the Centre for Research in Islamic Economics. My application to the Centre was successful, providing me with crucial financial support. During my 1997 meeting with Dr. Siddiqi, I learned that he had been a member of the committee that approved my grant, further exemplifying his commitment to fostering academic growth and supporting aspiring scholars.

Many years later, in March 2002, I joined the Islamic Research and Training Institute (IRTI). By that time, Dr. Nejatullah Siddiqi had retired from the Centre for Research in Islamic Economics and left Saudi Arabia. However, he returned as a visiting scholar at IRTI for six months starting in November 2002. This period proved invaluable, as I had numerous discussions with him and benefited greatly from his advice. During this time, he provided clarity on several issues related to the *mudarabah* (profit-sharing agency) contract and *mudarabah* financing while I was working on a related paper. Additionally, he completed his book Riba, Bank Interest, and the Rationale of its Prohibition (2004) during this period. Engaging with him on this work was particularly enlightening. In this concise yet comprehensive book, he addressed the major aspects of the prohibition of *riba* and the principles of a *riba*-free financial system, drawing from the purpose of Islamic law. A key takeaway for me was his detailed extraction and explanation of five reasons from the Qur'an for the prohibition of *riba*, which he articulated with remarkable clarity and depth:

i. *Riba* corrupts society.

ii. *Riba* implies improper appropriation of other people's property.

iii. *Riba*'s ultimate effect is negative growth.

iv. *Riba* demeans and diminishes human personality.

v. *Riba* is unjust.

Early Works

Dr. Nejatullah Siddiqi began his journey in the development of Islamic economics and finance during a time when the ideological rivalry between communism and capitalism was at its peak. Like many Muslim scholars of his era, he sought to present an Islamic system as a viable alternative, addressing the shortcomings of both communism and capitalism. This Islamic economic framework respected natural human desires while guiding them through divine principles within the legal, moral, social, and political dimensions. In advocating for the Islamic socio-economic system, Dr. Siddiqi initially focused on the Islamic financial system, particularly on how banks could operate without relying on interest. At the time, banks were a dominant component of the financial systems on the Subcontinent and globally. He proposed a model where deposit mobilization and fund utilization by banks would operate on a *mudarabah* (profit-sharing) basis.

In this two-tier *mudarabah* banking model, depositors act as fund providers, entrusting their money to banks on a *mudarabah* basis. The banks, in turn, use these funds to finance businesses and entrepreneurs through a second-tier *mudarabah.* Profits generated from the second-tier *mudarabah* are shared, with a portion retained by the bank as earnings and the remainder distributed to depositors. The brilliance of Dr. Siddiqi's work lay not only in his exploration of how individual banks could operate on this model but also in his explanation of how an entire banking system could function on this basis. He further detailed the role of a central bank in controlling profit-sharing ratios within the *mudarabah* contracts, ensuring a cohesive and regulated banking system.

While Dr. Nejatullah was a theoretician and model builder, he did not establish or run any Islamic bank. Practical implementation of Islamic banking was carried out in the private sector by able and resource-rich individual entrepreneurs who wanted to provide *riba*-free banking and investment opportunities to Muslims. The practitioners of Islamic banking soon realized the importance of offering products that are similar to fixed returns.

They also found easy ways of Islamizing finance by pushing for and structuring financial contracts and financial products that could avoid economic risks and transfer them as much as possible to the financed party. Dr. Nejatullah used to voice his concern that while variable returns risk-sharing products and fixed returns products both are needed in the Islamic financial system, excessive reliance on risk-shifting *murabaha* is not good.

Later works

The objective and purpose of Islamic law consistently served as the guiding force in Dr. Siddiqi's technical works. However, his later publications, such as *Dialogue in Islamic Economics* (2002) and the Urdu work *Maqasid-e-Shariat*, reflected a deeper focus on the objectives of the *Sharīʿah*, extending beyond finance to encompass economics as a whole (Siddiqi 2009). Dr. Siddiqi observed that Islamic economics had inadvertently become restricted to two primary aspects: the prohibition of interest and the imposition of zakat (compulsory alms-giving). He argued that its scope is far broader, addressing a wide range of economic and social challenges and dilemmas. Furthermore, he emphasized that Islamic economics should not be limited to the behavior of Muslims alone but should also consider the behavior of all participants in the economy. In doing so, it can draw upon the rich guidance provided by the Qur'an and Sunnah.

Dr. Siddiqi emphasized the importance of integrating *maqasid al-Sharīʿah* (the objectives of *Sharīʿah*) and economic reasoning alongside *fiqh* principles to ensure the proper development of Islamic finance. He argued that the principles of *fiqh al-muʿamalat*, as currently applied to determine *Sharīʿah* compliance in financial matters, are often focused on individual circumstances. Islamic legal opinions, or fatwas, are typically issued with consideration for the specific situation of the individual or organization seeking guidance. Consequently, such fatwas may not account for the fallacy of composition or, in other words, that which is permissible and *Sharīʿah*-compliant for an individual may not be appropriate or beneficial if adopted collectively without additional rules. For instance, if there are multiple halal methods of financing, public policy guided by the objectives of the *Sharīʿah* requires an evaluation of their macroeconomic effects. The method that generates greater collective benefits and minimizes harm should be prioritized. As an example, Dr. Siddiqi discussed *tawarruq*, a financial transaction where an individual purchases a commodity on credit and sells it to a third party for cash to meet immediate liquidity needs. While some *fuqaha* deem *tawarruq* *Sharīʿah*-permissible due to its historical use and its utility for individuals facing financial difficulties, its broader economic implications are concerning. *Tawarruq*, as a debt-creating instrument, is not linked to productive capacity and can lead to unlimited debt accumulation. Widespread adoption of *tawarruq* as a mainstream Islamic financial product could result in excessive debt burdens for individuals and society. This not only contradicts the *Sharīʿah* objective of wealth preservation but also undermines human life, dignity, religion, and future generations. Therefore, while legal principles help distinguish halal from haram, economic reasoning and the *maqasid al-Sharīʿah* are essential for selecting the most beneficial options.

Sukuk are Islamic financial certificates that offer fixed returns but differ from bonds in that they represent ownership in tangible assets, usufruct, services, or investments in specific projects, ensuring their *Sharīʿah* compliance. However, over time, certain questionable features have been introduced into sukuk structures. For instance, sukuk have been issued against receivable income, or clauses have been included that bind the issuer to repurchase the sukuk at their original price. While Dr. Nejatullah Siddiqi acknowledged the progress in sukuk development, he strongly advocated for addressing these concerns to uphold their *Sharī'ah* compliance and integrity:

> [D]istancing sukuk from debt is necessary to make them free of *riba* and elements of *maysir* (gambling). This can be done by making sukuk based on real assets to the exclusion of *murabahah* receivables.[2] It also requires doing away with the commitment to redeeming sukuk at their original price on expiry of their term. These steps may save Islamic finance from contributing to the trend towards inequity and instability germane to conventional debt based financial system (Siddiqi 2008).

In his Urdu book, *Maqasid-e-Shariat* he also covered many social, religious, and public policy issues beyond finance. He highlighted the need for dynamic thinking to make Islamic economics and finance contribute to the socio-economic development of Muslims and humanity as a whole.

In 2014, under the auspices of the Islamic Research and Training Institute (IRTI), we organized a series of workshops focused on developing a *maqasid al-shari'ah* index for socio-economic development. Dr. Nejatullah Siddiqi expressed keen interest in the initiative, engaging with us through email and phone, even though he was unable to attend in person due to his advanced age. During the workshops, most authors adopted an approach similar to the Human Development Index (HDI), enhancing it with Islamically desirable variables, while a few

---

[2] *Murabahah* as practiced now, is a sales-based Islamic financing method where a seller purchases goods requested by a buyer and then sells them to the buyer at an agreed-upon price, which includes a disclosed profit margin. The buyer typically pays this price over a specified period, making *murabahah* a form of cost-plus financing. *Murabahah* receivables are the amounts owed to a seller under a *murabahah* contract.

explored entirely different methodologies. Dr. Siddiqi later received our manuscript and offered his encouragement, though he expressed a reservation: quantifying the concept of *maqasid al-Sharīʿah*, with its significant policy implications, risked reducing it to mere statistical measurement. In response, we clarified that our approach differed from others. Rather than directly quantifying *maqasid al-Sharīʿah*, we applied the concept to measure economic development through its inverse: poverty. Our index evaluates deprivations across the five dimensions of *maqasid al-Sharīʿah*, with lower deprivation levels indicating reduced poverty and, consequently, higher economic development.

Islamic Economics and Alleviation of Poverty: Concepts and Challenges

This section builds on the ideas of Dr. Nejatullah Siddiqi, taking them in new directions. It introduces advancements in poverty measurement, with the *maqasid al-Sharīʿah* as the foundation. While most would agree that life is more than meeting basic physical needs, development is not merely about comfort and higher living standards, and poverty is not just low income that hinders maintaining a decent standard of living or meeting basic necessities. In Islam, life is about living with purpose and enjoying it without waste.[3] The purpose of life is to worship Allah ﷻ in both individual and collective contexts.[4] The essential protections of **(i)** life, **(ii)** religion, **(iii)** progeny, **(iv)** intellect, and **(v)** wealth are

[3] Qur'an 7:31

۞ يَٰبَنِيٓ ءَادَمَ خُذُواْ زِينَتَكُمۡ عِندَ كُلِّ مَسۡجِدٖ وَكُلُواْ وَٱشۡرَبُواْ وَلَا تُسۡرِفُوٓاْۚ إِنَّهُۥ لَا يُحِبُّ ٱلۡمُسۡرِفِينَ

O Children of Adam! wear your beautiful apparel at every time and place of prayer: eat and drink: But waste not by excess, for Allah loveth not the wasters.

See also Qur'an 6:141

[4] Purpose of life on earth, Qur'an 51:56. وَمَا خَلَقۡتُ ٱلۡجِنَّ وَٱلۡإِنسَ إِلَّا لِيَعۡبُدُونِ

And I did not create the jinn and mankind except to worship Me.

fundamental to this purpose. These protections underpin all *Sharīʿah* injunctions and prohibitions. Though the *Sharīʾah* primarily addresses Muslims, these protections are universal, ensuring freedoms for all to choose the right path as ordained by Allah ﷻ. A minimum level of protection in these five dimensions is essential for societal development. Thus, human progress combines material, spiritual, and moral development, which are key features of the Islamic economic and financial system, as emphasized by Nejatullah Siddiqi, who also proposed additional objectives beyond the well-known five.

In our work, we focused on the five well-known objectives of *Sharīʿah* to create a measurement method; otherwise, the discussion would have been too broad. If socioeconomic development is to be measured, it should be assessed across these five dimensions, rather than solely in terms of income or living standards. It is important to note that the Islamic concept of economic development extends beyond conventional economics, which often limits development to GDP growth, improved living standards (Kuznets 1934, 1941), longevity (Scott, Ellison, and Sinclair 2021), or freedom (Sen 1999), with the latter being its highest philosophical form in current economic theory. This conceptual difference arises from various factors, but the primary reason is Islam's worldview, which links this world to the hereafter, fundamentally shifting the human perspective.

Another challenge in measuring socioeconomic progress is that development has no upper limit, as its potential is constrained only by available resources and efforts. In contrast, poverty, as the inverse of development, has a conceivable upper limit and is relatively easier to measure. Poverty is also simpler to conceptualize compared to development because it is based on deprivation from necessities, which are inherently limited, unlike unlimited wants. Consequently poverty, in terms of its incidence, extent, and severity, can serve as a reverse indicator of socioeconomic development.

We now focus on measuring poverty more comprehensively using the five objectives of the *Sharīʿah* as criteria. This method will be outlined briefly, with details available in referenced papers. The core concept is that individuals require minimum levels of protection (guarantees) in the dimensions of **(i)** life, **(ii)** religion, **(iii)** progeny, **(iv)** intellect, and **(v)** wealth to function and develop. If someone falls below the required level in any dimension, they are considered "deprived" in that area. If they are deprived in multiple dimensions, i.e., falling below the minimum in a specified number of dimensions or key dimensions, then they are classified as "poor." Otherwise, they are considered nonpoor. At a societal level, progress can be defined as simultaneous development across all five dimensions for all members. Without this, development is either skewed or absent. While the definition of poverty is value-laden and has subjective thresholds both for minimum achievement in each dimension and the cutoff for the number of deprivations, the choice of evaluation dimensions is more universal and meaningful. This approach allows for a more comprehensive identification of the poor.

Measuring poverty along these dimensions requires indicators that are closely linked to each dimension. These indicators should be concise (a few well-chosen ones) and measurable. Conciseness ensures the poverty measure is sensitive to changes in key variables and cost-effective in data collection. However, measuring across five dimensions presents challenges in aggregation, especially with regard to how to combine them when each dimension differs in nature and units of measurement. To address this, we adopted the Alkire-Foster (AF) counting method (Alkire and Foster 2008). In this method, each dimension is assessed individually to determine an individual's level of achievement. Those falling below the set thresholds are classified as deprived in that dimension. The number of deprivations for each individual is then counted, and a pre-agreed cutoff is used to classify them as either poor or nonpoor. This approach avoids the complexities of interpersonal comparisons and interdimensional aggregations typically encountered in multidimensional poverty measurement. Appendix A provides a technical explanation of this method. Standard poverty measures such as poverty incidence, intensity, and the poverty gap can still be calculated, though with slightly different interpretations. For more details on applying this method to measure poverty based on *maqasid al-Sharīʿah* using actual data, readers can refer to the studies by Hasan, Ali, and Muhammad (2018) and Ali (2019). Currently, the main challenge is the lack of custom surveys designed for this purpose by international organizations and national statistical bureaus. As a result, the cited studies relied on data from variables closely aligned with the desired indicators from available surveys, such as the World Values Survey (WVS), which provides a valuable dataset for this work.

An Illustrative Example

To demonstrate that a *maqasid al-Sharīʿah*-based index for poverty measurement is feasible, practical, and more effective, we can use numerical results from a study by Ali and Hasan (2018). In their work, the dimension of faith protection is measured using three indicators from the World Values Survey (WVS), which capture both the profession of faith and its confirmation through actions. The dimension of life protection is assessed using nine indicators, while the remaining three dimensions (intellect, posterity, and wealth) are measured using 4, 6, and 4 indicators, respectively. A summary of these indicators is provided in Table 1. Some of these indicators fall under positive protection, while others are categorized as preventive protection. The dos and don'ts of the *Sharīʿah* are divided into four levels: Level 1 includes acts that are divinely punishable, such as *shirk* (associating partners with Allah ﷻ), *riba* (usury), and suicide. Level 2 covers legally punishable acts under *hudud* laws, such as theft, murder, and adultery. Level 3 consists of acts of religious goodness, like prayer, fasting, *zakat*, and *hajj*. Level 4 includes acts of moral goodness, such as kindness to parents, generosity, discipline, cleanliness, and good governance. The first two levels are considered preventive protection, while the last two are categorized as positive protection. Ideally, each dimension should have at least one indicator from all four levels.

Dimension	**Variable Name in the Survey**	**Indicator Hint (see the full question in the survey)**
FATIH	V145	attendance in religious services
	V146	frequency in prayer
	V147	religious, non-religious or atheist person
	V148	belief in God
LIFE	V55	freedom of choice in life
	V177	preferred not to go out at night
	V179	victim of crime last year
	V180	immediate family victim of crime last year
	V183	a war involving my country
	V184	a terrorist attack
	V185	a civil war
	V188	gone without enough food to eat
	V189	felt unsafe from crime in your home
INTELLECT	V182	not being able to give my children a good education
	V248	highest level of education
	V172	alcohol consumption in streets
	V175	drug sale in streets
POSTERITY	V203	Homosexuality: justifiable
	V203A	Prostitution:
	V204	Abortion:
	V205	Divorce:

Dimension	Variable Name in the Survey	Indicator Hint (see the full question in the survey)
	V206	sex before marriage:
	V209	parents beating children:
PROPERTY	V59	satisfaction with financial situation
	V171	occurrence of robberies
	V181	worry about losing job or not finding a job
	V239	which income group you belong to

Table 1: Maqasid al-*Sharī'ah* Dimensions and their indicators in WVS 2010-2012

For each indicator, a desired threshold level was decided upon. A person is said to be deprived in terms of an indicator if he or she falls short of a minimum desired level in that indicator. Then the poor are identified by putting the second cut-off at 40% of total deprivations (i.e., $k \geq 2$). That is, a person is identified as poor if he/she is deprived in 40% or more of the five dimensions. All the usual statistics of poverty can be calculated using this method. The incidence of poverty or the headcount (denoted by H) measures the percentage of poor in the total population. The intensity of poverty (denoted by A) measures the average number of dimensions of deprivations among the poor. Lastly, the multidimensional *maqasid al-Sharī'ah*-based poverty index (MSPI) measures the headcount adjusted for intensity (MSPI = H x A) i.e., the product of incidence and intensity of multidimensional *maqasid al-Sharī'ah*-based poverty. In other words, it is the proportion of deprivations a country faces out of the total potential deprivations it could experience overall.

Results and Analysis

Table 2 categorizes 20 OIC countries based on MSPI scores into very highly multidimensionally poor, highly multidimensionally poor, moderately multidimensionally poor, and weakly multidimensionally poor countries. The demarcation percentages for these categorizations are arbitrary and created for comparison and policy purposes only. The same data are also shown in Figure 1.

Ranking	Country	Head Count H	Intensity A	MSPI (at 40% deprivation)	Category*
1	Kazakhst	0.794667	0.540042	0.429153	1
2	Algeria	0.69	0.511836	0.353167	1
3	Malaysia	0.676923	0.517727	0.350462	1
4	Pakistan	0.644167	0.507555	0.32695	1
5	Kyrgyzst	0.637333	0.512511	0.32664	1
6	Lebanon	0.645833	0.505019	0.326158	1
7	Nigeria	0.645253	0.496996	0.320688	1
8	Tunisia	0.632365	0.506667	0.320398	1
9	Azerbaij	0.580838	0.485086	0.281757	2
10	Egypt	0.54826	0.491641	0.269547	2
11	Yemen	0.532	0.479436	0.25506	2
12	Iraq	0.49	0.48364	0.236983	2
13	Morocco	0.466667	0.491411	0.229325	2
14	Uzbekist	0.460667	0.486672	0.224193	2
15	Libya**	0.451901	0.493738	0.223121	2
16	Turkey	0.337072	0.481959	0.162455	3
17	Palestin	0.33	0.475333	0.15686	3
18	Jordan	0.285833	0.477201	0.1364	3

Ranking	Country	Head Count H	Intensity A	MSPI (at 40% deprivation)	Category*
19	Kuwait	0.092095	0.441667	0.040675	4
20	Qatar	0.015094	0.426875	0.006443	4

*1 = MSPI >=30% very highly multidimensionally poor.

2 = MSPI >=20% but <30% highly multidimensionally poor.

3 = MSPI >=10% but <20% moderately multidimensionally poor.

4 = MSPI <10% weakly multidimensionally poor.

** Since the data available in VWS is from 2010-14, therefore some countries, e.g., Libya is ranked better compared to its current situation.

Table 2: Poverty Headcount, Intensity, and MSPI scores of countries in four classes

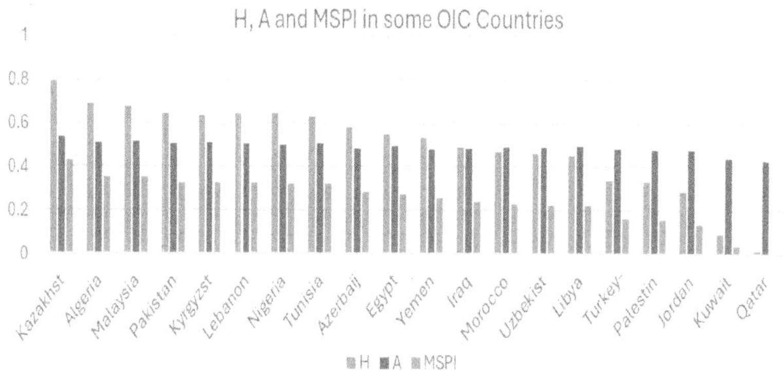

Figure 1

An individual is considered poor in terms of *maqasid al-Sharī'ah* protections if he/she is deprived in 40% or more out of the sum of weighted indicators of all dimensions. i.e., an individual with a deprivation score greater than or equal to 40% is multidimensionally poor in the light of the *maqasid al-Sharīʿah.* The MSPI for a country shows the proportion of deprivations a country faces as a percent of the total potential deprivations it could experience overall. MSPI is obtained from the product of the incidence and intensity of multidimensional poverty (H x A). It would be instructive to know how much information we can get from this analysis. For example, among the countries shown in Table 2, Kazakhstan has the highest MS-based poverty with an MSPI of 0.429. The headcount index (H) is 79.5%, which indicates the incidence of poverty. In other words, 79.5% of the sample population in Kazakhstan falls short of a desirable level of achievement in terms of the *maqasid al-Sharīʿah.* In the present example, it also means 79.5% of the sample population in Kazakhstan is deprived in two or more dimensions. The intensity of poverty is calculated by average deprivation (A) which turns out to be 54%, meaning that on average an MS poor person in Kazakhstan is deprived in 54% of the total dimensions. The MSPI which shows *maqasid al-Sharīʿah*-based multidimensional poverty is calculated by multiplying H and A; that is, the headcount (H) is adjusted for intensity (A). In the case of Kazakhstan, MSPI is 0.429. Similarly, the poverty statistics of other countries in Table 1 can be interpreted. Comparing H and A of a country provides further information. For example, Turkey has a much lower MSPI (0.162) than many countries. However, the intensity of poverty in Turkey (A = 0.4819) is higher than the incidence of poverty (H = 0.337) there. This means that while a small proportion of the population is poor in Turkey, its severity among the poor is much higher. It is also possible to find the proportion of deprivations in each dimension and across different areas and localities because the measure based on the Alkire-Foster counting methodology is additive. Thus, this approach not only allows for inter-country and inter-area comparison but also gives details of poverty composition in each country, which is useful for finding the weaker dimensions and formulating poverty alleviation policies.

Conclusion

This paper offers three key insights: it highlights Nejatullah Siddiqi's role as a mentor, provides a comprehensive overview of Dr. Siddiqi's contributions to Islamic economics, finance, and the *maqasid al-Sharīʿah*, and builds on his mission by summarizing recent advancements in measuring poverty and economic development from an Islamic perspective. Dr. Nejatullah Siddiqi's works were both accessible and inspiring, sparking interest in Islamic economics and banking for many. His mentorship and support had a profound impact on his students, while his innovative ideas, openness to dialogue, and steadfast commitment attracted numerous scholars to the field of Islamic economics and finance. In his early works, Dr. Siddiqi focused on developing an Islamic economic system as an alternative to communism and capitalism, with an emphasis on interest-free banking. He proposed a two-tier *mudarabah* banking model, where depositors provide funds to banks, which are then used to finance businesses, positioning banks as financial entrepreneurs rather than intermediaries. He also raised concerns when Islamic financial practices deviated from their intended objectives. In his later works, Dr. Siddiqi expanded on the broader objectives of the *Sharīʿah*, emphasizing that Islamic economics should address all economic and social issues, not just the prohibition of interest. He stressed the importance of the *maqasid al-Sharīʿah* and economic reasoning in shaping Islamic finance and integrating it into the broader socio-economic development of Muslims and humanity. He advocated for dynamic thinking and emphasized the holistic objectives of *Sharīʿah*, which extend beyond financial matters.

This paper builds on Nejatullah Siddiqi's mission by presenting a *maqasid al-Sharīʿah*-based framework for measuring poverty and economic development, developed by the author and Hamid Hasan. This approach extends beyond monetary and physical needs, focusing on the protections for life, religion, progeny, intellect, and wealth as defined by the *Sharīʿah*. Using the Alkire-Foster counting method, the framework assesses poverty through deprivations in these five dimensions, providing a comprehensive measure that goes beyond traditional economic metrics like GDP and the Global Multidimensional Poverty Index. This holistic framework integrates material, spiritual, and moral aspects, emphasizing the importance of tailored data collection to effectively measure and address poverty in line with Islamic principles. The index and its methodology are valuable for formulating actionable policies for poverty alleviation and evaluating the impact of those policies. It is hoped that further research in this area will enhance the application of Islamic concepts in the socio-economic development of countries and contribute to extending the ideas found in the writings of the late Nejatullah Siddiqi.

Appendix-A

Box 1: Steps in the calculation of multidimensional poverty

Step-1: Choose the unit of analysis

Step-2: Choose dimensions

Step-3: Choose indicators

Step-4: Set poverty lines (first cut-off)

Step-5: Apply poverty lines

Step-6: Count the deprivations for each person

Step-7: Set the second cut-off

Step-8: Apply the second cut-off (k) to obtain the set of poor persons and censor all nonpoor data

Step-9: Calculate the headcount (H)

$H = {}^{q}/_{n}$ where q is the number of people who are multidimensionally poor, and n is the total population

Step-10: Calculate the average poverty gap (A)

$A = \frac{\sum_1^q c}{q}$ where c is the deprivation score of multidimensionally poor and is obtained by adding the deprivation score in each dimension. If a poor person is deprived in three dimensions, then his score is obtained as follows: $c = c_1 + c_2 + c_3$.

Step-11: Calculate the adjusted headcount (Mo)

$M_0 = H \cdot A$

Step-12: Decompose by group and breakdown by dimension

$Contrib_j = \frac{\sum_1^q c_j/n}{M_0}$ It shows the contribution of dimension j to multidimensional poverty

References

Ali, Salman Syed, ed. 2019. Towards a *Maqāṣid Al-Sharī'ah* Index of Socio-Economic Development: Theory and Application. Cham: Palgrave Macmillan.

Ali, Salman Syed, and Hamid Hasan. 2018. "Measuring Deprivation from *Maqasid al-Sharī'ah* Dimensions in OIC Countries: Ranking and Policy Focus." *Journal of King Abdulaziz University: Islamic Economics* 2018 (1): 3-26.

Alkire, Sabina, and James Foster. 2008. "Counting and Multidimensional Poverty Measurement | OPHI Working Papers (2007, Revised in 2008)." https://ophi.org.uk/publication/WP-07.

Alkire, Sabina, and James Foster. 2011. "Counting and Multidimensional Poverty Measurement." *Journal of Public Economics* 95 (7): 476-87. https://doi.org/10.1016/j.jpubeco.2010.11.006. Chapra, M. Umer. 2008. *The Islamic Vision of Development in the Light of Maqāsid al-Sharī'ah.* (Research Paper). Jeddah: Islamic Research and Training Institute (IRTI).

Hasan, Hamid, Salman Syed Ali, and Malik Muhammad. 2018. "Towards a Maqasid al-*Shari'ah* Based Development Index." *Journal of Islamic Business and Management* 8 (1). https://journals.riphah.edu.pk/index.php/jibm/article/view/112.

Kuznets, Simon. 1934. National Income, 1929-1932. Cambridge, Massachusetts: USA: National Bureau of Economic Research (NBER). http://www.nber.org/books/kuzn34-1.

Kuznets, Simon. 1941. National Income and Its Composition 1919-1938. New York: National Bureau of Economic Research.

Scott, Andrew J., Martin Ellison, and David A. Sinclair. 2021. "The Economic Value of Targeting Aging." *Nature Aging* 1 (7): 616-23. https://doi.org/10.1038/s43587-021-00080-0.

Sen, Amartya. 1999. *Development as Freedom.* Oxford University Press.

Siddiqi, Muhammad Nejatullah. 1979. *The Economic Enterprise in Islam*, Lahore, Pakistan: Islamic Publications.

Siddiqi, Muhammad Nejatullah. 1983. *Banking without Interest.* Leicester (UK): Islamic Foundation

Siddiqi, Muhammad Nejatullah. 1985. *Partnership and Profit-Sharing in Islamic Law*, Leicester (UK): Islamic Foundation. (Originally in Urdu. 1968. *Shirkat aur Mudarabat kay Sharai Usul*, Lahore, Pakistan: Islamic Publications).

Siddiqi, Muhammad Nejatullah. 1985. *Insurance in an Islamic*

Economy, Nairobi, Kenya: Islamic Foundation. (Originally in Urdu. 1974. *Insurance Islami Maishet Main*, Lahore, Pakistan, Islamic Publications).

Siddiqi, Muhammad Nejatullah. 1996. *Role of the State in the Economy: An Islamic Perspective*. Leicester: Islamic Foundation.

Siddiqi, Muhammad Nejatullah. 2002. *Dialogue in Islamic Economics*. The Islamic Foundation & Institute of Policy Studies.

Siddiqi, Muhammad Nejatullah. 2004. *Riba, Bank Interest and the Rationale of Its Prohibition* No 205, Occasional Papers. Jeddah: The Islamic Research and Teaching Institute (IRTI). https://ideas.repec.org//p/ris/irtiop/0205.html.

Siddiqi, Muhammad Nejatullah. 2008. "A Note on Sukuk and Their Role in Islamic Finance." July 2, 2008. http://www.siddiqi.com/mns/NoteOnSukuk.htm.

Siddiqi, Muhammad Nejatullah. 2009. *Maqasid-e-Shariat (Objectives of the Sharīʿah)*. Islamabad, Pakistan: Idara-e-Tahqeeqat-e-Islami, International Islamic University, Islamabad.

Siddiqi, Muhammad Nejatullah. 2015. "My Life in Islamic Economics | Critical Muslim." Critical Muslim 15. https://criticalmuslim.com/explore/issues/educational-reform/my-life-islamic-economics.

EIGHT

The Contributions of Dr. Nejatullah Siddiqi to Islamic Finance Initiatives in India and His Universal Approach to Global Issues

H. Abdur Raqeeb

Introduction

Dr. Muhammad Nejatullah Siddiqi is internationally recognized as a leading authority in Islamic economics and finance. His contributions have received widespread acclaim from experts both nationally and internationally. This paper examines foundational activities undertaken under his visionary leadership and guidance. The author, who worked closely with Dr. Siddiqi for three decades, played an active role in these initiatives, including the establishment of the Indian Centre for Islamic Finance (ICIF) in New Delhi. This paper captures the author's experiences and reflections on working alongside Dr. Siddiqi. It serves as a primary documentary resource on Dr. Siddiqi's contributions, many of which may not have been previously documented. Additionally, the paper highlights his global perspective on societal challenges through excerpts from two key speeches and concludes with an overview of his insights on Islamic economics and wealth creation.

Brief Biography

Dr. Muhammad Nejatullah Siddiqi was born in Gorakhpur, India on August 21, 1931. After completing his primary and secondary education, he moved to Aligarh Muslim University for his higher education. He completed a B.A., M.A. and Ph.D. in economics. He also joined Sanwi Darsgah in Rampur, UP and Madrasat-ul-Islah, Saraimeer, Azamgarh, Uttar Pradesh for education in Shariah and Islamic studies. He joined as a lecturer (Assistant Professor) at the Department of Economics, Aligarh Muslim University (AMU), Aligarh in 1961 and became Reader (Associate Professor) in 1975 and professor in 1977. Later he moved to King Abdul Aziz University, Jeddah, Saudi Arabia and began as a professor of Economics in 1978 and served there till 2000. Thereafter he rendered his services at various institutions across the world in various capacities of academic professional and advisor such as the International Islamic University, Kuala Lumpur, Malaysia, American Islamic Finance, based in Los Angeles, Islamic Research and Training Institute, Islamic Development Bank, Jeddah, Saudi Arabia and Center for Near Eastern Studies, University of California, Los Angeles etc. Thus, he was a gifted academician and a scholar of repute. His academic contribution was recognized across the globe especially in the field of Islamic economics and finance. For his valuable contribution, he received the famous King Faisal International award in 1982.

Foundational Principles of Islamic Finance

Dr. Muhammad Nejatullah Siddiqi prioritized the foundational principles of Islamic finance, opposing any compromise on its core tenets to align with prevailing practices, as he believed this would compromise the system's uniqueness. He emphasized that the objectives of Shariah must be upheld in all circumstances, even in challenging situations. Dr. Siddiqi warned that tolerating deviations from the fundamental ethos of Islamic finance could lead to a gradual erosion of its principles, rendering the Islamic banking industry ineffective and undermining its credibility, a trend that he observed over the decades. Nevertheless, he advocated for innovative practices within Islamic finance, provided they adhered to its foundational principles. For instance, he criticized *tawarruq* as an Islamic finance instrument, highlighting its adverse effects. Similarly, he viewed *murabahah* (mark-up finance) as a temporary solution for short-term financing, stressing that participatory finance should be prioritized for long-term needs, such as entrepreneurship and business projects, to ensure sustainable growth. He cautioned that while certain instruments might yield short-term benefits, they could have detrimental long-term consequences for the industry. Furthermore, Dr. Siddiqi called for a modernized approach to *ijtihad*, arguing that in today's complex world, where specialized knowledge is critical, the process should involve experts and professionals from diverse fields. He believed that restricting *ijtihad* to religious scholars alone risked overlooking the multifaceted nature of contemporary issues, weakening the decision-making process.

Dr. Siddiqi consistently championed the movement for Islamic banking initiatives in India by providing key ideas and themes for seminars, conferences, and workshops, while encouraging meaningful efforts in this field. He envisioned essential concepts and laid the groundwork necessary for establishing Islamic finance institutions. Despite his demanding schedule, he meticulously drafted the themes, aims, and objectives for these institutions with remarkable attention to detail. He also recommended suitable individuals for key responsibilities but never sought high-profile positions such as president or chairman for himself. Preferring to work behind the scenes, he played a pivotal role in driving these initiatives and activities. A notable example is the establishment of the Indian Centre for Islamic Finance (ICIF), where he guided numerous events and programs that brought together intellectuals from around the world for in-depth discussions on Islamic banking and finance. The remainder of the paper is a chronological account of key events undertaken with the leadership and guidance of Dr. Siddiqi.

Islamic Banking and the Reserve Bank of India Report (2006)

The global financial crisis, triggered by the US subprime mortgage crisis between mid-2007 and early 2009, left much of the conventional banking system in disarray. It also reignited interest in Islamic banking as a viable alternative, with its focus on ethical investment, emphasizing openness, transparency, and the avoidance of unnecessary risk. In 2005, the Government of India (GOI) directed the Reserve Bank of India (RBI) to explore ways to introduce Islamic banking in the country. To assess its feasibility, the GOI established a Working Group chaired by Mr. Anand Sinha, then Executive Director of RBI, to examine financial instruments used in Islamic banking. The group submitted its report in July 2006, proposing how Islamic banking could be implemented in India and its potential benefits. However, the group concluded that "if banks in India are to undertake Islamic banking, appropriate amendments to the Banking Regulation Act of 1949 are required, and the taxation implications must be re-examined" (IFT, 2012).

Dr. Siddiqi monitored the developments and was eager to receive the RBI working group report on the feasibility of Islamic banking. Jamaʿat-e-Islami Hind (JIH) planned to organize an international conference on the theme "Justice and Equity—the Message of Islamic Banking" in February 2006, months before the RBI report was released in July 2006. Dr. Manmohan Singh, the then Prime Minister of India, was invited to inaugurate the conference, while Finance Minister P. Chidambaram was also approached but preferred to wait for the RBI report before attending. Eventually, the organizers, including the author of this paper, persuaded Mr. Palani Manickam, Deputy Finance Minister, to inaugurate the conference. He delivered a positive address highlighting the need and relevance of Islamic banking and finance. Following the release of the Anand Sinha committee report on Islamic Banking in India, Dr. Siddiqi and others organized a workshop in Mumbai in September 2006, just two months later.

The 2006 International Conference on Islamic Banking

The Jama'at-e-Islami Hind (JIH) organized an international seminar in New Delhi on February 18-19, 2006, titled "Justice and Equity: The Message of Islamic Banking." The event featured prominent international speakers, including Dr. Umar Chapra, Dr. Mabid Ali al-Jarhi, Dr. Monzer Kahf, Mr. Mohammed Ismail Shariff, and Dr. Mansoor Durrani. Dr. Nejatullah Siddiqi (in absentia) and Dr. Fazlur Rahman Faridi provided guidance for the program and proceedings (IFT, 2012). Dr. Siddiqi played a pivotal role in persuading international experts and practitioners in Islamic Finance to participate in the conference. His strong connections and efforts brought together a distinguished group of speakers from around the world. Following the Anand Sinha committee report, and on Dr. Siddiqi's advice, a workshop was held in Mumbai to harness the enthusiasm generated. Experts at the workshop proposed feasible options for introducing the concept of Islamic finance within the framework of existing regulations.

The 2006 Workshop on Islamic Banking in India

A two-day National Workshop planning a "Roadmap for Islamic Banking in India" was held on September 16-17, 2006, in Mumbai, featuring national and international legal experts and bankers as speakers (IFT, 2012). Special guests included Mufti Mohammed Barkatullah, Sharia Advisor at the Islamic Bank of Britain, and Mr. Mohammed Talha, representative of Qatar International Islamic Bank. Attendees also included Mr. K.M. Abdul Salam of the RBI from Kochi, Dr. Fazlur Rahman Faridi from Aligarh, and Dr. Ausaf Ahmed from New Delhi. Dr. M. Nejatullah Siddiqi, on his way to Malaysia, played a pivotal role by attending and guiding the proceedings. The workshop was organized through the initiative of Dr. Rahmathullah.

The Dr. Raghuram Rajan Committee (CFSR) 2007 and the Inclusion of Islamic Banking

The Committee on Financial Sector Reform (CFSR)[1] issued a public notice inviting suggestions and recommendations for submission. Dr. Siddiqi actively engaged with prominent figures and experts in Islamic finance and banking in India, including his teacher at AMU, Dr. Abdul Hasib, who later became Executive Director of the RBI, along with Dr. Rahmatullah and others, encouraging them to submit their proposals to the CFSR. As a result, Dr. Abdul Hasib, Executive Director of the RBI, Dr. M.I. Bag Siraj, and institutions like Indian Nationals Abroad, Qatar, represented by its President Nizar Kochrey, and Dr. Seetharam, CEO of Doha Bank, provided proposals to the Planning Commission Committee advocating for the inclusion of Islamic finance and banking. Dr. Rahmatullah and Mr. Zahid Ahmed

[1] This twelve-member committee on Financial Sector Reforms (CFSR) was constituted by the Planning Commission of India, in 2007 under the chairmanship of Dr. Raguram Rajan.

participated in the final CFSR meeting. Dr. Vijiya Mahajan, a member of the CFSR, emphasized the importance and relevance of Islamic banking and successfully ensured the inclusion of two key paragraphs in the final report. This effort, led by the author and their team under Dr. Siddiqi's guidance, marked one of the most extensive public relations initiatives in independent India to advocate for Islamic banking in the country.

The 2008 Establishment of ICIF

Dr. Siddiqi also played a pivotal role in establishing the Indian Centre for Islamic Finance (ICIF) in New Delhi.[2] Through his consistent guidance and encouragement, ICIF brought together experts in banking, finance, and law, advocating for Islamic banking in India for over a decade and submitting numerous reports to the government and regulators.

The 2010 Cheraman NBFC Case in 2010:

In 2010, the State Government of Kerala launched Al-Barakah, a Non-Banking Financial Company (NBFC), with the aim of operating in accordance with Shariah principles (now Cheramaan Financial Company). This initiative was challenged in the Kerala High Court by Dr. Subramanian Swamy, who argued that the NBFC contradicted the secular ethos of the country. To counter the negative perception, Dr. Nejatullah Siddiqi conducted a week-

---

[2] Dr. Nejatullah Siddiqi established the "Indian Centre for Islamic Finance (ICIF)" in October 2008 with the following aims and objectives

- To develop a research institution in the field of Islamic economics and finance.
- To undertake theoretical and empirical studies for the application of principles of Islamic economics and finance in India.
- To cooperate with other individuals, organizations and institutions in India and abroad.

long tour across Kerala, promoting the idea that Islamic Banking is not exclusive to Muslims but is intended for everyone, particularly marginalized communities. During his visit, he engaged with educational institutions like al-Jamia al-Islamia, Santapuram, and Hira Centre in Kozhikode, interacted with leaders of the Islamic movement, and met key stakeholders such as Justice Krishna Iyer. His efforts aimed to foster a positive understanding of Islamic Banking amidst the controversy stirred by Dr. Swamy's case. Ultimately, the Kerala High Court dismissed Dr. Swamy's petition, stating, "No specific prohibition contained in any statute which makes it impossible to carry out Islamic Banking" (Indian Kanoon, 2011).

The 2011 Establishment of the Sahulat Microfinance Society

Dr. Siddiqi was a strong advocate for marginalized and impoverished communities, striving to create opportunities for them to engage in economic activities creatively. He proposed the cooperative model as a viable option for interest-free microfinance, leveraging the legal provisions within the State and Multi-State Cooperative Society Acts. In his view, "A Cooperative Credit Society is formed by its members for pooling their funds, managing their liquidity requirements and creating loanable funds therefrom addressing their demands from time to time, mutually sharing the operational cost and owning the benefit and risk of operation" (Sahulat, n.d.). As a result of Dr. Siddiqi's vision, Sahulat Micro Finance Society, Al-Khair Cooperative Credit Society, Janseva Cooperative Credit Society Ltd. and Sanghamam Cooperative Credit Society *etc.* have been established and are successfully operating in several states of the country with scores of branches.

The 2012 Meeting with the Islamic Development Bank Chairman in Delhi

Dr. Nejatullah Siddiqi was eager for the Islamic Development Bank (IsDB) in Jeddah to take an interest in introducing Islamic Finance and Banking in India. During a visit to New Delhi by Dr. Ahmed Mohammed Ali, President of IsDBI, Dr. Siddiqi, along with Dr. K. Rahman Khan, the then Union Minister of Minority Affairs, and Dr. Manzoor Alam, Chairman of the Institute of Objective Studies, met with him. They discussed various topics of mutual interest, including the promotion of a Hajj Mutual Fund similar to Malaysia's Tabung Haji, which did not materialize. Similarly, when Mr. Zaffar Saleem from the Islamic Corporation for the Development of the Private Sector (ICD) visited India, Dr. Siddiqi persuaded Mr. Khurshid Najmi, the RBI's Legal Advisor, to develop a practical model for an NBFC in the Indian context with IsDB. Mr. Khurshid Najmi subsequently prepared a document specifically for IDB/ICD. (IFT, 2012).

The Response to the RBI Objections to Islamic Banking in 2012

In 2012, Dr. Subba Rao, the then Governor of RBI raised objections towards introducing Islamic Banking in the country (Times of India, 2012). In response, Dr. Siddiqi prepared a special note titled "Islamic Finance in India" (November 2012) and forwarded it to a number of experts (Personal Communication, 2012). Though lengthy, the note is reproduced in full below, to demonstrate Dr. Siddiqi's practical approach:

> The purpose of this note is to find a way around RBI objections to introduction of Islamic banking in India. It is divided into two parts.
>
> Part one: The Islamic position is that mere passage of time cannot entitle the lender to a return on the sum lent. Furthermore, the lender is guaranteed repayment of the

amount lent only in case no return on the sum lent is stipulated. Since the sums of money deposited in banks are construed as sums lent to the bank, banks cannot pay a return on these deposits. On the asset side banks cannot demand a return on the sums of money they give to the businessmen unless the banks bear the commercial risks to which the business so financed is exposed. Guaranteed repayment of the capital supplied and a return on the capital supplied cannot coexist. As clarified by Dr. Subbarao, the RBI governor, the above stance of Islamic banking sponsors cannot be accommodated within laws under which RBI currently operates. He is right, our way forward is to find an alternative way for Islamic finance in India. Some kind of non-bank financial institution authorized to accept deposits. This institution should be entitled to expose its capital to commercial risk, with the condition that the returns would be shared with those who supplied that capital in the first stance. The depositors will no longer be construed to be 'lending' to this institution. Rather, their relation with this institution will be, either based on *Wakalah*/agency or Mudarabah/profit-sharing. In either case, the institution managing the funds supplied can be assigned a pre-determined share of the returns on capital. To be successful in the current circumstances, this arrangement calls for a way of treating business losses that does not envisage the depositors losing part of the money they deposited. This can be done by building a loss-compensating reserve. Part of the profits earned in good years can be channelized into a reserve fund out of which the deficit occasioned in the deposits due to losses incurred in a particular year could be made up. Further safeguards against incurring losses can be built by subjecting the fund-users' decisions to some kind of review that audits accounts as well as policies.

Part two: We need interest-free investment vehicles to enable investors to park their savings. Sukuk should be able to serve this purpose. The range of sukuk currently available in the Gulf and South-East Asia should be examined with a view to selecting a few suitable for Indian conditions. The following criteria are suggested. Simplicity in understanding and handling. Being asset backed, i.e., there should be some property whose ownership is legally shared by sukuk owners. Unlike shares and stocks, sukuk issued should initially be confined to manufacturing and real estate sector in general and infra-structures in particular. Sukuk issuers should be barred from undertaking to buy back the sukuk at their face value. Sukuk should be allowed to find their current sale-price in the free market. It is presumed that sukuk will be regulated by the SEBI. Whether foreign-issued sukuk should be allowed to [be sold] in India, is a question that is for the authorities to decide. What we regard as important is to provide Indian businessmen who are not inclined to issue interest-bearing bonds or borrow from banks, a vehicle for mobilizing interest-averse savings for investing productively. Lastly, it may be pointed out that, irrespective of the name given to the proposed new facilities, their housing in some existing institutions may go a long way in making financial services inclusive and poor-friendly. We wish there were outlets available in geographically wide-spread locations within reach of the artisan class in particular and poor families in general. All banks should be encouraged to have investment accounts that promise not to earn interest for the depositor by lending but earn profit for them by partnering. They will pass on to the depositor a specified percentage of the profit they earn. But in case of loss the banks will compensate the loss by a portion of profits earned in the past. No loss to the depositor. Sukuk al-Ijarah as detailed by AAOIFI [should] be allowed in Indian financial markets. This will enable mobilization of funds on a non-interest basis. Lastly, the various government schemes to help the farmers and small entrepreneurs should have an alternative to interest-bearing loans based on *murabahah* or leasing (Personal Communication, 2012).

The 2014 Response to the SBI Shariah Mutual Fund

In 2014, the State Bank of India (SBI) introduced the SBI Shariah Mutual Fund in 2014, although it was withdrawn at the last moment. At the time, certain groups levelled significant criticisms over the Shariah standards in SBI's documentation. Here, Dr. Siddiqi's detailed note on addressing Shariah compliance within the Indian context is particularly noteworthy.

As a matter of principle, we operate on two levels: internal, at which we seek to correct the flaws in the current practice of Islamic finance all the world over, including practices okayed by Shariah Advisors. We stand against *Tawarruq*, *Murabahah* with saleable debt documents, and Sukuk that promise to buy back at a given value, the purchase price etc. We have argued our case in conferences and in journals. Our friend Dr. Mudassir Siddiqi has contributed a lot in this regard. We have a sincere wish that Islamic finance launched in India should be pure, free of capitalism-like characteristics.

However, on the external front, i.e., in dealing with the government of India and the Indian Public in general we do not disown Islamic Finance as projected by various Islamic Institutions like Islamic Development Bank,

> Islamic Financial Services Board (IFSB), Accounting and Auditing Organization for Islamic Financial Institutions (AAOIFI) etc. Someone needs to check the Standards issued by AAIOFI on issues such as permissible levels of debt, interest income, etc. In dealing with SBI initiative let us step back and make the AAIOFI Standard the norm. I advise all concerned to take such experts as Dr. Shariq Nisar, Dr. Mansoor Durrani, Mr. Khurshid Najmi and others into confidence and try evolving a joint stand.

When the former Finance Minister, Mr. Arun Jaitely asked Mr. Rahman Khan to substitute the word Shariah in 'SBI Shariah Mutual Fund' with another form of nomenclature, the matter was referred to Dr. Nejatullah Siddiqi who suggested the term "participatory."

> The essence is participation and co-operation since co-operative has been used for other activities at a large scale, I prefer to call it '*Participatory Finance*'. It catches the spirit; some people call it interest-free but interest-free is only representing the shifting risk phenomena and it is not necessarily describing the spirit or environment. so, a better name is '*Participatory Finance*' (IFT, 2018).

The 2014 Recommendation to Insurance Laws (Amendment) Bill 2008

The Government of India established a Select Committee comprising Rajya Sabha members to examine the Insurance Laws (Amendment) Bill 2008 during its fifth sitting on October 14, 2014. Dr. Shariq Nisar and the author represented ICIF, as documented in the committee's official report:

> A representative of the Indian Centre of Islamic Finance apprised the Committee about the benefits of the 'Takaful' system of insurance as compared to the conventional

> system of Insurance. He stated that the '*Takaful*' system is based on the mutual co-operation, responsibility, assurance, protection and assistance between groups of participants and across the globe. 26% to 33% of insurance comes from such mutuality and cooperation. He suggested that in addition to the conventional system, the other systems of insurance viz. 'Takaful' should be also allowed to promote competition, diversity and to stop fraudulent activities that has been reported in conventional insurance business. He submitted that homogenization of the insurance industry is not good for the country and all kinds of structures and products that are possible to help financial inclusion of people must be studied. The representative pointed out that the GIC is offering Islamic Insurance in the Middle-East and is doing good business there. He however added that before its introduction, the aspect of regulatory gaps may also be reviewed, as many insurance companies are offering products without registration. He suggested the hybrid model of Islamic insurance existing in almost 75 countries, especially in the Middle-East, which can bring huge investments in the country from many Islamic Insurance Companies, must be explored (Rajya Sabha, 2014).

Dr. Nejatullah Siddiqi appreciated the description of Takaful in the above report of select committee of Rajya Sabha on Insurance (Amendment), and subsequently persuaded the *Forum for Group Discussion on Economics Issue* (FGDEI)[3] to arrange a talk on the topic "*Justification for an Introduction of Takaful*" in Delhi on

---

[3] This was an informal forum founded by Sahulat Microfinance Society in association with Radiance Views weekly, New Delhi and envisaged by Dr. Nejatullah Siddiqi.

April 27, 2018, by Dr. Shariq Nisar.

The 2017 ICIF and IFA efforts for a Collective System of *Zakat* and Awqaf

Dr. Nejatullah Siddiqi was enthusiastic about the idea of *Zakat* institutionalization in India. In 2011, the Institute of Objective Studies (IOS), Delhi wrote to the Islamic Fiqh Academy (IFA), Delhi to initiate a discussion toward fulfilling this objective. In 2017, Mr. Ameen Usami, IFA secretary, prepared a program and requested the involvement of the Indian Centre for Islamic Finance (ICIF). Dr. Siddiqi responded:

> Most topics suggested by IFA are traditional, no need to repeat them. We should focus on unresolved issues. A survey of efforts elsewhere also in India of investment of zakat funds with a view to benefit the poor can be done by a research scholar. A paper can be invited on practical issues and how to deal with them in law here in India. Regarding getting money from outside for zakat funded projects legal issues can be dealt with in a paper (Personal Communication, 2018).
>
> Similar approach is needed about Takaful/Insurance. Shariah compliant forms adopted elsewhere should be surveyed and feasibility of adopting in India discussed. Number of participants should be cut down to give time for meaningful discussions, also parallel session should accommodate more participants. At least 4 months should be allowed between announcing and holding the seminars (Personal Communication, 2017).

Dr. Siddiqi also asked the ICIF to prepare a note on *Zakat* investment in Malaysia and other Muslim countries, though this aspect of Islamic finance is yet to be explored and Indian Muslims do not yet have a roadmap for a collective system of zakat.

Dr. Siddiqi's Universal Approach

Dr. Siddiqi emphasized that the activities and thoughts of Muslim intellectuals, organizations, and institutions should be inclusive and beneficial to all of humanity, both nationally and globally. He advocated against imposing beliefs or using force, instead urging the highlighting of shared values and commonalities among religions. He stressed the importance of respecting the good traditions, principles, and values of all religions, as each contributes uniquely to human culture and society. This was the central theme of his final message to ICIF. *Dr. Siddiqi's Last Message to ICIF:*

> I am grateful for having a chance to have worked with you and to have shared advice with some of you in the past. I am thankful to Allah ﷻ for the progress made by ICIF over the years and how far it has come. My advice is to not force domination by Islam. Instead, try to make the Prophet ﷺ a lovable person. Try to be inclusive and do what is good for all of humanity, not only for Muslims. What we need is a universal focus on a spiritually defined order that affords all religious traditions equal opportunity of contributing. Going back to the grass roots and seeking guidance directly from whatever is recognizably divine in human heritage, in the full glare of reason and intellect, aided by intuition, imagination and knowledge. This is the only course of action with some chance of success. Let us mobilize all our resources in favor of such an agenda. *Insha Allah*, we shall succeed (Personal Communication, 2020).

Dr. Siddiqi has highlighted the unique features of Islamic economics, emphasizing the contributions and economic ideas of Ibn Khaldun and early Muslim scholars, which were later adopted by Western economists. He specifically emphasized the ground breaking concept of Shah Waliullah Dehlavi, a prominent Indian Muslim thinker and scholar of his time, whose concept of *irtifaqat* is considered a masterpiece in economic development. The following is an excerpt from his speech delivered at the third Shah Waliullah award ceremony:

> Thanking the Institute for honoring him he enunciated some of his ideas on Islamic economics. He said that Islamic and economic thoughts have been serving human life for centuries but the two have come as close in the 20th century as never before. The books being written on the history of economic thought now acknowledge the contribution of Ibn Khaldun who lived some 400 years before Adam Smith. The Ulama, too have been writing on the prohibition of Riba and other economic issues like agriculture, market demand and pricing etc. But it was Adam Smith's contemporary, Shah Waliullah who presented an analytical study of the economic evolution of human society through his famous discussion on *Irtifaqat* in his *magnum opus*, *Hujjatullahil Baligha*. Some two hundred years after Shah Waliullah there developed the idea in the Indian subcontinent, which is known as Islamic economics in the world today, said Prof. Siddiqi. Islamic economics, unlike traditional economics, has the advantage of benefiting from the divine guidance. It deals with those areas of human life, which are affected the most by ever-developing technologies. That is why *Ijtihad*, intellectual reasoning, is always needed here, said Prof. Siddiqi.
>
> In the beginning of the 20th century Allama Iqbal wrote a book on economics in which he dealt with the problems of farmers in Punjab. At the same time Mufti Muhammad Abduh was thinking about *Shirkat wa-Mudharabat* in view of the interest accruing from the money deposited in

> the post office. After a few decades when the conflict between Capitalism and Marxism intensified in the Muslim world and India the Ulama and Muslim intellectuals started thinking about the economic teachings of Islam and authors like Anwar Iqbal Quraishi, Manazir Ahsan Geelani, Hifzur Rahman Seharvi, Sayyid Abul Ala Maududi and Muhammad Baqir al-Sadr produced their valuable works which may be regarded as the beginning of the Islamic economics. However, formally the subject was initiated on an international level when the first international conference on Islamic economics was held in Makkah in 1976. And now when the new century has just started its journey, this subject is respectfully taught everywhere.

The following is a summary of his speech, highlighting key aspects of Islamic economics, his critique of value-neutrality, other assumptions in conventional economics, and western globalization:

> Dr. Siddiqi further mentioned that some two hundred years ago a project was launched to "free" economics from moral values and social objectives and make it a subject like physics. However, the project, being unnatural, failed miserably. The project was initially adopted because it presented the hypothesis of maximizing individual wealth with the help of mathematics. However, what was not realized was that often hypotheses [...] affect human life. This new economics thus gave approval and sanctity to capitalism, intensified colonial expansion and ultimately the conflict of interests [that] led to the outbreak of two World Wars. After a great deal of damage and destruction, it was decided to put the brakes on market forces, which gave birth to the idea of the welfare state. However, this, too, would die its natural death under the weight of its

own weaknesses, said Prof. Siddiqi. He also said that apparently the world has achieved tremendous economic development but inequitable distribution of wealth has also increased both at the national and international [levels].

This is the reason that the hypotheses of economics and its methodologies are being reviewed today. The return to moral values is also a reflection of this "review mentality." Nobel Laureate Amratya Sen's ideas on drought and starvation are also being viewed in this very perspective. However, still a puritanical traditionalist economist finds it difficult to accept that his science of economics should have any business with morality and religion, said Dr. Siddiqi.

Dr. Siddiqi also said that Islamic economics is not against the search for efficiency and development; it only wants to tie it with social justice and the satisfaction of heart. It believes in maximization of wealth but it also wants the equitable distribution of wealth both between individuals and nations, said Prof. Siddiqi. He also threw light on globalization and its bad effects on the Muslim world. He said globalization is a by-product of the communication revolution and because of this the world is changing. However, America's hegemonistic mentality has hijacked the agenda of globalization because of which it has become harmful to the Islamic and the third world. Prof. Siddiqi, however expressed hope that that this situation would not last for long. Because of the communication revolution the world has become like a global village, where only a system that ensures justice, equality and democracy would survive and not the one that seeks to establish the hegemonic domination of any particular nation, said Prof. Siddiqi (IOS, 2003).

As noted above, Dr. Siddiqi was of the view that a universal focus must be adopted toward the issues being faced by humanity. The following is an excerpt from his speech delivered at the Golden Jubilee Conference of the All India Muslims' Majlis-e-Mushawarat:

> Better be humble and, instead of behaving superior and all–knowing, participate in solving the vexing problems of the day, benefitting everyone irrespective of race, region or religion. There are many, but I single out three areas of universal concern: climate change or/and ecological imbalances; finance and monetary management and Family and social relations. The deteriorations taking place in these aspects of living are so fast, so deep and so widespread that anyone able to contribute towards improving the situation is sure to earn people's regard and respect. Here is a chance to restore humanity's regard for Islam by projecting teachings of Islam capable of relieving humanity's distress and demonstrating how Islamic norms and values and the institutions that could be built on their basis can be able to serve humanity out of its predicament.
>
> The effects of global warming and related changes are now hitting people everywhere in the form of storms, out of season rains/ droughts. It is no longer possible to pretend nature will take care of these changes and mankind can continue living in comfort as before, relentlessly pursuing the insane objective of limitless accelerated growth. Something needs to be done, but what? And how to motivate people to accept the needed changes in lifestyle, etc.? No less tricky are the issues relating to the creation and management of money, [and the] provision of finance wherever and whenever needed. Both are currently debt–dominated. All debts carry interest and the whole system syphons income and wealth upwards

increasing inequality, making the rich richer and the poor poorer. Out of the seven billion plus humans inhabiting the earth presently five billion are poor, of whom 2 billion have to subsist on a dollar a day. In the globalized world what is happening within national boundaries gets projected internationally, making indebted nations default, forced into austerity measures, face rebellions of their people, and ultimately threatening world peace. Things can hardly continue as they are. Change is necessary, but what changes and how to get them accepted by those concerned: Monetary authorities, banks and other financial institutions, regulators and above all, the people in general?

Raising children in homes accommodating both parents and preferably, some of the grandparents would be the ideal setting for the health and wellbeing of the future generations. But, alas, it is becoming a rarity rather than the common setting due to frequent break-up of families, tight urban living conditions, career focused individuals and a host of other factors. Very few care for others, most individuals try to use others as instruments for promoting their own interests. Social relations are increasingly devoid of sympathy, sincerity, even honesty. The very fabric of civilized living is threatened with most people out there: legislators, regulators, judges, shopkeepers, workers ..., bent on cheating.

Religions, Islam in particular, have something to offer by way of motivating people to behave by making them feel accountable to a supernatural being and making them care about life after their earthly existence. Islam's teachings of simple living, moderation and sincerity in human relations can help redress the imbalances in men's relations with nature as well as their relations among

> themselves. Islam's emphasis on sharing the risks and uncertainties of life rather than shoving them all onto the shoulders of users of money and finance by making interest–bearing debts the kingpin of money and finance has the potential of relieving humanity from tyrannies of current arrangements. If only we could muster the courage to adopt a positive approach! Protests, airing grievances, demands..., all have had their day. The Founding Fathers of the Majlis-e-Mushawarat 50 years ago launched it primarily seeking goodwill. Time to explore the potentialities of service and participation in building a better future for all (AIMM Souvenir, IFT, 2015).

Dr. Siddiqi's Advice for Further Work in Islamic Economics

The following are some passages from Dr. Siddiqi's masterpiece *Maqasid-e-Shariat*, which highlights the untapped areas where scholars and researchers in Islamic economics should direct their focus:

> The attitude of profit maximization in relation to personal gain makes a person careless about the interests of his fellow man and sometimes even tramples them. On the contrary, moral values like truth, honesty, justice, equality, and compassion teach a person to take care of the welfare of others along with their interests. People with values and interests also care about other humans. Their concept of life teaches them to speak the truth, borrow to repay and give some of their wealth to the poor, weak and helpless. Instead of considering other human beings as a means to fulfil your goals, consider having good relations with human beings as the goal.
>
> From the very beginning, Islamic economics has been

against the concept that man is a slave to his interest only. It is a fact that moral and spiritual values guide man according to the requirements of his nature. The questions like when? How far? And why? require researched answers. The research needed to study the effects of moral values on the economic behavior of a person, full of will and authority, cannot be expected from the neo-classical economics that has dominated the world. The atmosphere in which modern economics has grown has declared moral values outside its scope of research. Due to this unrealistic attitude, man has suffered a lot. Since this position is associated with the capitalists' heavy individual and national interests, the foundations for liberating the West from their grip must be provided outside the realm of Western concepts.

The servants of Islamic economics should do this. That is, mapping such attitudes and institutions, which on the one hand, have Islamic credentials based on morals and spirituality. On the other hand, history and contemporary realities bear witness to their being and Islamic assets. It requires creativity and empiricism more than speculation and reasoning. What was done in the last century was mostly done for Muslims. In the middle of the last century, many Muslim communities emerged from neo-colonialism and could freely develop their economic systems. The proponents of Islamic economics presented guidelines that the Muslim states could find their way following the Sharia in the world faced with the emergence of capitalism and communism. Today, according to Islamic economics, behavioral markers must work for all human beings. On the one hand, this broader concept of leadership is a requirement of our Islamic mission. On the other hand, it is compatible with the fact

> that the world is no longer divided into households as it was a hundred years ago. Now different nation-states can't establish their own monetary and financial systems. Globalization has had a profound impact on financial transactions and economic systems. The world is becoming one. The challenge today is that if you want to fix your house, you should also worry about the neighbor's house. If you want to keep your street clean, you should take care of the whole neighborhood (Siddiqi, 2009).

Five Principles of Wealth Creation Endorsed by Dr. Siddiqi

Dr. Yaqub Mirza identified five pillars of prosperity: 'Earn, Save, Invest, Spend, and Give.' These principles, endorsed and highlighted by Dr. Siddiqi, are presented as a sequence that can bring positive outcomes for individuals and society. In the preface of Mirza's book, Dr. Siddiqi clarified this point and further discussed the motivation behind wealth creation. He countered the notion of asceticism and abstinence from worldly life and wealth, a concept borrowed from Christian austerity that has influenced Muslim society. Dr. Siddiqi addressed the misinterpretation of austerity by some who cite examples of the Prophet's companions, such as Abdur Rahman ibn Auf and Uthman ibn Affan (May Allah ﷻ be pleased with them), who adopted a simple lifestyle after earning wealth. He clarified that these companions followed the final principle, "Spend the wealth and give," rather than hoarding it, which offers no benefit to individuals or society.

> Earn, Save, Invest, Spend, and Give. What is unique about it that justifies writing a book? Well for a complete answer you have to read the book. But I can tell you something to begin with. The significance lies in the sequence. Also, each one of these five steps implies a certain mindset,

rather, an ethic. Focus on these and you have your answer. Earning requires working, which calls for some self-discipline, and that brings in the big question of motivation. History is witness to the interesting relationship between strength and weakness of motivation and the rise and fall of civilization, Islamic Civilization being no exception. The Prophet ﷺ had some strongly motivated people around him. Motivation is multi-dimensional, but here I am largely thinking of money making. Few remember that as many as four out of ten Companions of the Prophet who are congratulated as they were promised a place in Jannah died billionaires, in today's terms. There is ample evidence that they worked hard for that kind of wealth, especially as some of them, like Abdur-Rahman ibn Auf, had migrated to Medina empty handed. To the possible query, why earn so much? The answer is that Islamic History provides with reference to men like Abdur Rahman ibn Auf and Uthman ibn Affan, the celebrated third Caliph, lies in the last of the above sequence: Giving.

Unfortunately, the self-confidence that makes a conscientious Muslim a big money maker [who also lives] in preparation for the eternal life in the hereafter was soon lost under the influence of Christian asceticism and, possibly, Greek and Hindu Philosophies. A shadow was cast upon "Earning." This raised alarm bells among the wise and farsighted, inviting a spate of works titled *The Book of Earning*, beginning with *Kitab al-Kasb* by Imam Muhammad bin al-Hasan al-Shaybani (d.189 H/834 C.E.). These books, numbering a dozen over the next hundred years, argued in the light of texts from the Qur'an and Sunnah that it was all right for a Muslim to Earn, Save, and Invest (Mirza, 2014).

Conclusion

Dr. Siddiqi's contributions to Islamic economics as a pioneer, often regarded as the father of the discipline, are immense. He systematically introduced the field and provided practical models through his writings. Throughout his academic life, he presented innovative ideas and concepts, emphasizing their practical applications and implications. He openly criticized the dominance of *murabahah* and short-term financing in Islamic banking, arguing that these practices fail to reflect the essence of the Islamic economic system. Dr. Siddiqi consistently advocated for the participatory nature of Islamic finance, which has been gradually eroded in banking practices. He believed that participatory and risk-sharing activities alone are insufficient. To strengthen the Islamic finance industry, he emphasized the need for government and regulatory support to address dishonest practices and ensure ethical behavior in financing and business transactions. Maintaining a high level of transparency, in line with Islamic teachings, is crucial. Practical models must uphold the core principles of Islamic finance without compromise. However, in non-Muslim countries, more flexible practices may be adopted within the framework of each country's regulations. Dr. Siddiqi's ideas deserve serious consideration by scholars and researchers worldwide to transform them into practical applications. Further research on the various aspects of his work, presented over decades in his books, is essential to continue his legacy.

References

AIMMM Souvenir. 2015. Chennai: Islamic Foundation Trust (IFT). Accessed 05/01/2025. https://iftchennai.in/islamic-banking/.

Government of India. 2007. "Committee for Financial Sector Reform." Accessed 05/01/2025.

https://www.google.com/url?sa=t&source=web&rct=j&opi=8997844

9&url=https://www.jrvarma.in/reports/Raghuram-Rajan/cfsr_all.pdf&ved=2ahUKEwii4_WM3_CHAxVQUGwGHRINDUgQFnoECBUQAQ&usg=AOvVaw31WtsKsCstO1qcUwoTfrPM.

Islamic Foundation Trust (IFT). 2012. *Islamic Banking in India.* Chennai: Islamic Foundation Trust (IFT). Accessed 05/01/2025. https://iftchennai.in/islamic-banking/.

IFT Newsletter, Islamic. 2018. Chennai: Islamic Foundation Trust (IFT). Accessed 05/01/2025. https://iftchennai.in/islamic-banking/.

Indian Kanoon. 2011. "Dr. Surbramanian Swamy vs State of Kerala." Accessed 05/01/2025.

https://indiankanoon.org/doc/1816970/.

Institute of Objective Studies (IOS). 2003. "Report of the Ceremony of the Third Shah Waliullah Award 2001." Accessed 05/01/2025.

https://oldwebsite.iosworld.org/reportshah.htm.

Mirza, Yaqub. 2014. *Five Pillars of Prosperity.* London: White Cloud Press.

Parliament of Rajya Sabha. 2014. "Report of Select Committee on Insurance Laws (Amendment) Bill, 2008." Accessed 05/01/2025.

https://prsindia.org/files/bills_acts/bills_parliament/2008/Select_committee_on_Insurance_Laws.pdf.

Personal Communication with Author, November 28-29, 2012; March 4, 2015; August 1, 2017; April 18, 2018; November 2, 2020.

Radiance (2022). "Personality, Principles and Performance of Dr. Muhammad Nejatullah Siddiqi." *Radiance Weekly.* Accessed 05/01/2025. https://radianceweekly.net/dr-nejatullah-siddiqi-personality-principles-and-performance/.

Sahulat. "Interest Free Microfinance through Cooperatives." Accessed 05/01/2025.

https://sahulat.org/category/interest-free-microfinance-through-cooperatives.

Siddiqi, Nejatullah. 2009. "Maqasid Shariat." New Delhi: MMI Publisher. 274-276.

Siddiqi, Nejatullah. 2013. "Ma'ash Islam aur Musalman." New Delhi: MMI Publisher. 38.

The Times of India. 2012. "Islamic Banking not Possible." Accessed 05/01/2025.

https://timesofindia.indiatimes.com/business/india-business/islamic-banking-not-possible-subbarao/articleshow/17330704.cms.

NINE

Muhammad Nejatullah Siddiqi's Comprehensive Views on Developing Islamic Economics: Some Reflections

Mohamed Aslam Haneef

Background

I first came to know of the late Professor Siddiqi in the second half of 1983 when I joined the Department of Economics, International Islamic University Malaysia as one of the first batch of students taking the Bachelor of Economics programme. The dearth of reading materials made us read and re-read those few invaluable books that came out from the Markazi Maktaba Islami, India and the Islamic Foundation, UK, the various conference papers and publications of the then International Centre for Research in Islamic Economics, King Abdul Aziz University, Jeddah as well as publications from the Islamic Research and Training Institute, IDB, Jeddah. The name Nejatullah Siddiqi stood out as one of the handful of scholars (others like M.A. Mannan, M. Anas Zarqa, M. Umer Chapra, M. Baqir al-Sadr, Monzer Kahf, Mahmoud Abu Saud to name a few) who had pioneered this new discipline called Islamic economics.

I met Professor Siddiqi for the first time when he attended the 3rd International Conference on the Islamization of Knowledge in Kuala Lumpur in July 1984 where he presented a paper entitled "Islamizing economics." We met again when he came for another conference at the IIUM in July 1987, followed by a workshop on teaching Islamic economics. We also met in February 1989 at the International Centre for Research in Islamic Economics, KAU Jeddah when, as a young lecturer, I had the good fortune of joining a delegation of IIUM students on an educational visit to Saudi Arabia. By the late 1980s, Siddiqi had already established himself as one of the leading pioneers of Islamic economics and as one of the most prolific writers of Islamic economics reference materials.

Nejatullah Siddiqi's Intellectual Contribution as a Pioneer of Islamic Economics

Among his publications that became the main points of reference in those early days of study at IIUM were the following:

- Economic Enterprise of Islam (1972)
- Some Aspects of an Islamic Economy (1972)
- Muslim Economic Thinking (1981)
- Banking Without Interest (1983)
- Issues in Islamic Banking (1983)
- Insurance in an Islamic Economy (1985)

In the 1990s, he authored more publications that also became landmark studies for academics at the IIUM.

- Teaching Economics from an Islamic Perspective (1996)
- Role of the State in the Economy: An Islamic Perspective (1996)

- Economics: An Islamic Approach (1999)

In the 2000s, Siddiqi seemed to enter a new phase, one that saw him become more reflective and evaluative. This was something that was quite natural for someone who had been at the center of the development of this nascent discipline for more than four decades. His works began to present his thoughts on the future development of Islamic economics. Again, this is something quite natural for someone who has seen and discussed it all! While one could, and should, write a comprehensive account of Professor Siddiqi's invaluable contribution to the discipline, this article will focus specifically on his views regarding "how to develop Islamic economics" as seen from the perspective of a student who later became an academic at the IIUM.

Siddiqi's Advice on How to Develop Islamic Economics

At a conference at the Science University of Malaysia in 1994, Siddiqi presented a paper entitled "Nature and Methodology of Islamic Political Economy." The fact that he called the discipline "Political Economy" shows clearly that Siddiqi detracted from the neoclassical position that sees economics as an 'independent' discipline. By integrating the political dimension of society to the economic—and I would add, also integrating the social dimension—Siddiqi saw Islamic economics as part of a wider social/human science. In fact, one could also infer from his many other works, a general call for not reducing man to merely an economic agent, but rather to see the individual agent living in, and making decisions, as a social individual bound by a certain institutional and civilizational framework. I concur and think this is what Islamic economists should be looking into when trying to develop contemporary Islamic economics as part of a reclassification of knowledge and its disciplines. In the paper, Siddiqi (1994) laid out what I consider to be important guidelines that should always be kept in mind when developing Islamic economics as a science. The following eight guidelines clearly indicate Siddiqi's clarity in how one should approach the social sciences from an Islamic perspective.

1. **Observe reality as it is, do not let ideals lead you into an optical illusion** of seeing what is not there. Also, do not let yesterday's observation become the last word regarding tomorrow's possibilities.

2. **Make reality a starting point in your march towards an ideal**; do not make demands of it that it cannot fulfil here and now. Also, mapping out the entire landscape is not necessary for beginning the journey. You learn by doing. The important thing is to be clear about what you want to do.

3. **Do not expect from moral worldview to deliver more than it has in the past, look to history.** Lessons from history are not only found in success stories. Failures teach you how to avoid them.

4. **Focus on the individual: motivate him spiritually, enable him with skills, enrich him in resources, empower him by providing opportunities.** In the new global economy such individuals create their own jobs and improve their environment. They make whatever they carry—culture religion, dress, food habits tolerable, sometimes even loveable, to others.

5. **Statism has failed. Accept this.** Excepting the bare minimum of legitimate power ordained by the Qur'an and Sunnah, reduce government as much as possible and leave it to individuals through *Shura*—democratic process to assign to it what they think fit, when they choose, where they like. Also, it is not wise to make a change of

government in Muslim countries on the basis of the precondition being an "agenda for change." If you cannot change it, ignore it.

6. **Global confrontation is counterproductive**. Do not initiate it. Even if the "West" imposes, avoid it. In the global economy of the future there is no East or West. It is trade, interdependence, and the mixed metropolis—a metropolis teeming with people from all four corners of the world, professing all kinds of faiths, treasuring diverse heritages, etc.

7. **The craving for a *de novo* discipline of Islamic Economics is ill conceived. No such thing is possible.**

    a. The key to Islamic economics lies in positioning the Islamic vision in the place of the Anglo-Saxon economic vision.

    b. But, the Islamic economic vision has to be universal and contemporary, not chauvinistic and medieval. As we move in that direction, we may be pleased to discover we have good company from amongst modern economists in both the West and East.

    c. The search for a more humane political economy is now universal. The challenge is who leads the way.

8. **And, lastly, be practical.** Apply what you have, now. Do not wait for refinement and perfection.

The above guidelines clearly call for Islamic economics to be understood and developed as a social science. A social/human science, including from Islamic perspectives, must make actual human behavior a central part of its methodology. While our primary sources of knowledge, i.e., the Qur'an and the Sunnah of our Prophet ﷺ are central sources for the Islamic vision that is at the core of Islamic economics, Siddiqi warns us not to overexaggerate our reading of Muslim history and not to overburden our expectations from individual human behavior. Empirical observation of what is happening in society—today—must be given attention and understood correctly, especially in the social/human sciences. It is possible that what we observe in society may differ from the ideals that make-up our Islamic normative framework. It is the role and contribution of Islamic economists to actually bridge this gap in ways that give it a transformation role. In making that transformation, Siddiqi clearly shows his preference for starting with individual transformation, while avoiding dependence on what he calls "statism."

In making this transformation, Siddiqi also alludes to the importance of critical engagement with modern sciences, including economics. Although he had some criticisms regarding the Islamization of knowledge (2011), the criticisms seemed to be that there was not enough interaction, especially in trying to develop alternative solutions from Islamic perspectives for all humanity. Trying to create a "de novo Islamic economics discipline," as some scholars claim, is ill-conceived. Rather, we should critically engage, avoid confrontation and instead present Islam as a universal agenda that is meant to achieve the well-being of all humanity. This far-sighted advice from Siddiqi sometimes faces challenges among the over-enthusiastic segments of Muslims, who are keen to show the supremacy of Islam and Islamic civilization and are quick to dismiss contributions from others. This aspect of "engagement and collaboration" is very important as we move forward to develop curricula, research agenda and the next generation Islamic economists.

Siddiqi on the Need to Develop the Next generation of Islamic Economists

In the "Vote of Thanks" made at the end of the 5th International Conference on Islamic economics and finance held in Bahrain, 2003, Siddiqi—possibly seeing the decline in focus in Islamic economics and the popular urge to talk about Islamic banking—raised the urgent need to help produce the next generation of Islamic economists. Although not directly stating this, one could look at his earlier writings to confidently say that Siddiqi viewed Islamic banking as part of Islamic economics. Hence, trying to develop the former separately from the latter would only lead our reforms astray. Speaking on behalf of the International Association of Islamic Economics (IAIE) that he helped establish two decades earlier, Siddiqi (2003) made the following remarks, quoted in full.

1. We have the ambition of penetrating further into academia. One effective way of doing that is by instituting endowed chairs at some major institutions of learning. These chairs are for teaching and research in Islamic economics/Islamic finance.

2. Also, scholarships for attracting talented students in this field can be very effective. We have wide contacts and experience in this regard. All that we need to make a breakthrough are financial resources.

3. There is also a plan for donating or subsidizing the purchase of Islamic economic literature to universities which can follow along with the above two steps.

4. Through in-house research, round tables and appropriate publications to influence the future direction of the Islamic financial industry so that it becomes poor-friendly and pays special attention to the poorest among Muslim

countries and communities. This may require designing credit instruments and investment vehicles suited to the poor, a task that should not be left to the market forces as it would need some institutional support in the initial stage.

5. A forum where East meets West in a noble joint venture to develop economics using the latest of human knowledge guided by divine principles. The Association has the wherewithal of acting as a link between Muslim academia, and the economics profession, as well as between the financial community in general and Shariah scholars and jurists.

As an academic at the IIUM for almost four decades, I cannot agree more with these insightful proposals. Five years later, at the 7th ICIEF held at King Abdul Aziz University, Jeddah, I presented a paper calling for a specific endowment fund created to support a dedicated research agenda for Islamic economics (Haneef, 2008). We need to re-focus on the integrated framework of the 1970s and early 1980s to develop Islamic banking based within an Islamic economics framework. Demands from the commercial world about Islamic banking led to what Siddiqi termed "an Islamic economics movement being replaced by an Islamic banking industry." Some who were less diplomatic called it the "hijacking" of the noble Islamic economics agenda! I can vouch for this shift away from and neglect of, Islamic economics by looking at Malaysia. While Islamic Economics was the focus of the IIUM in the early to mid-1980s, the more commercially demanded aspects of Islamic banking and its related instrument development industry took over in the late 1980s. Islamic economics received less interest from academics and students. As far as curriculum and academic programs were concerned, the focus turned to business studies. Islamic banking specializations and, later, degrees became highly demanded by the booming Islamic banking industry.

It was only in the early 2000s, when growing criticism of the practice of Islamic banking—much of it due to scholars like Siddiqi himself—that academics and even practitioners of Islamic banking realized that Islamic banking and finance had to be developed as an integral part of an Islamic economics agenda, an agenda that focused on the general well-being of society, rather than just the well-being of shareholders of Islamic banks. This realization was also due to an overall critique of neoclassical economics and calls for corporate social responsibility. Siddiqi's earlier call for collaboration and engagement with a wider movement and the need to focus on justice and human well-being are so necessary here. At the IIUM, we established the Department of Economics in 1983, followed by Business Administration in 1984. However, following the trends at the time, we established the Management Centre in 1992 (now the Graduate School of Business) that had a very successful Masters in Business Administration with a highly demanded Islamic banking and finance specialization. Only in 2008, with the support of some dedicated pioneers of Islamic economics, was the Islamic Economics and Policy Research Unit (IEPRU) set up, which later became the Centre for Islamic Economics and Policy Research in 2013, demonstrating Siddiqi's (and other pioneers') views that there was an urgent need to re-focus on Islamic economics.

Research into topics such as *awqaf* and a wider discussion of social economics and finance have borne fruit. This has moved the agenda away from outmoded shareholder models to more effective stakeholder discourse. The 2010s saw much more support from the banking and finance community for a more holistic approach to Islamic banking and finance. In addition, there was an increased appreciation for Islamic economics. In Malaysia, research projects funded by a leading Islamic bank that focused on re-examining the works of Islamic economic pioneers is one example of this positive development. One project that I think should be a priority agenda is to write critical review articles in all areas of economics. Under the supervision of qualified supervisors, this could lead to a major output entitled "Critical Readers in Islamic Economics," a series of books that present key voices in Islamic economics plus reviews that indicate gaps and future research priorities. As far as scholarships are concerned, if the 2010s saw Islamic banks funding students to do graduate studies in Islamic banking and finance, the 2020s saw specific graduate scholarships for students to do Islamic economics at the Masters and PhD levels being instituted at the Department of Economics, IIUM, thanks to the support of the International Institute of Islamic Thought (IIIT) established in Herndon, USA in 1981. Also, the current government of Malaysia, since late 2022 headed by Prime Minister Anwar Ibrahim, has called for a re-evaluation of the Islamic banking and finance models used, clearly pushing for the re-integration of Islamic economics with the higher objectives of the Shariah and with Islamic finance so that Islamic finance can play a more comprehensive role in the overall development and well-being of all Malaysians. Prime Minister Anwar rarely speaks about Islamic economics and finance without quoting Siddiqi, someone he had known since the 1970s!

There are clear indications that Islamic economics, both in terms of scholarship and policy prescriptions, will be given more prominence in the Malaysian (and regional) context. Development of the next generation of Islamic economists is crucial in this regard. Despite these positive developments over the last 15 years or so, there is an urgent need for more collaboration and joint efforts to prepare the next generation of Islamic economists. These Islamic economists must have all the necessary knowledge and skills required, which calls for more effort in curriculum development and human resource issues, topics that require another paper. However, what is clear is that the next generation of Islamic economists must. in the framework of the Islamization of knowledge (the IOK agenda) master both the Islamic heritage as well as modern knowledge. This is a tall order despite the IOK agenda being discussed for 40 years. While serious attempts have been made to undertake Islamization/integration efforts, primarily at the IIUM, as Siddiqi (2011) points out and—as the many in-house studies at the IIUM have found—the task comes with many challenges. These challenges range from skepticism to an inability to understand what IOK is. However, there is no option but to correct misunderstandings, overcome skepticism and ensure critical engagement and collaboration.

Siddiqi on the Journey of Islamic Economics

In 2004, a roundtable was organized by IRTI-IDB to discuss "The Current State of Knowledge and Development of the Discipline." This topic would be repeated in many future conferences, but this roundtable was possibly the first time that a small group of scholars, mainly pioneers, were brought together to share their own views regarding what has been accomplished, what were the strengths and shortcomings and what needs to be done moving forward. Siddiqi (2004) made his views clear, although not everyone agreed. He chose to call his presentation "What Went Wrong." Islamic economics has been too focused on *fiqh*. Whether it was the behavior of economic agents such as the consumer or the entrepreneur, or the functioning of social institutions such as property or money. From microeconomics to macroeconomics, management of money to public finances, in each field we worked to derive rules from *fiqh*.

1. It is therefore safe to conclude that a finite body of rules framed over the earlier centuries of Islam to enable Muslims to live as Allah ﷻ wanted them to live could not

be used to derive general rules applicable in later times without first checking their background, socioeconomic conditions, etc.

2. Even those of us who knew the need to complement the *fiqhi* approach with the *maqasid* approach to deliver a meaningful agenda for economic development in modern circumstances, failed to deliver, generally speaking.
3. As a matter of fact, even those who frequently made recourse to *maqasid al-shari'ah* got trapped by the classical treatment of *maqasid*.
4. There is also a need to distinguish between Islam's objectives as a way of life and the objectives of Islamic Law. Envisioning the Islamic economy in the twenty-first century is better done with reference to the goals of Islam as a way of life rather than being done with reference to Islamic Law.

After more than 30 years of involvement in the development of the discipline and its practice, Siddiqi (and other pioneers) shared their views and reservations about the state of Islamic economics. Siddiqi's overall critique was of what he viewed as an over-emphasis on Islamic Law and Jurisprudence or, in other words, an overly *fiqhi* approach, toward both in Islamic economics and Islamic finance. While the pioneers themselves advocated for the need to base Islamic economics and finance on the Islamic worldview, and to then integrate its values, laws and norms into the canon of economics. However, it seemed to them that what gained dominance were the Islamic legal/*fiqhi* aspects. Hence, what became the 'Islamic' feature of Islamic economics and finance were its legal/*fiqh* rules. Siddiqi and other pioneers (for example his colleague at the then International Centre of Research in Islamic Economics and the King Abdul Aziz University, Jeddah, Anas Zarqa) warned that Islamic economics was not equivalent to *fiqh mu'amalat*, that is, the Islamic legal regulation of interpersonal transactions, nor merely a case of adding *fiqh mu'amalat* courses to modern economics courses in our curriculum. In fact, both Siddiqi and Zarqa, who on different occasions served as Visiting Professors at the Department of Economics IIUM in the mid-2000s, advised us to focus on developing qualified Islamic economists rather than overloading the Bachelor of Economics program with too many courses in *Fiqh* and *Usul al-Fiqh*. They rightly pointed out that we needed to improve the teaching of economics from an Islamic perspective, and to then try and integrate the *al-Turath al-Islami* (i.e., Islam's tradition and worldview) into the teaching of economics.

Later, Siddiqi called for the development of an approach rooted in the higher intentions and purposes of the Shariah (*maqasid al-shari'ah*), also known as a "*maqasidi* approach," which would view Islamic economics as a civilizational effort. While still a minority approach (both then and now), Siddiqi was also aware that the *maqasidi* literature available was in itself heavily dependent upon the historical views of past scholars of Islam. Hence, even calls to adopt a *maqasidi* approach were still confined to the discourse of more than 1000 years ago. Siddiqi takes the argument one step further by also clarifying that the *maqasidi* approach may better serve the development of Islamic economics if we refer to the *maqasid* or higher objectives of Islam as a way of life, and as a civilizational approach rather than merely looking at the higher objectives of Islamic law.

I fully agree with Siddiqi on his last point. On many occasions, I have stated that merely replacing a Shariah-compliant approach with a *maqasidi* approach to developing Islamic banking will not achieve the desired impact (i.e., to create genuine Islamic banking and economics) as long as we have misunderstood Shariah as limited to Islamic law. This statement may seem odd since nearly all Islamic scholars agree that Shariah is much more than law. Yet, when it comes to its application and to developing Islamic economics and finance, the legal/*fiqh* dimension always dominates. The *fiqh* and tradition is repeatedly referred to, but the understanding of *fiqh* and its *usul* is also always limited to the legal aspects of the Shariah. Hence, Muslim society has become very legalistic/*fiqhi* in its view of all aspects of life, including economics. We must first understand, and both interpret and apply Shariah as more than Islamic law. We should see the Shariah as guidance for life, which covers values, principles, norms and laws, so that we may bring in ethical and moral aspects of the Shariah as guidance. In fact, I have actually proposed the need to develop an *Usul al-Iqtisad*, as it were, rather than focus on *Usul al-Fiqh* (the sources of Islamic jurisprudence). After all, we are trying to study the social/human science of Islamic economics, not its *fiqhi* rules (Haneef, 1997; 2011). Developing an Islamic methodology for the behavioral sciences (see also Saud, 1993) is what Siddiqi also presents when he elaborates on his *maqasidi* approach.

How the *Maqasidi* Approach Can Contribute to the Future Development of Islamic Economics

Siddiqi advocates for a more "radical" approach to developing Islamic economics and its *maqasid* reference, challenging the dominance of the *fiqhi* approach and an over-reliance on the detailed views of past scholars. While he values the rich intellectual heritage of Islamic scholarship, Siddiqi acknowledges the limitations of treating the views of past scholars as absolute. Most scholars agree that the works of even the most renowned figures are fallible. However, there is often reluctance to adapt these views to contemporary contexts. Siddiqi calls for a more nuanced engagement with Islamic scholarship and its sources, stating: "I would suggest we have to make a fresh start and not just pool past wisdom." His proposed approach includes:

1. Starting with the Qur'an to identify the values and objectives it prescribes.
2. Focusing on economic goals such as sustenance for all, dignity, security, justice, equity, freedom of choice, moderation, balance, peace, progress, and reducing inequality in income and wealth distribution.
3. Drawing inspiration from the example of the Prophet ﷺ.
4. Addressing contemporary realities and asking how Islamic values and objectives can be realized in today's economic environment.
5. Using *fiqh* as a valuable but not exclusive resource. While it remains an indispensable source, modern knowledge and technology offer insights that past treasures cannot provide when identifying means to achieve these ends.

These above steps clearly establish the rules—according to Siddiqi—that are involved in developing an Islamic social science for contemporary times. It places the Qur'an, followed by the Sunnah of the Prophet ﷺ as the first two sources of reference when developing Islamic economics. However, it is in the next step that he departs from what he sees as the way used by many Islamic jurists to develop Islamic economics and finance.

He considers the dilemma as follows:

- "My immediate concern is to point out that what transpired during the last half century (in the development of Islamic economics) was not always in the sequence indicated above."
- For many, if not most of the scholars, *fiqh* came first and the contemporary reality came next. They sought to lay down how the rules and regulations detailed in our *fiqh* compendiums are to be implemented here and now *even*

in contemporary conditions and (this) was taken for granted."

According to Siddiqi, this approach was and is an error, taken as almost an "article of faith." In other words, it was assumed that the *maqasid al-shari'ah* could be realized in today's environment by putting into practice all the rules of personal conduct and public policy that are there in the books we inherited from our glorious past. In another paper, Siddiqi (2008) presented more details about why relying on previous scholars views could be deficient for contemporary times. The case of the proliferation of debt financing in today's Islamic banking practice was given. According to Siddiqi, opinions supporting the extensive use of debt financing today were based on "micro-*fiqh*" views in the past. For individuals with genuine needs, debt is permitted on an individual basis. However, in today's banking system, through the multiplier and accelerator principles discussed in economics, giving a "blanket individual debt green-light" shows a lack of "macro-*fiqh*" understanding. An individual borrowing RM1000 gives an impact of RM1000. However, if one million people borrow RM1000 each, the direct debt is now RM1 billion, not including its multiplier effects. The way our jurists are trained and their usage of the opinions of past scholars (who offered their opinions as individuals on individual cases) needs to be tempered by knowledge of the macro-impacts of these opinions.

I can certainly appreciate Siddiqi's views and concern when faced with similar challenges in a project to develop a *maqasid al-shari'ah* development index. The "economics" trained members in our team proposed to look beyond the five necessities (*darurat al-khams*) established by our famous scholars of the past and to add new components when talking about basic necessities today. Immediately, we were reminded that the five necessities were sufficient to cover all possible new components that we wanted to add. We also tried to suggest that we should not only talk about the category of necessities (*daruriyyat*) in this *maqasid*-based framework and index, but to look at the categories of needs (*hajiyyat*) and embellishments (*tahsiniyyat*) and to discuss, not only about their preservation, but to also include discussions about their development and enhancement. It seems that even when developing economic frameworks, tools and measurements in today's context, we still need to be bound by the details of what our scholars said hundreds of years ago. This is exactly one of the main issues that Siddiqi wanted to convey in his elaboration of "what went wrong."

Overcoming the Challenges in Developing a *Maqasidi* Approach to Islamic Economics

As with many of Siddiqi's later works, he highlights some steps he thinks would overcome the challenges in developing Islamic economics faced. **1.** An inadequate understanding of contemporary reality and, **2.** an inadequate understanding of Shariah sources. Siddiqi states that almost every scholar will agree with—that the contemporary human and social economies today are very different from what was in the past. This includes what was there in the first four centuries of Islamic history, when Shariah law codification was almost complete. However, beyond this general fact, scholars will still prefer, or even insist, that the works of past scholars and the old rules developed by them hundreds of years ago can accommodate contemporary situations. In other words, not only are we to refer to the Qur'an and Sunnah as reference points for today's situation, we must also accept past scholars views as reference points as well. Trying to use one's reason to derive new understandings of concepts found in the Qur'an and Sunnah by directly referring to the Qur'an, Sunnah and current realities, is not preferred.

Hence, according to Siddiqi, rather than focusing on the one issue which has always been the focus of the Prophetic Message i.e., justice, equity and how they can be reached in modern settings, too much emphasis is placed on *fiqh* rules and regulations formulated by scholars hundreds of years ago. These rules and views dominate the discourse. Instead of thinking about contemporary realities in society first with reference to what the Qur'an and Sunnah say, we instead try to fit them into frameworks developed by our past scholars. Hence, Siddiqi sees it as central to the development of modern Islamic economics that we develop core Islamic concepts which are found in our Islamic sources but always with reference to contemporary realities. We can benefit from past scholars' works, but they are not necessarily needed to be followed in every detail. This must be a priority research agenda in universities with Islamic Economics programs.

Consequently, according to Siddiqi, after referring to the Qur'an and Sunnah, Islamic economics needs to research the challenges faced in society and especially in Muslim societies. Islamic economics must serve to alleviate the current problems faced in society and not merely what appears important in theory or in history. Focusing on current problems from Islamic perspectives would also lead to an Islamic economic theory, if well-conceived. Siddiqi points out that while Islamic economics and banking have provided an excellent service by providing Muslims with a way to do banking, investment and insurance without involving *riba* (interest), it may have been subsumed by the conventional system. Instead of offering mankind an alternative to conventional finance that serves genuine production, exchange and distribution of wealth, it seems to have become subservient to that finance system.

The *Maqasidi* Approach to Developing Contemporary Islamic Economics: Dealing with Modern Knowledge

As early as his 1984 paper on "Islamizing economics," Siddiqi was very clear that we did not have to reject everything from contemporary economics that had developed over the last 250 years or more. In fact, in many conversations and meetings held when he came as visiting Professor to the Department of Economics in 2007/8, he reiterated that we need to be "fair" in our treatment of modern economics, including the neoclassical school. Unlike some scholars who feel that we can learn nothing from neoclassical economics, Siddiqi argues for critical engagement. In fact, he grew more dissatisfied of what he termed as a gradual inward-looking consequence of the Islamization of knowledge (IOK) process that seemed to have forgotten its critical engagement with the "other" and potential collaboration with other tradition scholars and instead, became more insular.

In his later assessment of the IOK agenda, Siddiqi (2011) re-emphasized Ismail al-Faruqi's (d.1986) call that the solutions sought via IOK were for all humanity. Just as we are to critically evaluate the views of Muslim scholars of the past, so too must we subject modern economics to a critical evaluation. However, in dealing with modern economics we need to do so by presenting their views correctly. We also need to better understand the context and bases of their views. We must systematically engage them in the same way we assess and evaluate the teachings and works of our past scholars, that is, with reference to the Qur'an, Sunnah and the Islamic worldview. Siddiqi (2011, p.19) laments the lack of emphasis on developing "new knowledge" through engagement and collaboration. Rather, he saw an increasing tendency to look inward. However, he was very clear that critical engagement meant just that, a critical and creative interaction to accept that others' views can also be used in developing new knowledge.

Taking the standard discussion of the normative and positive aspects of a social science, in this case economics, Siddiqi calls for the development of an Islamic normative framework. He talks of the need to develop the "Islamic paradigm." This Islamic paradigm, obtained primarily from the Qur'an and Sunnah, requires elaboration and detailed expansion. This normative framework also benefits from observing society as well as what scholars have written (both in the past and today). It is here that Siddiqi states that current assumptions in modern economics, for example about the concept of the rational economic man, are not "balanced." Rather than accepting the European view that the economic agent is merely self-interested or a selfish maximiser, Siddiqi argues that acts of caring about others, serving social interests while protecting one's own and avoiding any harm to man, animal or the physical environment are a part of the Islamic view of man. Indeed, this view is universally acknowledged, except in modern economics! This is where fundamental, critical evaluation of modern economic foundations are needed.

When these basic assumptions about the economic agent are replaced, the entire framework changes. The goals of the agents differ, and the behavioral norms to achieve those goals are also different. Hence, the meaning of what makes a correct, ethical, and rational decision also changes. The replacement of a pure focus on private gain and selfish interests with one that also requires attention to the social dimension of man, and to the well-being of others changes the paradigm. Once this fundamental normative framework represents the Islamic perspective, integrating institutions such as *zakat*, *waqf* and Islamic decision-making behaviors becomes natural. The outcome of the flawed modern, neoclassical economics framework is significant wealth production but increased inequality coupled persistent, rising relative poverty. In addition, it has reduced overall well-being, increased crime and corruption and insecurity. By changing the assumptions at the bases of economics, goals such as addressing poverty, inequality and environmental concerns now become part and parcel of the alternative Islamic framework.

Concluding Comments

M.N. Siddiqi has been a major inspiration for more than five decades. While his contributions have been in so many areas of this still nascent discipline, this article focused on his views on certain shortcomings regarding how the discipline has developed, and his suggestions on how the discipline should be improved moving forward. While a great deal has been achieved, more needs to be done. Siddiqi calls for moving beyond the *fiqh* emphasis that has dominated Islamic economics in the last half century and embracing a more comprehensive approach. In my view, we need a true integration between the Islamic tradition and heritage (*al-turath al-islami*) and modern knowledge. However, this requires us to break away from any "fear of original thinking." While the Qur'an and Sunnah will always be our main sources for contemporary Islamic economics, it is crucial to critically engage with and evaluate modern scholarship. In addition, it is crucial to critically evaluate the works of our past scholars. Greater emphasis should be given to contemporary realities faced by society since alternative solutions are needed. Islamic economics must be built on the foundations of Islam and its worldview, but also be presented as a solution for all humanity. To build the discipline, we must focus on developing the next generation of Islamic economists who have the requisite knowledge in both the Islamic tradition and modern knowledge. This next generation of Islamic economists will have to continue the legacy established by pioneers such as M.N. Siddiqi, may Allah ﷻ bless him with eternal paradise.

References

Abu-Saud, Mahmoud. 1993. "The Methodology of the Islamic Behavioral Sciences," *American Journal of Islamic Social Sciences,* 10(3): 382-395.

Islahi, Abdul Azim. 2010. "Review of Maqasid-e-Shariat by M.N. Siddiqi," *J.KAU: Islamic Econ.,* 23(2): 235-244.

Haneef, Mohamed Aslam. 1997. "Islam, the Islamic worldview and Islamic economics," *IIUM Journal of Economics & Management,* 5(1): 39-65.

Haneef, Mohamed Aslam. 2008. "Funding Research in Islamic Economics," *7th International Conference in Islamic Economics and Finance,* King Abdul Aziz University, Jeddah.

Haneef, Mohamed Aslam and Hafas Furqani. 2011. "Methodology of Islamic economics: overview of present state and future direction." *International Journal of Economics, Management & Accounting,* 19(1): 1-26.

Siddiqi, M.N. 1994. "The Nature and Methodology of Islamic Political Economy in A Globalized World Environment." Paper presented at the *International Workshop on Islamic Political Economy in Capitalist Globalization: An Agenda for Change,* Science University of Malaysia, Penang.

Siddiqi, M.N. 2003. "Vote of Thanks." Presented during the closing of the *5th International Conference of Islamic Economics and Finance,* Manama, Bahrain.

Siddiqi, M.N. 2004. "Keynote Address." Presented at the Round table on Islamic Economics: Current State of Knowledge and Development of the Discipline," Jeddah, Saudi Arabia.

Siddiqi, M.N. 2007. "Shariah, Economics and the Progress of Islamic Finance: The Role of Shariah Experts," *International Journal of Economics, Management and Accounting,* 15(1): 1-7.

Siddiqi, M.N. 2011. "Islamization of Knowledge: Reflections on Priorities," *American Journal of Islam and Society*, 28(3): 15-34.

TEN

From Islamic Economics to Fiqh: The Contributions of M.N. Siddiqi to the Fundamentals of Fiqh

Zulqernain Haider Subhani

Introduction

Dr Muhammad Nejatullah Siddiqi was an eminent Islamic economist and is regarded as one of the pioneering scholars in the field. His contributions spanned both the theoretical development and the practical application of Islamic economics. Siddiqi hailed from Uttar Pradesh (UP), India, and became associated with the Jamat-e-Islami Hind during his early youth. Unlike many other Islamic scholars in India, who typically received their Islamic education through the well-established Madrasah system with deep historical roots dating back to the British colonial period, Siddiqi's training in Islamic studies was achieved through special arrangements and his own personal efforts.

Although Siddiqi was primarily a scholar of Islamic economics and finance, his insights in *fiqh* and its fundamental principles are both profound and enlightening. While his reflections on the foundations of *fiqh* may not be systematically articulated, a closer and more careful examination reveals that his views are both exceptional and worthy of deeper study. This is particularly important in light of the stagnation and regression that Islamic *fiqh* has experienced, not only in India but throughout the broader Islamic world. In an intellectual climate where rethinking traditional and dominant notions of *fiqh*—let alone its very fundamentals—was often viewed as unacceptable by scholars (*'ulama'*), Siddiqi's reflections stand out as innovative and significant.

It is important to note that many early scholars, including Siddiqi, initiating the Islamic economics movement during the mid-twentieth century primarily focused on the Qur'an and Sunnah, emphasizing the general and broader aspects of Shariah. These emphases included *tawhid* (monotheism), human brotherhood, cooperation, and justice. Their main inspiration stemmed from the time of the Prophet ﷺ and the Rightly-Guided Caliphs. Classical *fiqh*, as developed in the past, was not their primary reference, except when it served to reinforce and support these general principles. Siddiqi's early work, *Islam ka Nazariyae Milkiyat*, exemplifies this approach, as it extensively engaged with classical *fiqh*, not in relation to specific or minor issues of Islamic economics, but rather to uphold the fundamental tenets of Islamic economic ideals.

However, with the expansion of the Islamic financial industry and its growing competition with conventional banks, Islamic financial institutions increasingly relied on *fatwa*s (Islamic legal opinions) to lend credibility to their products. As a result, *fiqh* became central to the practice of Islamic economics and finance. It was within this context that scholars of Islamic economics, such as Siddiqi, began to pay heightened attention to *fiqh*, critically analyzing the issues and challenges posed by its growing influence in the field of Islamic economics and finance (Siddiqi 2014a). Furthermore, in Siddiqi's conception of Islamic economics, two of its three key components are directly related to *fiqh*. According to Siddiqi, these components must also involve reason and intellect in order to adequately address contemporary economic challenges (Siddiqi 2001, 62-64). Given this context, this chapter examines Siddiqi's insights, remarks, and perspectives on *fiqh* and its methodology, primarily through his writings on Islamic economics, while also considering other relevant works. These insights will be analyzed and, where appropriate, situated within the broader framework of scholarly efforts to reform *fiqh* and its foundational principles (*usul al-fiqh*).

Fiqh: A Historical Human Construct

Fiqh is generally defined as the centuries-long legacy of *'ulama'* and other Muslim scholars in articulating and delineating Islamic rulings and perspectives on human actions. A significant number of contemporary scholars and individuals believe that *fiqh*, as an interpretation of the foundational texts of Islam—namely the Qur'an and Sunnah—has reached a state of finality. They contend that there is little room for revision or rethinking of what has been posited and prescribed by earlier scholars, relegating the role of contemporary scholars to merely copying and applying these views and rulings to modern situations. Siddiqi, on the contrary, was explicit in recognizing that *fiqh* is a human product, shaped by the particular time and place in which it was developed. Since human conditions are dynamic and subject to change, *fiqh* cannot and should not be regarded as immutable or final. He clearly stated:

> It's important to recognize a common misconception among people that jurisprudence is immutable and resistant to change. Jurisprudence is, in fact, a product of human thought from a particular era. Given changing circumstances, the need for fresh thinking and the

> development of new jurisprudence guided by *ijtihad* becomes essential. Nevertheless, existing jurisprudence will continue to serve as a model and guide (Siddiqi 2014b, 69).

Siddiqi (2014b, 70) further emphasized that, "Islamic jurisprudence traditionally evolved in response to changing life circumstances. Yet, for the past four centuries, this evolution has stagnated." He also further elaborated:

> Those who dumped the history in the dustbin once *fiqh* was considered to have been finalized by about the end of fourth/tenth century did so under a false assumption. The mission of law (*fiqh*) is to capture the divine will (what would please the Lord, *raza-i-ilahi*). No doubt the great Imams did so in a superb way harnessing reason (*'aql*), texts of the Qur'an and Sunnah, and public good (*maslahah*). But as the time moved on, not only our reasoning but our understanding of the Texts, and our perception of *maslahah* also changed (Siddiqi 2014a, 68).

In a dialogue on Islamic economics with an academic colleague, he argued that *fiqh* and the broader Islamic intellectual tradition are human constructs, shaped by preceding and contemporary human thought, which may not be entirely adequate for addressing present challenges. Instead, Siddiqi (2002, 16) emphasized the need to return to the fundamental and transcendent sources of guidance:

> You seem to pin greater hopes on what would result when Muslim economists acquire direct access to our entire heritage of *tafsir*, *fiqh* etc. etc. as well as the work of Muslim philosophers like al-Kindi, al-Farabi and others. Let us not forget that all those were human efforts, inspired by the divine guidance contained in the Qur'an and Sunnah as well as by the human thought, preceding

them or contemporary to them. Have not Farabi, Ibn Sina and Miskawaih drawn heavily upon Aristotle and other Greek philosophers? Why should we be inhibited in borrowing from modern economics? As a matter of fact, life has grown so complex (mainly due to large numbers, advanced technology and expanded information base) that the works of 11th-13th century A.D. do not have as much to offer as I suspect you are expecting them to offer. We have to go back to the primary source of guidance: The Book of Allah ﷻ and His Prophet.

He conveyed a similar sentiment in a response to another esteemed scholar of Islamic economics during their conversation, writing:

I take to heart your advice "give more of your time and talent to the 'Islamic theory' as basis for a system which is nothing but Islamic." I need your help. How to do it? I go again and again to the works of the Salaf. Recently I read even the Muslim Philosophers and Sufis to look for their economic ideas. But alas human thought, even those of Muslim jurists/Sufis/Philosophers always bears the imprint of time and place. Where to look for Islamic economic theory for the 21st century. If I look for it in my own head only, I am sure you will be the first to reject it? So we have to improvise and compromise (Siddiqi 2002, 166).

He recognized that a key issue hindering Islamic scholars in addressing questions of economics and finance is their unwarranted belief that *fiqh*—and Islamic history and tradition more broadly—are innocent and flawless. This stance obstructs a pragmatic engagement with and learning from history. Siddiqi (2015, 151) observed:

Even the way we examine history is seriously flawed. A

> selective approach is the norm. Modern historians find serious gaps between theory and practice in the Islamic past. Muslim scholars paint an idealized picture of history where everything was rosy. Truth suffers in both cases depriving us from the real benefits of history.

Another intriguing, albeit controversial, example in his writings presents *fiqh* as the human construction within specific historical and temporal contexts. Siddiqi (2017, 160) wrote:

> It is a reality that the division of the world into Darul-Harb and Darul-Islam, as well as the Dhimmi status assigned to non-Muslim residents within an Islamic government, found in jurisprudential texts, do not possess a permanent status. These were scholarly interpretations guided by practical necessity rather than divinely sanctioned permanent divisions.

So, in his writings on Islamic economics, as well as on Islamic thought in general, Siddiqi emphasized that *fiqh* is a human product. He argued against confining *fiqh*—the necessity of defining eternal values and immutable principles in terms of practical meanings and operable norms—to any specific period of Islamic history. He contended that it is inappropriate to regard the views and rulings of past scholars as final, eternal, or immutable, imposing them on today's Muslims.

Islamic Economics and Contemporary *Fiqh*

Building on his courageous, bold, and reasoned stance on *fiqh*, Siddiqi found it deeply problematic for Islamic economics and finance to rely on the classical or traditional legacy of *fiqh* to address modern needs and circumstances. He recognized that such reliance would ultimately lead to the mere emulation of conventional finance and the reinforcement of the status quo (Siddiqi 2014a). To effect meaningful change in unjust and inequitable economic systems, Siddiqi believed that one must go beyond traditional *fiqh* and refer directly to the foundational sources of Islamic guidance: the Qur'an and Sunnah. He stated: "The reality today is that Muslim scholars and *'ulama'* primarily rely on traditional *fiqh* literature to address contemporary issues. Instead of seeking guidance from the Qur'an, they predominantly turn to traditional *fiqh* literature for issues related to politics, society, economics, and finance" (Siddiqi 2015, 26).

Drawing on this perspective, Siddiqi critically analyzed contemporary *fiqh* and its role in Islamic economics and finance. He stated that contemporary *fiqh* falls far short of addressing modern realities, as it primarily revolves around the regurgitation of historical views and opinions, regardless of their relevance or utility today. Siddiqi daringly observed:

> A main problem is that Muslim aspiration is totally out of sync with contemporary reality ... (Even though many institutions and universities have adopted Islamic economics courses and programmes) however, a mist of artificiality surrounds the programmes, not to mention the superficiality of its content. There is a perception, partly thanks to the Islamization of knowledge project, that we can simply graft the new on to the old. That the old may need to be rethought, modified or trimmed does not occur to the legions of researchers working the field. Indeed, to question the old Islamic economic norms is almost regarded as blasphemous (Siddiqi 2015, 149-50).

Siddiqi (2015, 156) further stated that, "Unfortunately, the current approaches to economic management especially in money and finance fail to take cognizance of them. They remain beholden to conventional ideals and try to operate within the framework of *fiqh* or jurisprudence codified a thousand years ago under different circumstances." In his later reflections on the state of Islamic economics, Siddiqi noted that one of the key issues and challenges facing the field is the failure to adequately adapt centuries-old rules into a modern rule book.

According to Siddiqi, one of the main reasons contemporary *fiqh* fails to fulfil its intended role is scholars' disregard for the concept of change. The importance of change is a recurring theme in Siddiqi's works. He was firmly convinced that modern-day challenges cannot be addressed through traditional *fatwa*s, given the significant differences between past and present circumstances. Siddiqi (1971, 87) noted that, "With the expansion of knowledge and advance in sciences and technology the mode of production and distribution of wealth changes and so do the conditions of living. Old attitudes, moves and manners become obsolete and new ones are dictated by the changed circumstances. Islam is not committed to conserve outdated institutions or revive the dead ones." Siddiqi (2017, 164) further elaborated that, "Many Shariah rulings are based on the customs and practices of the community to whom the Prophet was sent. This is a natural and wise approach, but it requires that in situations where customs and practices differ, the original religion and objectives of Shariah should be taken into account while addressing issues of *ijtihad*."

Instead of putting labels of liberalism and westernization on those Muslims who are indifferent to *fiqh* in their lives, he holds religious leadership responsible for not being aware of the changes happening around them and not fully meeting the demands of the time. Siddiqi (2016, 10) said that, "The main issue is not whether knowledgeable and Muslims are equally influenced by modern civilization. The real issue is that in new circumstances, the old standards appear irrelevant, and our religious leadership has been reading the potential of ijtihad for a hundred years but is still not stepping forward in that direction. The real question is, what are the reasons for not moving ahead?" According to Siddiqi, contemporary *fiqh* is largely a mere replication of classical *fiqh*, lacking relevance and failing to account for the necessary consideration of change in modern contexts. As a result, many Islamic economists, including Siddiqi, found the developments within the Islamic financial industry unsatisfactory, as they continued to rely heavily on traditional *fiqh* and *fatwa*s.

The Way Forward: Imitation Or *Ijtihad*?

Having developed a clear understanding of *fiqh* and the challenges Islamic economics faced due to an inappropriate reliance on outdated *fiqh*, Siddiqi (2014a) adopted a straightforward stance on imitation (*taqlid*) and *ijtihad*. He unequivocally rejected any justification for imitation and called for *ijtihad*, which he defined as creative thinking for making moral values an operational, innovative way to serving the common good, and a fresh approach to the foundational sources of Islam. This was particularly within the context of Islamic economics, but also more broadly. Rather, he argued that imitation of ancient scholars was in no way different from emulating Western civilization and values. As Siddiqi (2014b, 134-35) clearly stated:

> The ailment afflicting Muslims, where they either emulate their forebears or Western societies, prevents them from forging new paths using their own wisdom. This affliction permeates all aspects of their individual and collective lives, impacting their worldly pursuits as well as their religious endeavors. Whether they engage in scientific or civil studies, or even when they seek knowledge of the Qur'an and Sunnah, their approach remains unaltered. Their consistent mode of operation persists whether they plan for economic growth or endeavor to rejuvenate Islam. The ability to think independently and generate novel ideas eludes them. Instead of taking initiative, they hesitate, and instead of engaging in independent

reasoning, they mimic others. This pattern is evident across all domains.

Similarly, he articulated that "The primary task is to liberate Muslims once again from mental bondage, both from Western influences and from the outdated aspects of Islamic tradition" (Siddiqi 2014b, 186). Not only this, but he also tended to equate imitation with church culture and boldly stated that, "Islam does not have a church, nor is there anyone infallible after the last Messenger of Allah ﷺ, whose interpretation of the Qur'an and Sunnah is binding on everyone" (Siddiqi 2009, 29). Despite his firm stance, his position on *taqlid* and *ijtihad* was not reactionary, as seen with many modern scholars. Rather, it was supported by well-grounded and logical arguments, as will be explained below.

Firstly, the Qur'an repeatedly urges individuals to use their intellect instead of imitating others blindly. Siddiqi (2014b, 130) wrote: "Consider the Holy Qur'an. It repeatedly urges individuals to use their intellect when addressing them. Its greatest invitation to believe in Allah ﷻ is also given by appealing to the intellect. The Qur'an invites people to think and contemplate, emphasizing that monotheism aligns with intellect, while polytheism opposes it." Secondly, the distinction between actual knowledge which transcends temporal and spatial bounds and historical implementation of it entails that *ijtihad* should never cease to continue. He elaborated:

> Actual knowledge transcends time, place, and numbers, while practical life places significant importance on time, place, and numbers. It is the role of ijtihad to extract relevant principles from eternal knowledge and adapt them to the context of time and place. Knowledge is eternal, *ijtihad* is its shadow under which our present grows up and daily life passes. Knowledge remains constant, but its interpretations evolve (Siddiqi 2012, 93).

Thirdly, the fact that life is in constant change demands an ongoing and renewed efforts to deal with varying and new situation instead of attempting to find solution of new problems in old books. Siddiqi (2012, 80) points out: "Attempting to find answers in existing books or relying solely on heuristic methods may prove ineffective because these problems have novel origins. Thus, confronting new situations and making informed decisions constitutes *ijtihad*, in my view." He elaborated in a different place:

> Finding a counterpart from the tradition for this purpose is futile because the historical context in which we find ourselves today has no exact parallel. This is an unprecedented situation in Islamic history, and it requires new forms of reasoning. If we are confident in our understanding of the current circumstances and have faithfulness to Allah ﷻ and a strong attachment, then we should trust in this effort and adopt this approach (Siddiqi 2022, 29).

Siddiqi (2012, 83) further reiterated this fact by highlighting the significance of creativity in *ijtihad*, as he said: "The need for *ijtihad* exists in every age and in every sphere of life. In our seminaries and schools, we often teach what is already known, neglecting to emphasize creativity. The philosophy of education, especially within Muslim circles, tends to assume that all facts are known and merely need to be reiterated."

Finally, one interesting and unique point which Siddiqi made in favor of *ijtihad* against imitation is that imitation hinders its followers from engaging and learning from other sources and experiments. Siddiqi (2016, 29) wrote: "By elevating the jurisprudential legacy of the past to a binding status, traditional religious circles have deprived themselves of the opportunity to learn from others." What makes Siddiqi's concept of *ijtihad* truly unique and distinct is his emphasis on a point that is nearly unprecedented in both classical and contemporary Islamic scholarship: *ijtihad* should be open to every believer, with no particular group or category of individuals holding a monopoly over its practice. Siddiqi (2009, 29) articulated that, "Each individual believer is free to interpret the divine instructions and apply them to their own life challenges. They can seek guidance from others but must not follow blindly."

In a slightly different context, Siddiqi (2005, 4) extended this invitation to the followers of all religions, encouraging openness and direct engagement with their respective texts and revelations. He stated:

> Let individuals reconnect to the divine. Let them do it on their own without imposing on them our dated interpretations of the sacred texts. Trust them. Make them aware of the stakes ... Religious mentors who deny these sources to the common man, claiming a monopoly of these sources, commit the gravest of all sins. They have no right to do so. They do not have a divine mandate for appropriating the role of interpreting God.

Siddiqi (2017, 146) categorically rejected the notion that *ijtihad* or fresh thinking might be harmful. Instead, he argued that the opposite could be risky, "Drawing a lesson from Islamic history, we can say with certainty that Muslims will not be harmed by embracing new thinking in new situations. On the contrary, there is a risk of harm if we refrain from thinking and taking action." Similarly, to counter the misconception that opening the door to *ijtihad* and allowing freedom of thought could lead to chaos, Siddiqi (2017, 258) contended: "History has shown us that intellectual harmony is not achieved through restricting thought or imposing intellectual constraints. Instead, it is fostered through free thought, the exchange of ideas, and deliberation. Chaos and disintegration result from rigidity and repression, not from openness and tolerance."

He also emphasized that it should not be a concern if new *ijtihad* does not align with the opinions of the great classical scholars of Muslim history. He explained that their works and *ijtihad* were shaped by the socio-political, cultural, and intellectual realities of their time, and their interpretations should never be viewed as transcendental or immutable, no matter how esteemed those scholars may be. Siddiqi (2012, 84) stated: "As a result of careful deliberation, your conclusions may differ from those of Imam Ghazali or even conflict with the views of previous Imams and Mujtahids. It's important to note that economists generally agree that innovation is the path to development."

Revisiting the Fundamentals of *Fiqh* for Islamic Economics

It is important to highlight the ongoing, though controversial, debate among contemporary scholars regarding whether the fundamentals of *fiqh* (*usul al-fiqh*) can be revisited, challenged, or reformed, or whether they are ahistorical and transcendental, thus immune to revision or reform. A group of scholars, beginning with Muhammad Abduh, passing through Ibn Ashur, and including figures like Hasan al-Turabi, have strongly advocated for revisiting and reforming the principles of *fiqh*. They argue that the profound changes in contemporary realities, circumstances, and issues necessitate a re-evaluation of these fundamentals. Al-Turabi (1984, 13) for instance, argued that "The traditional science of *Usul al-Fiqh* (fundamentals of Islamic jurisprudence), from which we seek guidance, is no longer fully suited to meet our contemporary needs. This is because it bears the imprint of the historical circumstances in which it developed, as well as the nature of the legal issues that were the focus of *fiqh* research at that time." Siddiqi seems deeply influenced by this line of thinking as he did not merely advocate for *ijtihad* at the level of practical issues and rulings, commonly referred to as partial *ijtihad* (*ijtihad juz'i*). Rather, he called for *ijtihad* at a more fundamental level, concerning the principles of *fiqh—usul al-fiqh*. In this context, Siddiqi (2022, 39) noted: "It is our peculiar psychology that we engage in *juz'i ijtihad* but shy away from *kulli ijtihad* and a shift in attitude, which the circumstances demand. I am afraid that this hesitation is driven less by fear of God and more by fear of social backlash." In short, Siddiqi was a strong proponent of rethinking *usul al-fiqh*. As we will explore below, some of his remarkable insights reflect his disposition and aspirations for reform in this foundational area.

Rethinking *Qiyas*

One of the recurring themes in Nejatullah Siddiqi's writings on Islamic economics and finance is the imperative to move beyond *qiyas* (analogical reasoning) by embracing broader interpretations of harm (*mafsadah*) and benefit (*maslahah*). This idea, while discussed in some detail by several reformers of Islamic jurisprudence (*fiqh*) and legal theory (*usul al-fiqh*), remains a relatively niche topic. Although Siddiqi addresses this point only briefly, readers familiar with contemporary debates on the renewal of *usul al-fiqh* will recognize the depth of his insights regarding the limitations of qiyas and the potential for more expansive legal reasoning. *Qiyas* has historically been one of the most significant, if not the most essential, tools of *ijtihad* in Islamic jurisprudence. As defined by scholars, qiyas refers to the process of applying the legal ruling of a precedent case found in scriptural sources to a new, unprecedented case, based on a shared, definitive reason (*'illah*) between the two. In premodern times, when life was relatively simpler and legal issues shared more similarities, *qiyas* proved to be a highly effective and sufficient tool for *ijtihad*. However, with the advent of modernity, society has undergone profound changes—many of which lack clear historical parallels—

while also becoming increasingly complex. In light of these developments, many scholars of *fiqh* and *usul al-fiqh* have recognized the limitations and inadequacies of traditional *qiyas* in addressing contemporary issues. They have thus called for reforming the concept of qiyas, advocating for a more expansive and comprehensive approach to qiyas that moves beyond its narrow classical formulation.

Taha Jabir al-Alwani, Muhammad al-Dassuqi, Ahmed al-Raysuni, Nuruddin al-Khadimi are among few prominent scholars who have contributed to this ongoing discussion. These scholars have called for a more inclusive and flexible interpretation of *qiyas*, as opposed to the narrow and rigid definition often maintained by traditional scholars. The conventional approach has rendered qiyas almost ineffective in addressing contemporary issues. By advocating for a broader understanding of qiyas, they aim to revitalize its application, making it a more dynamic tool for addressing modern challenges. For instance, al-Dassuqi (2001, 101) notes:

> As for *qiyas* (analogical reasoning), what has been transmitted from scholars about it has been confined to a narrow scope, which is the transference of a ruling from an original case to a new case based on a common, well-defined *'illah* (legal reason). This type of *qiyas* is limited to analogizing a specific new issue with a particular precedent that has a ruling established by a legal text, thereby extending the ruling to the new case. Such a restricted form of *qiyas* may be suitable for complementing interpretive principles in clarifying certain rulings, such as those related to marriage, etiquette, and rituals. However, broader domains of religion require a more natural form of *qiyas*, free from the complex conditions that some early *usul* scholars derived from Aristotelian logic during their era of fascination with it...

> The expansion of *qiyas* (analogical reasoning) is based on the established principles of legal causes, wisdom (*hikmah*), benefits (*masalih*), and objectives (*maqasid*) that have been derived from scriptural texts through inductive reasoning (*istiqra'*).

Nejatullah Siddiqi was explicit in his view that *qiyas*-based *fiqh* in its narrow traditional sense was insufficient for developing theories and rulings in Islamic economics and finance. He consistently advocated for a broader, more flexible approach to *fiqh*, rather than one that relies on analogical reasoning derived from early rulings. Siddiqi made it clear that *fiqh* can only remain effective if the traditional application of *qiyas* is relegated to a secondary role, while greater emphasis is placed on the broader considerations of benefits (*masalih*) and welfare (*maslahah*). As Siddiqi (2014a, 68) articulated this notion:

> In order to revitalize *fiqh* and reinvigorate the Islamic community, it is necessary to approach all sources afresh. There is a great role *fiqh* is destined to play in our efforts to create a modern Islamic society. But the way to do so is not to treat *fiqh* as a body of rules valid for all times and places but a context-bound exercise of capturing God's will. This requires analogical reasoning (*qiyas*) being given a second place after taking into consideration private benefits (*manafi'*), public good (*maslahah*), social consequences (*ma'alat*) and the other objectives of Islam (*maqasid*). micro and macro-economic analyses, sociological and psychological studies and impact on the environment are better guides for reaching the right decisions under new conditions than logic and old precedents.

In another instance, Siddiqi (2015, 153) suggests, "So, dealing with the issue of regulating the banking industry on the basis of analogical reasoning does not help and a consideration of consequences (*ma'alat*) and the public interest (*masalih*) becomes necessary."

Siddiqi emphasized the need to move beyond analogical reasoning not only in the context of Islamic economics and finance, but also in addressing a wide range of new challenges and situations. While discussing a comprehensive Islamic framework for Muslims in India, Siddiqi (2022, 31) pointed out:

> The system in which Muslims in India are living are unlike any experience during the time of any Prophet or any jurist from the past. Therefore, making deductions and analogies (*qiyas* and *istinbat*) based on historical precedents is not possible; only general guidelines can be derived. The method of deriving from the compiled *fiqh*, which is not based on divine revelation or the Prophetic tradition but is a product of human intellect, cannot be considered accurate when determining the legal status of India, such as whether it is *Dar al-Harb* (land of war) or *Dar al-Islam* (land of Islam) and this is contrary to what Allah wants from us.

This brings us to the second key point in the reform of *usul al-fiqh*, which is highly stressed in the *maqasid*-based framework of *ijtihad*: the integration of general principles with specific evidence (al-Raysuni 1995).

Integrating General Principles with Specific Evidence

This heading refers to a fundamental question: If a ruling is established by specific evidence and arguments concerning a particular issue, is it sufficient for that ruling to be upheld, regardless of whether its consequences are desirable or undesirable, and regardless of whether it aligns with the general principles and values of the Shariah and contributes to its goals and objectives? In addressing this situation, Siddiqi (2017, 188) wrote:

> The fundamental principle that we must always keep in mind and consider is that valid and permissible transactions, whether independent or combined with another contract, if their outcomes include anything that opposes justice and fairness, or leads to injustice, oppression, and the usurpation of rights, or goes against the general objectives of Shariah, then such contracts lose their legitimacy and fall into the category of prohibited and forbidden contracts.

Siddiqi also emphasized that it was wrong to assume that rules will always lead to the achievement of goals. He intriguingly argues that while goals are God-given, rules are man-made. He stated:

> The anomaly of something conforming to rules failing to realize the goals (for which the rules were supposedly set) is not something new in Islamic legal development. A look at Imam Malik's approach to *maslahah* (good cause) or Imam Abu Hanifa's concept of *istihisan* (preferring the better option) tells us that it takes more than following a set of rules to realize the objectives of Shariah. The ground reality too does not support the claim that following rules always ensures the realization of *maqasid al-shari'ah.* The goals are God-given while the rules are man-made (Siddiqi 2014a, 63-64).

He further argued that the classical great imams adhered to this approach, whereas the contemporary focus on strict adherence to rules while neglecting their outcomes and broader objectives is a recent development among Muslim jurists and muftis. Siddiqi (2017, 196) said:

> The truth is that the great Islamic jurists, such as Abu Hanifa, Malik, and others, when they exercised *ijtihad* (independent reasoning) in the field of transactions, would undoubtedly consider the consequences and outcomes in their efforts to resolve jurisprudential issues. Abu Hanifa's theory of *istihsan* (juridical preference) and Malik's theory of *masalih mursalah* (unrestricted public interest) are examples of this approach. It is not sufficient to only examine the validity of the contracts themselves when issuing a *fatwa* or providing a solution, as the harm may outweigh the benefit.

On the contrary, Siddiqi criticized modern jurists and Shariah experts for their narrow focus on specific issues within Islamic banks, which often overlooks the general principles and overarching objectives of the Shariah. This narrow approach has ultimately led Islamic banks to produce results similar to those of interest-based conventional banks. Siddiqi (2017, 195-97) observed:

> As for the esteemed jurists or Islamic legal researchers, they contributed to the establishment and promotion of these banks based on the fatwas (religious rulings) of jurists and consultants associated with these institutions. Their primary focus was on specific and minor issues, for which they proposed solutions in light of the detailed rulings found in Islamic jurisprudence books. However, the fundamental principles and broader issues that were the concern of the pioneers of Islamic banking and finance, whom we have mentioned, were absent from these fatwas or not addressed... The truth is that focusing all efforts on fatwas that address minor and specific issues and daily matters over the past thirty years has led us to the same outcome reached by conventional, interest-based banks.

Siddiqi's (2017, 199-212) discussion on *tawarruq* profoundly exemplifies this principle, illustrating how, despite its legality and permissibility in *fiqh*, it produces outcomes that contradict the intended goals of the *maqasid al-shari'ah* in finance and economics. *Tawarruq* contributes to credit creation and operates in a manner similar to interest-based banking, ultimately undermining the entire monetary system that Islam seeks to present to the world.

It is important to highlight that many *maqasid*-focused scholars, including Ibn Ashur, al-Alwani, and Ahmed al-Raysuni, among others, have argued that the integration of general principles with specific evidence is essential for any valid *ijtihad*.

Context-based and Realities-based Approaches

Fiqh is broadly divided into three key components: the understanding of the texts of the Qur'an and Sunnah (*fiqh al-nass*), the understanding of context or realities (*fiqh al-waqi'*), and the understanding of the possibilities and modalities of applying these texts to real-life situations (*fiqh al-tanzil*). It is important to note that the latter two components are directly related to understanding context and realities through various available tools and methods of learning and knowledge, such as empirical sciences, sociological analyses, and other analytical approaches. Nonetheless, the harsh reality is that apathy toward empirical studies and any form of engagement with understanding context and realities appears to be embedded in religious scholarship in general and *fiqh* studies in particular, as clearly noted by Siddiqi (2015) and many other contemporary scholars. Consequently, most of the research in these studies becomes hollow. Siddiqi (2014a) identified this as a major challenge for contemporary Islamic *fiqh*, observing that many jurists and scholars "refuse to acknowledge the context-specific nature of their interpretations of various Islamic norms of behavior." This refusal, he argues, leads to confusion regarding what can be regulated and what should be left to individual discretion.

Anas Zarqa aptly commented on Siddiqi's approach to Islamic *fiqh*, noting that Siddiqi gave due consideration to the significance of context and realities in applying the Shariah in the modern era (see further the foreword by Anas Zarqa in the Arabic translation of *Maqasid-e-Shariat*). Notably, Siddiqi did not merely advocate for contemporary scholarship to consider current realities and engage in context-bound exercise of translating the divine guidance into practical solutions; he also encouraged scholars to explore traditional *fiqh* in its historical context to better understand the positions of classical jurists. Siddiqi (2014a, 68-69) elaborates on this point by stating:

> Meanwhile, analogy-focused *fiqh* must be supplemented by a heavy dose of history. *Fiqh* rulings of great Imams and those cherished by different schools of *fiqh* need to be reported along with full disclosure of when where and under what socio-political circumstances the rulings were given… The more detailed and clearer picture we have of how Muslims tried to establish God's will in changing circumstances in economic affairs, in different times and spaces, the more our current economic thinking will be on the mark. Unfortunately, it has not been in the past.

In my humble view, one crucial yet underexplored aspect of integrating knowledge between Shariah studies and the social sciences is the incorporation of empirical studies into the domain of Islamic *fiqh*, thereby linking it more closely to social realities. Siddiqi recognized this need with remarkable clarity and repeatedly lamented the current state of Muslim scholars, as well as the prevailing educational culture and research practices within Islamic studies departments.

The Centrality of the *Maqasid* in *Ijtihad*

Nejatullah Siddiqi's intellectual contributions to Islamic economics and *fiqh* reflect a deep commitment to the *maqasid al-shari'ah* (the higher objectives of the Shariah). He emphasized the significance of the *maqasid* and also proposed new additions to the traditional categories of overarching and fundamental objectives that are essential in the contemporary world. Siddiqi argued that the *maqasid* should not merely be peripheral considerations in Islamic law, but central to both the formulation of new rulings and the re-evaluation of existing ones. His contributions in this domain demonstrate his vision for a more dynamic and context-sensitive Shariah that aligns with the needs of modern society. Siddiqi identified several key objectives that he believed should be integrated into the traditional understanding of *maqasid al-shari'ah*. These include human dignity and honor, fundamental freedoms, justice and fairness, poverty alleviation, public welfare, social equity, equitable wealth distribution, peace and security, and international harmony and cooperation. His proposed additions expand the scope of the *maqasid* beyond individual acts of worship and legal rulings to encompass broader social and economic concerns, reflecting his holistic view of the Shariah as a moral framework designed to uplift humanity in all spheres of life.

One distinguishing aspect of Siddiqi's conception of the *maqasid* lies in his emphasis on a broader, more inclusive approach. He advocated for a *maqasid* framework that prioritizes the welfare of humanity as a whole, with the well-being of the Muslim ummah situated within this universal approach. To achieve this, Siddiqi (2014a; 1971; 2016; 2012; 2017) argued for collaboration with all human communities based on universal values and principles—values that are not only intrinsic to the *maqasid al-shari'ah* but are also shared and recognized by all human beings. Siddiqi elaborated on the *maqasid*-based approach, emphasizing the flexibility of Islamic legal principles in responding to changing conditions. He argued that every Islamic rule serves a specific purpose and should circumstances evolve such that a rule no longer achieves its intended purpose, the rule must be adapted or replaced. Siddiqi (2015, 156) stated:

> *Maqasid* impacts the human situation on a number of levels. First, every rule serves some purpose; Islamic rules are neither arbitrary nor random. Second, should a rule cease to serve its purpose due to changed conditions, it has to be replaced by one designed to serve the original purpose. Third, a situation not covered by existing rules is to be handled by devising a new rule rooted in the relevant *maqasid*. Fourth, if implementation of a rule results in a perverse or an undesirable outcome, that rule has to be abandoned in favor of one suited to the relevant *maqasid*. These points are well argued in the literature on *maqasid*.

This framework, deeply rooted in the *maqasid*, challenges the conventional approach to *fiqh* that is often constrained by the strict adherence to classical rulings without considering their modern applicability. Siddiqi's critique extended to contemporary Islamic economic practices, particularly in the realm of banking and finance. Siddiqi (2015, 156-57) stated:

> Unfortunately, the current approaches to economic management especially in money and finance fail to take cognizance of them. They remain beholden to conventional ideals and try to operate within the framework of *fiqh* or jurisprudence codified a thousand years ago under different circumstances. Classical jurists gave due weight to *manafi'* (interests), *masalih 'ammah* (public interests) and *ma'alat* (consequences), but the current generation of jurists advising decision-makers do

not have the courage to do so.

Siddiqi emphasized that the classical jurists, such as Imam Malik and Imam Abu Hanifa, demonstrated flexibility in their legal reasoning through concepts like *maslahah* (public interest) and *istihsan* (juristic preference), showing an awareness of the broader objectives of the Shariah. He critiqued contemporary jurists for lacking the courage to adopt similar approaches, arguing that mere adherence to legal rules is insufficient to realize the objectives of the Shariah. Siddiqi (2014a, 63-64) noted:

> The anomaly of something conforming to rules while failing to realize the goals (for which the rules were supposedly set) is not something new in Islamic legal development. A look at Imam Malik's approach to *maslahah* or Imam Abu Hanifa's concept of *istihsan* tells us that it takes more than following a set of rules to realize the objectives of Shariah. The ground reality, too, does not support the claim that following rules always ensures the realization of *maqasid al-shari'ah*. The goals are God-given, while the rules are man-made.

Siddiqi's (2015) critique of capitalism, particularly its focus on economic growth at the expense of human dignity and equity, further illustrates his commitment to the *maqasid*. He argued that an Islamic approach, rooted in the *maqasid*, could avoid the pitfalls of capitalism by prioritizing justice, fairness, and the well-being of all members of society. Moreover, Siddiqi emphasized that the Qur'an and foundational Islamic texts are better suited for providing guidance at the level of the *maqasid*, rather than specific, day-to-day practical solutions. He believed that the overarching ethical and moral guidance found in these texts should form the basis of Islamic legal rulings, particularly in modern contexts where new challenges and realities arise. Siddiqi (2016, 14) noted that: "Indeed, those who read or listen to the

Qur'an today will not find specific solutions to their daily life issues, but they will find an emphasis from God on commitment through justice, avoidance of injustice, fulfilling promises, speaking the truth, good treatment of parents, and similar fundamental human qualities that can have an impact." In conclusion, Siddiqi's emphasis on the centrality of the *maqasid* represents a call for a more dynamic, adaptable, and contextually aware approach to Islamic jurisprudence. By focusing on the *Maqasid al-shari'ah*, Siddiqi tries to ensure that Islamic *fiqh* remains relevant in addressing the complex realities of the modern world, particularly in areas such as economics, finance, and social development.

A Deeper Understanding of the Hadith

Discussions of the Hadith are central to the discourse on *fiqh* and the principles of *usul al-fiqh*. As a matter of fact, *ijtihad* in traditional *fiqh* was largely synonymous with *qiyas* as a tool, while *fiqh* itself was predominantly based on the Hadith as a source. Although discussions of the Hadith have always been an integral part of Islamic discursive traditions, their importance became even more pronounced with the advent of modernity, as debates surrounding the Hadith now run parallel to those over *fiqh*. Among contemporary Muslim scholars, diverse camps have emerged regarding their stances toward the Hadith, ranging between two extremes. On one side, there are those who lean towards outright rejection of all the Hadith, while on the other, there are those who embrace an unquestioning acceptance of all the Hadith compiled in so-called authentic collections or those with claims of verified chains of transmission. Between these two extremes lie various intermediate positions and differing scholarly camps.

Siddiqi adopted a nuanced and comprehensive approach to

the Hadith, carefully navigating between extreme positions. He rejected the outright dismissal of *fiqh* and Hadith in favor of a sole reliance on the Qur'an. As Siddiqi (2002, 327) put it in a conversation with a prominent scholar: "But turning away from *fiqh* does involve turning away from Hadith wholesale. How can a recourse to the Qur'an remain credible in such a situation?" Simultaneously, he also dismissed the notion of unconditional acceptance of all proclaimed Hadith. Siddiqi (2017, 124-25) articulated this perspective with profound clarity, stating:

> Sunnah serves as the explanation of the Qur'an. Without considering the exemplary life of the Prophet, divine guidance cannot be fully understood. However, three factors that may lead to differing interpretations of the Sunnah should not be overlooked: language, time, and space. Additionally, several other considerations must be taken into account when engaging with the Sunnah. The *Ahadith* that contain the Sunnah vary in terms of the degree of authenticity of their chains (*sanad*), and this variation must be acknowledged. Moreover, regardless of their strength, *Ahadith* can never attain the same level of authority as the Qur'an. Beyond the differences in chains, many other potential areas of variation exist in the Hadith, as can be seen in proper references. In this context, I would like to highlight another aspect of the issue. The Prophet's understanding of the Qur'an and his practical applications of that understanding serve as an authority for us. However, this understanding and its application were specific to a particular time and place, and they should be interpreted within that context. There are instances where decisions were made that differed from the practices of the Prophet due to changes in context. It is also noteworthy that determining the context in which the Sunnah was observed or narrated may itself be a point of

potential disagreement. All of these factors contribute to the diverse ways of engaging with the Sunnah.

He also emphasized that our focus in understanding the Sunnah should not be to merely imitate specific rulings and forms; instead, we should strive to comprehend the process of translating eternal and fundamental principles into realities and examine how the Prophet accomplished this. As Siddiqi (2016, 24) explained:

> In this context, the question becomes highly significant: does the Sunnah refer to the methods of translating objectives and benefits in a way aligned with the spirit of Shariah that the Prophet relied on for the purification and organization of governance, politics, economics, and social life during his time, or is it solely about the specific rules and regulations that the Prophet established?

He further emphasized the importance of considering both the realities of the Prophet's time and our contemporary context to better understand the Hadith and effectively apply them today. This understanding is crucial for interpreting these teachings in a way that aligns with the goals and objectives of the Shariah, which are central to its essence. As Siddiqi explained:

> To understand the Sunnah, especially if it relates to constitutional, political, social, and economic issues, it is essential to first examine the Arab realities of the 7th century AD concerning the issue at hand. We must understand the customs and prevailing norms of the people during that time. What changes were necessary in light of the commandments given by the Prophet? What was the purpose of the Prophet's intervention? The next step is to comprehend the contemporary realities of our time, taking into account today's customs and norms, and then assess what changes are needed in light of the prophetic purpose. What policies should be adopted to

implement this?

It is clear that Siddiqi advocated for a much deeper and more nuanced approach to engaging with the Sunnah and the Hadith, steering clear of the binary extremes of outright rejection or unconditional acceptance. He encouraged a perspective that acknowledges the potential for differing interpretations while emphasizing the importance of context. Furthermore, he urged a focus on the essence of the Sunnah in relation to the objectives of the Shariah and the overarching principles of Islam.

Revisiting Claims of *Ijma'*

The concept of *ijma'*, or consensus, has been pivotal in Islamic *fiqh*, regarded as one of the foundational sources of the Shariah alongside the Qur'an and Sunnah, as acknowledged by scholars of *usul al-fiqh*. However, a significant number of contemporary scholars are increasingly questioning and challenging the classical understanding of *ijma'*, advocating for a redefinition that emphasizes collective consultation and *ijtihad* without imposing binding authority. Critics argue that the very definition and conditions of *ijma'* render it an impractical notion, highlighting that the idea of majority is inherently relative and subject to change over time (Subhani and al-Fijawi 2021). Although Siddiqi did not explicitly address the concept of *ijma'* or its implications, a careful examination of his works reveals that he does not regard claims of *ijma'* as binding. He does not view issues labelled as *ijma'* or majority opinion as beyond reproach or discussion. On the contrary, Siddiqi actively challenges and questions many rulings considered to be based on *ijma'* or majority opinion, demonstrating a willingness to confront these notions without regard for their established status.

One example of this is the issue of stoning (*rajm*) for married adulterers, which has a very strong claim to *ijma'* among traditional scholars. However, many contemporary scholars have presented the opposite views on this matter. Siddiqi (2016, 30-31) emphasizes the need of revisiting this issue with fresh analysis stating:

> The Qur'an does not explicitly mention the punishment of *rajm* (stoning) for married adulterers. Therefore, it is essential to re-examine the nature of this punishment as applied by the Prophet ﷺ to specific offenders. It is crucial to determine whether this punishment was intended solely for the act of adultery or whether it encompassed a more complex nature of the crime. Additionally, further research is needed to establish whether the prescribed punishment is just death or if this specific method of punishment also holds a binding status within Shariah.

Similarly, regarding the issue of apostasy, the claim of *ijma*ʿ is very strong, and traditional scholars are often harshly opposed to anyone who deviates from the established position that apostasy warrants a death penalty. Despite this prevailing consensus, Siddiqi firmly believes that the claims of *ijma*ʿ or majority opinion are problematic. He emphasized the importance of conducting fresh ijtihad on this matter, explicitly supporting the opposing view. He stated:

The Holy Qur'an does not specify a particular punishment for apostasy. While it guarantees freedom of conscience, labelling apostasy as a punishable crime and enforcing penalties that eliminate opportunities for future reform raises significant ethical concerns … How can the freedoms enjoyed by Muslims in non-Muslim-majority countries be denied to non-Muslims in Muslim-majority countries? Justice and fairness dictate that double standards should not be applied.

At the same time, he also indicates that he is against the punishment of isolated apostasy, not the punishment of warriors and rebels, as Siddiqi (2016, 31-32) wrote: "The matter of rebellion against the Islamic state and anti-Islamic sentiments is distinct from the act of leaving Islam—an extremely sensitive issue involving the punishment for changing one's religion and abandoning Islam."

It is important to note that, historically, the majority of scholars and jurists have supported the death penalty for apostasy. However, in the modern era, there has been a significant divergence of opinion, with many scholars now rejecting this punishment. Prominent figures such as Allama Rashid Raza Misri and Imam Abu Zahra have taken a firm stance against the death penalty for apostasy. In the 1990s, this issue gained renewed attention through two influential books that sparked extensive discussion. The first, Dr. Inayatullah Subhani's *Tabdeeli-e-Mazhab aur Islam* (and a slightly revised version, *Murtad Ka Hukm Islami Qanoon Mein*), was initially published in Urdu and later translated into English and Arabic. The second, authored by Dr. Taha Jaber al-Alwani, was first published in Arabic and later in English under the title La Ikraha Fi Al-Din. Interestingly, despite there being no direct collaboration between the two authors, these books, published around the same time, present remarkably similar arguments and reasoning.

Conclusion

In conclusion, Nejatullah Siddiqi was one of the pioneering scholars in the field of Islamic economics and finance. Although Siddiqi did not specifically write on *fiqh* or *usul al-fiqh*, his contributions to Islamic economics and finance, as well as his broader works, contain numerous insightful and critical observations about the fundamentals of *fiqh*. Siddiqi understood classical *fiqh* as a historical, human construct shaped by the conditions of its time. Consequently, he viewed the reliance on classical *fiqh* for addressing contemporary issues in Islamic economics and finance as problematic and impractical. Siddiqi called for *ijtihad*, not only by scholars but by all Muslims, encouraging them to contribute to this process in any capacity they could. His call for *ijtihad* extended beyond practical, everyday matters to the core principles of *fiqh*. He particularly emphasized the need for reforming *qiyas*, integrating general principles with specific evidence, promoting context-based and empirical research, and focusing on the *maqasid al-shari'ah*. He also advocated for revisiting views considered as *ijma'* or widely accepted by the majority.

References

Al-Dassuqi, Muhammad. 2001. *Al-Tajdīd Fī Al-Fiqh Al-Islāmī.* Cairo: Wazaratul Awqaf Al-Misriyyah.

Al-Raysuni, Ahmed. 1995. *Naẓarīyyat Al-Maqāṣid 'inda Al-Imām Al-Shāṭibī.* Herndon VA: International Institute of Islamic Thought.

Al-Turabi, Hasan Abdullah. 1984. *Tajdīd Uṣūl Al-Fiqh.* Jeddah: Al-Dar Al-Saudiyah.

Siddiqi, Muhammad Nejatullah. 1971. "Jamaat-e-Islami in Secular India." *Aligarh Law Society Review* II: 74-93.

Siddiqi, Muhammad Nejatullah. 2001. *Economics: An Islamic Approach.* Islamabad: Institute of Policy Studies & The Islamic Foundation.

Siddiqi, Muhammad Nejatullah. 2002. *Dialogue in Islamic Economics.* Islamabad: Institute of Policy Studies & The Islamic Foundation.

Siddiqi, Muhammad Nejatullah. 2005. "Relevance and Need for Understanding The Essence of Religious Traditions in the Contemporary World." In *Inter-Civilizational Dialogue in a*

Globalized World. Institute of Objective Studies.

Siddiqi, Muhammad Nejatullah. 2009. *Maʿāsh Islam and Musalman*. Delhi: Markazi Maktaba Islami Publishers.

Siddiqi, Muhammad Nejatullah. 2012. *Ikkiswīn Ṣadī Men Islam Muslamān Awr Tahrīk-e-Islami*. Delhi: Markazi Maktaba Islami Publishers.

Siddiqi, Muhammad Nejatullah. 2014a. "Islamic Economics: Where From, Where To?" *JKAU: Islamic Economics* 27 (2): 61-72.

Siddiqi, Muhammad Nejatullah. 2014b. *Tahreek Islami Asr-e-Hazir Me*. Delhi: Markazi Maktaba Islami Publishers.

Siddiqi, Muhammad Nejatullah. 2015. "My Life in Islamic Economics." *Critical Muslim*, 143-58.

Siddiqi, Muhammad Nejatullah. 2016. *Muʿāṣir Islami Fikr*. Delhi: Hidayat Publishers and Distributors.

Siddiqi, Muhammad Nejatullah. 2017. *Maqāṣid-e-Sharīʿat*. Delhi: Markazi Maktaba Islami Publishers.

Siddiqi, Muhammad Nejatullah. 2022. "Mulk Ka Maujooda Nizam Awr Tahreek-e-Iqamat-e-Deen." *Zindagi-e-Nau* 48 (12): 25-39.

Subhani, Zulqernain Haider, and Mohammad Farid Ali Al-Fijawi. 2021. "Zahirat Ikhtilaf Al-Ulema Al-Muʿāṣirin Fi Taʾwīl Al-Nuṣūṣ." *Journal of Islam in Asia* 18 (2): 93-121.

ELEVEN

The Contribution of Muhammad Nejatullah Siddiqi to Islamic Economics, Banking, and Finance in Indonesia

Murniati Mukhlisin

Background

Islamic economic activities, including banking and finance, are based on the principles of the Shariah (Islamic law), which emphasize ethical and equitable financial practices. These principles date back to early Islamic societies, where economic transactions were guided by justice, equity, and community welfare. Over time, they evolved into a formal system distinct from conventional banking by prohibiting interest (*riba*), uncertainty (*gharar*), speculation (*maysir*), harm (*darar*), injustice (*zulm*), impermissible acts (*haram*), and promoting profit-loss sharing and commission.

Three Key Phases in the Development of Islamic Economics

a. Early Practices: Islamic economic principles were informally practiced in early Islamic societies. Interest-free lending societies emerged in the 19th century, laying the foundation for modern Islamic banking (Islahi, 2018: 411; Siddiqi, 1981: 29-30).

b. Formal Establishment: The formal establishment of Islamic banks began in the 1960s, driven by a desire to create financial institutions aligned with Islamic principles. This period marked a significant shift toward institutionalizing Islamic finance as an alternative to conventional banking systems (Siddiqi, 2001: 401).

c. Modern Growth: Today, there are over 500 Islamic banks worldwide, along with numerous non-interest-bearing financial institutions, reflecting the widespread acceptance of Islamic finance principles. Islamic finance assets have now reached USD 3.9 trillion (SGIER, 2024: 9).

Muhammad Nejatullah Siddiqi is often regarded as a pivotal figure in the development of modern Islamic banking and finance. His contributions have been crucial in bridging theoretical concepts with practical applications. As a professor at institutions like Aligarh Muslim University and King AbdulAziz University, he played a vital role in shaping academic discourse on Islamic finance (Abdullah, 2022: 1). His teaching and mentorship laid the groundwork for future research and inspired a new generation of scholars in the field.

Siddiqi's Key Contributions in Indonesia

Muhammad Nejatullah Siddiqi made significant contributions to the early development of Islamic banking through his works, including *Banking Without Interest* (1983), *Issues in Islamic Banking* (1983), and *Riba, Bank Interest and Rationale of Its Prohibition* (2004). He played a pivotal role in advancing the concepts of *mudarabah* (profit-sharing) and *musharakah* (joint venture), which are central to ethical financial practices under

Shariah law. *Mudarabah* is a profit-sharing arrangement where one party provides capital and the other contributes expertise and management. Profits are shared based on a pre-agreed ratio, while losses are borne solely by the capital provider. Siddiqi highlighted that this model promotes entrepreneurship, aligns the interests of both parties, and enhances economic stability by synchronizing payment obligations with revenue. He argued that such arrangements reduce the risk of default common in conventional debt-based systems, thereby improving economic resilience (Siddiqi, 2001: 420). *Musharakah* refers to a partnership where all parties contribute capital and share profits and losses proportionate to their contributions. Siddiqi emphasized that *musharakah* fosters cooperative investment, risk-sharing, and social equity. This model democratizes access to finance, minimizes individual risk, and promotes collective responsibility, creating a more stable economic environment (Siddiqi, 2001: 409).

Siddiqi's work laid the theoretical foundation for Islamic banking by emphasizing *mudarabah* and *musharakah* as mechanisms for a stable financial system. He argued that aligning financial obligations with actual economic performance could mitigate the instabilities of conventional banking systems reliant on fixed interest rates (Darwis & Zulaeha, 2022: 56). His seminal book, *Banking Without Interest*, remains a cornerstone text that outlines these profit-sharing concepts and their application in modern financial institutions (Islahi, 2018: 417). Beyond theory, Siddiqi advocated for the practical implementation of Islamic banking principles. His influence contributed to the establishment of over 500 Islamic banks worldwide, which operate based on the principles he championed. He also stressed the importance of policy advocacy, urging the development of financial products that prioritize macroeconomic stability and equitable wealth distribution. Siddiqi believed financial practices should align economic growth with ethical considerations, emphasizing inclusivity and social welfare (Darwis & Zulaeha, 2022: 52). Siddiqi's legacy continues to inspire scholars and practitioners in Islamic economics. His vision for an ethical banking system has driven innovation in Islamic finance, promoting financial inclusivity, equity, and stability. His work on *mudarabah* and *musharakah* remains central to modern Islamic banking, shaping its development as a viable and ethical alternative to conventional financial systems.

In addition to his academic contributions, Siddiqi was a prolific author whose influential works have been translated into Indonesian and serve as key references for establishing Islamic banks in Indonesia. His books explore Islamic banking concepts, including money and banking, interest-free banking, and the functions of the Islamic Development Bank (IDB). Widely available in Indonesian libraries, these texts remain cornerstone works in Islamic finance literature, offering critical insights into economic theories and practices from an Islamic perspective. Siddiqi also emphasized justice and equity in economic systems, transforming abstract principles into practical frameworks that promote financial inclusion for marginalized communities (Abdullah, 2022: 1). His ideas have been widely cited in postgraduate theses. To illustrate the impact of Siddiqi's work, this chapter used Google Colab to analyze patterns, trends, and networks in scholarly literature authored by Indonesian researchers. Google Colab combines executable code with rich text, images, and other formats in a single document.[1] Ten papers published in local journals were analyzed using coding to identify key themes. The results provide the following insights:

---

[1] See this link: https://colab.research.google.com/drive/1OPP6Qt-ZfNxjsbYGAIZtHwnkRBOd1BZI?authuser=1#scrollTo=3qUMLo7e8iHZ

Picture 1. Google Colab Keyword Pattern

> Picture 1 above describes the most common words used by the authors namely: "ekonomi," 877, "Islam," 729, "Siddiqi," 347, "syariah," 248, "bank," 219, "pemikiran," (thought) 213, "Muhammad," 207, "Nejatullah," 193, "zakat," 169, "sistem," 163, "keuangan," (finance) 156), "manusia," (man) 154, "sosial," 151, "Islamic," 141, "perbankan," (banking) 134, "produksi," (products) 133.

The authors published the papers between 2017 and 2024, both before and after Covid-19, making them relatively recent. The terms ekonomi and Islam reflect the current usage in Indonesia following the successful establishment of Islamic banking between 1992 and 2010. In the past five years, the Indonesian government has expressed strong support for the development of Islamic economics, extending beyond banking and finance to include sectors such as halal food and beverages, modest fashion, halal pharmacy and cosmetics, Muslim-friendly tourism, and halal media and recreation. The following summaries are based on the ten papers analyzed using Google Colab, highlighting the key themes identified:

a. "*Perbankan Syariah: Studi Perbandingan Pandangan Nejatullah Siddiqi dan Afzalur Rahman*" ("Shariah Banking: A Comparative Study of the Views of Nejatullah

Siddiqi and Afzalur Rahman" Sirajuddin & Muh. Syarif Nurdin, 2017). The authors compare the views of Nejatullah Siddiqi and Afzalur Rahman on Islamic banking, focusing on their shared rejection of *riba* and advocacy for profit-sharing financial structures. While both scholars support transitioning from interest-based banking to profit-loss-sharing mechanisms, their approaches differ. Siddiqi emphasizes a macroeconomic perspective, while Rahman adopts a *fiqhi*-oriented approach. The paper also critiques the prevailing notion that investors alone should bear financial losses, proposing instead that losses should be shared between investors and borrowers. Finally, the study examines the evolution of Islamic banking and its theoretical foundations in modern financial systems.

b. "*Esensi Zakat sebagai Instrumen Finansial Islami dalam Pandangan Muhammad Nejatullah Siddiqi*" ("The Essence of *Zakat* as an Islamic Financial Instrument in the View of Muhammad Nejatullah Siddiqi" Havis Aravik, 2017). In the paper, *zakat* is highlighted as a central element in Siddiqi's economic thought. He views it as a key financial instrument for wealth distribution and poverty alleviation. Siddiqi also proposes that *zakat* should serve as a public finance tool, helping to prevent economic crises by stimulating consumption during downturns. In contrast, he distinguishes *zakat* from conventional taxation, which, in his view, does not inherently promote social equity.

c. "*Pendekatan Pemikiran Ekonomi Islam Muhammad Nejatullah Siddiqi*" ("Muhammad Nejatullah Siddiqi's Islamic Economic Thought Approach" Rizal Darwis & Zulaeha, 2022). The paper outlines Siddiqi's economic philosophy, which is grounded in the moral and ethical obligations of Islamic economics. He combines Islamic law with neoclassical economic principles, emphasizing market trust and ethical production. The paper highlights Siddiqi's advocacy for *zakat*, his rejection of *riba*, and his focus on an economy that prioritizes societal welfare over individual wealth accumulation. He promotes an Islamic economic paradigm that balances social responsibility with financial growth.

d. "*Konsep Etika Produksi Menurut Pemikiran Muhammad Nejatullah Siddiqi*" ("The Concept of Production Ethics According to the Thoughts of Muhammad Nejatullah Siddiqi," Mega Silvia et al., 2022). The paper highlights Siddiqi's approach to production ethics, which emphasizes fairness and social responsibility. He argues against profit maximization as the primary goal for producers, instead advocating for an ethical framework that ensures access to essential goods, employment opportunities, and social justice. For Siddiqi, Islamic production should align with moral values and contribute to community welfare, rather than focusing solely on high profits.

e. "*Polemik Masa Depan Ekonomi Islam*" ("Polemics on the Future of Islamic Economics," Ahmad Ubaidillah, 2024). The paper examines Siddiqi's contributions to Islamic economics and the diverse responses from Islamic economists. Siddiqi highlights the importance of integrating Islamic values into economic practices, particularly through *zakat* implementation and the prohibition of *riba*. He advocates for a fair market mechanism where consumer behavior aligns with Islamic principles, supported by governmental intervention to ensure economic stability. While some scholars support Siddiqi's vision, others criticize his emphasis on historical Islamic precedents over contemporary applications.

f. "*Pemikiran Ekonomi Ilmuwan Muslim Kontemporer Mazhab Mainstream*" ("Economic Thought of Contemporary Muslim Scientists of the Mainstream School," M. Ariel Ramadhani et al., 2024). The authors examine the ideas of Nejatullah Siddiqi and other contemporary Muslim economists, such as Monzer Kahf and Umer Chapra. The mainstream Islamic economic school seeks to balance Islamic law with modern economic practices. It critiques neoclassical models that overlook Islamic principles and emphasizes sustainable economic development, social justice, and equitable wealth distribution.

g. "*Eksistensi Lembaga Keuangan Syariah dalam Membangun Ekonomi Nasional*" ("The Existence of Islamic Financial Institutions in Building the National Economy," Riki Maulana et al., 2024). The authors highlight the crucial role of Islamic financial institutions (IFIs) in developing national economies, particularly in Indonesia today. Siddiqi views IFIs as vital for promoting ethical financial transactions, fostering economic stability, and preventing exploitative practices like interest-based lending. The article also explores the strengths and challenges of IFIs, including regulatory issues and the need for greater financial inclusivity.

h. "*Studi Kritis Mazhab Mainstream dalam Ekonomi Islam*" ("A Critical Study of Mainstream Schools in Islamic Economics," Rizka Amelia et al., 2024). This research critically examines the mainstream school of Islamic economics, which blends conventional economic theories with Islamic teachings. The paper highlights criticisms that mainstream Islamic economics closely mirrors neoclassical economics, substituting interest (*riba*) with profit-sharing mechanisms like *zakat*. The authors also discuss how mainstream scholars advocate for the practical application of Islamic finance.

i. "*Jejak Muhammad Nejatullah Siddiqi dalam Perekonomian Islam Modern*" ("Muhammad Nejatullah Siddiqi's Footprint in Modern Islamic Economics," T. Rizkan Polem et al., paper published in 2024). The authors explore Siddiqi's contributions to modern Islamic economics, highlighting his efforts to integrate classical Islamic economic principles with contemporary financial systems. Siddiqi's work advocates for a just and sustainable economic model based on *zakat*, ethical finance, and profit-sharing mechanisms. The research underscores his role in shaping Islamic banking, particularly in transitioning from interest-based transactions to equity-based financial structures. It also examines the implementation of his ideas in modern economies, especially in Indonesia, where Islamic financial institutions have embraced his principles to promote financial inclusivity and economic justice.

j. "*Studi Kritis Mazhab Mainstream dalam Ekonomi Islam*" ("A Critical Study of Mainstream Schools in Islamic Economics," Rizki Amelia et al., 2024). The authors highlight that Siddiqi's economic thought focuses on integrating Islamic ethics with modern financial systems, emphasizing social justice, wealth redistribution, and financial inclusivity. Siddiqi strongly opposes *riba*, advocating instead for profit-and-loss sharing models like *mudarabah* and *musharakah*. He views *zakat* as a vital tool for economic stability and poverty alleviation while promoting ethical business practices that prioritize community welfare over profit maximization. Known for his pivotal role in shaping Islamic banking, Siddiqi championed interest-free institutions rooted in justice and fairness. He also supports state intervention in regulating the economy to prevent exploitation and ensure social equity. Siddiqi envisions an economic system that balances ethical, spiritual, and financial goals, positioning Islamic economics as a sustainable alternative to conventional models, which he criticizes for their focus on material wealth.

In summary, the articles collectively highlight key aspects of Muhammad Nejatullah Siddiqi's Islamic economic thought. Central themes include his emphasis on *zakat*, rejection of *riba*, and the integration of ethics into finance. While some scholars critique his reliance on historical economic models, Siddiqi's contributions to modern Islamic banking, financial justice, and social equity continue to shape contemporary Islamic economics. Additionally, the discussion on ethical production, financial inclusivity, and economic sustainability underscores the growing relevance of Islamic economic principles in today's modern economies.

Ethical Dimensions

Siddiqi's work has greatly influenced the ethical dimensions of Islamic finance, particularly regarding the prohibition of usury (*riba*) and the principles of social justice. His insights also enable a comparative analysis between Islamic and conventional banking systems. According to Siddiqi, the ethical dimensions of Islamic finance include:

a. Prohibition of Usury

The prohibition of usury is fundamental to Islamic finance, as it seeks to eliminate exploitative practices that lead to economic injustice. Siddiqi argued that *riba* is not only a financial issue but also a moral one, as it creates an imbalance in economic relationships. He highlights several key points:

i. Usury can cause significant economic disruption by increasing the burden of debt on borrowers, often resulting in cycles of poverty and financial instability (Wigati, 2021: 229). Siddiqi emphasized that the Qur'an explicitly prohibits *riba* due to its harmful effects on society, advocating for financial practices that promote fairness and equity.

ii. Siddiqi argued that interest-based lending lacks a moral foundation since it generates profit without contributing to productive economic activity. This perspective aligns with the broader Islamic principle that financial transactions should be based on mutual benefit and risk-sharing rather than exploitation (Maksum & Hidayah, 2023: 235).

b. Principles of Social Justice

Siddiqi's work emphasizes the central role of social justice in Islamic finance, advocating for systems that promote equitable wealth distribution. He argued that the prohibition of *riba* is a fundamental principle designed to ensure that wealth circulates fairly within society, reducing economic disparities and fostering social cohesion (Siddiqi, 2001: 2). This emphasis on equity reflects the ethical foundation of Islamic finance, which seeks to create a stable and inclusive economic environment. In addition to addressing wealth distribution, Siddiqi highlighted the importance of supporting underprivileged communities through ethical financing methods. He emphasized the role of instruments like *zakat* (charity) and *qard al-hasan* (interest-free loans) in alleviating poverty and promoting social welfare. By prioritizing the needs of marginalized groups, these practices embody the ethical and compassionate principles at the heart of Islamic finance, demonstrating its potential to contribute meaningfully to broader societal well-being (Siddiqi, 2001: 23).

The following Table 1. shows a comparative analysis between Islamic banking and conventional banking based on the insights of Muhammad Nejatullah Siddiqi.

Aspect	**Islamic Banking**	**Conventional Banking**
Interest (*riba*)	Prohibited; relies on profit-sharing models	Interest-based; profits derived from loans
Risk Sharing	Emphasizes risk-sharing between parties	Risk transferred to borrowers; lenders bear less risk
Investment Focus	Investments must comply with Islamic principles	Investments can include any profitable ventures
Social Responsibility	Strong emphasis on ethical investments	Primarily profit-driven without ethical constraints

Table 1. Fundamental Differences;
Islamic Banking vs. Conventional Banking

Siddiqi offers critical insights into how these differences manifest in practice, particularly in the application of profit-sharing models, risk-sharing, and ethical approaches:

a. Siddiqi argued that Islamic banking operates within an ethical framework that promotes social responsibility, transparency, and accountability, contrasting sharply with the often profit-centric approaches of conventional banks.

b. Siddiqi posited that the principles of risk-sharing inherent in Islamic finance contribute to greater financial stability, as they align financial obligations with actual economic performance, thereby reducing the likelihood of defaults and crises associated with excessive debt burdens in conventional systems.

Siddiqi's Impact on the Global Recognition and Influence of Islamic Finance

Siddiqi's ideas have had a significant impact on the global recognition and development of Islamic finance, particularly in promoting ethical banking practices and social justice. His contributions have been instrumental in establishing a framework for Islamic banking that stands in contrast to conventional banking systems. Key aspects of Muhammad Nejatullah Siddiqi's foundational contributions include:

a. Siddiqi is widely regarded as the "Father of modern Islamic banking." His seminal work, Banking Without Interest, published in multiple editions since 1973, has played a crucial role in popularizing Islamic finance concepts worldwide. This book outlines the principles of Islamic banking, emphasizing profit-sharing and ethical financial practices.

b. His academic career, which included positions at Aligarh Muslim University and King AbdulAziz University, enabled him to influence generations of scholars and practitioners. He also established the International Centre for Research in Islamic Economics, promoting rigorous research and education in the field.

c. With over 63 significant books and numerous articles, Siddiqi's writings cover various aspects of Islamic economics, including critical examinations of profit theories and the role of the state in Islamic economies. His works have become essential reading for those studying Islamic finance.

Siddiqi's ideas have profoundly influenced the operation of financial institutions, driving the remarkable growth of Islamic financial institutions worldwide. From being virtually nonexistent at the start of his career, there are now over 500 Islamic banks and numerous non-interest-bearing financial institutions, reflecting the widespread acceptance and implementation of Islamic finance principles (Islahi, 2018: 408). Additionally, his advocacy has encouraged major financial players to explore and integrate Islamic finance products, thereby enhancing their legitimacy and appeal in global markets.

The Contemporary Relevance of Siddiqi's Ideas

Siddiqi's ideas remain highly relevant in addressing contemporary challenges and opportunities in Islamic finance. His insights provide a framework for navigating the complexities of modern economic systems while adhering to Islamic principles. Key aspects of the contemporary relevance of Siddiqi's ideas include:

a. Siddiqi emphasized the need for contemporary Islamic economic thought to integrate Islamic values with modern economic developments. This approach is crucial as the global economy becomes increasingly complex, requiring a system that is not only efficient but also ethical and just. His advocacy for a comprehensive economic system rooted in Islamic principles offers a viable alternative to conventional financial practices that often prioritize profit over social welfare (Amelia et al., 2024: 95).

b. Siddiqi's critical examination of conventional banking practices highlights the risks associated with interest-based lending, which can lead to economic instability. He argued that Islamic finance, through its prohibition of *riba*, presents a more stable framework by aligning financial transactions with real economic activities, thereby mitigating speculative risks (Siddiqi, 1999: 3). This perspective is increasingly relevant as the global financial system grapples with volatility and crises.

c. His focus on social justice within Islamic finance addresses growing concerns about inequality and exploitation in economic transactions. By promoting profit-sharing models like *mudarabah* and *musharakah*, Siddiqi's ideas encourage equitable wealth distribution and active participation in the economy, which are essential for fostering social solidarity and stability (Siddiqi, 2004: 59).

Finally, Siddiqi called for seizing the opportunities in the rapid growth of Islamic finance today to continue his legacy in promoting justice, practicing social welfare, and innovating Islamic finance products and services. Key aspects of this call include:

a. Siddiqi proposed that Islamic finance offer holistic solutions to modern economic challenges by emphasizing ethical investment and social responsibility. His vision includes mechanisms like *zakat* and *waqf*, which not only redistribute wealth but also enhance community welfare. This aligns with the current global trend towards sustainable and socially responsible investing.

b. The establishment of numerous Islamic-compliant financial institutions worldwide reflects the growing acceptance of Islamic finance as a legitimate alternative to conventional banking. Siddiqi's foundational work has influenced the development of these institutions, which are now positioned to address diverse market needs while adhering to ethical standards.

c. Siddiqi has called for ongoing research into Islamic finance practices to bridge the gap between theory and application. His emphasis on empirical evidence and innovative financial products encourages continuous improvement within the industry, fostering resilience against external shocks and enhancing its credibility.

Conclusion

Muhammad Nejatullah Siddiqi's contributions have greatly influenced the understanding and implementation of ethical principles in Islamic finance. By emphasizing the prohibition of usury and advocating for social justice, he established a framework that distinguishes Islamic banking from conventional practices while promoting a more equitable economic system. His work has elevated the global status of Islamic finance, providing a foundation that aligns ethical considerations with practical financial solutions to address societal needs.

Siddiqi's legacy is celebrated in Indonesia, where his academic works have become key references in establishing Islamic banks. His efforts have shaped academic discourse and influenced policy-making, as well as the establishment of financial institutions that prioritize ethical considerations in economic transactions. His vision continues to inspire scholars and practitioners in the field of Islamic economics worldwide, influencing the evolution of Islamic finance as a viable alternative to conventional systems. His advocacy for integrating ethical principles with modern economic practices has positioned Islamic finance to address contemporary challenges, fostering stability, social justice, and sustainable development. As scholars and practitioners build upon his insights, Siddiqi's legacy remains a guiding force in shaping the future of Islamic finance in an increasingly complex global economy.

From the current SGIER report, Islamic finance has now gained significant traction, reaching a stage of rapid development and widespread adoption, while other sectors of the Islamic economy are actively exploring opportunities to integrate and expand within this evolving financial landscape. It is notable that the influence of Muhammad Nejatullah Siddiqi's contributions extends far beyond the realm of Islamic finance itself; his legacy has played a crucial role in shaping the broader Islamic economic framework. His ideas on ethical finance, social justice, and the integration of Islamic principles into economic policies have not only guided financial institutions but have also influenced economic governance, entrepreneurship, and market regulations within Islamic economies. The transformation is particularly evident in Indonesia, where other Islamic economic initiatives that capture the *halal* lifestyle have flourished, reflecting the widespread application of Siddiqi's vision in a modern economic context.

Despite being home to the largest Muslim population in the world, the Indonesian government continues to implement a predominantly secular economic system that aligns with global financial practices. Nevertheless, alongside this framework, there has been a growing call for greater inclusivity in economic participation. The Islamic economic system has emerged as an alternative that is not limited solely to Muslims but is designed to benefit society as a whole, including individuals from diverse religious backgrounds, various age groups, and different socioeconomic statuses. This unique and inclusive approach ensures that Islamic economic principles, such as ethical finance, profit-sharing, and social justice, can be accessible to all, regardless of faith. Today, the entire Islamic economic ecosystem in Indonesia has been actively promoting financial literacy and inclusion for marginalized groups, including individuals with special needs, the underprivileged, and those who lack access to conventional financial services. Employing principles of fairness, equity, and sustainability, the Islamic economic system continues to offer a viable model that complements the existing secular framework while addressing social and economic disparities. For this, Indonesia owes a debt of gratitude to Muhammad Nejatullah Siddiqi for his influence in setting up the Islamic economic system in the country.

References

Abdullah, Aslam. "Dr. Muhammad Nejatullah Siddiqi: The Father of Modern Islamic Banking." (2022).

https://www.muslimobserver.com/dr-muhammad-nejatullah-siddiqi-father-modern-islamic-banking/

Aravik, Havis. "Esensi zakat sebagai instrumen finansial islami dalam pandangan Muhammad Nejatullah Siddiqi." Ekonomica Sharia: *Jurnal Pemikiran dan Pengembangan Ekonomi Syariah*, no. 2 (2017): 101-112.

Darwis, Rizal & Zulaeha, Zulaeha. "Pendekatan Pemikiran Ekonomi Islam Muhammad Nejatullah Siddiqi. *Al Buhuts*. 18: 1, (2022): 51-68.

Islahi, Abdul Azim. "History of Islamic Banking and Finance. *Intellectual Discourse."* 26:2 (2018) 403-429.

Maksum, Muhammad & Hidayah, Nur. "The Mechanism of Avoiding Riba in Islamic Financial Institutions: Experiences of Indonesia and Malaysia." *JURIS (Jurnal Ilmiah Syariah)* 22, no. 2 (2023): 235-244.

Mukhlisin, Murniati. "Exploring Reflexivity and Resistance of Indonesian Islamic Financial Institutions towards IASB and AAOIFI Financial Reporting Standardization Projects." PhD Thesis in Accounting (Islamic). University of Glasgow, Scotland, UK (2014). Available at: https://theses.gla.ac.uk/5991/, accessed on 18 February 2024.

SGIER, "State of the Global Islamic Economy 2023 Report." Accessed on January 14, 2024, available at: https://www.dinarstandard.com/post/state-of-the-global-islamic-economy-report-2023. (2024).

Siddiqi, Muhammad Nejatullah, "Muslim Economic Thinking, Leicester", The Islamic Foundation, (1981).

Siddiqi, Muhammad Nejatullah. "Islamic Finance and Beyond

Premises and Promises of Islamic Economics." Islamic Finance: Local Challenges, Global Opportunities: *Proceedings of the Third Harvard University Forum on Islamic Finance* (1999).

Siddiqi, Muhammad Nejatullah "Recent History of Islamic Banking and Finance." *Islamic Economic Studies*, (2001). Vol. 13 No. 2, pp. 1-48.

Siddiqi, Muhammad Nejatullah. "Riba, Bank Interest and the Rationale of Its Prohibition." Occasional Papers 205, *The Islamic Research and Teaching Institute (IRTI).* (2004). 15-18.

Siddiqi, Muhammad Nejatullah. "Issues in Islamic Banking." *The Islamic foundation, Leicester, London, U.K.*, (2004), pp.152.

Wahid, Abdurrahman, Yadi Janwari, and Dedah Jubaedah. "Mazhab dan Pemikiran Ekonomi Islam Kontemporer." *Rayah Al-Islam*, 7, no. 3 (2023): 804-825.

Wigati, S. "The Concept of Usury (*Ribā*) According To MTR." *Maliyah Jurnal Hukum Bisnis Islam.*(2021) 11: 02

Ten papers analyzed by Google Colab:

Sirajuddin, Sirajuddin, and Muhammad Syarif Nurdin. "Perbankan Syariah: Studi Perbandingan Pandangan Antara Nejatullah Siddiqi dan Afzalur Rahman." *LAA MAISYIR: Jurnal Ekonomi Islam* 4, no. 1 (2017).

Aravik, Havis. "Esensi zakat sebagai instrumen finansial islami dalam pandangan Muhammad Nejatullah Siddiqi." *Ekonomica Sharia: Jurnal Pemikiran dan Pengembangan Ekonomi Syariah*, no. 2 (2017): 101-112.

Darwis, Rizal & Zulaeha, Zulaeha. "Pendekatan Pemikiran Ekonomi Islam Muhammad Nejatullah Siddiqi. *Al Buhuts.* 18: 1, (2022): 51-68.

Silvia, Mega, Yadi Janwari, and Ayi Yunus Rusyana. "Konsep Etika Produksi Menurut Pemikiran Muhammad Nejatullah Siddiqi." *Papatung: Jurnal Ilmu Administrasi Publik, Pemerintahan dan Politik* 5, no. 1 (2022): 1-8.

Ubaidillah, Ahmad. "Polemik Masa Depan Ekonomi Islam." *Jurnal Ilmiah Ekonomi Islam* 10, no. 3 (2024): 2543-2553.

Ramadhani, M. Ariel, Arifal Anugerhana Putra, Rafiffi Ali Hanan Santosa, Muhammad Taufik Abadi, and Muhammad Aris Syafi'i. "Pemikiran Ekonomi Ilmuwan Muslim Kontemporer Madzhab Mainstream 1." *Jurnal Ilmiah Research Student* 1, no. 3 (2024): 437-445.

Maulana, Riki, Jaih Mubarak, and Ayi Yunus Rusyana. "Eksistensi Lembaga Keuangan Syariah Dalam Membangun Ekonomi Nasional Ditinjau Dari Pemikiran Muhammad Nejatullah Siddiqi." *Iqtishodiyah: Jurnal Ekonomi dan Bisnis Islam* 10, no. 1 (2024): 131-144.

Amelia, Rizka, Fathonah Nur Imamah, Winda Sari, Alma Meiliani, Octaviar Wilmar Ervanni, and Innek Safitri. "Studi Kritis Mazhab Mainstream dalam Ekonomi Islam." *Anuitas: Jurnal Ekonomi, Bisnis dan Manajemen* 1, no. 1 (2024): 87-104.

Polem, T. Rizkan, Azhari Akmal Tarigan, and M. Ridwan. "Jejak Muhammad Nejatullah Siddiqi dalam Perekonomian Islam Modern: Relevansi dan Adaptasi Teori Klasik dalam Konteks Kontemporer." *Jurnal Masharif Al-Syariah: Jurnal Ekonomi dan Perbankan Syariah* 9, no. 4 (2024).

Amelia, Rizka, Fathonah Nur Imamah, Winda Sari, Alma Meiliani, Octaviar Wilmar Ervanni, and Innek Safitri. "Studi Kritis Mazhab Mainstream dalam Ekonomi Islam." *Anuitas: Jurnal Ekonomi, Bisnis dan Manajemen* 1, no. 1

TWELVE

Muhammad Nejatullah Siddiqi and the Foundation of Islamic Economics

Hafas Furqani & Syamsul Idul Adha

Introduction

The rise of modern Islamic economic thought in the Islamic world began in the mid-1990s, focusing on the discussion of economics from an Islamic perspective. Scholars initiated numerous Islamic economic writings, with notable contributions from Urdu writers such as Hifzur Rahman Seoharwi with *Islām kā Iqtiṣādī Niẓām* (The Islamic Economic System), Yusufuddin with *Islām ke ma'āhī Naẓarīye* (The Theory of Islamic Economics), and Manazir Ahsan Gilani from Osmaniya University with *Islāmi Ma'āshiyāt* (Islam and Economy) (Islahi 2015b). In the Malay Archipelago, scholars also began exploring economics through an Islamic lens. Furqani (2017) noted that Haji Oemar Said Tjokroaminoto published *Islam and Socialism* in 1924. Kahrudin Yunus authored *Hidup bermasjarakat menurut Islamisme, Pantjasilaisme atau bersamaisme* (*Living in Society According to Islamism, Pancasilaism, and Bersamaism*) in 1955, while Dr. H. M. Rasjidi published *Islam dan Sosialisme* (*Islam and Socialism*) in 1966.

Early Islamic economics emerged as a response to the capitalism introduced by colonialism and sought to provide an Islamic perspective on life and living (Hamidullah 1955). Thinkers of this era worked to develop their own epistemology of economics (*uṣūl al-iqtiṣādiyyah*) based on primary Islamic sources (*al-maṣādir al-awwaliyyah*), such as the Qur'an and Sunnah. Through this epistemological approach, they formulated theoretical assumptions to foundational construct the principles of economic theory. Muhammad Suleiman al-Ashqar et al. advanced economic theories using this methodology publishing texts like *Buḥūth Fiqhiyyah fī Qaḍāyā Iqtisādiyyah Mu'āṣirah* (Studies in Islamic Jurisprudence and Contemporary Economic Issues) (Sholihin 2014). These foundational Islamic economic theories also aimed to deconstruct the Neoclassical economic paradigm, shifting financial practices in Muslim communities as part of a post-colonial response to Western influence on the Islamic World (Islahi 2015a).

A number of critics of Islamic economics consider the development of Islamic finance ideas and practices among Islamic scholars to be nothing more than socio-political engineering in the 20th century oriented towards efforts to separate the Islamic World from Western cultural influences, without producing any contribution to the development of analytical models of business theory. Thus, the efforts are nothing more than *ad hoc* theories, which rely on normative value judgements and prescriptive approach (Kuran 1997; 1995). The systematization and conceptualization of Islamic doctrines related to economics aims to produce a coherent and functional financial model as an alternative to capitalism and Marxism. To it critics, the developing of an Islamic economic paradigm is merely rhetorical because, these reformist scholars completely ignore socio-political problems, and instead focus on conservative technocratic trends (Roy 1994). Even Muslim reformers are not immune to proposing an economic system approach, particularly regarding ownership and modes of production, that aligns with a capitalist economy supported by welfare state intervention and a jurisprudential law enforcement approach necessitating radical reform in Islamic institutions (Behdad 1989).

During the 1950s-1970s, a paradigm shift emerged among economic scholars that led to the development of Islamic economics as an independent discipline. Scholars involved in the development of Islamic economics sought to integrate the methodology of mainstream economics into the Islamic economics framework. The economists involved in this activity include Kahf (1993), Mannan (1980), Naqvi (1981), Chapra (1985), and Choudhury (1986). In their writings, these scholars emphasized the urgent need for the development of a scientific foundation of Islamic economics as an integrated framework which is capable of uniting Islamic teachings with economic theories and systems (Furqani 2015; Islahi 2015a). One of the economists who also played a major role during the 1970s and 1980s was Muhammad Nejatullah Siddiqi. Siddiqi was involved in a crucial role in building a pluralistic methodological approach as a scientific foundation for Islamic economics. Siddiqi played a key role in the agenda of the Islamization of knowledge by integrating Islamic tradition, knowledge and heritage with modern economics in order to realize the goal of economic welfare from an Islamic perspective (Haneef and Furqani 2011).

Although Siddiqi does not specifically describe an Islamic economic methodology in his writings, he pays tremendous attention to the need to develop a scientific foundation for the future development of Islamic economics as a discipline (Haneef and Furqani 2011). He initiated a move toward a methodological pluralism approach by integrating empirical analytical tools from Neo-Keynesian economic theory, while maintaining the primacy of Islamic jurisprudential principles, values and methodology.

Today, Siddiqi is recognized as a leading figure in mainstream Islamic economics for his efforts to integrate Islamic doctrines with modern economic principles. (Haneef 1995). Siddiqi presents Islamic economics as a distinct discipline within a comprehensive, multidisciplinary scientific framework. It incorporates the moral dimension of the economy, aiming to achieve both material and spiritual well-being. Consequently, the scientific foundation of Islamic economics is rooted in divine revelation as its overarching structure, complemented by empirical observation and rational reasoning. (Furqani 2015).

Some scholars have recently criticized the framework of Islamic economics proposed by Siddiqi and others. Ziauddin Sardar considers Islamic economics developed through positivistic frameworks to be overly descriptive and focused on Western epistemology. Sardar believes that scholars such as Siddiqi have been excessive in applying a descriptive and reductionist analysis (Sardar 1985). He even called Siddiqi a Keynesian *par excellence* because his understanding of the economy and financial activities is solely based on the Keynesian analytical framework. This criticism shows Sardar's assumption that Siddiqi and other mainstream scholars are unable to articulate Islamic concepts as analytical tools or original and distinctive policy foundations. For Sardar, these are carried away by the Western economic paradigm and without realizing that the analytical methodology developed is actually a replication of western values. Thus, Islamic economics becomes nothing more than a subdiscipline of orthodox economics approved by some mainstream scholars (Sardar 1985; Haneef 1995; Kahf 2003). Zaman (2019) also re-evaluates the empirical model framework in mainstream scholarship as the second generation of modern Islamic economics. This shift follows the failure of the first generation of scholars, favoring a compromise approach by modifying the capitalist economic system. This is presented as a form of Islamization, which negatively impacts the development of a scientific foundation as a consensus for the means and approaches in Islamic economics.

The study of Siddiqi's contributions to the scientific foundation of Islamic economics is limited and rare. This is partly due to the lack of comprehensive records of his writings on this topic, particularly regarding ontology, epistemology, and methodology. Haneef (1995) systematically outlines Siddiqi's contributions, including the worldview, methodology, and theoretical frameworks of Islamic economics, such as models of the Islamic economic system, distribution theories, and interest-free banking. Haneef & Furqani (2011) and Ustaoğlu (2023) briefly discuss Siddiq's methodological and theoretical frameworks, distinguishing Islamic economic and financial systems from modern economic models. Nabi (2018) also offers a detailed survey of Siddiqi's writings in Urdu and English but provides minimal analysis of his methodology in Islamic economics. The study aims to address the gap in understanding Siddiqi's role in developing the scientific foundation of Islamic economics. It reviews Siddiqi's writings on the philosophical and scientific foundations of Islamic economics, covering worldview, ontology, epistemology, methodology, and assumptions. The goal is to create a more comprehensive model and analysis of Siddiqi's contributions as a guide to future studies.

The Field of Islamic Economics Before the Impact of Siddiqi

The development of modern Islamic economics in the pre-1970s, particularly during the 1940s-1960s, was significantly shaped by traditionalist scholars, particularly in Islamic jurisprudence. These scholars independently studied Islamic economics without institutional support and actively promoted its ideas (Furqani 2015; Islahi 2015a). During this period, Islamic economic thought aimed to challenge Eurocentric Western ideologies, offering a distinct vision rooted in equity and justice, guided by Islamic law, and separate from the capitalist and socialist systems (Zaman 2019). The Islamic economic thought of this era was not just ideological, but also initiated a philosophical and doctrinal discourse on developing an idealistic and comprehensive scientific foundation for economics (Sholihin 2014). Scholars in this time analyze capitalism and socialism, concluding that Islamic economics needed to develop through Islamization, guided by the Qur'an and Sunnah. This approach was based on the understanding that the materialist worldview of modern economic thought, rooted in Graeco-Roman values like self-interest, could not address contemporary socio-economic issues effectively (Islahi 2015b). Thus, the early development of Islamic economics focused on identifying and formulating Islamic economic systems, critiquing capitalism and socialism (Islahi 2015a). First-generation scholars emphasized theorizing Islamic economics and banking through a narrative approach, and did not prioritize empirical testing of their developing ideas (Islahi 2015a; Sardar 1985; Kuran 1995).

Hamidullah (2015) highlights certain issues with modern economic methods, noting their lack of holistic and comprehensive approaches. He argues that the development of Islamic economics addresses these weaknesses by integrating the strengths of modern economic methods in a more cohesive manner. The epistemological foundation of Islamic economics relies on divine revelation, that is, the Qur'an and Sunnah, alongside legal reasoning (*ijtihad*) to resolve legal challenges, all within a framework informed by rational, logical economic models. At the axiological level, Islam's emphasis on moral values distinguishes it from materialistic economic systems like capitalism and communism, which are criticized as sources of societal harm (Islahi 2017).

Yunus (1992) defines economics as the product of modern

thinkers, shaped by the dynamics and changes of the zeitgeist. Therefore, understanding the spectrum of economic ideologies is crucial for critiquing and formulating an independent Islamic economic system. Yunus emphasizes that Islamic ideology extends beyond religious worship to include respect for economic institutions, particularly in addressing socio-economic issues (Yunus 1955). He views economics as a societal common sense from a phenomenological perspective. This leads him to critique both scholars who interpret economics solely through normative doctrine and those who approach it as a purely theoretical discipline (Addiarrahman 2018). According to Yunus, economic problems should be analyzed through a socio-institutional approach, examining the hierarchy of social structures that creates conflicts of interest due to limited resources, hindering prosperity. This approach aims to develop Islamic economic theory by constructing social models that explain human behavior within specific institutional contexts. Yunus argues that this methodology offers distinct advantages over the predictive models of positive economics, which are often constrained by biased assumptions and over-generalized conclusions (Dugger 1979; Addiarrahman 2018).

The Islamic economic system, as an economic ideology, is founded on two ontological principles: spirituality and materiality, or spiritualization and materialization. These principles aim to mediate between the economic systems of capitalism and socialism by combining their benefits while addressing their weaknesses (Yunus n.d.). The ontological dimension of Islamic economics forms the basis for its epistemology, which is rooted in Islamic teachings on economics derived from the Qur'an and Sunnah. This foundation produces an axiology that emphasizes real economic activities, fostering genuine prosperity rather than the mere circulation of capital or factors relating to the ownership of production, as seen in the capitalist system (Yunus n.d.;

Addiarrahman 2018). The focus on real economic activity, rather than the ownership of production and capital assets, stems from the understanding that ownership is a consequence of such activity. Consequently, real economic activity underpins the development of both positive and normative theories in Islamic economics (Yunus 1959).

Some studies on the scientific foundation of Islamic economics apply a historical-legal analysis to understand the emergence of Islamic economic theory. Max Weber utilized sociology and historical methodology to examine the social and institutional structures of Muslim communities, providing a more accurate foundation for economic activity in Islam (Turner 1974). This historical-legal analysis, by observing the sociological and institutional development of economic activity in Islamic society, positions economics as a practical science *('ilm 'amalī)*, that is, a discipline focused on organizing societal relationships to meet life's needs (Spengler 1964). This perspective views Islamic economics as a synthesis of the classical Graeco-Roman tradition of economic order (*oikos-nomos*) within a community, but Islamized through shifts in worldview and value paradigms, combined with the guidance of the Qur'an and Sunnah (Baeck 1991).

Historically, Ahmad (1969) notes that the development of Islamic economics is closely tied to the historicity of Islamic civilization and culture since the 7th century AD. It originates from three main sources: (a) the Qur'an, (b) early religious texts that followed the Qur'an, and (c) writings that treat economics and its subject matters as a distinct discipline. The Qur'an offers a philosophical perspective by presenting a worldview and ontology of economics, situating God within economic reality and establishing ethical and axiological norms. Post-Qur'anic texts further elaborate by constructing Islamic legal institutions to regulate economic activities. Meanwhile, early Islamic writings on economics provide their own perspective on economic matters through a theorizing process rooted in a worldview and theological paradigm, balancing the material and non-material dimensions that form the most fundamental economic problems. For his part, Fazlur Rahman provides an ontological foundation for Islamic economics as a system of socio-economic justice, not merely a theoretical discipline. He defines economic value as the integration of efforts to seek wealth and profit through production activities guided by unique moral qualities, making it valuable as a form of worship. Rahman outlines theories on the production and distribution of wealth based on the Qur'anic values of economic activities (Faẓlurraḥmān 1969). Islam offers a distinct worldview and paradigm for interpreting social justice in the economy, separate from Socialism. In the Islamic perspective, economic activity involves accumulating sources of prosperity but is always guided by ethical and moral principles, along with the social system, such as *Zakat*, which ensures social welfare (Rahman 1970).

The Foundation of Islamic Economics

The development of modern Islamic economics during the 1950s-1970s aimed to create an idealistic system to counter the influence of capitalist and socialist systems on Muslim thought (Nienhaus 2000). This period saw Islamic economics driven more by a political agenda against Western imperialism than by scientific research (Kuran 1995). As a result, Islamic economics was viewed as a doctrinal narrative rather than a scientific analysis. Its somewhat *ad hoc* nature and casuistical approach fell short of the criteria for a scientific discipline, making it unsuitable for understanding economic behavior (Iqbal 2014; Mahomedy 2013).

After the 1970s, Islamic economics shifted towards integrating Islamic principles with modern economics, accompanied by the use of tools like econometrics. This change aimed to establish Islamic economics as an economic discipline with a strong theoretical and methodological framework (Furqani 2015). Muhammad Nejatullah Siddiqi was a pioneer in this field and contributed significantly to developing more scientific and sophisticated theories (Ustaoğlu 2023). Haneef (1995) highlights two key approaches of Siddiqi's in developing Islamic economics:

- The reception of Neoclassical analytical tools in Islamic economics, while also modifying assumptions and models to highlight the limitations of the Neoclassical framework (Haneef 1995). However, this approach has been criticized by some for overly replicating Neoclassical methods, leading to an overemphasis on Western positivist and empiricist paradigms. Critics argue that this shift has sometimes sidelined the Islamic worldview and doctrinal principles in the development process (Alatas 2006; Sholihin and Furqani 2020; Sardar 1985).

- The development of Islamic economics through the modern Islamization approach involves building hypotheses from Qur'anic and Sunnah sources, while also applying empirical evidence to arrive at scientific statements (Haneef 1995). However, Siddiqi's Islamization approach has been criticized for its unclear methods. As a result, critics argue that it often replicates modern economic theories without sufficiently engaging the Islamic worldview, limiting its impact on the structure of economics (Furqani and Man 2008).

The application of these two approaches is an important foundation for Siddiqi in developing the discipline of Islamic economics. This is especially the case regarding its foundational elements including its worldview, epistemology, methodology and assumptions (Ustaoğlu 2023). Unlike previous Islamic economics scholars, who tended more towards ideological goals, Siddiqi focused more on the scientification of Islamic economics through the integration of Islamic doctrines within the framework of modern economic models. This effort resulted in an Islamic economics discipline that was not only doctrinal but also scientific. Siddiqi achieved this through the adaptation of Neoclassical and Keynesian theories and methodologies within the framework of an Islamic economic analysis (Haneef 1995).

The Worldview of Islamic Economics

The development of Islamic economics is deeply connected to worldview, which serves as the philosophical foundation for understanding reality (Furqani 2021). Worldview helps humans interpret the relationship between the universe and human nature, guiding them to find meaning and purpose in life, manage limited resources, and establish social relations (Chapra 1998). It also shapes social reality by providing a framework for society to organize and interpret life's order, forming the basis for regulating the world order (Burke 2013). Economic vision, shaped by worldview, provides a foundation for developing economic analysis frameworks. In the Islamic economic vision, the concept of *dīn* is foundational, emphasizing human submission to God's will by living under the guidance of His Law (Al-Attas 1978; Haneef 1997). This ethical foundation in the economic framework aligns with the seeking of knowledge, showing harmony between religion as a worldview and scientific inquiry in economic analysis (Naqvi 2016; Furqani 2021). Worldview shapes how humans perceive reality, influencing both abstract theoretical concepts and practical changes in behavior and institutions (Swidler 2010). In Islamic economics, worldview establishes a knowledge structure that connects human understanding with the transcendental dimension of divinity (Nasr 1986).

Siddiqi views worldview as a foundation of Islamic economics, defining it as a transformation of thought and practice. He emphasizes that the Islamic worldview, rooted in the Qur'an and Sunnah, provides general principles for economic activity that importantly should adapt to changing contexts and conditions (Haneef 1995; Ustaoğlu 2023). While the Islamic worldview itself does not change, its derivative aspects such the economic require flexibility (Haneef 1997). Unlike Neoclassical economists who see economic activity as autonomous or Marxists who view it as deterministic, Siddiqi asserts that the economic behavior is inseparable from the determination of worldview, not *vice-versa* (Haneef 1995). He also stresses that developing disciplines like Islamic economics requires careful integration of worldview, spirituality, and moral perspectives (Siddiqi 2011).

Al-Attas (1978) asserts that the Islamic worldview is closely related to the ontological relationship between God as the creator and humans as creation. In the Islamic worldview, humans are required to surrender themselves, and desire to always live both in body and soul as a representation of obedience to God's law. Siddiqi (1970) asserts his perspective on the Islamic worldview:

> God, the Almighty, is the creator and the master of entire universe including man. Man's span of existence is not merely this worldly life but it extends to eternity. Man though free to choose his attitude and approach in life is nevertheless accountable for his behavior in the life hereafter where enduring felicity or unending punishment shall be his share according to his behavior in this world.

The core concept of the Islamic worldview is *Tawhīd* (the Oneness of God), which is demonstrated in the manifestation of His attributes and actions. God is the Creator, Sustainer and Judge of all things. He is also the cause and end of everything. Every Muslim is obliged to surrender to God by obeying all commandments and avoiding all prohibitions. This idea has consequences for Muslims' economic behavior, which relies on Islamic economic moral and ethical norms (Haneef 1997). Belief in the Oneness of God inspires the Muslim economic perspective and regulates social behavior. This is due to the belief that every human action will be rewarded by God, not only in worldly life but also in the afterlife (Naqvi 2016).

The Islamic worldview provides a sufficient foundation for determining methodological approaches. Purely neutral-scientific and rational economics is a myth, as economic vision, epistemology, and methodology are inherently shaped by a particular worldview (Al-Daghistani 2021). Integrating Islamic principles and worldview into the scientific framework of Islamic economics involves building knowledge aligned with Islamically defined nature, scope, and subject matter. However, adapting Neoclassical theory and methodology in Islamic economics, though seemingly aligned with Islamic principles, is unjustifiable. This is because the scientific basis of conventional economics stems from Western empiricism and materialism, which conflict with the Islamic worldview (Salleh 2011).

The Ontology of Islamic Economics

Ontology is the study of existence and the nature of things we know (Lawson 2003). It helps define knowledge, including its nature, scope, and key topics, by exploring questions about existence and how things exist (Kalin 2010). The true essence of knowledge lies in the objects being studied, which is called primal ontology or the theory of being. The interconnectedness, or purposiveness (*teleology*), of the world signals how knowledge is unified (Choudhury 2019). We can understand this truth through intellectual activities that connect logical reasoning with the reality of what is being studied (Lahham 2021).

The study of ontology as a theory or science is the effort to understand the reality that makes that theory or science valid. For economics, this involves exploring its philosophical foundations to grasp its worldview, vision, definition, nature, scope, framework, and purpose (Furqani 2006). This inquiry provides a comprehensive understanding of economics as a scientific discipline, addressing its epistemological and methodological challenges. Ontology, including worldview, determines the methods used in economics, not the other way around. Therefore, economics cannot be purely scientific or neutral, as its foundation is rooted in a specific worldview (Al-Daghistani 2021). The key focus of ontology in Islamic economics is defining its nature as a scientific discipline. This involves identifying its nature, scope, and subject matter to distinguish it from other economic disciplines and to justify its study and development scientifically (Furqani 2006). While Siddiqi (1970) does not offer a specific definition of Islamic economics, he does provide a general understanding of economy as a concept: "Economy… is a part, rather than an aspect of culture. Culture is nothing less than life, life as it manifests itself in all its variety and vigor."

Here, Siddiqi emphasizes that the economy is intertwined with the cultural aspects of human life. The subject matter of Islamic economics, like Neoclassical and Keynesian economics, as a study of human behavior with a focus on achieving social welfare amid scarce resources for well-being. The only difference lies in Islamic objectives, problem-solving approaches, and institutional frameworks. The implication inherent in this perspective has led to the adaptation of Neoclassical and Keynesian theories and methodologies within the Islamic economics framework, albeit incorporating some distinct behavioral factors (Furqani 2018; Khan 2015). Siddiqi (1970), then, from this vantage point asserts that:

The spirit of any culture is the outlook towards life, and

> the relationships involved therein. It is the way of looking at goods and materials. It is a tendency towards certain ends selected from amongst many; an inclination towards a particular set of means, exclusive of all other alternatives. It is the guiding principle of all individual human behaviors.

Siddiqi views the economy as an element of culture that shapes human behavior. This cultural element itself stems from a worldview that interprets both material and spiritual realities, including how human needs are met (Haneef 1995). In defining economic behavior, Siddiqi leans toward the Neoclassical definition by Robbins (2007), who describes economics as the study of human behavior in achieving ends with limited means. However, Siddiqi diverges from Neoclassical scholars like Marshall (2013) and Pareto (2014), who assume that the ultimate goal of economic behavior is to maximize utility. Instead, Siddiqi argues that human behavior aims not only to fulfill material and physical needs but also non-material and spiritual ones. Thus, Siddiqi (1970) asserts:

> The Islamic individual is always conscious of the fact that a materially prosperous life is not an end in itself, that a high standard of living is no value in itself. Our life-end being success in the life hereafter, the value of everything is determined by the contribution it makes towards that end. It is virtue and goodness that count. So all efforts to satisfy our material needs can contribute this end only if they are properly directed. We can make our economic activities subservient to our life-end if we focus our attention to the higher ends.

The ultimate goal of Islamic economics is *falāḥ* (prosperity), achieved by organizing economic resources through cooperation and participation. The proper use of resources should guide humans toward *falāḥ*, addressing the challenge of scarcity (Khan 1984). Meeting human needs, including both worldly and spiritual welfare, is essential for maximizing *falāḥ* (Hasan 2020). Siddiqi (1970) emphasizes that economics studies human behavior with the aim of achieving *falāḥ*, encompassing both this world and the hereafter. The Qur'an views all economic activities, whether individual or collective, as directed toward realizing *falāḥ*. Therefore, Islam does not restrict efforts to achieve prosperity through social change and community institutions.

The Methodology of Islamic Economics

Methodology is a part of epistemology, which forms the scientific foundation of knowledge. Epistemology is the study of the theory of knowledge, its sources, applications, and limitations. In contrast, methodology focuses on how to develop and test knowledge to create robust theories (Haneef and Furqani 2011). It involves designing scientific methods with specific procedures for studying natural and social phenomena. Methodology ensures that the methods used in research are applied correctly to understand the object of knowledge (Safi 2014).

The methodology of economics, as a subfield of the discipline, focuses on how economists justify their theories and why they prefer one theory over another. A methodology can be a positivist statement that is descriptive and factual, or a prescriptive statement that is justificative and normative (Blaug 1993). The term "methodology" is often confused with methods, procedures, approaches, or techniques of modeling. However, methodology is fundamentally about evaluating and appraising theories to establish them as scientific knowledge, rather than being a method itself (Fox 1997). It provides a rationale for justifying the preference for certain theories based on intellectual rules, including concepts, model frameworks, hypothesis formulation, and critical appraisal of theories (Machlup 1978).

One approach to developing Islamic economics is the pluralism or mixed methodology. This approach is influenced by the tendency toward Neo-Keynesian synthesis, whereby some non-mainstream economists to adopt a pluralistic methodology to better understand economic reality (Shah 2006; Hausman 1989). Siddiqi advocates for a pluralistic or flexible methodology by integrating Neoclassical and Keynesian methodologies with developing classical Islamic methods (Haneef 1995). Siddiqi (2014) believes that Islam is compatible with various modeling approaches, including both doctrinal and positivistic methods. He argues that completely rejecting modern economic theory is not feasible; instead, a critical approach is needed to assess and select elements of modern economic theory. For Siddiqi (1981) This accommodative approach in intended to avoid accepting implicit, non-neutral values in modern economic analysis. Siddiqi (1988a) identifies at least three main methodological approaches for the development of Islamic economics:

- The methodology of the Islamic sciences is used to establish the theoretical foundation for rules of conduct and individual behavior norms. This approach involves applying logical reasoning (*qiyās*) to derive rules from the Qur'an and Sunnah, institutionalizing norms, and using analytical reasoning to identify social benefits (*maṣlaḥah*) in areas where *qiyās* and *ijtihād* are not applicable. This methodological framework is essential for integrating Sharia and economics in developing the scientific foundations of Islamic economics.
- Economics is applied as a tool to analyze human behavior, social relations, and processes related to economic activities such as production, consumption, and distribution. This approach primarily falls under positive

economics but is limited by its scope, requiring insights from other disciplines to provide a more comprehensive understanding.

- The integration of Islamic sciences and positive economics aims to transform positive theory into normative theory. This involves two stages: first, evaluating the behavior of economic agents based on Sharia principles, and second, aligning their behavior with Islamic values to achieve the objectives of the Sharia.

These critical approaches to modern economic theory and methodology have led Siddiqi to modify key assumptions, behavioral norms, and objectives to highlight the perspective of Islamic economics and address the weaknesses of the Neoclassical model, thereby creating a new theoretical and economic analysis framework (Haneef 1995; Siddiqi 1970). Islamic economics, as both a scientific discipline and a normative doctrine, aims to establish a new economic system. For Siddiqi (1996), modern economic methodologies can produce theories relevant to Islamic economics, focusing on achieving specific ends and utilizing appropriate means. Meanwhile, Islamic sciences institutionalize behavioral norms for economic agents in line with Islamic doctrine.

Siddiqi's advanced methodological approach focuses on developing Islamic economics as an "agent of Islamization." The Qur'an and Sunnah serve as the primary epistemological foundation, providing a distinct framework and worldview for Islamic economics (Siddiqi 1988a). These sources are used to establish scientific criteria for evaluating the consistency between doctrinal principles and empirical evidence. Unlike Neoclassical and Keynesian methodologies, which rely solely on empirical testing, Islamic economics requires theories to first pass tests of doctrinal integrity and logical validity (Furqani and Haneef 2012).

Hypotheses are derived from correct interpretations of Qur'anic and Sunnah texts and serve as postulates for translating ideal and practical realities into theoretical models (Siddiqi 2014). These models are then empirically tested, with feedback used to refine and develop Islamic economic theory (Furqani and Haneef 2012). Siddiqi (2014) emphasizes the importance of empirical studies to support textual evidence and advocates for refining data and procedures if empirical tests contradict hypotheses, rather than discrediting the hypothesis itself (Haneef 1995; Furqani and Haneef 2012).

The Fundamental Assumptions of Islamic Economics

The core assumption of Islamic economics is defining its micro-foundation, focusing on the behavior of economic agents in an Islamic society as a key factor in how the Islamic economic system operates (Arif 1985a). This behavioral model is essential for both estimating and predicting behavior within theoretical and practical frameworks, as well as for establishing institutional norms for economic behavior (Dugger 1979). The model should adopt a holistic approach, incorporating social and institutional perspectives on human behavior, emphasizing values like caring and sharing, and engaging in social and economic activities (Siddiqi 2014).

Siddiqi rejects the concept of the rational economic man in Neoclassical economics, considering it both unrealistic and undesirable. This concept relies on complex assumptions about values, as well as specific times and places, making it difficult to observe in reality (Haneef 1995; Braun 2021). Additionally, Siddiqi addresses the issue of transaction costs in New Institutional economics, noting that economic agents lack complete information about the implications of their decisions for themselves or society. As a result, Siddiqi and other New

Institutional economists reject the idea of the rational economic man as a foundation for economic systems (Siddiqi 2014; Braun 2021).

Siddiqi tends to propose a prototype of Islamic man (*homo islamicus*), characterized by altruistic and socially-oriented traits. He emphasizes that Qur'anic virtues promote altruism and caring behavior alongside individual interests. Islamic doctrines also guide economic life by encouraging consumption moderation, minimizing waste, and prioritizing social utility (Haneef 1995; Siddiqi 1988b). The concept of the Islamic man, with its foundation in moral values, offers a promising approach to addressing social and economic issues through consensus and a universal inclination toward ethical conduct and moral values (Siddiqi 2014). This concept of the Islamic man reflects the behavior of economic agents in an Islamic society, which differs from the characteristics of the traditional economic man (Arif 1985b). However, Siddiqi does not explicitly define the epistemological framework of the Islamic man. He describes economic agents as agents of Islamization, where their behavior varies depending on the context of Islamization and the diversity of interpretations based on the level of Islamicity in their actions. Siddiqi's perspective makes the concept of the economic agent a challenging framework, as it lacks consistency and predictability for behavioral analysis (Haneef 1995).

Siddiqi introduces the concept of social utility as a key foundation for economic decision-making, contrasting with Neoclassical economics' focus on utility maximization (Haneef 1995). He argues that producers should prioritize the availability of essential goods for the community, even if it means not maximizing profits, as economic decisions should adhere to moral principles like honesty and fairness. Practices that contradict the goal of maximizing social interests are strictly prohibited (Haneef 1995; Siddiqi 1988b). Siddiqi also advocates for mutual consultation and cooperation as an alternative to the laissez-faire competitive model of Neoclassical economics, criticizing the concept of the invisible hand for failing to optimize economic equilibrium. He emphasizes the importance of prioritizing social justice, efficiency, economic development, stability, and freedom in Muslim societies (Haneef 1995). Achieving these goals requires economic agents to sincerely uphold the values of justice and benevolence in their decision-making (Siddiqi 1988c).

Conclusion

The development of Islamic economics as a modern discipline occurred in two stages. The first generation, from the 1940s to the 1970s, was led by traditionalist scholars with expertise in Islamic law. The second generation, from the 1970s onward, involved scholars in modern economics (Furqani 2015). Muhammad Nejatullah Siddiqi, a leading figure of the second generation, played a pivotal role in establishing a comprehensive and systematic scientific foundation for Islamic economics. He transformed Islamic economics from a socio-political opposition to capitalist and socialist systems into a philosophical approach to modern economics (Furqani 2006). Siddiqi's contributions include developing the scientific framework of Islamic economics, encompassing worldview, ontology, methodology, and basic assumptions. While his work is not as comprehensive as later scholars like Syed Nawab Haidar Naqvi, Akram Khan, Umer Chapra, and others, his significance lies in bridging the transition of Islamic economics from a doctrinal and ideological framework to a modern economic discipline. His openness to integrating Neoclassical and Keynesian theories, with necessary modifications to assumptions and values, highlights his critical role. However, his approach also underscores the need for further refinement through a deeper study of Islamic economic philosophy's ontological and epistemological foundations.

References

Addiarrahman, Addiarrahman. 2018. "Ekonomi Kemakmuran Bersama: Indonesian Islamic Economic Thought of Kahrudin Yunus." *Shirkah: Journal of Economics and Business* 3(3): 283-306.

Ahmad, Rafiq. 1969. "The Origin of Economics and The Muslims: A Preliminary Survey." *The Punjab University Economist* 7(1): 17-49.

Alatas, Syed. 2006. "Islam and the Science of Economics." In *The Blackwell Companion to Contemporary Islamic Thought*, 1st ed., 587-606. Malden: Blackwell Publishing.

Al-Attas, Muhammad Naquib. 1978. *Islam and Secularism*. Muslim Youth Movement of Malaysia.

Al-Daghistani, S. 2021. The Making of Islamic Economic Thought: Islamization, Law and Moral Discourses. Cambridge University Press.

Arif, Muhammad. 1985a. "Toward a Definition of Islamic Economics: Some Scientific Considerations." *Journal of King Abdulaziz University: Islamic Economics* 2(2): 79-93.

Arif, Muhammad. 1985b. "Toward the Shari'ah Paradigm of Islamic Economics: The Beginning of a Scientific Revolution." *American Journal of Islamic Social Sciences* 2(1): 79-99.

Baeck, Louis. 1991. "The Economic Thought of Classical Islam." *Diogenes* 39 (154): 99-115.

Behdad, Sohrab. 1989. "Property Rights in Contemporary Islamic Economic Thought: A Critical Perspective." *Review of Social Economy* 47(2): 185-211.

Blaug, Mark. 1993. *The Methodology of Economics*. Cambridge Books.

Braun, Eduard. 2021. "The Institutional Preconditions of Homo Economicus." *Journal of Economic Methodology* 28(2): 231-46.

Burke, Kenneth. 2013. "Comment by E. Roy Weintraub." In *Economics as Discourse: An Analysis of the Language of Economists*, 117-28. Springer Science & Business Media.

Chapra, M. Umer. 1985. *Towards a Just Monetary System*. Vol. 8. International Institute of Islamic Thought (IIIT).

Chapra, Muhammad Umar. 1998. "Relevance and Importance of Islamic Economics." In *Lessons in Islamic Economics*, 1:99-114. Islamic Development Bank.

Choudhury, Masudul Alam. 1986. "The Micro-Economics Foundations of İslamic Economics: A Study in Social Economics." *American Journal of Islam and Society* 3(2): 231-45.

Choudhury, Masudul Alam. 2019. *Methodological Dimension of Islamic Economics*. World Scientific Publication Ltd.

Dugger, William M. 1979. "Methodological Differences between Institutional and Neoclassical Economics." *Journal of Economic Issues* 13(4): 899-909.

Faẓlurraḥmān. 1969. "Economic Principles of Islam." *Islamic Studies* 8(1): 1-8.

Fox, Glenn. 1997. Reason and Reality in the Methodologies of Economics. Edward Elgar Publishing Ltd.

Furqani, Hafas. 2006. "Ontology and Methodology of Contemporary Islamic Economics: A Preliminary Exploration." *Unpublished Master Thesis. International Islamic University Malaysia.*

Furqani, Hafas. 2015. "The Discipline in the Making: Appraising the Progress of Islamic Economics." *Journal of Islamic Monetary Economics and Finance* 1(1): 1-24.

Furqani, Hafas. 2017. *The Current Situation of Islamic Economics in Indonesia*. Istanbul: Report. IKAM Research Centre for Islamic Economics Istanbul Turkey.

Furqani, Hafas. 2018. "Defining Islamic Economics: Scholars' Approach, Clarifying the Nature, Scope and Subject-Matter of The Discipline." *Turkish Journal of Islamic Economics* 5(2): 69-94.

Furqani, Hafas. 2021. "Islamic Economics: Is It A Doctrine or A Science?" *Jurnal Ekonomi Malaysia* 55(2): 137-44.

Furqani, Hafas, and Mohamed Aslam Haneef. 2012. "Theory Appraisal in Islamic Economic Methodology: Purposes and Criteria." *Humanomics* 28(4): 270-84.

Furqani, Hafas, and Zakariya Man. 2008. "The Emergence of Contemporary Islamic Economics: A Sketch of Its Historical Development." In *1st International Workshop on Islamic Economics: Exploring Islamic Economic Theory.*

Hamidullah, Muhammad. 1955. "Haidarabad's Contribution to Islamic Economic Thought and Practice." *Die Welt Des Islams* 4(2/3): 73-78. https://doi.org/10.2307/1569538.

Hamidullah, Muhammad. 2015. "Islam's Solution of the Basic Economic Problems: The Position of Labour." In *Muhammad Hamidullah and His Pioneering Works on Islamic Economics*, 69-116. Scientific Publishing Centre King Abdulaziz University.

Haneef, Mohamed Aslam. 1995. Contemporary Islamic Economic Thought: A Selected Comparative Analysis. Alhoda UK.

Haneef, Mohamed Aslam, and Hafas Furqani. 2011. "Methodology of Islamic Economics: Overview of Present State and Future Direction." *International Journal of Economics, Management and Accounting* 19(1): 1-26.

Haneef, Mohamed Aslam Mohamed. 1997. "Islam, the Islamic Worldview, and Islamic Economics." *IIUM Journal of Economics and Management* 5(1): 39-65.

Hasan, Zubair. 2020. "The Nature and Signiicance of Islamic Economics: Integrative Approach." *Leading Issues in Islamic Economics and Finance: Critical Evaluations.* Singapore: Springer Singapore.

https://doi.org/10.1007/978-981-15-6515-1_2.

Hausman, Daniel M. 1989. "Economic Methodology in a Nutshell." *Journal of Economic Perspectives* 3(2): 115-27.

Iqbal, Munawar. 2014. "Development of Theory of Islamic Economics: Problems and Proposals." *International Journal of Behavioural Accounting and Finance* 4(3): 259-80.

Islahi, Abdul Azim. 2015a. "First vs. Second Generation Islamic Economists: Deviations and Differences in Thoughts." In *Islamic Economics: Theory, Policy and Social Justice*, 2:11-22. Bloomsbury Qatar Foundation Journals.

Islahi, Abdul Azim. 2015b. "The Genesis of Islamic Economics: Revisited." *Islamic Economic Studies* 23(2): 1-28.

Islahi, Abdul Azim. 2017. "The Legacy of Muhammad Hamidullah in Islamic Economics." MPRA Paper 80149, University Library of Munich.

Kahf, Monzer. 1993. The Islamic Economy: Analytical Study of the Functioning of the Islamic Economic System. American Trust Publications.

Kahf, Monzer. 2003. "Islamic Economics: Notes on Definition and Methodology." *Review of Islamic Economics* 13(1): 23-47.

Kalin, Ibrahim. 2010. Knowledge in Later Islamic Philosophy: Mulla Sadra on Existence, Intellect and Intuition. Oxford University Press.

Khan, M. Fahim. 2015. "Revisiting the Foundational Concepts and Thoughts in Islamic Economics: Where Islamic Economics Should Originate in Terms of Theoretical Content." In *Islamic Economics: Basic Concepts, New Thinking and Future Directions*, 12-57. Cambridge Scholars Publishing.

Khan, Muhammad Akram. 1984. "Islamic Economics: Nature and Need." *Journal of King Abdulaziz University: Islamic Economics* 1(2): 55-61.

Kuran, Timur. 1995. "Islamic Economics and the Islamic Subeconomy." *Journal of Economic Perspectives* 9(4): 155-73.

Kuran, Timur. 1997. "The Genesis of Islamic Economics: A Chapter in the Politics of Muslim Identity." *Social Research* 64(2): 301-38.

Lahham, Karim. 2021. The Anatomy of Knowledge & Ontological Necessity of First Principles. Tabah Foundation.

Lawson, Tony. 2003. *Reorienting Economics*. Routledge.

Machlup, Fritz. 1978. Methodology of Economics and Other Social Sciences. New York: Academic press.

Mahomedy, Abdulkader Cassim. 2013. "Islamic Economics: Still in Search of an Identity." *International Journal of Social Economics* 40(6): 556-78.

Mannan, Muhammad Abdul. 1980. *Islamic Economics: Theory and Practice*. Ashraf.

https://books.google.co.id/books?id=IZMe0AEACAAJ.

Marshall, Alfred. 2013. *Principles of Economics*. Springer.

Nabi, Nasir. 2018. "Faisal Laureate Muhammad Nejatullah Siddiqi: Life and Works." *Journal of Islamic Banking & Finance* 35(3): 42-54.

Naqvi, Syed Nawab Haidar. 1981. *Ethics and Economics: An Islamic Synthesis*. United Kingdom: The Islamic Foundation.

Naqvi, Syed Nawab Haider. 2016. Perspectives on Morality and Human Well-Being: A Contribution to Islamic Economics. Vol. 24. Kube Publishing Ltd.

Nasr, Reza Vali. 1986. "Whither Islamic Economics?" *Islamic Quarterly* 30(4): 211-20.

Nienhaus, Volkaire. 2000. "Islamic Economics: Dogma or Science?" In *The Islamic World and The West: An Introduction to Political Cultures and International Relations*, 86-99. Leiden: Koninklijke Brill NV.

Pareto, Vilfredo. 2014. Manual of Political Economy: A Critical and Variorum Edition. OUP Oxford.

Rahman, Fazlur. 1970. "Islam and Social Justice." *Pakistan Forum* 1(1): 4-9.

Robbins, Lionel. 2007. An Essay on the Nature and Significance of Economic Science. Ludwig von Mises Institute.

Roy, Olivier. 1994. *The Failure of Political Islam*. Harvard University Press.

Safi, Louay. 2014. The Foundation of Knowledge: A Comparative Study in Islamic and Western Methods of Inquiry. International Institute of Islamic Thought (IIIT).

Salleh, Muhammad Syukri. 2011. "Islamic Economics Revisited: Re-Contemplating Unresolved Structure and Assumptions." In *8th International Conference on Islamic Economics and Finance. Doha, Qatar*, 1-21.

Sardar, Ziauddin. 1985. Islamic Futures: The Shape of Ideas to Come. Mansell.

Shah, Mohd Hazim. 2006. "Science as Episteme and Science as Techne: The Differing Roles of Scientific Knowledge in Pre-Modern and Modern Cultures." *History, Philosophy and Social Studies of Science: Essays in Honour of Ungku Aziz, University Malaya Press, Kuala Lumpur*, 79-103.

Sholihin, M. Sholihin M. 2014. "Positivism or Normativism Economics: An Appraisal toward Islamic Economics Methodology." *Turast: Jurnal Penelitian Dan Pengabdian* 2(2): 131-51.

Sholihin, Muhammad, and Hafas Furqani. 2020. "The Realism of Islamic Economics: Abbas Mirakhor's Methodological Structure of Islamic Economics." *Journal of Islamic Finance* 9(2): 89-100.

Siddiqi, Muhammad Nejatullah. 2011. "Islamization of Knowledge: Reflections on Priorities." *American Journal of Islam and Society* 28(3): 15-34.

Siddiqi, Muhammad Nejatullah. 1970. *Some Aspects of the Islamic Economy*. Islamic Publications.

Siddiqi, Muhammad Nejatullah. 1981. "Restructuring the Study of Economics in Muslim Universities." In *Social and Natural Sciences: The Islamic Perspective*, 71-86. Hodder and Stoughton.

Siddiqi, Muhammad Nejatullah. 1988a. "An Islamic Approach to Economics." In *Islam: Source and Purpose of Knowledge*, 153-74. International Institute of Islamic Thought.

Siddiqi, Muhammad Nejatullah. 1988b. "From Contemporary Economics to Islamic Economics." In *Today's Problems, Tomorrow's Solutions*, 108-17. Mansell Publishing Ltd.

Siddiqi, Muhammad Nejatullah. 1988c. *The Economic Enterprise in Islam*. Islamic Publications.

Siddiqi, Muhammad Nejatullah. 1996. *Teaching Economics in Islamic Perspective*. Scientific Publishing Centre.

Siddiqi, Muhammad Nejatullah. 2014. "Methodology of Islamic Economics." In *Handbook on Islam and Economic Life*, 71-89. Edward Elgar Publishing.

Spengler, Joseph J. 1964. "Economic Thought of Islam: Ibn Khaldūn." *Comparative Studies in Society and History* 6(3): 268-306.

Swidler, Leonard. 2010. "Toward a Universal Declaration of a Global Ethic." *Journal for the Study of Religions and Ideologies* 3(7): 19-45.

Turner, Bryan S. 1974. "Islam, Capitalism and the Weber Theses." *The British Journal of Sociology* 25(2): 230-43.

Ustaoğlu, Murat. 2023. "Muhammad Nejatullah Siddiqi." Edited by Murat Ustaoğlu and Cenap Çakmak. *The Palgrave Encyclopedia of Islamic Finance and Economics.* Springer International Publishing. https://doi.org/10.1007/978-3-030-93703-4_468-1.

Yunus, Kahrudin. 1955. *Sistem Ekonomi Kemakmuran Bersama.* 1st ed. Vol. 1. 2 vols. Fikiran Baru.

Yunus, Kahrudin. 1959. Bersamaisme Alias Ekonomi Terpimpin: Guided Economics. Lembaga Sukses Indonesia.

Yunus, Kahrudin. n.d. *Konsepsi Ekonomi Islam.* Fikiran Baru.

Yūnus, Qahar ad-Dīn. 1992. "al-Niẓām al-Iqtiṣāḍī fī al-Islām." In *al-Islām wa-al-Mu'aḍalāt al-Ijtimā'ī al-Hadīthah bi-Aqlām 'Asharah min 'Ulamā' al-Islām*, 1st ed., 125-33. Dar Katib al-'Aziz.

Zaman, Asad. 2019. "The Methodology of Third-Generation Islamic Economics." In *Methodology of Islamic Economics*, 18-30. Routledge.

THIRTEEN

Rethinking Early Islamic Banks in the Ottoman World: The Case of Cash *Waqfs*

Mehmet Bulut

Historical Background

The Ottoman Empire introduced a new financial system during the construction of the modern capitalist world economic system. This system was based on *vakf-ı nukud*/cash *waqfs* (CWs), *iltizam*/tax farming, and *esham*/*sukuk*. Without understanding the Ottoman heritage and experience, modern scholarship will face a significant gap in the history of Islamic banks and financial history. This paper focuses on the Ottoman experience, particularly CWs as early Islamic financial institutions and banks. Criticisms of capitalist economic theory have increased, especially during times of economic and financial turmoil. These critiques range from partial applications to complete condemnation of the capitalist system. However, systematic criticism of capitalist economic theory remains difficult due to its entrenched authority and the marginalization of alternative viewpoints. Despite this, there are viable alternatives to capitalism, including the Islamic economic mentality. Islamic economics provides a substantial alternative to prevailing economic philosophies such as capitalism and socialism. It highlights the significance of historical practices in addition to the teachings of the Qur'an and Sunnah. Throughout history, the economic practices of the Ummah have facilitated the resolution of economic and financial problems within Islamic borders. One such practice is CWs, which acquired extensive popularity during the Ottoman era and has existed for more than five centuries.

Cash *waqfs* (CWs) reflect both Islamic and Ottoman economic thought, preventing the introduction of banks, crucial institutions within capitalism, into Ottoman territory until the late 19th century. These *waqfs* derive their capital, in whole or in part, from cash, and the income generated is used for the designated purpose. Modern Islamic financial instruments are influenced by the revenue strategies employed by CWs. Frequently, these *waqfs* benefited small businesses, allowing Muslim entrepreneurs to access financing opportunities compliant with Islamic principles. Moreover, archival sources demonstrate that CWs sustained production and commerce in addition to consumption. The methods utilized by CWs within an economic framework that prohibits interest exemplify the adaptability of Islamic law, or *fiqh*. This study examines the Islamic economic mindset, with an emphasis on the *waqfs* established by the Ottomans in the Balkans. The founding documents of *waqfs* found in the Ottoman archives serve as the primary source material for this investigation. This study sheds light on the Islamic economic mentality as an alternative to capitalist systems by examining the historical and economic significance of financial *waqfs* in the Ottoman context. It demonstrates the resilience and adaptability of the Islamic legal framework in addressing economic challenges and offers valuable insights for contemporary discussions on Islamic economic and financial systems.

Islamic Economic System Amidst Expanding Financial Sector and Political Dynamics

Competition and cooperation have influenced the evolution of human societies throughout history. Based on these variables, diverse societies have shaped their economic and social structures, with some emphasizing competition and others emphasizing cooperation. Individualism and collectivism, as characterized by Greif (1994), have been used to describe these societies through a variety of scholarly studies. However, these studies frequently overlook the values recommended by religions to their adherents. Additionally, Kuran's (1997, 2003) assertions that Islam and Islamic law/*fiqh* contribute to underdevelopment lack a solid foundation. Nevertheless, the Islamic economic and financial system integrates a broader spectrum of values. The purpose of this paper is to examine the influential institutions that have shaped the Islamic economic and financial system, with a focus on the microfinance mentality. To achieve this, an analysis of the prevalent mentality and current condition of the conventional economic and financial system is required.

Recent global financialization has reached a level that poses a potential threat to nations. The primary purpose of the financial system is to mobilize and distribute funds, predominantly in the form of debt or loans, via a variety of mechanisms. Nonetheless, it is crucial to recognize that the financial system's influence extends beyond its financial dimensions. When evaluating the economic and financial system as a whole, it becomes clear that the financial system has significant effects on production, employment, and psychological, sociological, and social factors. Consequently, it is essential to recognize and address the multidimensional effects resulting from financial system challenges.

Globally, the scale and impact of the financial sector have grown substantially due to remarkable technological advancements. Especially for developing nations that are integrated into the global financial system, capital movements play a crucial role. While full integration frequently promotes economic growth, it also exposes these nations to external financial vulnerabilities. The close relationship between the economy and politics accentuates the political and economic influence of the individuals or groups that control the financial system. Therefore, the influence of the financial sector, particularly capital proprietors, on economic decision-making can result in sovereignty and moral concerns. Current attempts to resolve these issues are frequently confined to the existing system and lack viable alternatives. Nevertheless, the Islamic system provides a remedy for economic issues resulting from individualism and competition throughout history. This study investigates cash *waqfs* (CWs) as potential alternatives to the microcredit mechanism.

The expanding influence of the financial sector raises concerns about power concentration and its impact on economic decision-making and political dynamics. Developing nations that are integrated into the global financial system are especially susceptible to external financial operations, which can compromise their economic sovereignty. Current efforts to resolve these obstacles frequently fall short and do not offer viable alternatives. The Islamic economic system, on the other hand, provides a comprehensive solution to economic issues, particularly those originating from individualism and competition. Examining institutions such as CWs in the context of the microcredit mechanism can shed light on alternative economic and financial system approaches. By investigating these institutions and their function within the Islamic economic system, this study seeks to highlight potential alternatives that address the system's flaws. It also emphasizes the significance of analyzing the prevalent mindset and the current state of the conventional economic and financial system as the basis for proposing alternative models that promote sustainable and inclusive economic development.

Waqfs and CWs

Capitalism, which has encircled the globe since the 18th century and established its systematic superiority in the latter half of the 20th century, has increased desires to maximize individual well-being, such as unlimited production and consumption, acquiring private property, earning money, and being wealthy without value. This mindset is not at all altruistic. *Waqfs* prioritize cooperation. A competitive viewpoint is incompatible with the waqf system. Capitalism prioritizes the individual's well-being through unrestricted production, consumption, and accumulation of wealth and frequently disregards altruistic considerations. In contrast to the competitive nature of capitalism, *waqfs* represent a cooperative philosophy. *Waqfs*, which are based on Islamic economic principles, combine resources for the greater benefit of society, with an emphasis on collective welfare and equitable distribution. This alternative strategy encourages sustainable development, social justice, and community participation. By recognizing these divergent values, we can examine alternative economic models that prioritize cooperation and societal well-being, resulting in a more inclusive and well-balanced system. The study of *waqfs* offers insights into advancing collective progress and adopting altruistic values.

In the Islamic world, *waqfs* have a lengthy history and have played an important role in molding society, especially during the Ottoman era. *Waqfs*, which are charitable Islamic social institutions, have been an integral part of the Islamic world for centuries. *Waqfs* have served as crucial mechanisms for attaining sustainable development in Islamic societies throughout history (Walaa 2021). *Waqfs* became an element of government policy during the Ayyubid Dynasty, and their use peaked during the Ottoman Empire. During this time period, nearly one-third of the Ottoman state's total revenue was generated through waqf donations. This demonstrates the significant role performed by *waqfs* in the financing and maintenance of diverse social welfare initiatives. In addition, *waqfs* in the Ottoman Empire were effectively managed to ensure that the founder's intentions were carried out. They were indispensable for promoting social welfare, enhancing access to education and healthcare, and sustaining the livelihoods of diverse social groups. During the golden era of the Ottoman Empire, the waqf institution's wealth was solidly established, allowing for the financing of a vast array of facilities and social services (Bulut et al. 2019). The services for cities such as infrastructure development, community services, education, cultural initiatives, and religious services are provided by *waqfs*. The *waqfs* had important role for development of cities.

Waqfs not only provided essential social amenities but also played a crucial role in meeting the requirements of families and members of society at large. In addition to their monetary contributions, *waqfs* held considerable cultural and religious significance in the Islamic world. They were viewed as acts of piety and devotion, reflecting a belief in the value of contributing to society (Suryanto, Rahmat & Marlina 2020). By establishing *waqfs*, individuals could ensure that their fortune is utilized in perpetuity for the community's advantage. In general, the history of *waqfs* in the Islamic world, especially during the Ottoman era, demonstrates their profound significance. *Waqfs* exemplified acts of piety and devotion, enabling individuals to leave a lasting impression on their communities. In addition, *waqfs* served to promote communal cohesion and address societal requirements. The establishment and administration of *waqfs* played an essential role in enhancing the well-being of the ummah. The *waqfs* facilitated the delivery of essential services, including education, healthcare, infrastructure development, and community services. In addition, *waqfs* supported disadvantaged members of society, such as the impoverished, orphaned, and indigent. Through their financial partnerships, such as CWs, *waqfs* in the Ottoman Empire ensured that these services were available to all members of society, regardless of their economic status.

Waqfs are institutional structures that exemplify altruism and solidarity, reflecting the Islamic economic mindset and playing a crucial role in the development of Islamic societies. *Waqfs* have served as civil initiatives throughout history, financing various educational, religious, and infrastructural institutions, especially during the Ottoman Empire (Günay 2012; Yediyldz 2012). These institutions supported by waqf not only created jobs but also contributed to economic vitality. During the latter half of the 19th century, the Ottoman Empire, renowned for its *waqfs*, developed CWs in response to the advent of joint-stock companies, banks, and insurance institutions in the West. The revenues generated by CWs, which consist of capital in the form of cash, are the result of operations conducted in accordance with Islamic principles and procedures (Bulut & Korkut 2019a). The religious discussions surrounding CWs served as an important indicator of their legitimacy and religious foundation (Şimşek 1985; Ozcan 1999, 2000; Kudat 2015), which contributed to the adoption of CWs in Muslim society. This religious legitimacy played a crucial role in facilitating the approval and pervasive use of CWs within the Muslim community, thereby ensuring their continued importance in influencing economic and financial systems. The enduring presence and influence of CWs demonstrate the enduring significance of religious values and practices in shaping economic structures and promoting societal well-being.

In contrast to contemporary financial institutions, the most significant characteristic of CWs was that their founders were not motivated by profit. The primary objective of CWs is to use the revenues generated from financial capital to further the objectives of the waqf. Regard was paid to the Islamic prohibition on interest in the methods of income generation. CWs have paved the way for many interest-free financial institution practices. Despite the fact that the primary purpose of the CWs was to provide charity services, these *waqfs* played an essential role in meeting the requirements of those in need of funds. The CWs, which determined the borrowing rate and prohibited usurers on the financial market, formed the basis of the Ottoman financial system for several decades. In the eighth century, Imam Zufar issued a fatwa recognizing the significance of pecuniary *waqfs* (Tekdogan 2020). The emergence and acceptance of CWs in the Ottoman Empire represented a significant change in the financial system of that era. Despite the initial impediment posed by the prohibition on interest, CWs progressively gained popularity in the Ottoman Empire, especially beginning in the sixteenth century. As the Ottoman Empire grew and changed over time, these financial *waqfs* gained widespread acceptability and popularity, contributing to their enduring influence.

Financial Contributions of CWs

CWs arose as an alternative to the expanding banking sector in the West, offering a different financial strategy that contradicted the notion that only affluent individuals could establish *waqfs* and perpetually accumulate capital, as is the case with conventional banking systems. In contrast, CWs enabled even modest savers to establish *waqfs* on their own or in conjunction with other benefactors. This Ottoman-established financial system adhered to the principle the "economy is for humans" as opposed to the modern economic principle "humans are for economies" (Tabakoğlu 2012, p. 192). Its implementation was based on the principle of enhancing the conditions of devotees (*ibadullahın terfi-i ahvali*), which sought to improve the welfare of individuals.

The worldview of societies played a crucial role in the establishment of an interest-free financial system, as society's adoption of such institutions is closely linked to their fundamental worldview (Bulut, Akkemik & Göksal 2016). CWs offered a distinct alternative to the conventional banking system by providing a financial structure based on the principles of equity and inclusion. In contrast to conventional banks, CWs did not restrict participation on the basis of wealth, enabling individuals with modest savings to contribute to the establishment of *waqfs*. This approach emphasized the inherent social responsibility of economic activities and was consistent with the larger principle of improving human welfare. The acceptance and success of the interest-free financial system, exemplified by CWs, were contingent on its values and principles aligning with the worldview and societal norms of the communities in which it operated. This compatibility between the interest-free financial system and the worldview of society facilitated the development and widespread adoption of CWs as a viable alternative to conventional banking systems.

CWs offer an alternative system of financing based on the ontological foundations of Islam, avoiding manipulative practices and interest-based financial transactions, and refraining from financing the production of prohibited goods. At their core, the principles of CWs are derived from Islamic ethical values and standards. In accordance with Islamic financial principles, CWs are founded on risk-sharing, partnership, and profit-sharing. This system eschews interest-based lending and borrowing, fostering a community-centered approach that places a greater emphasis on servicing society than on market dynamics. In addition, the CW system employs a development-oriented framework rather than a singular focus on growth, placing poverty reduction policies, transactions, and practices at the vanguard of its operations (Asutay 2012, p. 99; Korkut & Kar 2018, p. 190). CWs reflect a comprehensive approach to finance that is consistent with Islamic values and seeks to advance economic and social justice.

By averting transactions based on interest, CWs promote a more equitable distribution of resources and reduce the likelihood of exploitation. This system emphasizes the importance of shared prosperity while promoting risk-sharing and collaboration. CWs prioritize societal welfare and address the requirements of marginalized individuals and communities within a community-based framework. Microfinance initiatives, *qard al-hasan* (charitable loans), and *zakat* (mandatory almsgiving) play a crucial role in the CW system's efforts to reduce poverty. CWs empower individuals and contribute to sustainable development at the grassroots level by diverting funds to initiatives that support entrepreneurship, education, healthcare, and essential necessities. Unlike conventional growth-oriented models, the CW system promotes a more inclusive and balanced approach to economic development. This system encourages responsible and ethical investment practices that consider the long-term well-being of individuals, communities, and the environment rather than profit maximization at all costs. CWs provide an alternative vision for a more just and equitable economic system based on Islamic principles by promoting ethical finance and social solidarity.

Despite the existence of CWs with substantial capital, the majority of them were modest in size and catered to small-scale loans. This emphasizes their crucial function in assisting aspiring entrepreneurs with financing. However, there are debates regarding the beneficiaries of CWs, specifically whether they served predominantly consumer financing or played a significant role in financing production and commerce (Çizakça 2000; Faraqhi 2004; Bulut & Korkut 2016a). Although it is not uncommon for CWs to be involved in consumer financing, it is essential to highlight their holistic contribution to production and trade via the financial system. Notably, particular provisions in waqf establishment documents (*waqfiyas*) serve as important indicators of this. These *waqfiyas* stipulate that only artisans and merchants are eligible for financing, emphasizing the emphasis on supporting productive activities (Table 1; Bulut et al. 2019). As a result, CWs play a larger role in the economy as they supplement financing institutions by providing loans to entrepreneurs. In addition to providing financial support, CWs cultivate an environment that is conducive to economic development and stability. CWs empower individuals with limited access to conventional financing by providing loans to small entrepreneurs, thereby fostering economic diversification and cultivating entrepreneurial endeavors. In addition, their emphasis on trade and production financing contributes to the growth of local industries and markets, resulting in increased employment opportunities and sustainable economic growth. The distinctive characteristics of CWs, such as their concentration on modest loans and alignment with ethical and value-based principles, contribute to their broader socioeconomic impact. CWs play a vital role in nurturing inclusive growth, reducing inequality, and promoting economic resilience within communities by channeling resources towards productive sectors and providing assistance to individuals at the grassroots level.

	The *Waqf* of Ibrahim b. Hadji Bali	**The *Waqf* of Mudarris Abdurrahman Agha b. Mehmed**	**The *Waqf* of Hadji Ahmed Effendi b. Mehmed Effendi**
Source	*Shar'iyyah* (Court) Records of Edirne: 4646, Page: 7	*Shar'iyyah* (Court) Records of Edirne, Register: 4675 Page: 21-22	VGMA, Register: 737, Page: 155-164, Serial: 61
Date	5 Ramadhan 1048 / 10 January 1639	Last ten days of Safar 1056 / 29 March-7 April 1646	15 Sha'ban 1126 / 26 August 1714

	The *Waqf* of Ibrahim b. Hadji Bali	**The *Waqf* of Mudarris Abdurrahman Agha b. Mehmed**	**The *Waqf* of Hadji Ahmed Effendi b. Mehmed Effendi**
Subject	40.000 akches endowment of Ibrahim b. Hadji Bali from Hasanpasha Neighborhood of Edirne for reparation of the Bozacı Bridges on the Arda River, and for the Orta Bridge on the Meriç River.	23.000 akches in silver endowment of Mudarris Abdurrahman Agha b. Mehmed from Edirne for attendants of the mosque around the Sheikh Ibrahim Tomb, and for Qur'an recitation.	Various real estates and 2.000 qurushes endowment of Hadji Ahmed Effendi b. Mehmed Effendi from Yunus Bey Neighbor-hood of Rodosçuk City for the mosques throughout the city and several charity services in Mecca and Madinah.
Operation rate	15%	15%	15%
Conditions	Conditions to be fulfilled by persons who can borrow from the foundation in the foundation certificate: 1. Capital must be operated within the framework of interest-free/shariah provisions.	Conditions to be fulfilled by persons who can borrow from the foundation in the foundation certificate: 1. Capital must be operated within the framework of interest-free/shariah provisions.	Conditions to be fulfilled by persons who can borrow from the foundation in the foundation certificate: 1. Capital must be operated within the framework of interest-free/shariah provisions.

	The *Waqf* of Ibrahim b. Hadji Bali	The *Waqf* of Mudarris Abdurrahman Agha b. Mehmed	The *Waqf* of Hadji Ahmed Effendi b. Mehmed Effendi
	2. The person who will receive the financing must live in the region where the waqf was established. 3. The person receiving the financing must be a trader. 4. The person receiving the financing should be a reliable person. 5. The person who will receive the financing must show a mortgage or guarantor	2. The person who will receive the financing must live in the region where the waqf was established. 3. The person receiving the financing must be a trader or an artisan. 4. The person receiving the financing should be a reliable person. 5. The person who will receive the financing must show a mortgage and guarantor.	2. The person who will receive the financing must live in the region where the waqf was established. 3. The person receiving the financing must be a trader or a wealthy person. 4. The person receiving the financing should be a reliable person. 5. The person who will receive the financing must show a mortgage or guarantor. 6. Risky investments should be avoided.

Table 1. Sample of CWs that provided cash for entrepreneurs (Bulut et al., 2019)

During the Ottoman Empire, CWs played a crucial role in meeting the cash requirements of merchants, artisans, and craftsmen. These foundations served as a means of wealth transfer, effectively compensating for a potential cash scarcity in the economy. By providing access to funds, CWs protected entrepreneurs from prevalent usury practices in the market, ensuring equitable profit rates for both small and large depositors. The stability of the profit rates offered by CWs remained consistent over extended time periods, frequently remaining at approximately 15% (Graph 1; Bulut & Korkut 2016b). Graph 1 also shows the fluctuation of borrowing rates in other countries in the same period as in the Ottoman Empire.

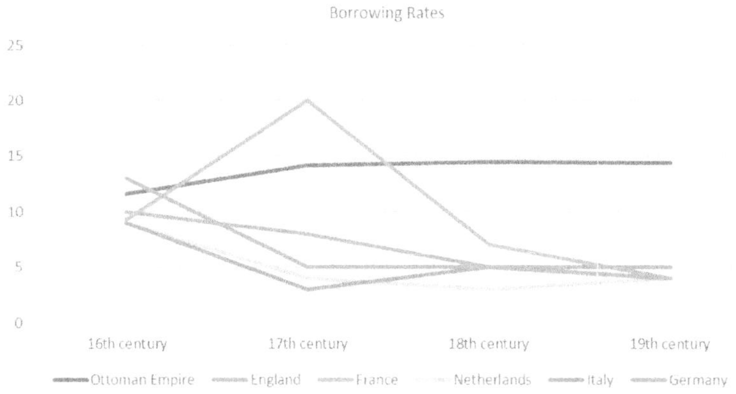

Graph 1. Borrowing rates of CWs
(Bulut & Korkut 2016b)

The stability of CWs was influenced by the state regulations that governed them. By restricting the use of cash from the CWs to merchants and artisans while excluding civil servants, CWs supported the economy's trade and production. The enduring stability of financing costs in the Ottoman Empire created a predictable investment climate for merchants, artisans, and business owners. State regulations and the guidance of the Ottoman *ulama* in discouraging exorbitant interest rates played crucial roles in preserving this equilibrium over a lengthy period of time (Bulut & Korkut 2022). Additionally, the practice of lending in exchange for commodities contributed to the system's stability. The ability to borrow at a stable and reasonable interest rate not only facilitated economic activity but also contributed to financial stability. It enabled individuals to confidently plan and invest, fostering entrepreneurship and economic expansion. The sustainability of this system was made possible by the state's efforts to regulate lending practices and discourage exploitative interest rates. Overall, CWs served as a crucial mechanism for microcredit, supporting the financial requirements of entrepreneurs and allowing them to contribute to commerce and production. The stability and equity of the financing costs, coupled with state regulations and social norms, fostered economic growth and financial stability in the Ottoman Empire.

A Structural Analysis of CWs in Comparison to Conventional Systems and Institutions

It is essential, when comparing institutions and systems, to consider not only their practical applications but also their mental and structural characteristics. The mental infrastructure and structural characteristics play a crucial role in defining the operation of these institutions. Focusing solely on surface-level applications may not yield a comprehensive understanding of their true nature and effectiveness. By mentally and structurally comparing institutions and systems, we can acquire a deeper understanding of their underlying principles, values, and organizational frameworks. This analysis allows for a more comprehensive evaluation of their strengths, weaknesses, and societal impact as a whole. It enables us to evaluate the extent to which these institutions adhere to ethical standards, social values, and long-term sustainability. A mental and structural comparison also reveals the underlying motivations, decision-making processes, and power dynamics of these institutions. It illuminates the processes of policy formulation, resource allocation, and stakeholder engagement. Understanding the mental and structural dimensions enhances our ability to identify potential biases, systemic issues, and opportunities for development within these institutions. The broader implications and long-term effects of institutional frameworks can be evaluated with the assistance of a comprehensive analysis that incorporates both mental and structural elements. It offers a more nuanced comprehension of how institutions operate, adapt, and contribute to the evolution of society. By considering mental and structural components, we can obtain a more accurate and comprehensive understanding of institutions and systems, thereby fostering more informed decision-making and policy formulation.

The CW financial system was a precursor to the prevalent interest-based financial systems of the present day. Recognizing the responsibilities of these historical institutions can offer an alternative to conventional economic systems. To fully grasp the potential of these institutions, a comprehensive understanding of their functions, mechanisms, and historical contributions is required. By reexamining their historical significance, we can examine how these institutions can be revitalized to address the faults of the current economic system and offer a viable alternative for the future. Understanding their positions and adapting them to the current environment can pave the way for economic frameworks that are more inclusive, sustainable, and equitable.

CWs were crucial to the Ottoman Empire's ability to challenge the fundamental financial institutions of the capitalist system. Their adaptability contributed significantly to their success. CWs were not limited to funding only charitable services; their methods of generating income also facilitated financing for entrepreneurs with currency shortages. As a result, financial *waqfs* contributed to the empire's sustained industrial and commercial growth. The capacity of CWs to assist entrepreneurs and meet their financial needs was essential to economic expansion. By providing access to capital, CWs empowered small-scale enterprises and facilitated their expansion. This, in turn, stimulated economic activity and increased society's overall prosperity. In addition, the revenue generated by CWs served as a dependable source of funding, ensuring the continuation of productive endeavors, and promoting the long-term viability of businesses. By providing an alternative to conventional capitalist financial institutions, CWs facilitated economic development in accordance with the principles of Islamic finance and equitable access to resources. The success of CWs in promoting production and trade demonstrates their significance as a viable financial system that transcends philanthropic purposes. Their ability to provide a bridge between entrepreneurs and much-needed capital demonstrates their potential for constructing robust, inclusive economies. Understanding the role of CWs in challenging capitalist financial institutions illuminates the significance of alternative systems that prioritize economic justice and sustainable development.

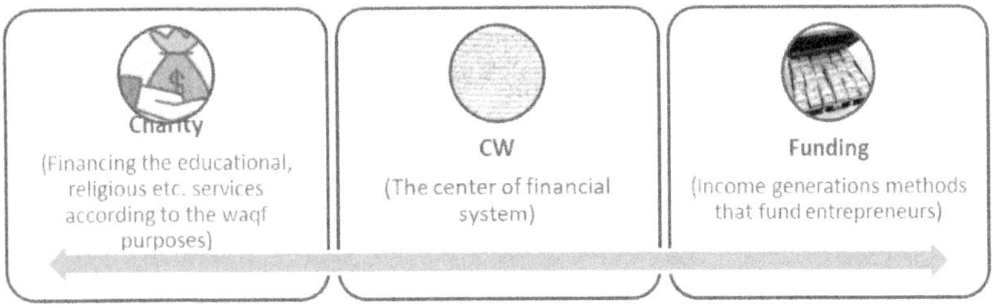

Figure 1. The Two-Way Benefits of CWs

With their dual benefits, CWs exerted a profound influence on the financial system. As microcredit institutions, CWs provided financial assistance to microbusinesses, including guild-affiliated individuals, thereby promoting regional development. In an era characterized by unequal capital accumulation in institutions such as banks, CWs served as a redistribution mechanism. By providing access to financial resources for microbusinesses, CWs significantly contribute to economic inclusion and inequality reduction (Bulut & Korkut 2019a). The assistance provided by CWs enabled individuals to establish and expand their enterprises, thereby contributing to the expansion of the local economy and the creation of jobs. Contrary to the consolidation of wealth in conventional banking systems, CWs served to more equitably distribute financial resources. Moreover, CWs represented an alternative paradigm that countered the unjust accumulation of capital associated with certain institutions.

CWs operated in accordance with the broader objectives of social and economic development by employing a system based on the principles of cooperation and communal welfare. Their function as a redistribution mechanism was consistent with the values of equity and inclusion, providing an alternative narrative to the dominant capitalist structures. Meanwhile, Islamic financial institutions that are trusted to manage CW have not been fully effective in empowering the socio-economic community (Fawwaz et al. 2020). The impact of CWs transcended individual microbusinesses and contributed to the resilience and sustainability of local economies. CWs supported the development of productive sectors and mitigated the negative effects of concentrated wealth by addressing the financing requirements of small-scale entrepreneurs. This approach fostered economic inclusivity and bridged the gap between different socioeconomic groups (Bulut & Korkut 2019b). Their presence within the financial system as a viable alternative provided a view of a more balanced and socially just economic framework (Table 2).

Feature	Benefits against conventional economic and financial system
The financial system is based on Islamic/ethical methods.	*It can re-establish the link between the real economy and the financial sector.*
Financing institutions and instruments fund microenterprises.	*Capitalism enabled a small number of firms to dominate the market. This system can change this pattern.*
The system consists of regional institutions that benefit regional development.	*Detecting regional needs will be easier.*
There are provisions for the needs of the society.	*The waste of resources is one of the problems that the economy seeks to solve. The need-focused system can solve the problem of wasting resources.*
It has a human-centered approach, not a human centrist.	*Human centrist systems raise the problem of individualization. The human-centered system solves problems socially.*
The main motivation is moral-based financing and production, not profit/money.	*Profit-oriented economic systems consider any method legitimate. In contrast, this system aims human welfare in a holistic manner.*
It is based on material and spiritual development. Quantitative growth is not required without values.	*It reveals a healthy growth path. In this way, it establishes fair income distribution.*
It is based on cooperation, not competition.	*It prevents unfair profit appetite and passion for excessive earnings.*
It appeals to all humanity.	*Many features of conventional financial system do not comply with the orders of divine religions. However, this system is concerned with all humanity.*

Table 2. The microfinance system of Ottoman CWs

Source: (Bulut & Korkut 2019a, p. 107) and adapted by the author.

The overarching framework of CWs incorporates Islamic microfinance principles and the microenterprise mechanism. These characteristics reflect the fundamental principles of Islamic economics, which emphasize cooperation over competition. This model has the potential to benefit all humanity. The primary objective of the Islamic economic worldview is to establish a balance between limited resources and limitless desires by applying moral standards to find the most suitable solutions in the financial, economic, and social spheres. Islamic finance is a significant alternative because it facilitates the establishment of this equilibrium and generates suitable solutions. In this context, the emphasis on microfinance and microenterprise support is of particular importance. These mechanisms contribute to economic inclusion and stability by addressing the requirements of individuals and small enterprises. As an alternative to the modern financial system, the Islamic economy and finance system, which is profoundly ingrained in Islamic civilization, provides a set of values and a mental infrastructure that propose solutions for the greater good of humanity. The implementation of microfinance and microenterprise mechanisms grounded in Islamic principles can facilitate the transition to this system, which prioritizes the well-being of individuals. This strategy is anticipated to promote peace and prosperity by ensuring that economic activities adhere to ethical and fair principles.

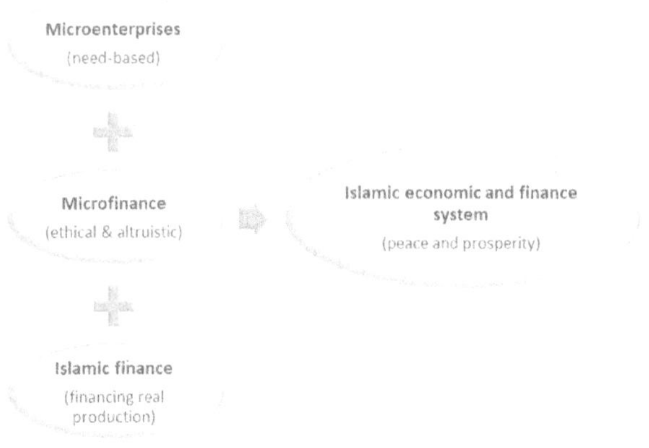

Figure 2. The Model of the Islamic Economic and Finance system

Conclusion

The conventional capitalist economic system views and characterizes humans as beings devoid of intrinsic value, driven solely by self-interest and the pursuit of personal profit. In contrast, Islam considers humanity to be the most cherished of all creations, imbuing everyone with inherent dignity and worth. The Islamic economic system mandates the administration of crucial economic mechanisms, such as distribution, solidarity, and redistribution, within the context of justice and equity. The insatiable pursuit of profit and practices aligned with capitalist ideologies have gained increasing dominance in the current global economic landscape. Markets now wield greater influence and control over the economic affairs of the world than nation-states. This shift has perpetuated a system in which profit-seeking is prioritized over human welfare and ethical responsibility. Adopting the tenets of the Islamic economic system is a viable alternative to the prevalent capitalist mentality. By placing a premium on justice, equity, and human dignity, Islamic economics seeks to establish a more morally grounded and balanced economic order. It emphasizes the significance of administering economic activities with a focus on societal well-being, equity, and the satisfaction of fundamental requirements. Adopting this perspective can foster a more humane and inclusive economic system that prioritizes human worth.

The urgent problems of consumerism, resource waste, unequal income distribution, and global inequality necessitate a new economic paradigm. The principles of the financial system advocated by Islamic economics offer comprehensive and targeted solutions to these problems. In addition to the absence of interest and Shariah-compliant financial transactions, the Islamic financial system incorporates a holistic worldview that prioritizes universal moral values pertinent to all societies, not just Muslim ones. This perspective acknowledges the inherent worth of individuals and seeks to establish social justice as a fundamental goal. Islamic economics provides a comprehensive framework that emphasizes moral behavior, responsible resource management, and an equitable distribution of wealth. It promotes sustainable consumption patterns by fostering moderation and responsible resource management. In this system, economic decision-making is guided by the principles of fairness, solidarity, and social justice, with the goal of minimizing wealth disparities and ensuring a more equitable distribution of resources. Moreover, Islamic finance principles extend beyond monetary transactions. They include ethical investment, risk-sharing, and the promotion of economically productive activities that benefit the entire society. By placing a premium on human well-being and social welfare, the Islamic financial system endeavors to resolve the underlying causes of economic imbalances and cultivate a more inclusive and equitable economic order. Adopting the Islamic perspective toward economics can pave the way for a more sustainable and equitable future. It calls for a transition to a value-driven economic system that recognizes the inherent worth of individuals, promotes responsible resource utilization, and endeavors for global social justice.

The modern financial system and capitalist mentality frequently assimilate emergent alternative currents in the world, but their intent is not to adopt a genuine alternative system. Instead, they seek alternative solutions to specific problems within the existing system that do not challenge its fundamental principles. As a result, these new systems are viewed as complementary as opposed to genuinely alternative, thereby serving to maintain the status quo. Nevertheless, Islamic economics and finance deny the label of complementarity, as they offer a holistic approach that transcends religious boundaries and seeks to achieve the broader objectives of humanity. To create a viable alternative to the current system, it is essential to reevaluate historically effective institutions and adapt them to the current context. CWs are one institution that can assist in establishing an alternative economic and social structure. By reconsidering the principles and practices of CWs, we can utilize their distinctive values and mental infrastructure to compensate for the shortcomings of the contemporary system. With their emphasis on cooperation, equitable distribution, and communal welfare, CWs offer a viable alternative to the profit-driven nature of the contemporary financial system. They provide a foundation for inclusive economic development in which resources are allocated in accordance with principles of justice and societal welfare. By incorporating the lessons learned from the historical success of financial *waqfs* into modern economic structures, we can nurture an alternative path that challenges the dominance of the contemporary system. With its distinctive values and mental infrastructure, social financial practices in history continues to be the one of the humanitarian alternatives to the contemporary system. By embracing and revitalizing the principles of moral economics, we can pave the way for a more equitable, inclusive, and morally founded economic order that transcends the limitations of the current system. By doing so, we can create a more harmonious and just world in which the well-being of humanity takes precedence over limited profit-driven motives.

References

Archival Documents

Shar'iyyah (Court) Records of Edirne: 4646, Page: 7

Shar'iyyah (Court) Records of Edirne, Register: 4675 Page: 21-22

VGMA, Register: 737, Page: 155-164, Serial: 61

Books and Articles

Asutay, M. (2012). Conceptualizing and locating the social failure of Islamic finance: Aspirations of Islamic moral economy vs the realities of Islamic finance. *Asian and African area studies, 11*(2), 93-113.

Bulut, M., Akkemik, K. A., & Göksal, K. (2016). The relation between worldviews and intergenerational altruism in Turkey: An empirical approach. *Journal for the Study of Religions and Ideologies, 15*(45), 234-256.

Bulut, M., et al. (2019). *Osmanlı Dönemi Rumeli Para Vakıfları (Cash Waqfs in Ottoman Europe)* (14 Vols). İstanbul Sabahattin Zaim University Pub., Istanbul.

Bulut, M., & Korkut, C. (2016a). A comparison between Ottoman CWs (CWs) and modern interest-free financial institutions. *Vakıflar Dergisi*, 46, 23-45.

Bulut, M., & Korkut, C. (2016b). Finansal İstikrar ve Para Vakıfları Etkisi: Rumeli Para Vakıfları Örneği. *İslam Ekonomisi ve Finansı Dergisi*, *2*(1), 55-76.

Bulut, M., & Korkut, C. (2019a). Ottoman CWs: An Alternative Financial System. *Insight Turkey, 21*(3), 91-112.

Bulut, M., & Korkut, C. (2019b). A Look at the CWs as an Indicator of Ottoman Financial Mentality. *Vakıflar Dergisi*, Special Issue, 115-132.

Bulut, M., & Korkut, C. (2022). The Impact of the Elite (Ulema) Class on the Ottoman Economy: The Case Study of the CWs. *International Journal of Economics, Management and Accounting, 30*(1), 27-54.

Çizakça, M. (1998). Awqaf in history and its implications for modern Islamic economies. *Islamic Economic Studies, 6*(1), 43-70.

Çizakça, M. (2000). A History of Philanthropic Foundations: The Islamic World from the Seventh Century to the Present. İstanbul. Boğaziçi University Press.

Faroqhi, S. (2004). Bosnian Merchants in the Adriyatic. *International Journal of Turkish Studies, 10*(1-2). 225-239.

Fawwaz, M. F. A., Juliana, J., Cakhyaneu, A., Muhammad, M., & Marlina, R. (2020). *Waqf* as Alternative Financing Resource for Infrastructure Development in Indonesia: Analytical Hierarchy Process Approach. *Islamic Research, 3*(2), 50-58.

Greif, A. (1994). Cultural beliefs and the organization of society: A historical and theoretical reflection on collectivist and individualist societies. *Journal of political economy, 102*(5), 912-950.

Günay, H. M. (2012). Vakıf. *TDV İslâm Ansiklopedisi, 42*, 475-479.

Korkut, C., & Kar, M. (2018). İnsani Finans ve Değerler. *Kurumlarda Değerler* (pp. 179-197), Konya: Necmettin Erbakan Üniversitesi Yayınları.

Kudat, A. (2015). Bir Finans Enstrümanı Olarak Nukûd Vakfı ve In'Ikâd Formülasyonu. *İslam Ekonomisi ve Finansı Dergisi 1*(2). 1-22.

Kuran, T. (1997). Islam and underdevelopment: an old puzzle revisited. *Journal of Institutional and Theoretical Economics, 153*(1), 41-71.

Kuran, T. (2003). The Islamic commercial crisis: institutional roots of economic underdevelopment in the Middle East. *The Journal of Economic History, 63*(2), 414-446.

Özcan, T. (1999). Sofyalı Bâlî Efendi'nin Para Vakıflarıyla İlgili Mektupları. *İslâm Araştırmaları Dergisi*, 3, 125-155

Özcan, T. (2000). İbn Kemal'in Para Vakıflarına Dair Risâlesi. *İslâm Araştırmaları Dergisi*, 4, 31-41.

Suryanto, A., Rahmat, B. K., & Marlina, L. (2020). Islamic Philanthropy *Waqf* Empowerment of Madina Minimarket In Tasikmalaya—Indonesia. *IKONOMIKA: Jurnal Ekonomi dan Bisnis Islam, 5*(1), 1-16.

Şimşek, M. (1985). Osmanlı cemiyetinde para vakıfları üzerinde münakaşalar. *Ankara Üniversitesi İlahiyat Fakültesi Dergisi, 27*(1), 207-220

Tabakoğlu, A. (2012). *Türkiye İktisat Tarihi*. İstanbul: Dergâh Publications.

Tekdoğan, Ö. F. (2020). The Introduction of *Waqf* into Fractional and Full Reserve Banking Systems to Achieve Economic Stability. *Journal of Islamic Monetary Economics and Finance, 6*(3), 531-554. DOI: 10.21098/jimf.v6i3.1132

Tuğrul, M., & Bulut, M. (2017). Bir Mikrofinans Modeli Olarak Osmanlı Para Vakıflarının Karşılaştırılmalı Analizi: Edirne, Filibe, Selanik, Tekirdağ ve Üsküp Para Vakıfları. *ADAM AKADEMİ Sosyal Bilimler Dergisi, 7*(2), 289-302. DOI: 10.31679/adamakademi.356595

Walaa, J. A. (2021). Using Blockchain in WAQF, Wills and Inheritance Solutions in the Islamic System. *International Journal of Economics and Business Administration, 9*(2), 101-

116. DOI: 10.35808/ijeba/691

Yediyıldız, B. (2012). Vakıf. TDV *İslâm Ansiklopedisi, 42,* 479-486.

Appendix

The *waqfiya* of Ibrahim b. Hadji Bali *Waqf,*
Shar'iyyah (Court) Records of Edirne: 4646, Page: 7

FOURTEEN

An Unfinished Agenda? Islamic Economics and the Alleviation of Poverty: Challenges and Proposals for Resolution

Khurram Shahzad

Introduction

Poverty remains a critical issue in developing nations, with forty percent of the world's population living on less than $2 per day (Raimi, Patel, and Adelopo 2014). Nearly a billion people lack access to clean water, and millions of children are deprived of education and die from preventable illnesses (World Bank 2010). Within Muslim-majority countries, 44% of the 1.7 billion population lives below the poverty line despite these nations holding 70% of the world's natural resources (S. Hassan and Yılmaz 2019; The Nation 2013). Poverty's impact is extensive, affecting education, social cohesion, mental health, and national economic stability (Duncan, Magnuson, and Votruba-Drzal 2017; Mood and Jonsson 2016). Two main policy strategies are implemented to combat poverty: indirect strategies promoting sustainable macroeconomic growth, and direct strategies focusing on credit access, health, and literacy (M. K. Hassan 2006). Examples of successful indirect approaches include stable macroeconomic policies in Indonesia, Malaysia, and Thailand. In contrast, Bangladesh's direct approach exemplifies effective partnerships between governmental and non-governmental organizations to aid the underprivileged (CPD 1996).

Poverty alleviation is rooted in Islam on ethical and social justice principles. Islamic economics tends to provide a framework around individual needs and societal welfare (Obaidullah and Khan 2008). It differs from conventional economics by putting an emphasis on the equal distribution of resources and social welfare, not profit maximization. It defines poverty as the inability to meet five essential human needs: health, religion, knowledge, offspring and wealth (M. K. Hassan and Ashraf 2010) In Islamic economics, poverty alleviation includes a program to increase incomes, to achieve income distribution fairness and equality of opportunity (M. K. Hassan 2006). Despite that, many Muslim countries have used *Zakat*, *Waqf* and Islamic social finance tools to reduce poverty. Although these frameworks have been tried, challenges remain in how to execute them.

This study is organized into five sections. The introduction provides a general overview of poverty and Islamic approaches to alleviating it. The second section explores the roles of *Zakat*, *Waqf*, Islamic microfinance, and integrated Islamic financial models in poverty reduction. The third section analyzes *Zakat* and *Waqf* systems in various Islamic countries, while the fourth section addresses challenges in utilizing Islamic social finance tools. Finally, the last section offers insights from recent models addressing these challenges and provides recommendations for advancing poverty alleviation through Islamic finance.

1. Poverty Alleviation and Tools of Islamic Social Finance

Using the principles of Islamic economics as its basis, Islamic Social Finance (IsSF) attempts to create social justice and sustainable development between public and private sectors (Gündoğdu 2019). Charity based instruments such as *Zakat*, *Waqf*, donations, alongside commercial mechanisms such as *Qard al-Hasan*; and Islamic microfinance using profit sharing modes such as Musharakah and Mudarabah are all part of IsSF. In terms of ethical practice and economic activity, these instruments make Islamic finance a powerful instrument for poverty reduction and economic equity (Hasibuan 2010). Islamic social finance plays a crucial role in promoting financial inclusion, ethical investments, and equitable wealth distribution. *Zakat* and *Qard al-Hasan* serve as direct assistance mechanisms, providing swift aid to the poor (Mohseni-Cheraghlou 2017). Additionally, profit-sharing models like Mudarabah and Musharakah encourage entrepreneurship without burdening the disadvantaged with debt, fostering individual empowerment and driving economic growth (M. M. Rahman 2020). This following section reviews studies and models related to *Zakat*, *Waqaf*, Islamic microfinance, as well as some integrated models that address poverty.

2. *Zakat*

Zakat is a vital financial tool for promoting socioeconomic development in Islamic countries, enhancing short-term well-being, and reducing poverty (Ahmad 2019). Historically, effective *Zakat* administration under leaders like Hazrat Umar bin Khattab (R.A) and Umer bin Abdul Aziz resulted in such prosperity that eligible recipients became scarce, demonstrating its impact on poverty alleviation (Arif 2017). Studies by Akram and Afzal (2015) reveal that *Zakat* significantly reduces poverty by supporting the poor, orphans, and widows, showing an inverse relationship between poverty levels and *Zakat* distribution in both short- and long-term contexts. This relationship highlights *Zakat*'s role in stimulating economic activity, lowering unemployment, and improving living standards.

Empirical research by Azam, Iqbal, and Tayyab (2014) in Pakistan highlights *Zakat*'s significant potential to improve household welfare. However, Akram and Afzal (2015) argue that many Islamic countries need to enhance their *Zakat* collection and disbursement systems to maximize its impact, as current collections fall short of potential contributions. Siddiqui (2009) underscores *Zakat*'s role as a social security mechanism in Islam, emphasizing its ability to reduce poverty through direct wealth transfers from the rich to the poor. Several Islamic countries, such as Saudi Arabia, Pakistan, Jordan, and Malaysia, have established state-level *Zakat* systems that support millions of vulnerable individuals, showcasing *Zakat*'s vital role in social support networks across Islamic societies.

2.2 Waqf

Waqf, a form of Islamic social finance, is a perpetual charitable endowment where assets such as land, buildings, cash, books, and shares are dedicated for philanthropic purposes. Embraced by both Muslim and non-Muslim communities, Awqaf institutions today serve a variety of roles, from providing religious education to supporting community services and maintaining mosques, as observed in North America (Kahf 1992). Modern approaches to *Waqf* aim to enhance its poverty-alleviating potential while adhering to Islamic principles. El-Gari (2004) proposed integrating *Qard al-Hasan* (interest-free loans) with *Waqf*, allowing banks to fund poverty-alleviation efforts with capital derived from *Waqf* donations. Mohd Thas Thaker (2018) recommends that micro enterprise development be funded with integrated cash *Waqf* models.

Cash *Waqf* has been effectively utilized in Muslim countries to address liquidity challenges by generating income for microfinance and Takaful initiatives that directly contribute to poverty reduction (Mohsin 2013). The "Integrated *Waqf*-based Islamic Microfinance Model" (IWIMM), developed by Haneef et al. (2014), aims to combat poverty in OIC member countries by offering Shariah-compliant microfinance within the framework of poverty alleviation and empowerment. IWIMM leverages *Waqf* funds to lower capital costs, making financial services such as microenterprise training, Takaful, and project financing more affordable. In subsequent research, M.A. Haneef et al. (2015) tested the IWIMM model, incorporating six elements: Islamic Microfinance Project Financing (PF), Human Resource Development (HRD), Poverty Alleviation (PA), Islamic Micro Finance (IsMF), Takaful Financing (TF), and *Waqf* Resources (WR). The findings suggest that the integrated model is efficacious and have implications regarding borrower education, size of loans, social networks awareness, and channeling *Waqf* funds to Islamic microfinance institutions consistent with Mudarabah principles. This comprehensive approach suggests that *Waqf* could play a role in the sustainable positive poverty alleviation.

2.3 Islamic Microfinance

Based on the concepts of micro finance and Islamic banking, Islamic microfinance helps to achieve their common objectives including social development, motivation of target clients, risk bearing and integration of excluded people in the development process (Abbas and Shirazi 2015). This approach offers an exceptional way to achieve micro-financial and financial intermediation as well as poverty reduction in line with Islamic culture and tradition (Ashraf, Hassan, and Hunt-Ahmed 2013). Shariah-compliant microfinance programs offer a very viable form of poverty eradication since ethical finance complements poverty eradication approaches which recognize the need to create sustainable income generating streams for the excluded sectors of society.

Islamic Microfinance Institutions (IMFIs) utilize diverse funding sources such as *Waqf* and *Zakat*, distinguishing them from conventional funds (Wilson 2013). The *Wakala* model facilitates the efficient administration and disbursement of donor funds alongside other sources like *Zakat*, Sadaqah, and Awqaf (Obaidullah 2008). These funds can be mobilized through deposit-based systems, including *Wadiah, Qard al-Hasan, and Mudarabah,* or through equity-based *Musharakah*, offering multiple avenues for sustainable financing. However, challenges arise in their implementation, such as borrowers receiving insufficient funds for income-generating activities (Rehman & Rahim 2023).

The Mudarabah financing model used in IMFIs allows for profit-sharing between the institution and the entrepreneur, typically for a fixed period, after which the shares can be resold to the entrepreneur or a third party. The funds are then directed toward microfinance activities, significantly impacting poverty reduction and reducing government welfare expenses, thereby fostering independence for low-income groups (Kakembo & Ahmad 2023). However, the model's effectiveness depends on strong fund management, effective supervision, and well-trained staff. Without these, issues such as poor management, lack of oversight, and inadequate training can lead to high default rates and a decline in the model's ability to improve welfare. To address these limitations, Butt (2017) proposes combining Islamic charity with Corporate Social Responsibility (CSR) funds, creating a dual-source funding model that draws from both individuals and companies. This approach aligns with the principles of the Qur'an and Sunnah, aiming to eradicate poverty and enhance the profitability of microfinance. Through this model, economically disadvantaged individuals receive vocational training and funding for microenterprise development, contributing to community improvement while ensuring compliance with the standards of Muslim countries.

The study by Naveed Aslam (2014) examined the impact of Islamic microfinance on poverty and concluded that it improves living standards and per capita income, thereby contributing to poverty reduction. However, the study highlights the need for a strong regulatory framework to ensure the effective implementation of Islamic microfinance. Aslam suggests that combining Islamic microfinance with traditional poverty alleviation methods, such as *Zakat* and Awqaf, could amplify its impact. Despite its potential, Islamic microfinance faces challenges, including limited outreach, high operational costs, insufficient funds, and a lack of skilled personnel, which hinder its scalability and sustainability. In Bangladesh, Mizanur (2011) conducted an empirical study involving 1,020 clients and 34 managers from Islamic Bank Bangladesh Limited (IBBL), demonstrating that Islamic microfinance programs positively impact clients' income, expenditure, productivity, and ethics. The Rural Development Scheme (RDS) of IBBL serves as a key example of enhancing economic activities among disadvantaged rural communities. Despite these successes, IMFIs face challenges related to regulatory clarity, capacity building, and scalability. Obaidullah (2008) identifies three main challenges: product diversification at the micro-level, improved coordination with rating agencies at the meso-level, and a unified regulatory environment at the macro-level. Hailey (2009) further highlights issues such as financial literacy, funding sources, legal frameworks, product standardization, and Shariah-compliant audit procedures. While these challenges persist, Islamic microfinance has significant potential to sustainably improve income generation and reduce poverty.

2.4 Integrated Models of Islamic Finance

Islamic Social Finance (IsSF) encompasses both charity-based tools, such as Zakah, *Waqf*, and other donations, as well as commercial-based tools like *Qard al-Hasan* and Islamic microfinance models, including Musharakah and Mudarabah (Gündoğdu 2019). These IsSF instruments are powerful tools for addressing major challenges such as poverty, unemployment, and limited access to business financing. In Indonesia, the Baitul Maal at Tamwil (BMT) cooperative model integrates Islamic social finance with commercial finance to support underserved micro and small businesses. BMTs combine charitable funds through Baitul Maal with non-commercial financing solutions via Baitul Tamwil. They also utilize cash *Waqf* to fund social programs, promote financial inclusion through micro-Takaful, and provide income protection for borrowers. A study by Adnan and Ajija (2015) confirms that BMT financing reduces poverty, with beneficiaries experiencing income growth post-financing. BMTs provide capital, infrastructure, and training to economically disadvantaged individuals, often using collateral or joint liability, with charitable endowments covering defaults when necessary (Wulandari et al. 2016). However, challenges such as limited capital, low public engagement, and regulatory barriers persist. These issues, along with underdeveloped entrepreneurial skills and lack of ownership, hinder the effectiveness of BMTs (Razak & Dawami 2019).

Diniyya (2019) examines models like the IWIMM framework for sustainable Islamic microfinance, which integrates *Waqf*-based finance with microfinance initiatives to improve access to education, healthcare, and human resources. Sadeq (2002) proposes structured *Waqf* projects comprising primary and secondary initiatives funded by *Waqf* certificates, aimed at sustainable poverty alleviation through organized voluntary efforts. M.A. Haneef (2014) highlights the IWIMM model's four components: *Waqf*, microfinance, human resources, and Takaful as essential for poverty reduction. These elements strengthen microfinance institutions (MFIs) by enabling affordable financing and income security for low-income populations. M.A. Haneef et al. (2015) argue that integrating Takaful and *Waqf* within MFIs could further alleviate poverty. However, challenges such as credit risk, moral hazard, and funding shortages necessitate coordinated efforts from national and international bodies.

Pakistan's primary Islamic redistribution tools are *Zakat* and interest-free loans, though *Waqf* lacks significant private-sector involvement (Munir, Sapar, and Majeed 2023). Integrating Islamic social finance with government support could mobilize private-sector resources for sustainable development in Muslim-majority countries. M.K. Hassan and Ashraf (2010) suggest combining *Zakat*, Awqaf, and microfinance to address both immediate poverty relief and long-term economic empowerment. This model provides immediate support through *Zakat*, community infrastructure through Awqaf, and economic stimulation through microfinance. However, its success depends on sound governance and management to ensure state funds reach the intended beneficiaries with minimal costs to the poor. Challenges include bureaucratic inefficiencies, reliance on voluntary contributions, and the need for culturally tailored solutions. While these Islamic microfinance models focus on poverty reduction, they face limitations such as joint liability lending pressures, scaling issues, profit-sharing complexities, and rigid repayment patterns. These constraints may limit flexibility and the ability to maximize impact on borrowers. Additionally, the models often overlook broader necessities like wage increases or alternative income sources for part-time employees. Addressing these limitations through appropriate scaling, effective monitoring, and meaningful beneficiary engagement is crucial for ensuring the long-term effectiveness and sustainability of Islamic microfinance.

3. Evaluation of *Zakat* and *Waqf* Systems in Different Countries

This section examines how the systems of *Zakat* and Awqaf have been implemented in various Muslim countries to alleviate poverty and strengthen the Islamic social fabric.

3.1 Saudi Arabia

These social institutions play a crucial role in the social and economic development of communities in Saudi Arabia. *Zakat* is managed and coordinated by the Department of *Zakat* and Income Tax (DZIT), which allocates funds for social welfare, poverty alleviation, education, and healthcare (Al-Filali and Gallarotti 2012). The Saudi government leverages advanced technology to streamline the collection and distribution of *Zakat*, enhancing the system's efficiency. The Ministry of Islamic Affairs, Dawah, and Guidance oversees the *Waqf* system in the kingdom. Recently, the government has modernized the traditional *Waqf* system by enacting new laws and establishing the General Authority of Awqaf to manage and develop *Waqf* assets effectively (Çizakça 2011). These initiatives have strengthened the roles of *Zakat* and *Waqf* in driving socioeconomic development and supporting the needy and less fortunate.

3.2 Malaysia

Zakat and *Waqf* systems are well-organized in Malaysia and integrated into the country's social and economic framework. State Islamic religious councils employ modern management practices and technology to efficiently collect and transparently distribute *Zakat* to eligible beneficiaries, including the poor and needy (Saad and Abdullah 2014). Similarly, Malaysia's *Waqf* system, managed by state religious authorities, has been modernized through government initiatives, such as the establishment of the *Waqf*, *Zakat*, and Hajj Department under the Prime Minister's Office. This department strengthens *Waqf* governance and optimizes asset utilization for public welfare and development projects, introducing innovative financial instruments like cash *Waqf* to encourage public participation (Shatzmiller 1993). Four Malaysian universities have successfully established *Waqf* endowments, with one example being the construction of rentable buildings to generate *Waqf* income. For instance, the International Islamic University Malaysia supports 4,000 students annually with scholarships funded by *Waqf* resources. This highlights Malaysia's leadership in effective Islamic social finance management (Aziz, Johari, and Yusof 2013).

3.3 Turkey

Rakhmat and Beik (2022) compared *Zakat* and *Waqf* management in Malaysia and Turkey using a qualitative descriptive method with secondary data. *Zakat* is mandatory in Malaysia but voluntary in Turkey, though both countries allow tax deductions for *Zakat* contributions. In Malaysia, the government oversees *Zakat* management, whereas the Turkish government does not. However, both governments manage *Waqf*, with Malaysia's *Waqf* overseen by the Ministry of Religion and Turkey's by the Ministry of Culture and Tourism. Secularism has influenced *Waqf* practices in both countries, with *Waqf* issues handled by civil courts instead of Shariah courts. Additionally, Turkey's shift in terminology from "*Waqf*" to "ta'sis" has led to a decline in *Waqf* collections.

3.4 Pakistan

Pakistan's *Zakat* and Awqaf systems face several challenges that hinder their effectiveness and potential as tools for social welfare and poverty alleviation. A major issue is the lack of a consistent regulatory framework and oversight mechanisms, which erodes public confidence and often leads to mismanagement and corruption (Aman and Ullah 2016). Additionally, the absence of a centralized database for tracking *Zakat* and Awqaf assets results in inefficiencies and increases the risk of fund misuse (Rahman and Dean 2013). Public awareness about the importance and proper channels for *Zakat* and Awqaf contributions remains low, limiting their utilization for socioeconomic development (Miah 2019). Political interference and the lack of professional training for those managing these institutions further exacerbate the system's problems (Adnan and Ajija 2015). Weak legal frameworks, poor resource management, inadequate governance, and disregard for Shariah principles in *Waqf* development also constrain the potential of these institutions (Rehman and Rahim 2023). Addressing these challenges requires a comprehensive understanding and adherence to *Waqf* principles within the framework of Shariah. Strengthening legal frameworks, improving governance, and fostering public awareness are essential steps to unlock the full potential of *Zakat* and Awqaf as instruments of social welfare in Pakistan.

3.5 Indonesia

In Indonesia, *Zakat* and Awqaf play vital roles in the social welfare system, involving collaboration between the government and the community. *Zakat* is managed, collected, and distributed by the National *Zakat* Board (BAZNAS) and the National Amil *Zakat* Agency (LAZNAS) to alleviate poverty and promote social development (Firdaus et al. 2012). Legal frameworks have formalized and standardized *Zakat* management to enhance transparency and accountability. Similarly, the Indonesian *Waqf* Board (BWI) oversees *Waqf*, with cash *Waqf* mechanisms attracting financial resources for socioeconomic projects through public participation (Çizakça 2011). Indonesia's collaboration between the government, religious institutions, and the community has established the country as a pioneer in Islamic social finance. An innovative example is the Baitul Maal at Tamwil (BMT), an Islamic cooperative that integrates social and commercial finance. Baitul Maal handles charitable funds, while Baitul Tamwil provides financing solutions, supported by cash *Waqf* from Baitul Maal. This structure enables the implementation of both nonprofit and profit-oriented initiatives, protected by micro-Takaful. Profits from cash *Waqf* are reinvested in social programs to promote financial inclusion for micro and small businesses (Adnan and Ajija 2015). For instance, BMT MMU Sidogiri, in collaboration with institutions in East Java, has improved recipient incomes by providing capital, infrastructure, and training to economically disadvantaged individuals. Financing defaults are mitigated through collateral, joint liability options, and charitable endowments. Wulandari et al. (2016) highlight that integrating BMTs into religious capacity-building efforts strengthens their positive impact on community development.

3.6 Bangladesh

In Bangladesh, the government-administered *Zakat* Board oversees the collection and distribution of *Zakat* to support poverty alleviation, education, healthcare, and other social welfare initiatives (M.K. Hassan and Khan 2007). Despite its contributions, the system faces challenges such as low public awareness, inefficient collection, and administrative barriers. There are calls for greater transparency, improved management, and increased public engagement to enhance its impact (Ahmed 2004). The Awqaf system, managed by the *Waqf* Administration under the Ministry of Religious Affairs, includes initiatives like Cash *Waqf* Certificates (CWC) introduced by Social Investment Bank Limited (SIBL) in 1995. These certificates enable public contributions to socioeconomic projects, mobilizing resources for development. However, the Awqaf system struggles with inadequate legal frameworks, poor management, and corruption, highlighting the need for comprehensive reforms (Mannan 2005). Bangladesh is also recognized for pioneering microfinance through the Grameen Bank, a globally adopted model for poverty alleviation. A Shariah-compliant variant has emerged, integrating Islamic social finance tools. Islamic Bank Bangladesh Limited (IBBL) introduced Islamic banking and microfinance through the Rural Development Sangstha (RDS) program, which provides goods and assets via Mudarabah profit-sharing arrangements, ensuring funds are directed toward income-generating activities. RDS members participate in training, maintain Mudarabah savings accounts, and contribute to the *Qard al-Hasan* fund for the extremely poor. A 12.5% profit-sharing return applies, with a 2.5% rebate for timely repayments, reducing the effective rate to 10%. The RDS program, through initiatives like the Micro Enterprise Investment Scheme, has raised funding caps from 50,000 to 300,000 taka, supporting small entrepreneurs, particularly women, in expanding their SMEs (UNDP 2017). Targeting unemployed women and youth within 10 km of branches, the RDS program fosters poverty reduction, women's empowerment, and financial inclusion, demonstrating the potential of Islamic microfinance in advancing socioeconomic development.

3.7 Brunei Darussalam

Kakembo and Ahmad (2023) examined the potential of Islamic microfinance to reduce poverty in Brunei Darussalam through a proposed Mudarabah financing model. This model leverages funds from Zakah, Sadaqah, and *Waqf*, contributed by the government and relevant individuals or organizations, to support three key poverty alleviation institutions: Jabatan Pembangunan

Masyarakat (JAPEM), Majlis Ugama Islam Brunei (MUIB), and Yayasan Sultan Haji Hassanal Bolkiah (YAYASAN).[1] The model emphasizes utilizing *Waqf* assets, including land and monetary contributions, to support development initiatives and establish training centers for capacity building and skills development. These centers would collaborate with academic and professional institutions to provide entrepreneurship and financial management training to micro-entrepreneurs from disadvantaged backgrounds. This training helps them develop viable business proposals, which are then evaluated by Islamic Microfinance Institutions (IMFIs). Successful entrepreneurs demonstrating sufficient expertise can enter Mudarabah contracts with IMFIs, promoting job creation and reducing unemployment. Profits from the Mudarabah contracts, along with other charitable community contributions, are reinvested in society. Specifically, funds are allocated to MUIB, JAPEM, and YAYASAN to assist the most vulnerable groups, such as the disabled, elderly, sick, and children, who are unable to engage in business activities. This model aspires to become a sustainable approach to poverty alleviation while advocating for social support for the neediest segments of society.

3.8 Comparisons Between Key Countries:

Islamic social finance (ISF) instruments such as *Zakat*, *Waqf*, and Sadaqah play a crucial role in addressing social issues like poverty, education, and health. However, effective management of these funds requires robust institutional frameworks (Razak and Dawami 2019). Razak and Dawami (2019) examine how these ISF

---

[1] *The Yayasan Sultan Haji Hassanal Bolkiah*, also known as the Yayasan Foundation Brunei Darussalam, is a charitable organization in Brunei. Established by Sultan Haji Hassanal Bolkiah, the foundation supports charitable and social activities within the country. It has played a significant role in assisting communities affected by disasters such as floods, landslides, and fires, providing essential services to those living in poverty.

tools are mobilized and utilized across Malaysia, Indonesia, and Pakistan, highlighting differences in implementation but emphasizing their shared reinforcement of ISF objectives. In Malaysia, the amount collected through *Zakat* and disbursed by state-level SIRC institutions is the highest. In contrast, in Indonesia and Pakistan, *Zakat* and Sadaqah are distributed by governmental committees or voluntary organizations. Funding consistency varies across countries and depends on the differing structures of Islamic microfinance institutions. For example, Baitul Maal wat Tamwil (BMT) in Indonesia and Akhuwat in Pakistan rely heavily on fluctuating sources such as member deposits and Islamic charities. In Malaysia, funding structure issues are mitigated by government subsidies provided to institutions like AIM (Razak and Dawami 2019). The implementation of ISF also poses challenges to governance standards, human resource quality, transparency, and funding structures. Marenza (2024) adds a comparative perspective, noting significant differences between Indonesia and Pakistan in managing *Zakat* and *Waqf*. While Indonesia leads in institutional frameworks and regulations, Pakistan faces challenges related to transparency and effectiveness. This comparison highlights the evolution of ISF and the lessons learned, emphasizing the need for robust governance and funding structures to maximize ISF's impact across diverse contexts.

4. The Challenges Faced by Different Islamic Finance Models

The *Zakat* and Awqaf systems in various countries face challenges that undermine their effectiveness in poverty alleviation. Early Islamic states managed *Zakat* collection and distribution, but post-colonial governments in countries like Yemen, Saudi Arabia, Pakistan, and Malaysia introduced state-led *Zakat* systems with mandatory participation. Conversely, countries such as Egypt, Jordan, and Bangladesh employ voluntary, state-administered systems, though public engagement remains limited due to low donor trust and confidence in government. Additionally, National *Zakat* Funds often lack the capacity to accurately assess recipient eligibility (Ashraf, Hassan, and Hunt-Ahmed 2013). In Bangladesh, the voluntary nature of *Zakat*, combined with weak integration into poverty programs and reliance on foreign aid, coexists with low public awareness (Mohsin et al. 2016). Pakistan's *Zakat* system is prone to premature deductions from bank accounts and exemptions for key economic sectors. Malaysia, however, offers voluntary contributions with tax incentives, leading to annual growth in *Zakat* collections (Iqbal and Nor, 2024). Pakistan's Awqaf system faces similar challenges, including weak legal frameworks, governance issues, and non-compliance with Shariah (Rehman and Rahim 2023). Islamic microfinance also struggles with significant challenges. For instance, the Mudarabah financing model suffers from high default rates and limited impact due to insufficient supervision and high operational costs (Kakembo and Ahmad 2023). Limited staff expertise and underdeveloped regulatory frameworks hinder scalability and sustainability (Naveed Aslam 2014). Solutions such as product diversification, regulatory coordination, and a unified policy framework are needed across micro, meso, and macro levels (Obaidullah and Khan 2008).

In Indonesia, BMTs face capital constraints and management issues, further compounded by regulatory limitations (Adnan and Ajija 2015). Colonial legacies and nationalization have historically weakened Awqaf institutions, while modern Awqaf efforts are impeded by limited government credibility, insufficient research on modernization, and conflicting interpretations of Awqaf laws (M.K. Hassan and Ashraf 2010). Islamic microfinance faces funding and knowledge gaps, with Murabahah and Ijarah contracts being the most commonly used to support micro-entrepreneurs (Abbas and Shirazi 2015). While there is potential for growth, integrating *Zakat*, Awqaf, and Islamic microfinance requires addressing governance, regulatory, and empowerment challenges to ensure sustainable impact (Miah 2019). Shabbir et al. (2018) critique integrated models, arguing that reliance on *Zakat* and Awqaf alone may limit their reach and effectiveness due to inconsistent funding. Tackling the systemic causes of poverty—such as resource access, education, and policy reform—may require a holistic approach that combines Islamic microfinance with broader poverty reduction strategies, fostering sustainable poverty eradication through balanced social support and skills development.

5. Ways Forward

Various solutions exist to address the challenges of Islamic finance models while reducing poverty. However, the primary objective is to promote the socioeconomic development of impoverished communities and ensure the long-term sustainability of the organizations involved, enabling them to continue delivering their services effectively (Miah 2019). The success of an Islamic finance model in alleviating poverty depends on several factors, including socioeconomic conditions, the needs of the target population, and the capabilities of the implementing organizations. Despite these variables, *Zakat* is widely recognized as the most impactful approach due to its direct and immediate benefits for the underprivileged (Widyatama, Baso, and Haq 2020).

An integrated approach to Islamic microfinance can more effectively address poverty alleviation by incorporating Shariah-compliant funding sources such as *Zakat*, *Sadaqah*, *Waqf*, *Mudarabah*, *Musharakah*, *Bai-Muajjal*, and *Qard al-Hasan*. Countries can draw valuable lessons and insights from the successful implementation of Shariah-compliant products in Malaysia, Indonesia, Bangladesh, and Sudan to better serve underprivileged populations. For instance, Islamic Bank Bangladesh Limited (IBBL) has launched the Rural Development Scheme (RDS) to support rural clients. Amanah Ikhtiar Malaysia (AIM) has achieved significant success in reaching the most impoverished communities. Indonesia has established an extensive network of Islamic microfinance institutions, including microfinance divisions of Islamic banks, Islamic rural banks, and Islamic financial cooperatives. Similarly, Islamic banks in Sudan play a prominent role in microlending. The Sudanese Islamic Bank (SIB) has applied *Musharakah* and Mudarabah financing models to assist impoverished families in improving their living standards.

A recent model based on *Zakat*, proposed by Salim et al. (2024), addresses urban poverty through a *Zakat*-Based Urban Farming Logic Model. This approach utilizes *Zakat* and CSR funds from Islamic financial institutions to enhance economic sustainability, improve quality of life, and alleviate poverty. The model focuses on empowering poor urban communities through urban farming, combining Islamic social finance with urban agriculture. It offers a promising solution for Malaysia's urban landscape and has the potential for global replication. By providing financial relief and equipping participants with sustainable skills and income sources, the model plays a significant role in poverty alleviation. It improves food security by increasing access to food and reducing food prices, as participants can grow their own produce. Additionally, the model transforms urban spaces both environmentally and aesthetically by introducing green spaces, enhancing urban sustainability, and contributing to environmental health. This scalable and replicable model has already shown success in Malaysian communities and holds potential for addressing global urban poverty and food security challenges.

Collaboration with Islamic financial institutions is crucial for channeling *Zakat* and CSR funds, as they play a significant role in community welfare and socioeconomic development. The success of the model relies on the willingness of fund providers, participant motivation, adaptability to local conditions, and the capacity of market demand for produce. Positive outcomes from the pilot study suggest that this approach can empower urban poor communities and promote sustainable development. However, the model faces challenges, including participants' limited knowledge of farming and marketing. Its collaborative nature, involving multiple stakeholders, presents coordination difficulties and underscores the need for clear communication and aligned objectives. Environmental factors, such as heavy rainfall and storms, can cause minor damage to greenhouse structures, creating logistical issues. Additionally, Islamic social finance encounters challenges such as lack of transparency, trust, informal fund collection and disbursement, and inadequate management practices.

The model proposed by Mohi-ud-Din Qadri (2022) emphasizes four key elements for revitalizing Islamic Social Finance (ISF): Shariah, technology, social impact, and finance. These elements, often missing in current Islamic Social Finance models, are integrated into Qadri's blended approach, which combines *Zakat* and Islamic microfinance to address poverty and create employment innovatively. While earlier models sometimes overlooked social welfare and technology, Qadri's model uniquely incorporates these aspects to achieve greater impact. The proposed model suggests using *Zakat* funds as capital for Islamic microfinancing, with *Qard al-Hasan* or similar financing modes serving as its foundation. A key objective is to reduce the number of *Zakat* recipients over time, transforming them from recipients into *Zakat* payers. The model comprises several components: the *Zakat* Agency, *Zakat* Funds, *Zakat* Managers, Funds Disbursement, and the adoption of technology for *Zakat* collection and disbursement. In this framework, *Zakat* payers deposit their contributions into the *Zakat* Agency, which could be a government body such as the Ministry of Religious Affairs or the *Zakat* and Usher Department. *Zakat* Managers within the agency register and scrutinize beneficiaries, providing training to develop skills for self-reliance, such as enabling unemployed individuals to earn livelihoods. Funds are then disbursed after thorough scrutiny and skill development. These funds are categorized into refundable and nonrefundable types. Nonrefundable funds serve as seed money, while refundable funds are reinvested into microfinancing for business operations. Continuous monitoring and assessment ensure the repayment of funds in installments, supporting sustainable business growth and long-term impact.

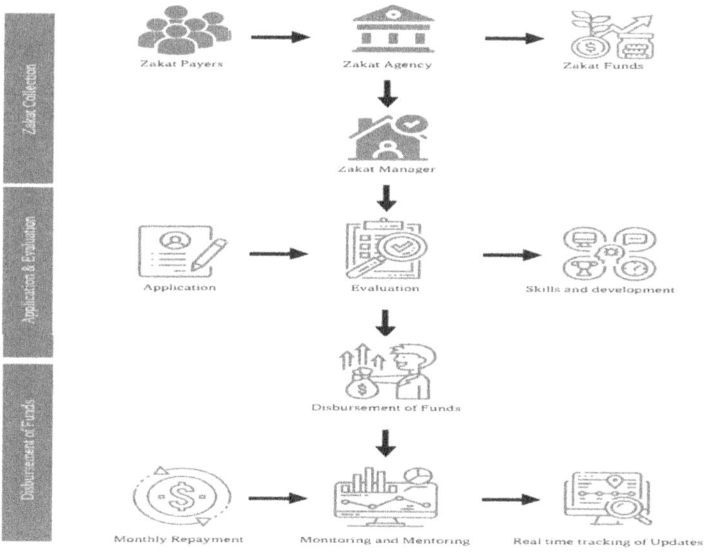

Figure 1. Qadri's Integrated Model of *Zakat* and Islamic Microfinance

To conclude, integrating technology with *Zakat* management can revolutionize its transparency, efficiency, and impact. By leveraging portals and apps, *Zakat* givers can monitor fund utilization, track disbursements, and review business progress.

Qadri proposes a FinTech-enhanced model to improve transparency, automation, and fund disbursement and recovery, ultimately transforming *Zakat* beneficiaries into *Zakat* givers, thereby actively reducing poverty over time. This model addresses key challenges in traditional *Zakat* and *Waqf*-based systems, such as effective fund management and empowering beneficiaries to achieve economic independence. *Zakat*, as a legally mandated almsgiving activity with strong moral and spiritual appeal, serves as a significant tool for poverty alleviation. When managed efficiently and distributed transparently, *Zakat* provides immediate assistance, bolsters essential networks, and offers a robust safety net for those in need.

Integrated *Zakat*-based Islamic microfinance models, like Qadri's, suggest that governments should collect and authorize *Zakat* funds to generate sustainable income for beneficiaries. Rather than focusing solely on daily needs, funds should first be directed toward business ventures or skill development, enabling recipients to earn income and eventually contribute *Zakat* themselves. Countries such as Malaysia, Indonesia, and Bangladesh have implemented this approach. By incorporating technology within a framework aligned with Shariah, finance, and social welfare principles, the model can be further enhanced. An expanded version of this model could integrate *Zakat*, *Waqf*, and *Qard al-Hasan* funds with Islamic microfinance, creating a comprehensive Islamic social finance framework for social welfare in accordance with Shariah. Technology, AI, and big data hold immense potential to improve governance, banking, and social welfare systems. To advance the future of Islamic social finance in poverty alleviation, adopting these technologies is essential for enhancing system efficiency and maximizing impact.

References

Abbas, Kausar, and Nasim Shirazi. 2015. "The Key Players' Perception on the Role of Islamic Microfinance in Poverty Alleviation: The Case of Pakistan." *Journal of Islamic Accounting and Business Research* 6 (2): 244-67.

Adnan, Muhammad Akhyar, and Shochrul Rohmatul Ajija. 2015. "The Effectiveness of Baitul Maal Wat Tamwil in Reducing Poverty: The Case of Indonesian Islamic Microfinance Institution." *Humanomics* 31 (2): 160-82.

Ahmad, Suhail. 2019. "Developing and Proposing *Zakat* Management System: A Case of the Malakand District, Pakistan." *International Journal of Zakat* 4 (1): 25-33.

Ahmed, Habib. 2004. *Role of Zakah and Awqaf in Poverty Alleviation.* Islamic Development Bank, Islamic Research and Training Institute Jeddah.

Akram, Mian Muhammad, and Muhammad Afzal. 2015. "Dynamic Role of *Zakat* in Alleviating Poverty: A Case Study of Pakistan." *Research Journal Social Sciences* 4 (1).

Al-Filali, Isam Yahia, and Giulio M Gallarotti. 2012. "Smart Development: Saudi Arabia's Quest for a Knowledge Economy." *International Studies* 49 (1-2): 47-76.

Aman, Naveed, and Karim Ullah. 2016. "Challenges Faced by the Islamic Microfinance Institutions in Pakistan." *Asian Journal of Islamic Finance* 1 (1): 1-13.

Arif, Muhammad. 2017. "*Zakat* as a Mode of Poverty Alleviation." *International Journal of Economics & Management Sciences* 6 (06): 57-65.

Ashraf, A L I, M Kabir Hassan, and K Hunt-Ahmed. 2013. "An Integrated Islamic Poverty Alleviation Model." *Contemporary Islamic Finance*, 223-44.

Azam, Muhammad, Nasir Iqbal, and Muhammad Tayyab. 2014. "*Zakat* and Economic Development: Micro and Macro Level Evidence from Pakistan." *Bulletin of Business and Economics (BBE)* 3 (2): 85-95.

Aziz, Muhammad Ridhwan Ab, Fuadah Johari, and Mohd Asyraf Yusof. 2013. "Cash *Waqf* Models for Financing in Education." In *The 5th Islamic Economic System Conference (IECONS2013)*, 835-42.

Butt, Q T A. 2017. "Integrating Model of Religious and Corporate Charities in Islamic Microfinance Institutions for Poverty Reduction." *J. Bus. Financ. Aff* 6: 293.

Çizakça, Murat. 2011. Islamic Capitalism and Finance: Origins, Evolution and the Future. Edward Elgar Publishing.

CPD. 1996. "Experiences with Economic Reform: A Review of Bangladesh's Development, 1995 | The University Press Limited." 1996.

https://uplbooks.com/shop/9789840513086-experiences-with-economic-reform-a-review-of-bangladesh-s-development-1995-2997#attr=13871.

Diniyya, Aulia Arifatu. 2019. "Development of *Waqf* Based Microfinance and Its Impact in Alleviating the Poverty." *Ihtifaz: Journal of Islamic Economics, Finance, and Banking* 2 (2): 107-24.

Duncan, Greg J, Katherine Magnuson, and Elizabeth Votruba-Drzal. 2017. "Moving beyond Correlations in Assessing the Consequences of Poverty." *Annual Review of Psychology* 68 (1): 413-34.

El-Gari, Mohamed A. 2004. "The Qard Hassan Bank." In International Seminar on Nonbank Financial Institutions: Islamic Alternatives, 1-3.

Firdaus, Muhammad, Irfan Syauqi Beik, Tonny Irawan, and

Bambang Juanda. 2012. "Economic Estimation and Determinations of *Zakat* Potential in Indonesia." *Jeddah: Islamic Research and Training Institute*, 1-75.

Gündoğdu, Ahmet Şuayb. 2019. "Determinants of Success in Islamic Public-Private Partnership Projects (PPPs) in the Context of SDGs." *Turkish Journal Of Islamic Economics-Tujise.*

Hailey, Paul. 2009. "Microfinance and Islamic Finance: Can They Be Reconciled and How Can They Benefit One Another." *HEC Social Business Certificate* 1.

Haneef, M A, A H Pramanik, M O Mohammed, M F Bin Amin, and A D Muhammad. 2015. "Integration of *Waqf*-Islamic Microfinance Model for Poverty Reduction: The Case of Bangladesh." *International Journal of Islamic and Middle Eastern Finance and Management* 8 (2): 246-70. https://doi.org/10.1108/IMEFM-03-2014-0029.

Haneef, Mohamed Aslam, Aliyu Dahiru Muhammad, Ataul Huq Pramanik, and Mustafa Omar Mohammed. 2014. "Integrated *Waqf* Based Islamic Microfinance Model (IWIMM) for Poverty Alleviation in OIC Member Countries." *Middle-East Journal of Scientific Research* 19 (2): 286-98.

Hasibuan, Sayuti. 2010. "Poverty Alleviation: The Islamic Way." Abdul Ghafar Ismail Mohd Ezani Mat Hassan Norazman Ismail Shahida Shahimi, 243.

Hassan, M Kabir. 2006. "The Role of *Zakat* in Poverty Alleviation in Bangladesh." In *A Conference in Dhaka, November*, 24-26.

Hassan, M Kabir, and A Ashraf. 2010. "An Integrated Poverty Alleviation Model Combining *Zakat*, Awqaf and Micro-Finance." In *Seventh International Conference-The Tawhidic Epistemology: Zakat and Waqf Economy, Bangi, Malaysia*, 261-81.

Hassan, M Kabir, and Juanyed Masrur Khan. 2007. "*Zakat*, External Debt and Poverty Reduction Strategy in Bangladesh." *Journal of Economic Cooperation Among Islamic Countries* 28 (4).

Hassan, Syed, and Sema Yılmaz. 2019. Poverty In Muslim Countries: Policy Recommendations Over The Gulf Cooperation Council.

Kahf, Monzer. 1992. "Waqf and Its Sociopolitical Aspects." Dalam Essential Readings in Contemporary Waqf Issues, Ed. Kahf, Monzer & Siti Mashitoh Mahamood (Kuala Lumpur: CERT Publications, 2011).

Kakembo, Ssemambo Hussein, and Abu Umar Faruq Ahmad. 2023. "Employing Islamic Microfinance in Addressing Poverty Challenges in Brunei: A Mudarabah Approach." In *Research Anthology on Microfinance Services and Roles in Social Progress*, 613-26. IGI Global.

Mannan, M A. 2005. "The Role of Waqf in Improving the Ummah Welfare." In Presentation at the International Seminar on Islamic Economics as Solution, Organised by Indonesian Association of Islamic Economists and Muamalat Institute, Jakarta Medan, Indonesia, 18-19.

Marenza, Silvya Eka. 2024. "A Comparative Analysis of Zakat And Waqf Management in Indonesia and Pakistan." *Jurnal Syarikah: Jurnal Ekonomi Islam* 10 (1): 12-20.

Miah, Abdul Awal. 2019. "Integration of *Zakat* and Awaqf for Poverty Alleviation and Development." *Revitalization of Waqf for Socio-Economic Development, Volume I*, 215-42.

Mizanur, M R. 2011. "Islamic Microfinance: A Tool for Poverty Alleviation." *Berlin, Germany: LAP LAMBERT.*

Mohd Thas Thaker, Mohamed Asmy Bin. 2018. "A Qualitative Inquiry into Cash *Waqf* Model as a Source of Financing for Micro Enterprises." *ISRA International Journal of Islamic Finance* 10 (1): 19-35.

Mohi-ud-Din Qadri, Hussain. 2022. Zakat & Microfinance: A Blended Model of Islamic Social Finance to Alleviate Poverty in Pakistan.

Mohseni-Cheraghlou, Amin. 2017. "Financial Inclusion and Poverty Alleviation in Muslim-Majority Countries: The Role of Islamic Finance and Qard Hassan." *Financial Inclusion and Poverty Alleviation: Perspectives from Islamic Institutions and Instruments*, 141-97.

Mohsin, Magda Ismail Abdel. 2013. "Financing through Cash-*Waqf*: A Revitalization to Finance Different Needs." *International Journal of Islamic and Middle Eastern Finance and Management* 6 (4): 304-21.

Mohsin, Magda Ismail Abdel, Hisham Dafterdar, Murat Cizakca, Syed Othman Alhabshi, Shaikh Hamzah Abdul Razak, Seyed Kazem Sadr, and M Obaidullah. 2016. "Financing the Development of Old *Waqf* Properties." *New York: Palgrave Macmillan US. Retrieved March* 27: 2021.

Mood, Carina, and Jan O Jonsson. 2016. "The Social Consequences of Poverty: An Empirical Test on Longitudinal Data." *Social Indicators Research* 127: 633-52.

Munir, Sahar, Resul Sapar, and Muhammad Imran Majeed. 2023. "Blended Islamic Finance: A Tool for Poverty Reduction." In *Islamic Accounting and Finance: A Handbook*, 677-721. World Scientific.

Naveed Aslam, Muhammad. 2014. "Role of Islamic Microfinance in Poverty Alleviation in Pakistan: An Empirical Approach." *International Journal of Academic Research in Accounting, Finance and Management Sciences* 4 (4).

Obaidullah, Mohammed. 2008. "Introduction to Islamic Microfinance." Mohammed Obaidullah, Introduction to Islamic Microfinance, IBF Net Limited.

Obaidullah, Mohammed, and Tariqullah Khan. 2008. "Islamic Microfinance Development: Challenges and Initiatives." *Islamic Research & Training Institute Policy Dialogue Paper*, no. 2.

Rahman, M Mizanur. 2020. "Financial Inclusion for Poverty Alleviation: The Role of Islamic Finance in Bangladesh." *Enhancing Financial Inclusion through Islamic Finance, Volume II*, 17-50.

Rahman, Rashidah Abdul, and Faisal Dean. 2013. "Challenges and Solutions in Islamic Microfinance." *Humanomics* 29 (4): 293-306.

Raimi, Lukman, Ashok Patel, and Ismail Adelopo. 2014. "Corporate Social Responsibility, *Waqf* System and *Zakat* System as Faith-Based Model for Poverty Reduction." *World Journal of Entrepreneurship, Management and Sustainable Development* 10 (3): 228-42.

Rakhmat, Adrianna Syariefur, and Irfan Syauqi Beik. 2022. "Pengelolaan *Zakat* Dan Wakaf Di Malaysia Dan Turki: Studi Komparatif." *ILTIZAM Journal of Shariah Economics Research* 6 (1): 48-58.

Razak, Dzuljastri Abdul, and Qosdan Dawami. 2019. "Achieving Islamic Social Finance Goals through Zakah, *Waqf*, and Sadaqah in Selected Countries: Issues and Challenges." In *Proceedings of the 7th ASEAN Universities International Conference on Islamic Finance (7th AICIF 2019)-Revival of Islamic Social Finance to Strengthen Economic Development Towards a Global Industrial Revolution*, 38-45.

Rehman, Fazal Ur, and Faiz Ur Rahim. 2023. "*Waqf* in Pakistan: Contemporary Issues and Challenges from Shari'ah Perspective." *Research Journal of Religious Thoughts* 2 (1): 97-109.

Saad, Norma, and Naziruddin Abdullah. 2014. "Is *Zakat* Capable of Alleviating Poverty? An Analysis on the Distribution of *Zakat* Fund in Malaysia." *Journal of Islamic Economics, Banking and Finance* 10 (1): 69-95.

Sadeq, AbulHasan M. 2002. "*Waqf*, Perpetual Charity and Poverty Alleviation." *International Journal of Social Economics* 29 (1/2): 135-51.

Salim, Kinan, Baharom Abdul Hamid, Ziyaad Mahomed, and Wiaam Hassan. 2024. "*Zakat*-Based Urban Farming: A Tool for Poverty Alleviation, Community Empowerment, Financial Inclusion, and Food Security." *Review of Islamic Social Finance and Entrepreneurship.*

Shatzmiller, Maya. 1993. *Labour in the Medieval Islamic World.* Vol. 4. Brill.

Siddiqui, Saif. 2009. "Islamic Economic System and Poverty Reduction." *Available at SSRN 1332618.*

The Nation. 2013. "44pc of Poverty-Hit Live in Muslim Countries." 2013. https://www.nation.com.pk/25-Apr-2011/44pc-of-povertyhit--live-in-muslim-countries.

UNDP. 2017. "IFN—*Zakat* for the SDGs: The UNDP Can Help." 2017. https://www.islamicfinancenews.com/zakat-for-the-sdgs-the-undp-can-help.html?login_error=PHN0cm9uZz5FUlJPUjo8L3N0cm9uZz4gVGhlIGVtYWlsIGFuZCBwYXNzd29yZCBjb21iaW5hdGlvbiBpcyB3cm9uZy4%3D.

Widyatama, Arif, Andi Sabirin Baso, and Fathiatul Haq. 2020. "The Other Side of *Zakat* in Poverty Reduction: A Phenomenology Study." *Iqtishadia* 13 (1): 77.

Wilson, Rodney. 2013. "Making Development Assistance Sustainable through Islamic Microfinance." In *Shari'a Compliant Microfinance*, 63-75. Routledge.

World Bank. 2010. World Development Indicators 2011. World Development Indicators 2011. https://doi.org/10.1596/978-0-8213-8709-2.

Wulandari, P, N I S Putri, S Kassim, and L A Sulung. 2016. "Contract Agreement Model for Murabahah Financing in Indonesia Islamic Banking." *International Journal of Islamic and Middle Eastern Finance and Management* 9 (2): 190-204. https://doi.org/10.1108/IMEFM-01-2015-0001.

FIFTEEN

Professor Nejatullah Siddiqi's Vision for the Future of Islamic Economics

Jasser Auda

Introduction

T*o Allah we belong and to Him we return*, (Al-Baqarah 156). The Muslim Ummah lost one of its intellectual leaders, Prof. Dr. Muhammad Nejatullah Siddiqi, on November 12, 2022. We ask Allah ﷻ to shower His mercy on him, accept his good deeds, and reward him for his struggle for His sake and for the sake of a stronger Muslim ummah and a better world. Ameen. The late Professor Nejatullah Siddiqi is undoubtedly one of the most influential voices that shaped the thought/jurisprudence (*fiqh*) and practice (*tatbiq*) of the Islamic economics and finance in our times. His views contributed to the founding and growth of thousands of Islamic financial institutions around the world over many decades.

I am quite familiar with Professor Nejatullah's approach to Islamic economics and finances. It is a valuable continuation of the legacy of what I labelled in some of my works as "Islamic Modernism In Economic Thought," starting with Sheikhs Mohammad Abduh and Rashid Rida, all the way till the great jurists of our times who contributed to the Islamic economic thought, such as Sheikh Yusuf Al-Qaradawi, Sheikh Mustafa Al-Zarqa, Sheikh Wahba Al-Zuhaili, Sheikh Abdus-Sattar Abou-Ghuddah, Sheikh Muhammad Taqi Usmani, Sheikh Ali Al-Qaradaghi, and many notable others. Contemporary Islamic economics is a project that—in my view—was an important step forward for the ummah to deal with the colonization project, and it contributed in a crucial way to the financing of the Islamic movements and Islamic projects of every kind over the past half a century. I do believe that it is time, however, for our Ummah to wean itself from the Islamic economics' "capitalist apologism," if I may call it that, with all due respect to its proponents, and start to envision a different economics and a different future.

Therefore, I was delighted when I studied the latest ideas that our late Professor Siddiqi proposed in the form of "A Vision for the Future of Islamic Economics." It is not unusual for great scholars of Islam to look back at a certain point of maturity in their life/career and reflect upon the fundamentals of their own thought and legacy. For one example, scholars familiar with Imam al-Ghazali would know that there are two Ghazalis: the younger Ghazali who is essentially a Greek philosopher—after some "Islamization"—and a strictly Shafi'i follower *faqih*/jurist, versus the Ghazali of his later years, in which he issued a radical critique of philosophy and philosophers, and in which he took a much more "*maqasidi*" or purposive approach. In other words, he increasingly foregrounded the objectives of the Shariah (God's law) in his approach to *fiqh* (jurisprudence) and *usul* (methodological principles) to the extent his *qiyas* (analogical reasoning) was purely based on the *maqasid* in his "*al-Mustasfa min 'Ilm al-Usul*," his seminal work on *Usul al-Fiqh*. Al-Ghazali's critique of his contemporary (mainstream) *fuqaha'*/jurists in the introduction of his "*Ihya' Ulum al-Din*" is quite remarkable and presents quite a different everlasting, and genuine Ghazali.

In the later part of his blessed life, Professor Nejatullah Siddiqi followed the tradition of the great scholars of Islam; he took a step back and issued a high-level critique of the very foundations of the *fiqh*/jurisprudence of contemporary Islamic economics and finance. The clearest presentation for this critique is his "Vision for the Future of Islamic Economics." In it, Professor Nejatullah proposed five strategic changes: **1.** Family rather than market as a starting point in economic analysis; **2.** Cooperation playing a greater role than competition in the economy; **3.** Debts playing a subsidiary rather than the dominant role in financial markets; **4.** Interest and interest-bearing instruments playing no role in money creation and monetary management; and **5.** Maqasid-based thinking supplanting analogical reasoning in Islamic economic jurisprudence. This essay is in honor and memory of Professor Nejatullah, in which I argue how his vision is essentially a rejection of the capitalist basis upon which contemporary "Islamic economics" was built! It is a vision for the ummah today to re-assert its unique economic principles, and this is how his legacy continues.

Professor Siddiqi expanded the scope of traditional and modernist *fiqh* (jurisprudence) of Islamic economics, and presented a comprehensive, holistic and *maqasid*-based approach towards a new Islamic economic thought. He introduced a basic critique in the form of "A Vision for the Future of Islamic Economics." He proposed five strategic changes: **1.** Family rather than market as the starting point for economic analysis; **2.** Cooperation playing a greater role in the economy than competition; **3.** Debts playing a subsidiary rather than the dominant role in financial markets; **4.** Interest and interest-bearing instruments playing no role in money creation and monetary management; and **5.** *Maqasid*-based thinking supplanting analogical reasoning in Islamic economic jurisprudence.

In my view, this vision is no longer capitalist economics, which was the methodological basis of the mainstream Islamic economic theories and popular Islamic financial instruments that we witnessed over the past half a century or so. This essay in honor and memory of Professor Nejatullah offers a few thoughts to support his vision towards a unique and unapologetic economic contribution of the Muslim Ummah based on Islam.

1. Family Rather Than Market as The Starting Point for Economic Analysis

To quote Professor Nejatullah on this fundamental vision, he writes:

> The individual person is born in a family. His/her relationships with things as well as persons and other animate beings originate and flourish towards maturity in familial environment. This brings forth gift relationships and reciprocity before exchange relationships that characterize the market as conceived by economics. Economics as it developed in the Western milieu during the last three centuries lost much by ignoring this fact and focusing exclusively on exchange and market. It lost its humanity. It also lost in terms of realism. There is no reason the values nurtured in family entirely evaporate in the market. Insofar as these values are ineffective and dormant for now, can they be activated and energized? (Siddiqi 2013)

In my view, the "gift relationships and reciprocity" that Professor Nejatullah is calling for, is a call for the return of the *awqaf* (endowments) to the center of economics, instead of markets. Professor Nejatullah also contributed to *awqaf* thought throughout his blessed journey. *Waqf* has personal faith objectives such as seeking rewards in the hereafter, expressing gratitude to

Allah ﷻ, purification, etc. But the Prophet's stipulation that the *waqf* is "not to be sold, nor given as a gift, nor inherited" is meant to free wealth from its previous owner to Allah's ownership, and in practical terms, the jurisdiction of the ummah. This means granting financial and administrative independence to the *waqf* body against authorities with selfish and narrow interests. It also means guaranteeing sustainability for waqf projects through continuous investments that yield plentiful returns.

These objectives have special importance in our time where nation states and global companies have snatched the material and moral destinies of people. They have shrunk—either willingly or by force—the terrains of civic and indigenous action to the lowest limit. Modern politicians, regardless of whether it is democratic or autocratic, and whether in the East or the West, try to maintain ruling over social organizations outside the state's authority. This happens in civic organizations, non-governmental bodies, and especially in Islamic institutions of all sorts. This dominance is important to them since it guarantees them a continued existence in their posts—notwithstanding their blunders—against civic, juristic and philanthropic movements. Global corporations also exercise authority over states and other bodies to continue with their vested interests and earnings, and to achieve their trade objectives wherever they may be.

The Islamic world has witnessed a vicious attack on its *awqaf* from nation states in the "post-colonial" period. But a resurgence of family-oriented economics, i.e., *waqf* institutions, would reverse this trend. The problems of the poor, the indigent and those with excessive debt cannot be effectively addressed in matters of food, clothing, and housing on an individual or piecemeal basis. There must be bodies that undertake broad human development for them and their societies. This must not involve feeding the poor person some morsels until his hunger returns the next day. It also must not involve meeting a person's debts until he takes up a loan the following month. Naturally, priority must be given to providing the urgent needs of these groups. However, after doing so the welfare bodies must undertake to develop their capabilities and enable them to extricate themselves from the cycle of poverty and debt. This strategy must be far removed from "growth" standards as defined by global or special organizations based on un-Islamic standards. This is a matter treated by Islamic institutions, whose continuity is guaranteed by *awqaf.* Priorities are based on the Islamic *maqasid* of essentials, necessities, and embellishments.

Besides, education today is purely a profit-oriented system built on society's economic and political interests. The labor market does not strive to produce a person attentive to the Divine trust in humans' role on earth as envisaged by Islam. These educational institutions produce graduates that are merely cogs in the machinery of modern "growth," exploitation and consumerism while observing current capitalist standards. For this reason, it is one of the priorities of our time that we help *waqf* bodies that spend on present-day educational institutions. Professor Nejatullah's proposal and its implications certainly create a different social and economic reality than the current status quo.

2. Cooperation Playing a Greater Role in the Economy Than Competition

To quote Professor Nejatullah once again, he writes:

> The next possibility: a restoration of mutual understanding and cooperation in economic activities. A realization by individual economic actors that they owe something to others, a sense of obligation, leading to benevolent/beneficial conduct and a regard for public as distinct from private good—are likely to inspire and

> motivate economic agents. I am aware of the information problems involved, yet it is hoped the state and other semi-public agencies can meet the information deficit by pooling available knowledge, to an extent sufficient enough to enable joint action. We have a vast literature on both the above issues, familial ethics inspiring economic action and cooperative instinct in economic agents, produced by anthropologists and sociologists. But these trends of thought are not reflected in standard economic text books. The main reason is economic craving for quantification and its marriage with mathematics. The rethinking inspired by the recent crisis is expected to overcome this obduracy. Quantification is welcome, but not at the cost of realism and a human touch. Islamic economists can play a role in the search of a balanced approach. There exist advocates of 'holistic' approach similar to those emphasizing 'communitarian'ways in contrast to 'individualism.' (Siddiqi 2013)

The key idea for "cooperation versus competition" is Professor Nejatullah's call for a "holistic approach." The methodological analysis of the Qur'an and the Prophetic tradition proves the truth, fundamentality and depth of connectivity that takes systematic patterns between absolutely everything: the seen and the unseen, the material and the non-material. It also proves that the study of these patterns of connectivity results in the emergence of complex (*murakkab*) and holistic (*kulli*) meanings through the relationship between the parts. A primary component of these holistic meanings are the objectives/*maqasid*.

A human, for example, emerges from the connection and integration of his or her parts and dimensions. Allah ﷻ says in the Qur'an: *"In whatever form He willed, He composed you (rakkabak)"* (82:8) and *"So, We donned the bones with flesh, and then We made another creation emerge (ansha'nahu) so glory to*

Allah, the best of creators" (23:14). Then, He explained the objectives of that complex composition, the human. To know Allah ﷻ and to worship Him, to rectify earth and preserve life, and to connect what Allah ﷻ orders to be connected, are objectives at a higher level of awareness and integration. These are meanings higher than the functions of each of the organs. The idea that the constitutive parts cooperate—rather than compete—to rise to a holistic entity is very much embedded in the Qur'an. This whole is then characterized not only by these parts but more importantly by the connectivity or relationships among them and the higher objectives that are an integral and inseparable part of all creation, both the animate and the inanimate.

Studying the Revelation in this way for the sake of developing new economic theories, results in the emergence of webs of meaning that exhibit two universal laws: interconnectivity (*tawasul*) and emergence (*tawallud*) of holism from the parts. This is true in the realm of interrelations between the revealed meanings and higher objectives in all textual and deduced levels. Basically, that is how the universal meanings and the higher objectives emerge in the cognition of scholars of Islamic jurisprudence and thought (*fiqh*), who are reflecting on the interrelationships and the holistic picture. This also applies, according to the Revelation, to the interrelationships in the universe and how researching them reveals holistic patterns and causes objectives to emerge in the cognition of seekers of knowledge.

One cannot study the Qur'an and Sunnah properly without pondering upon the endless interrelationships and internal references, both the textually expressed and the inferred. The Qur'an also makes references and connections to the Sunnah. The Prophet ﷺ also made connections between certain sections of his Sunnah. All such relationships articulated within the texts can be read directly or inferred through mindful and detailed readings.

Then, by connecting all references to the meaning of "names" mentioned in the texts, the researcher comes to see the connection between Allah ﷻ and everything in the Book and in the universe, with everything emerging as an interconnected web and inseparable whole. The Revelation also teaches us essential knowledge about the universe. It does not leave us to explore based on our natural faculties only. As with its approach to itself, the Revelation addresses the universe by connecting all of its components at the most intricate and sublime levels. This exposition shows us how holistic meanings are constructed via the integration of the parts. In the true knowledge about the universe, the material world is not separate from what we classify as non-material elements. In fact, the correct classification of these realms is not physics versus metaphysics, but rather seen (*shahadah*) verses unseen (*ghayb*).

The universe is alive, connected and interacting by way of its divine creation. This is a different worldview that is based on Professor Nejatullah's vision for 'holism,' which is different from the purely material capitalist worldview that sees no such life and makes no such connections, and that difference has an impact on all aspects of life. It follows that everything in this universe is purposeful, with complex relational expressions with all other related matter. Each relation or set of relations gives rise to greater and greater holistic manifestations. Thus, all cognition, as I have detailed elsewhere, should be based on seven universal elements, namely: concepts, objectives, values, commands, universal laws, parties and proofs (Auda 2021). These are key elements of the fundamental premises of knowledge, awareness and scholarship that lead to more adequate understandings of Revelation and reality: past, present or future. The logical depth of this methodological shift is a worldview that is more suited to the needs of Muslims and humanity, especially as it shapes thought, education and action in today's economies.

3. Debts Playing a Subsidiary Rather Than the Dominant Role in Financial Markets

Professor Nejatullah writes:

> Conventional debt-ridden financial arrangements, with a speculative market for debt-instruments to boost, have played havoc with the economy of man. They are the primary cause of increasing levels of inequality within and between nations. By obliging borrowers to pay back what they borrowed with interest added in an environment characterized by uncertainty that does not guaranty additional wealth creation in all circumstances, the current system empowers capitalists at the cost of everybody else. The pressure for additional wealth creation pushes entrepreneurs to accelerate growth in utter disregard of the planet earth's ecological health and sustainability of a pollution-free environment. History testifies that the greatest threat to world peace emanates from the unequal and unfair financial transactions between nations. Debt-centered financial system is inhuman, a threat to the planet earth and anti-peace (Auda 2021).

The key here is Professor Nejatullah's rejection of a "debt-centered financial system." In my view, this is a rejection of the very system of central banks and fiat currencies, which is precisely the next item in Professor Nejatullah's vision:

4. Interest and Interest-Bearing Instruments Playing No Role in Money Creation and Monetary Management

Here, Professor Nejatullah writes:

> Recently when the Federal Reserve in the US wanted to increase the supply of money, it printed currency notes worth billions of dollars and purchased debt instruments

> promising repayment with interest. When the new supply of money originating from the central bank ultimately finds its way into commercial banks, they are able to finance business by creating more money—essentially entries in their ledger books enabling the borrower to write checks against them. These days (August 2013) it decided to end its policy of 'Quantitative Easing' and started selling those assets (bonds) at attractive prices causing a withdrawal of dollars from all over the world. Baring differences in some details, monetary management works that way all over the world. Interest is involved in creation of money as well as in its extinction. Almost all money in circulation is interest bearing debt transferring wealth from fund users to the owners of capital (Auda 2021).

The question, "What is usury (*riba*)?" is foundational and open to ongoing *ijtihad* (independent reasoning). The wisdom in keeping the answer open in the Qur'an and Sunnah lies in allowing scholars to adapt to the evolving circumstances of different eras in light of fixed principles and guiding objectives. In my view, the answer can be summarized in the principle that usury is the opposite of trade. The English economist Jeremy Bentham, the founder of utilitarian philosophy, argued that justice in trade cannot be achieved due to the inherent inequality between goods and prices, and because prices are subject to irrational whims, as he said. This philosophical approach served as the basis for contemporary capitalism's analysis of usury in the form of open bank interest rates, under the falsely termed concept of "maximizing utility" for the greatest number of people.

Bentham's view differed from the Aristotelians, who believed that the value of goods and prices must be equal. He also disagreed with those who limited interest rates, like the Scottish economist Adam Smith (Smith 2009). Consequently, Utilitarians saw trade as being similar to usury in its injustice, which is precisely what this verse rejects: "*Allah has permitted trade and forbidden usury*" (Qur'an 2:275). The distinction between trade and usury is the key to defining usury; trade is the exchange of goods for different prices, whereas usury is the exchange of goods for identical prices with an increase in weight, volume, or value, known as "*riba al-fadl,*" or an increase in value through unjustified delay, known as "*riba al-nasi'ah.*"

Riba al-Fadl encompasses any exchange where there is an increase of the same kind, such as interest on bank deposits, or loans from banks to companies and individuals with an increase. This is why the Prophet Muḥammad ﷺ reacted as he did when a man brought him some fine dates. The Prophet's dates were known as "*al-Lawn.*" A man told the Prophet that he had exchanged two measures of his dates for one measure of this superior quality date, to which the Prophet replied, "You have engaged in *riba* (usury)." This hadith should not be understood in our era as merely referring to the barter system common in the time of the Prophet, but as a foundational explanation of *riba*. *Riba* involves giving one date and taking two in return, which is an unjustified increase or *riba*. While the date may be of better quality, such considerations are irrelevant for the Sharia when the goods are of the same kind. That is, exchanging one date for two, regardless of quality, is *riba*, just as exchanging a pound of pure gold for two pounds would be, regardless of the shine of the metal. Similarly, in the modern financial system, exchanging one dollar for more than one dollar is *riba*.

A legitimate sale would involve selling the good date for a dirham, then using that dirham to buy two lesser-quality dates if that is the market price. The difference here is that these two transactions involve trade, which is a mutually agreed exchange between a buyer and seller where prices can vary based on market consensus. Only Allah ﷻ knows the true value or price. That is why the Prophet ﷺ viewed government pricing of goods when prices soared in Medina as a form of injustice, stating: "Indeed, Allah ﷻ is the One who fixes prices, withholds, gives abundantly, and provides. I hope to meet Allah ﷻ without anyone claiming against me for an injustice regarding blood or property," and in another narration: "Allah ﷻ is the One who sets prices." This means that Allah ﷻ determines the true value of things. However, if one date is exchanged for two dates, this is undoubtedly *riba* because the value unit is the same—the value (weight or volume) of one date—and any perceived difference is *riba*.

As for *riba al-nasi'ah*, it involves buying a present good with a deferred payment, which is contrary to the Prophet's command "hand to hand" mentioned in the hadith above, and the other prophetic directive: "Do not sell what is not in your possession." In a hadith from Umar ibn al-Khattab, the Prophet Muḥammad ﷺ said: "Do not sell gold for gold except like for like, or weight for weight, and do not sell silver for silver except like for like, or weight for weight, and do not sell something absent for something present unless it is hand to hand. I fear for you the practice of *riba*." Here, the form of *riba* involves selling a pound of gold today for a pound of gold tomorrow, which is not hand to hand or "deliver and take" as we say in contemporary transactions. The *riba* here is the unjustified increase of time. This means that selling a commodity for a deferred payment (debt) is *riba al-nasi'ah* due to the delay in converting the debt into a tangible item. Only selling a tangible item for a tangible item, hand to hand, is lawful.

In an incident narrated by Imam Malik, during the time of Marwan ibn al-Hakam, people started trading documents representing government grain distributions before actually receiving them. Zaid ibn Thabit and another companion entered upon Marwan and asked him, "Are you permitting *riba*, O

Marwan?" He replied, "I seek refuge with Allah ﷻ; what is that?" They said, "These documents are being traded before they are received." Marwan then ordered his guards to retrieve these documents from the people's hands and return them to their owners. The *riba* here was identified in Islamic jurisprudence as the prohibition of selling debt until it is received, as these documents had no intrinsic trading value but were simply a promise of debt payment. Similarly, the Prophet ﷺ prohibited selling a commodity before taking possession of it. In a hadith narrated by Hakim ibn Hizam, he said: "I bought some food from the charity and made a profit on it before I took possession of it, so I asked the Prophet about selling it, and he said: 'Do not sell it until you take possession of it.'"

The concept of *riba* from the time of the Prophet's message up until the pre-modern era differed significantly from how it is understood in modern Islamic thought. Historically, there was no distinction between what the Qur'an explicitly mentioned and what is established by authentic hadiths of the Prophet Muḥammad ﷺ, like those previously cited. However, Sheikh Rashid Rida, for example, differentiated between *riba* as mentioned in the Qur'an and *riba* in the Sunnah, limiting *riba* to the *riba* of the pre-Islamic era (i.e., traditional debt usury) and confining it to compounded interest. Consequently, the understanding of *riba* shifted from encompassing all transactions involving any unlawful increase to focusing solely on bank interest, particularly when it is high. This change mirrors what Protestantism did by altering the original concept of *riba* in the Judeo-Christian tradition.

Historically, *riba* included schemes like exchanging money with a difference, as illustrated by Ibn Abbas's statement about exchanging dirhams with an added silk garment. The concept of "*murabahah*" (cost-plus financing) was redefined to permit such arrangements, and more than ninety percent of Islamic banking investments today are based on this structure. But these transactions often involve the "two sales in one" that the Prophet prohibited: "Whoever sells two sales in one transaction, let him have the lesser value or *riba*." Even more problematic than *murabahah* in Islamic banks is the practice of *tawarruq*—an Islamic finance transaction, a buyer (borrower) buys an asset (typically a freely tradeable commodity such as platinum or copper) on credit from a lender on a deferred payment basis and then immediately resells the asset on the spot market for cash to a third party, which Professor Nejatullah was vehemently against. It is essentially a scheme to lend money with *riba* disguised in a permissible format. Moreover, as an Islamic bank operates within the modern state system, one of its challenges is that it deals with national central banks using *riba* in various forms of interest-bearing loans. Additionally, it creates money out of nothing, similar to conventional banks, thereby devaluing the currency and boosting financial markets, at the expense of real markets. These are some of the implications of the Islamic bank's integration into the *riba*-based capitalist system. Professor Nejatullah's vision for "Interest and interest-bearing instruments playing no role in money creation and monetary management" solves all of these problems, even though these basic ideas do require a great deal of development and research, something of which he was well aware, and called for.

5. *Maqasid*-Based Thinking Supplanting Analogical Reasoning in Islamic Economic Jurisprudence

Lastly, Professor Nejatullah writes:

> It will be appreciated that reliance on analogical reasoning in deciding about novel financial transaction sometime leads to perverse results. *Tawarruq*, which leads Islamic finance to an undesirable situation in which debts

> dominate the market, is one such example. An enquiry into consequences (*ma'alat* i.e., the consequences of an action) and a recourse to what Hanafis call *istihsan* (to consider something good) and Malikis characterize as *istislah* (seeking goodness and benefit for the public) is needed to preserve the capability of the Law to serve the objectives (*maqasid*) it is meant to serve [...] Muslim masses feel Islamic banking and finance has not served such goals as poverty alleviation and reduction of inequality in the distribution of income and wealth. Many accuse that, instead of setting priorities in the light of Islamic teachings that make wealth a means to universal need fulfillment, Islamic finance too is led by the greedy whims of the free market, like its conventional counterpart. If these deficiencies are not met, Islamic banking and finance runs the risk of alienation and loss of credibility in its home base (Auda 2021).

Here, Professor Nejatullah's call for a "*Maqasid*-based approach" to Islamic studies is much appreciated, and the writer of this essay has made it a life-long project (Auda 2021). A true "*Maqasid*-approach" is essentially a methodology that integrates, looks towards the future and levels critiques based on the fulfilment of the purposes of connections, or the lack thereof. The *maqasid*/objectives are utilized to integrate all phenomena, disciplines, dimensions, proofs, and the signs of Allah ﷻ in the Book and the universe. These objectives also serve as the basis for critically assessing current realities and planning for future rectification. Thus, a true "Maqasid-approach" to Islamic scholarship is achieved by critiquing shortcomings and promoting their achievements in approaches and methodologies. The following are the dimensions of these shortcomings versus achievements: **1.** blind imitation of the Islamic heritage without reference to the Revelation, versus utilizing criteria from the

Revelation to critique the Islamic intellectual history in a nuanced and balanced way; **2.** fragmentation and partialism in the Islamic approach, versus promoting synergy and integration between evidences, disciplines and specializations, **3.** apologism for the status quo on all levels, versus promoting critical studies of modernity and all systems that it produced in the current realities; **4.** contradiction in referencing between "transferred knowledge" and "rational knowledge," defined according to historical and secular views, respectively, versus the integration of these references under the guidance and hegemony of the revealed knowledge; **5.** deconstructionist critiques without differentiating between Revelation and culture, given that the Revelation—Qur'an and its illustration in the Sunnah—is outside the realm of this critique, versus human interpretations that would benefit from this level of critique in Islamic scholarship. It is to be noted that these five dimensions of critique apply as well to the new studies in the *Maqasid* field.

Finally, a true "*Maqasid*-approach" to Islamic scholarship must return to covering all disciplines, specializations, phenomena and forms of organization. The definition of Islamic scholars, therefore, must expand accordingly to include all researchers and activists, each in their respective field and level. The outcomes of Islamic scholarship must be primarily formative principles and theories in all realms of thought and action. These formative principles and theories are the basis of rules, whether they are legislative rules ranging between the obligation and prohibition, or public good rules ranging between benefit and harm. The development of these formative principles and theories should be the purpose of the methodological steps of research. These are all implications, in my view, of the principle that Professor Nejatullah Siddiqi outlined in his "A Vision for the Future of Islamic Economics." Building on these principles toward a new Islamic economics is the best way to honor his legacy.

References

Auda, Jasser. 2021. *Re-Envisioning Islamic Scholarship: Maqasid Methodology as a New Approach*. Edited by Sharif H. Banna. Claritas Books.

Siddiqi, Muhammad Nejatullah. 2013. "A Vision for the Future of Islamic Economics." In *9th International Conference in Islamic Economics*. Istanbul, Turkey. http://www.siddiqi.com/mns/AVisionForTheFutureOfIslamicEconomics.htm.

Smith, Adam. 2009. *The Wealth of Nations*. Thrifty Books.

SIXTEEN

Publications of Muhammad Nejatullah Siddiqi

Complied by Zulqernain Haider Subhani

Urdu Books

Maqasid-e-Shariat, 2017, Markazi Maktaba Islami, Delhi.

Muasir Islami Fikr, 2016, Hidayat publishers, Delhi.

Ma'ash, Islam awr Musalman, 2013, Markazi Maktaba Islami, Delhi.

Ikkiswin Sadi me Islam, Musalman awr Tahreek-e-Islami, 2012, Markazi Maktaba Islami, Delhi.

Islam aur Funoon-e-Lateefa, 2012, Idara-e-Abad-e-Islami Hind, Delhi.

Asr-e-Hazir Mein Islami Fikar, 2002, Qaumi Press, Lahore.

Deeni Madaris: Masail aur Taqaze, 2001, Markazi Maktaba Islami, Delhi.

Islam, Maashiyat aur Adab Khutoot ke Aaine Mein, 2000, Educational Book House, Aligarh.

Tahreek Islami Asr Hazir Men, 1995, Markazi Maktaba Islami, Delhi.

Qur'an aur Science, 1978, Markazi Maktaba Islami, Delhi.

Nash'at Saniyah Ki Rah, 1974, Markazi Maktaba Islami, Delhi.

Insurance Islami Ma'ishat Mein, 1974, Markazi Maktaba Islami, Delhi.

Ghair Sudi Bank Kari, 1969, Markazi Maktaba Islami, Delhi.

Shirkat aur Mudarabat Ke Shar'i Usul, 1969, Markazi Maktaba Islami, Delhi.

Islam ka Nazarriyah Milkiyat, (2 vols.), 1969, Islamic Publications, Lahore.

Islami Adab, 1960, Markazi Maktaba Islami, Delhi.

Translation Works

Islam Ka Nizam-e-Mahasil, 1966, Islamic Publications, Lahore, translation of Abu Yusuf's *Kitab al-Kharaj*.

Islam Men `Adl-e-Ijtimat'i, 1963, Islamic Publications, Lahore, translation of Syed Qutb's al-Adalah al-Ijtima'iyyah fi al-Islam.

Urdu Articles

Naye Hindustan ki ta'meer aur Muslim Nau Jawan, 2023, Zindagi-e-Nau, Delhi, Feb.

Mulk ka Mawjooda Nizam awr Tahreek-e-Iqamat-e-Deen, 2022, Zindagi-e-Nau, Delhi, Dec.

Maqasid-e-Shariah: Ek ‘Asri Mutala‘a, 2004, Fikr-o-Nazar, Islamic Research Institute, Islamabad, vol.41, no. 4, April-June.

Tashaddud aur Musalman, 2004, Zindagi Nau, Delhi.

Jihad, Ijtihad aur Mujahida e Nafs, 2003, Zindagi Nau, Delhi, Sep.

Ekkisween Sadi Mein Islam—Musalman aur Tehreek-e-Islami, 2002, Zindagi Nau, Delhi.

Mu'asir Islami Fikr: Chand Gaur Talab Pehlu, 2001, Tarjumanul Qur'an, Lahore, October-November.

Mussalman aur Ma'ashi Awamil, 2001, Zindagi Nau, Delhi, May-Jun.

Islami Tarjeehat, 1997, Zindagi Nau, Delhi, July.

Books in English

Islamic Banking and Finance in Theory and Practice: A Survey of the Art, 2006, Islamic Economic Studies. Jeddah.

Riba, Bank Interest and the Rationale of its Prohibition, 2004, Islamic Development Bank, Islamic Research & Training Institute, Jeddah.

Dialogue in Islamic Economics. 2002, Institute of Policy Studies, Islamabad & Islamic Foundation, Leicester, U.K.

I*slamic Public Economics.* 2001, Idara-i-Adabiyat-I-Delli (Translated from Urdu by AfzalPeerzade) Delhi, India.

Relevance and Need for Understanding the Essence of Religious Traditions in the Contemporary World, 2005, Institute of Objective Studies, New Delhi, India.

Economics—An Islamic Approach. 2001. Institute of Policy Studies, Islamabad & The Islamic Foundation, Leicester, U.K.

Teaching Economics in Islamic Perspective. 1996, Centre for Research in Islamic Economics, KAAU, Jeddah.

Role of the State in the Economy. 1996, The Islamic Foundation, Leicester, U.K.

Insurance in an Islamic Economy. 1985, The Islamic Foundation, Leicester, U.K.

Partnership and Profit-Sharing in Islamic Law. 1985, The Islamic Foundation, Leicester, U.K.

Banking Without Interest. 1983, The Islamic Foundation, Leicester, U.K.

Issues in Islamic Banking. 1983, The Islamic Foundation, Leicester, U.K.

Muslim Economic Thinking. 1981, The Islamic Foundation, Leicester, U.K.

Contemporary Literature on Islamic Economics. 978, The Islamic Foundation, Leicester, U.K.

Economic Enterprise in Islam, 1972, Markazi Maktaba Islami, Delhi, India, and Islamic Publications, Lahore, Pakistan.

Some Aspects of the Islamic Economy, 1972, Markazi Maktaba Islami, Delhi, India, and Islamic Publications, Lahore, Pakistan.

Muslim Personal Law, 1972, Markazi Maktaba Islami, (Edited) Delhi, India.

Recent Theories of Profit: A Critical Examination, 1971, Asia Publishing House, Bombay, India.

Articles in English

"My Life in Islamic Economics," *Critical Muslim* (London) 15 (September 2015),

https://criticalmuslim.com/explore/issues/educational-reform/my-life-islamic-economics.

"Islamization of Knowledge: Reflections on Priorities" *American Journal of Islam and Society*, 28 (3), (2011) 15-34.

"Violence and Muslims" *American Journal of Islam and Society*, 21 (2), (2004)137-143.

Siddiqi, M. Nejatullah, and S. M. Ghazanfar. "Early Medieval Islamic Economic Thought: Abu Yusuf's (731-798 Ad) Economics of Public Finance." *History Of Economic Ideas* 9, No. 1 (2001): 13-38 http://www.jstor.org/stable/23723591. Also published as a book chapter in *Medieval Islamic Economic Thought* edited by S.M. Ghazanfar and published by Routledge Curzon (2003).

Islamic Banks: Concept, Precept and Prospects, *Review of Islamic Economics*, No. 9, 2000, pp.21-35.

"Evolution of Islamic Banking and Insurance as Systems Rooted in Ethics" April 2000, *Takaful Forum*.

Role of Islamic Financial Institutions in Financing Economic Projects, (1999) *Proceedings King Abdulaziz University Seminar on Cooperation between Private Sector and Government* https://conference.ibfnet.group/wp-content/uploads/2022/01

Islamic Finance and Beyond: Premises and Promises of Islamic Economics, Harvard *University Forum on Islamic Finance* (1999) https://conference.ibfnet.group/wp-content/uploads/2022/01/Islamic-Finance-and-Beyond.pdf

"Future of the Islamic Movement" *Encounters* (Leicester) Vol. 4, No. 1, March 1998.

"Muslim Minorities in the 21st Century: A Case Study of Indian Muslims" *Encounters* (Leicester) Vol. 3, No. 2, September, 1997.

Towards Regeneration: Shifting Priorities in Islamic Movements, *Encounters* (Leicester) Vol. 1, No. 2, September, 1995.

"Islamic Economics and Finance" 1995, *Encyclopedia of Islamic Banking and Insurance*, London, pp. 1-9.

An Overview of Public Borrowing in Early Islamic History, *Review of Islamic Economics*, Vol. 2, No. 2, 1993.

Impact of Islamic Modes of Finance on Monetary Expansion, *Journal of King Abdulaziz University: Islamic Economics,* Vol. 4, 1992.

"Some Economic Aspects of *Mudarabah*" Review of Islamic Economics, Vol. 1, No. 2, 1991. (Also published in *The Political Economy of the Middle East* (1999) edited by Timothy Niblock and Rodney Wilson and published by Edward Elgar, London.)

The Muslim Situation in India, Some Observations, in The Muslim Situation in India (1989), Sterling Publication Co. Delhi. Edited by Iqbal A. Ansari.

"Christian Mission to Islam: A Muslim Response—Comment", *Journal Institute of Muslim Minority Affairs, London*, Vol. IX, No. 1, January1988.

"An Islamic Approach to Economics", in *Islam: Source and Purpose of Knowledge*, International Institute of Islamic Thought, Herndon, VA, 1988.

"From Contemporary Economics to Islamic Economics" in *Today's Problems Tomorrows Solutions*, London, Mansell, Edited by Abdullah O. Naseef, 1988.

"Islamic Banking: Theory and Practice" in *Islamic Banking in Southeast Asia*, edited by Mohamed Ariff, Singapore: Institute of Southeast Asian Studies. 1988.

"Guarantee of a Minimum Level of Living in an Islamic State" in *Distributive Justice and Need Fulfillment an Islamic Economy*, Munawar Iqbal (ed.) Leicester, U.K, The Islamic Foundation, 1988.

"Sources of Islamic Jurisprudence" in *Management and Development of Awqaf Properties*, Hasmat Basar (ed.) Jeddah, IRTI, Islamic Development Bank, 1987.

"Public Expenditure in an Islamic State" in *Economic Journal* (Government College, Lahore) Vol. XIX, Nos. 1 & 2, 1986.

"Banking and Monetary Policies in Islamic Economics" Faisal Islamic Bank, Sudan. English Series No. 2. (1983).

"Restructuring the Study of Economics in Muslim Universities" in Ismail R. Al-Faruqi and Abdullah Omar Nasseef, eds., Social and Natural Sciences: The Islamic Perspective, (Sevenoaks, Kent: Hodder and Stoughton : King Abdulaziz University, Jeddah, 1981).

"Jamaat-e-Islami in Secular India" *Aligarh Law Society Review*, (1971).

An Overview of Contemporary Islamic Finance in the Light of *Maqāsid al-Sharīah* (Objectives of Islamic *Sharī'a*)[1]

This chapter will attempt to critically examine contemporary economic thought and practices focusing on practical issues. For convenience and due to its importance, we have chosen the world of finance for this analysis. First, some fundamental aspects of finance will be presented, followed by an exploration of the differences between the situation in the early centuries of Islam and the present. Future trends will also be discussed. The chapter will then review efforts being made to reorganize Islamic finance in the modern era. In the light of this review, the challenges and problems faced will be considered, and the role of returning to the *Maqāsid al-Sharī'ah* in addressing these issues will be examined.

[1] Mohammad Nejatullah Siddiqi's, *Maqasid-e-Shariat* (revised edition, 2017) chapter no. 6 titled, "*Maqasid-e-Shariah ki Roushni mein Muasir Islami Maaliyaat kaa Jaiza*" translated by Mohammad Ahmadullah Siddiqi and Mufti Barkatullah.

Finance

It is well understood that producing wealth—through agricultural products, industrial goods, educational services, healthcare and other activities—is essential for sustaining life. Since no individual can produce everything they need or desire on their own, exchange becomes necessary. Bartering goods was cumbersome and time-consuming, leading to the use of money. The production process takes time, and during that period, the factors of production involved need to be compensated, and raw materials must be purchased.

Finance refers to the act of investing money in the organization of the production process. It also applies to the capital that a businessperson acquires to cover expenses, which may come from personal savings or from others. When this occurs directly between the saver and the businessperson, it is referred to as direct finance. When an intermediary is involved between the saver and the user of the capital, it is called indirect finance.

In the early stages of human civilization, direct finance was common, but as populations, products, and production times grew, indirect finance became more prevalent. In fact, direct finance shares some of the same drawbacks as bartering, being cumbersome and time-consuming (BusinessWeek, 2006, p.64)

Conversely, society benefits when savers entrust their savings to intermediaries and businesses seek capital through these intermediaries. This saves time and facilitates access to the necessary amount of finance.

Just as the use of money contributed significantly to human progress and economic prosperity, finance, especially indirect finance, has also played a vital role. Through financial intermediation, human capabilities, factors of production, financial resources, and development opportunities are utilized more effectively, ensuring that none of them are wasted. In addition to its primary function of transferring excess wealth from its owners to productive enterprises, financial intermediation also provides other valuable services, which will be discussed later.

Credit

The provision of finance is often described as the provision of credit, as finance usually involves lending cash or providing goods on credit. One of the key functions of finance is to bring together individuals and institutions to share the burden of uncertainty and risk in business. Often, the risks in business are so great that one individual cannot bear them alone, hence when multiple people or institutions participate in financing a business, they can collectively shoulder the risk.

In modern times, certain business activities require vast amounts of capital to be invested over long periods of time, and the outcomes are often uncertain. Financial corporations make these ventures possible by selling millions of shares, distributing the risk across many people. The market for shares allows anyone to buy and sell shares, which means no one must lock their money into a risky venture for an extended period. Moreover, in case of a business failure, the loss is spread over so many people that it becomes easier to withstand. As humanity advances, this aspect of finance—risk-sharing—continues to develop, bringing individuals and institutions together to face uncertainty and risk. Successful financial intermediation requires more than just offering finance and related services like risk-sharing. The provision of finance and risk-sharing must be based on justice and compassion so that the negative effects of uncertainty, which cannot be precisely calculated, can be borne collectively.

Additionally, the poor, underprivileged, and those unable to participate in the productive process should not be entirely excluded from its benefits. Conventional finance is highly deficient in this regard. Under the influence of capitalist ideology and neoclassical economic theory, individuals focus solely on profit-making. They see it as neither appropriate nor feasible to factor in social justice or societal welfare when making business decisions.

Consequently, the responsibility of protecting public interest from the negative impacts of individual decisions falls on the state, which often tries to regulate financial activities. However, capitalist philosophy and its accompanying economics generally discourage state regulation. In recent decades, awareness of the harmful effects of this approach has grown, and various movements have emerged that emphasize the consideration of collective interests and ethical values in financial and business decisions, such as Ethical Investment and Socially Responsible Investment (SRI). A study of human history provides valuable lessons in this regard, although we cannot do full justice to it here.

However, two points are worth noting. First, economic progress has largely depended on the widespread provision of finance and the efficient functioning of financial intermediation. Periods in history where this was lacking saw economic progress come to a halt. Agrarian and feudal societies bear witness to this fact. Second, economic development based on an unjust and compassionless financial system ultimately became a curse for humanity. Historical examples of commercial societies show that those relying on interest-based loans flourished for a shorter time compared to systems based on partnership or profit-sharing (such as Mudarabah), as seen in Mediterranean trade between the 12th and 14th centuries. (Goitein, 1967, v 1)

The System of Finance in Islamic History

From the 7th to the 10th century CE, covering the first four centuries of Islamic history, the human economy was divided into three sectors: agriculture, industry (craftsmanship) , and trade. Financial support for individuals involved in these activities was provided by those who had surplus wealth and sought to generate more income through it. Historically financial transactions between wealthy individuals and business operators were typically based on the following models:

- *Salam*: Advance payment for agricultural production
- *Istisna'*: Advance purchase of industrial goods
- Loan: Provision of cash for a specified period
- *Shirkah* (Partnership): Partnership where both parties share profit and risk
- *Mudarabah* (Profit-sharing): A partnership where one party provides capital, and the other provides labor, with profit-sharing between them
- *Muzara'ah and Musaqat*: Agricultural and irrigation partnerships
- *Ijarah* (Leasing): Leasing of production factors such as land, transportation, and irrigation animals.
- Supply on credit, meaning the supply of required items on credit:

Trade credit is perhaps one of the oldest forms of financing. The difference between the above-mentioned credit and trade credit is that the latter was generally known only between large-scale manufacturers or wholesalers and regular traders, while supply on credit was available to both consumers and businesses. A notable point about the supply of required items on credit is that it was not considered objectionable for the credit price to be higher than the price in a cash transaction. No objection to this ancient custom has been reported from the Prophet Muḥammad. This practice continued without restriction under his observation and was rightfully considered as approved by him. Some scholars believe that due to this position, avoiding interest-based transactions did not negatively impact trade expansion in Islamic states. They argue that the difference between credit and cash prices serves the same economic purpose as interest, providing compensation to the lender for the risks associated with the transaction and the time they are deprived of their capital. (Udovitch, 1975, 1-21)

As mentioned above, contracts like *salm*, *istisna'*, and *mudarabah* can also be considered methods of supplying credit, as the term "credit" is not limited to interest-based or non-interest-based loans. Economists apply the term to all methods by which an entity (consumer or business) can acquire the required goods and resources, regardless of the conditions under which they are obtained.

In addition to these contracts, other transactions like *ju'ala* (wage-based contracts), *wakalah* (agency), *kafalah* (guarantee), *hawalah* (debt transfer), *wadi'ah* (deposit), *amanah* (trusteeship), *rahn* (pawn), and *ibzaa'* (merchandising) were also in use. It is not necessary to delve into the details of these contracts here, as they can be easily understood with the help of appropriate books. What is common in all these forms is that through one or more of these contracts, the businessperson ultimately obtains the resources needed to complete the production process before they can sell their products and repay the cost of these resources, as will be discussed further. Even earnest money (*arabun*) becomes a form of financing. The prohibition of "*Bay' al-Arbun*" (earnest money sales) in a hadith of the Prophet is evidence that this practice was also prevalent in ancient times (*Sunan Ibn Mājah*).

It is important to note that all of these are forms of direct finance. However, over time, historical sources began mentioning "*al-mudarib yudharib*" (a *Mudarib* who provides *mudarabah* capital to another person), which is an indirect form of finance. To the best of our knowledge, this is first mentioned in the fifth Islamic century (eleventh century CE) in *fiqh* books (Siddiqi, 1968, 83-84). However, from the very beginning, *fiqh* references mention a specific issue: if the capital provider permits, the *mudarib* may give the capital received to someone else under *mudarabah*. It is worth investigating when "*al-mudarib yudharib*" became common as a profession or independent business practice. Various financing methods such as *salm*, *istisna'*, *muzara'ah*, etc., were likely used together as needed, resulting in the development of new forms of financial intermediation and indirect financing. It is hoped that further historical research will clarify the situation.

Now we need to examine the relationship between these financing methods that were prevalent in the early Islamic centuries, and the risks and uncertainties associated with production-related business. Only after this review can we understand the reforms Islam introduced to the pre-Islamic methods of financing.

It is important to note that the value of a financing method has two aspects:

1. Efficiency, and
2. Fairness.

Islam's reforms in pre-Islamic financing methods aimed to improve these two aspects, though it prioritized justice over efficiency. Where necessary, Islam accepted some reduction in efficiency for the sake of justice.

The most significant reform Islam introduced was the prohibition of interest on loans. There is extensive literature on the wisdom of this prohibition. Rather than repeating or summarizing it, we will move forward by simply reminding that the aim was both to eliminate injustice and ensure better efficiency (El-Gamal, 1999, 29-40)

In *salam*, it was made mandatory for the quantity of the purchased goods and the time of supply to be known and fixed. The same is true for *istisna'*. The general principle is that, as far as possible, vagueness and unknown factor (lack of precise information) in transactions should be avoided, as these lead to disputes. In fact, situations may arise where each party feels that they have been wronged. When the situation is unclear to both parties, they cannot engage in the transaction with peace of mind, which may reduce efficiency.

All these types of partnerships sought to reduce ambiguity and uncertainty. When transactions are conducted based on full knowledge, and the prices, goods, and their characteristics are clearly defined, people work wholeheartedly, and no one feels that they are being wronged. In other words, ambiguity in transactions negatively affects efficiency and creates doubts in the minds of the parties about possible injustice. Therefore, in partnerships and *mudarabah*, it is essential to know how much ownership each partner holds and to clearly determine the ratio of profit distribution among the partners. In Mecca's commercial environment, partnerships, *muzara'ah*, and *musaqat* were also common. Many hadiths of the Prophet Muḥammad emphasized the need to keep *mudarabah*, *muzara'ah*, and *musaqat* free from ambiguity, unknown factor, and indeterminacy, and to establish them on fair foundations. There is no need to go into the details of these issues here, as they can easily be studied in the appropriate books. However, one must keep in mind that it is impossible to guarantee that any specific financing method will never be used for exploitation and injustice.

That is why Prophet Muḥammad forbade taking undue advantage of a buyer's duress and dire need (*Sunan Abu-Dawud*, # 3382). He made the purity of intention and the goodness of purpose the foundation of the correct Islamic method (*Sahih al-Bukhari*, #1). Now, if someone cunningly crosses all these boundaries and adopts unjust methods, government intervention and regulation will become necessary. Thus, in Islamic history; such examples could be found in the books on *hisbah* (Islamic doctrine of accountability). There are several examples of regulation and government oversight regarding contracts with unjust terms, such as partnership (*shirkah*), profit-sharing (*mudarabah*), sharecropping (*muzara'ah*), advance payment (*salam*), commissioned production (*istisna'*), lease (*ijarah*), etc. Renting existed of animals of transportation, residential houses, and, in some cases, land was permitted. The issue of giving land on fixed rent for agricultural purposes is disputed. However, where renting is permissible, the terms of rent and duration should be clear. According to researchers who believe that the Prophet forbade giving land for farming on fixed rent, the reason is that if, for any reason, such as a lack of rainfall, there is no crop production, then charging rent for the land would be an injustice (because the land itself does not produce anything. Moreover, the farmer, even in the case of no production, would avoid using the land due to the responsibility of paying rent, which would affect productivity).

In this regard, we see that, like other financing methods, the regulations imposed on the provision of productive factors on rent aim to establish justice and enhance performance. In the organization of productive businesses, when borrowing raw materials or factors of production, it was considered necessary to ensure that the price and the time of payment were clearly determined. The same condition applies to trade credit, which was common between wholesalers and retailers. As for the price, it was left to mutual agreement.

In the current methods of finance, Islamic reforms also aim to avoid uncertainty (*Gharar*). *Gharar* refers to the risk that arises due to a lack of information or inability to control the environment. This lack or absence of information can pertain to the nature, quantity, price, time of payment, time of delivery, etc., of the goods under transaction. Due to this lack or absence of certainty In this regard, the risk of loss increases for either party. In such a case, engaging in a transaction often results in injustice to one of the parties involved. Since most economic transactions are based on estimates about the future, some degree of *Gharar* (uncertainty) is usually present. If it is minimal and the loss (or gain) resulting from this risk is also small, it can be overlooked.

However, in cases of significant *gharar*, transactions are not allowed. This principle applies to a type of exchange that is inherently connected to real goods and services in such a way that it cannot be avoided. As for pure *gharar*, which has no connection to any real exchange but exists solely for the purpose of gambling, it is prohibited. Gambling or "*maysir*" in Qur'anic terminology is not a productive activity. In other words, it is a zero-sum game that merely transfers wealth from one party to another without adding any value to society's overall prosperity.

Alongside these reforms and regulations, a major goal of Islamic reforms has been to safeguard the overall welfare of humanity. Collective interest is to be prioritized over the promotion of individual interests. Thus, in some cases, Islam has prohibited traders from engaging in actions that they would ordinarily be permitted to do. An example of this is the prohibition of *talaqqi jilb*, which is the practice of going out of town to meet traders bringing (mostly agricultural) goods to town and trying to make deals with them, and the prohibition of hoarding foodstuffs, or '*ihtikar*.' For details, see the book, "*Al-*

Mausooah Al-Fiqhiyah (The Encyclopedia of Islamic Jurisprudence) published by the Ministry of Awqaf, Kuwait in 1982.

Another example in the field of finance is the prohibition of combining loan and sale contracts in a single contract. The Messenger of Allah ﷺ said: "It is not permissible to combine a loan and a sale in one contract)." (*Jami` at-Tirmidhi*, #1234). As noted above, along with justice, benevolence is also a part of the Islamic value system. Human life cannot be balanced on justice and fairness alone, as there are always some weak and destitute people in society who may not have anything to offer but still have the right to receive something. Furthermore, the vast uncertainty that surrounds our environment (such as weather changes, fluctuations in human tastes and temperament, new technological innovations, and political upheavals (for which no one can be held responsible, nor can anyone control them) necessitates not only justice but also the provision of benevolence to collectively address their consequences. One example of this in the context of Islamic financial regulations is the following verse of the Qur'an: "And if the debtor is in difficulty, then [let there be] postponement until [a time of] ease. But if you remit it as charity, that is better for you, if you only knew." (Qur'an, 2:280; Ahmad, 2010, 69). This is a significant difference between the Islamic financial system and the capitalist financial system. The capitalist system leaves benevolence entirely at the discretion of individuals, whereas Islam makes it an integral part of its system at both individual and collective levels. In the above verse, the forgiving of a loan is left to the discretion of the lender, but in the case of the debtor's hardship, the law mandates the postponement of repayment, which can be enforced through the courts.

This was our brief review of the methods of providing finance in the early period of Islamic history and how Islamic reforms purified them from injustice and inefficiency and adorned them with benevolence to make them fit for a moral society. We have seen that it was considered essential to cleanse transactions of deception, uncertainty, and indeterminacy as far as possible. To justify a transaction, mutual consent was not considered sufficient; it had to be evaluated based on collective welfare, and efforts were made to enhance its ethical quality. If a transaction affected not only a few individuals but the interests of the entire society, it was considered a matter of public policy, and the expected benefits and harms or the balance of advantages and disadvantages were used as criteria for allowing or prohibiting it, as is evident from the examples of '*Ihtikar*' (hoarding) and '*Talaqqi Jilb*.

Provision of Finance through Complex Methods and Their Regulation

With the expansion and development of the economy, some methods became prevalent in Islamic societies, which were not mentioned during the prophetic era. Some of these are as follows:

1. *Jahabeza*—Account Auditing
2. *Suftaja* a crucial, negotiable financial instrument used in the early and medieval Islamic world (roughly from the 7th century onwards, peaking in the Abbasid period). It functioned as a bill of exchange, letter of credit, or travelers' check.
3. *Bay' Al-Arboon* (Down Payment), which was also mentioned during the Prophetic era.
4. *Saraf*—Money Exchange.

Though these methods have different characteristics and functions, their commonality relevant to our topic is that they provide or obtain cash flow for running businesses. Their historical significance parallels the rise of banking in Italy and

Europe. Below is some detail:

Suftaja

Suftaja is a type of promissory note. For instance, Zaid has some wealth in City A, but he wants to use it in City B. Umar has the same type of wealth in City B. Zaid gives his wealth to Umar, who provides him with a written note that allows Zaid to present it to Umar's agent in City B to receive the wealth there. The benefit to Zaid aside, Umar, for the duration between receiving and paying (which could be a long time in ancient periods), is able to use the wealth for profitable business. In other words, whoever deals in issuing *Suftaja* could easily engage in providing finance. As will be explained later, *sarrafs* (money changers), whose main job was currency exchange, also began issuing *suftajas.* Thus, *sarrafis* and *suftaja* issuers emerged as small-scale bankers.

Bay' Al-Arboon (Down Payment)

In the Indian subcontinent, this transaction is known as *bayana.* Instead of completing the purchase, the buyer gives a small portion of the agreed price to the owner and a time is set between them. If the buyer completes the payment within the agreed period, then the deal is finalized. Otherwise, if the deal is cancelled, the seller keeps the amount paid by the buyer. Although a Hadith has been narrated about this, it is considered weak.

The connection of *bay' al-arboon* with finance is that a businessman who collects down payments from buyers on a large scale can invest the accumulated cash in business, even though the assets are still in his ownership. Additionally, if the right to purchase by down payment could be transferred to another, a new market could be created.

Saraf (Money Exchange) and Jahabeza

Saraf refers to the exchange of one currency (like *Dirhams*) with another (like *Dinars*). Mentioned in Hadith, *Saraf* refers to large-scale transactions where a *saraf* holds different currencies and provides them to those who need them, earning profit through this exchange. This business is mentioned in early Islamic sources, though there is no documented evidence that it was common in Mecca or Medina during the prophetic era. The *saraf 's* relationship with finance is indirect. a *saraf* holding multiple currencies could potentially offer loans or provide financing on some other basis. if a *saraf* delivers the required currency and agrees to receive the equivalent later, this also constitutes a loan, meeting the definition of finance. Historically, *Saraf* played a major role in the beginnings of banking.

Although the business of *jahabeza* (account auditors) and *saraf* often overlapped, one could exist without the other. The *jahabeza* are mentioned in Islamic history during the Abbasid era, where in 913 AD (300 AH), the Caliph established a separate office for them, the *Diwan Al-Jahabeza* (Office of the auditors). For more details, see (Chachi, 2005, 165). Over time, the Jahabeza also took over issuing *suftaja*, originally initiated by the *sarrafs*. *suftaja* were also known as *sukuk*, a term that later evolved into "cheque." as the use of *sukuk* increased, the business of *jahabeza* expanded further.

As noted earlier, in ancient methods of financial dealings, Islamic reforms focused on two main aspects, namely fairness and efficiency. The regulation of relatively complex methods after the prophetic era was imbued with this same spirit. The purpose of the regulations regarding *surf* (currency exchange), as mentioned in Hadith, was to keep the transaction free from *riba* (usury), which Allah ﷻ forbade. Researchers have pointed out that these regulations ensure better efficiency as well. El-

Gamal, op. cit., 29-40.

Steps were taken to prevent financial transactions from being tainted by unfair practices, such as interest, gambling, fraud, coercion, the sale of distress, hoarding, rigged auctions, deceit, and the lack of proper knowledge leading to disputes or harm. These regulations were necessary for fairness and efficiency.

In finance-specific markets, certain additional regulations were enforced. For example, in the exchange of one currency for the same kind (like gold for gold or dollars for dollars), it must be exchanged in equal amounts and hand-to-hand. When the currencies differ (like gold for silver or dollars for pounds), amounts can differ, but the exchange must still be hand-to-hand. These conditions are stipulated in the various Hadith of the Prophet.

The Complex Nature of Transactions

In financial markets, incomplete knowledge and uncertainty are greater than in goods markets. This combination of incomplete knowledge and uncertainty leads to *gharar* (excessive uncertainty). Transactions tainted by *gharar* are prohibited if the uncertainty cannot be controlled. However, minor *gharar* is permissible, while major *gharar* makes the transaction invalid. This topic is complicated, and there is considerable debate among jurists regarding its practical application.

Islamic financial regulations aim to promote fairness, but in certain cases, potential reductions in efficiency are tolerated to maintain justice. This tension between fairness and efficiency is considered on a case-by-case basis by analyzing the individual and collective benefits and harms associated with a transaction. Additionally, these analyses rely on economic theories alongside other fields of study.

Islamic jurisprudence shows that combining otherwise permissible individual transactions can sometimes be prohibited if the combination leads to *riba*, excessive *gharar*, or results in unfair practices. Although such transactions may be permissible individually, their combination or the circumstances in which they occur can violate Islamic principles of fairness. Thus, the permissibility of financial transactions ultimately depends on balancing their benefits and harms and their alignment with Islamic objectives.

In this context, it is also necessary to mention those contracts that are not specific to financial transactions but are related to them and work in conjunction with the methods, some of which have already been mentioned above. contracts like *hawala* (debt transfer), *kafala* (guarantee), *daman* (surety), and *wa'ad* (promise) belong to this category. These contracts are used in non-financial matters as well, and all of them have been in use since ancient times. There is no reason why they could not have been used in conjunction with the above financial transactions. Even in such cases, it was necessary to ensure that transactions were kept free from as many flaws as possible that might lead to injustice or decrease efficiency. Consequently, several regulations were enforced in this regard:

1. There should not be two interdependent transactions at once (i.e., two sales in one transaction),
2. There should be no condition attached to the sale,
3. Both the price and the object of sale should not be deferred (i.e., *Bay' al-Kali bil-Kali* or a sale in which both the payment and the delivery are deferred).

In most cases, these prohibited transactions involve injustice and result in decreased efficiency. This is because such transactions increase indeterminacy or unknown factor (which can lead to disputes), raise *gharar* (excessive uncertainty), and increase the likelihood of fraud, etc. Hence, the jurists, in their discussions on prohibited forms of sales (*bay' al-manhiyya 'anha*), have highlighted these matters. A detailed study of books on Islamic *fiqh* will be useful (Rushd, 1985, 124-333).

The importance of studying these details today lies in the fact that transactions that appear entirely valid and beyond doubt when done separately are sometimes prohibited when combined because they seem to become a means for *riba* (interest), or they lead to such *gharar* (uncertainty) that can be avoided, or they result in fraud or some other kind of injustice. It is also possible that while there may be no doubt about the permissibility of the contracts, the results (perhaps due to changes in circumstances) may not align with public welfare. Naturally, as time and place change, the nature of transactions changes as well. However, it must always be kept in mind that even those transactions that are correct individually or under normal circumstances do not remain acceptable if their combination or specific circumstances lead to violations of justice and fairness, cause injustice and deprivation, or explicitly harm the objectives of Shariah. Since there is no objective measurement for these factors, considerable differences of opinion exist among jurists. We have already discussed earlier how to address such disagreements.

The conclusion of that discussion was that, in such matters, the final decision depends on the assessment of public welfare (*masalih*). It is necessary to estimate what individual and collective benefits are associated with the prevalence of a certain transaction. If there are some potential harms as well, they must be assessed and weighed against the expected benefits. If the benefits outweigh the harms, the transaction may be permitted; otherwise, it is not. We also clarified that, in assessing and evaluating these *masalih* (benefits) and *mafasid* (harms), apart from the science of economics, other intellectual and analytical sciences must also be employed. Furthermore, both microeconomic and macroeconomic analysis will be required. The reality is that the connection of a financial transaction with justice and fairness, or injustice and deprivation, in any era and in any country, and its impact on efficiency and productivity, and the extent to which it aligns with public welfare and the objectives of Shariah, can only be determined after thorough analytical study, extensive examination, and empirical verification.

New Trends in Islamic Finance

So far, the Islamic reforms in the field of finance that we have discussed were implemented during the first four centuries of Islamic history. Now, we will study in some detail the search for Sharia-compliant methods of finance and the Islamic organization of financial markets in the last few decades of the 14th century AH/20th century CE. It would have been ideal if, in this context, we could study the evolution of Islamic finance during the intervening centuries, that is, from the 5th to the 14th century AH. These thousand years are significant because the attention given to Sharia-compliant financial methods and the Islamic organization of financial markets in the last decades of the 14th century AH (the results of which we will study in detail in this chapter) can be seen as a continuation of the entire previous history of Islamic development. Unfortunately, the historical material available from the past thousand years has not been sufficiently researched or examined. The documents from the Ottoman Caliphate in the heart of Islam, Islamic India in the East, especially the Mughal era, and the buried treasures in the *Nawazil* (unprecedented issues) and jurisprudential literature of the Maghreb can reveal the evolution in financial methods in response to changing circumstances.

It is not possible here to review the changes that occurred in the world over the past thousand years, and their impact on the supply and demand of finance and financial methods. Briefly, it can be noted that there was an extraordinary expansion in national, regional, and international trade. In the Middle East context, the backbone of this commercial expansion is considered the trade with India (which historians refer to as the "India Trade," where India includes the entire subcontinent, including present-day Pakistan, Bangladesh, and Burma), which extended from the Red Sea to Sumatra (Goiten, 1968, pp. 328-332). This trade itself was connected to Mediterranean trade. This commercial activity relied on an extensive system of partnerships (Goiten, 1968, p.7) Muslims were also involved in the banking business, with banking in Tunis being in their hands. Around the 5th and 6th centuries AH, financial instruments like *sakk* (checks) and *suftaja* (letters of credit) became more common. The need for their exchange increased, and various jurists permitted their use under certain conditions.

In later centuries, two new financing methods emerged:

1. *Bay' al-wafa* (sale with buy back deals), and
2. *Waqf al-nuqud* (Cash endowments).

In the former, a sale would occur on the condition that the seller could repurchase the item later, receiving back the amount he had initially paid. A residential property, for example, could generate rental income for the buyer for a year, and after a year, the seller would get back the amount he had given, and the property would return to its original owner. In this way, the financier would earn extra income in exchange for the amount given for a year (like how interest-bearing loans worked, which Islam prohibited). Most jurists declared *Bay' al-wafa* impermissible, but some issued fatwas in favour of it. (For more details about *Bay-al-Wafa*, see *Mawsu'ah al-fiqhiyyah*. Vol.9, 1982) The *Majalla* (Ottoman legal code) mentions *Bay' al-*

wafa, indicating that it was quite prevalent during the 18th and 19th centuries CE.

Those who endowed cash for charitable purposes wanted to ensure that the principal amount remained intact and that the profits generated from its investment would be spent on charitable activities. To achieve this, they stipulated that the capital be invested in *mudarabah* at a fixed percentage of profit. Some jurists, considering the charitable objectives and the protection of the principal, allowed this practice. It seems that later on, *waqf al-nuqud* became acceptable for commercial purposes as well, based on these fatwas. Both *bay' al-wafa* and *waqf al-nuqud* were mostly practiced in Turkey. (Cizakca, 2000) There is no evidence of their widespread use in other Islamic regions.

We will not delve here into the jurisprudential debates surrounding these two financing methods, but it is important to note that under certain needs, financing was allowed that yielded a predetermined percentage of profit. Alongside these, other pre-existing methods of finance continued to be practiced.

As trade, particularly maritime trade and international transactions, increased, new methods were adopted to manage risk. Many of these methods were based on mutual cooperation (Rispler-Chaim, 1991, pp.142-155). Between the 14th and 17th centuries CE, a Sufi group on the Malabar coast managed a system of mutual insurance among maritime traders on some ports of the Chinese coast (Rispler-Chaim, 1991, p. 155). The 13th-century AH jurist Ibn 'Abidin al-Shami also discussed insurance. We mention this because in a world filled with risk and uncertainty, insurance and finance cannot be separated from each other.

Revival of Islamic Finance in the Modern Era

In the third decade of the twentieth century, most Muslim-majority countries were under foreign domination, yet movements to break free from colonial rule were gaining momentum in these regions. Alongside the struggle for independence, the question arose: upon what principles should the economies of free Muslim nations be organized? During the second and third decades of the twentieth century, capitalism and socialism were being widely debated worldwide. It was generally assumed that the soon-to-be-independent countries would have to choose between one of the two systems. Consequently, in countries with significant Muslim populations, such as pre-partition India, intellectuals advocating both systems were raising their voices.

In this atmosphere, the famous poet and philosopher Allama Iqbal, who was also well-versed in economics, proclaimed that Islam offers its own economic system, free from the excesses of both capitalism and socialism, and one that could provide greater justice and prosperity. Alongside this, powerful Islamic movements that emerged at that time also promoted the idea that Islam offers a comprehensive way of life. These movements rejected both capitalism and socialism, calling for the adoption of an Islamic economic system. Part of this call included the rejection of interest-based banking and finance, and the promotion of an interest-free banking and financial system based on Islamic principles. Muslim intellectuals and economists played a leading role in advancing this idea.

Some initial frameworks emerged in the fourth decade of the twentieth century, but detailed blueprints for interest-free Islamic banking and finance, supported by economic analysis, began to appear in the fifth and sixth decades (For details refer to, Siddiqi, 1988). In the 1960s, several experiments were conducted to establish interest-free financial institutions in Egypt, Malaysia, India, and Pakistan, and by the 1970s, the establishment of Islamic banks began. Along with this, Islamic insurance companies, Islamic investment companies, and later Islamic mutual funds spread throughout the Muslim world and beyond (For details refer to, Siddiqi, 2004, Chapters. 3, 4, 5, & 6).

In the following pages, we will shed light on the structure of modern Islamic finance and its theoretical and jurisprudential foundations.

Initially, the model for Islamic banking was based on *mudarabah* (profit-sharing investment manager). That is, the public would deposit their savings in Islamic banks, which would then provide these savings to entrepreneurs on a *mudarabah* basis to generate profit. The banks would keep a portion of the profit and give the rest to the depositors. Islamic banks would provide capital to businesses based on profit-sharing. However, in case of losses, the loss would be borne by the depositors. However, the practical implementation took place with this amendment that the Islamic bank would adopt all permissible methods to make the capital obtained from account holders on a *mudarabah* (profit-sharing) basis profitable. These methods included directly engaging in commercial businesses, running industries, purchasing real estate, and renting them out, among others.

But soon, most Islamic banks shifted away from direct, high-risk business activities towards methods that ensured a more secure and predictable profit. This was the method of *bay' al-murabaha* (cost-plus financing). The Islamic bank would buy the required goods for the customer and then sell the goods to the customer at a deferred price with a fixed profit margin. Over time, other financing methods such as *ijarah* (leasing), *istisna* (manufacturing contracts), and *salam* (advance purchase) were also adopted. By the end of the twentieth century, Islamic bonds (*sukuk*) based on these structures were being issued, which played a significant role in popularizing Islamic banking and bringing it closer to the masses.

By the mid-2000s, several hundred Islamic financial institutions were operating globally, managing assets worth more than $300 billion. The number of their customers, their geographical spread, and the range of financial services they offered continued to grow (Iqbal and Molyneux, 2004)

While the early Islamic banking model was indebted to Muslim intellectuals, economists, philosophers, and poets, the credit for bringing it to its current level belongs mainly to the Muslim industrialists and businesspeople who established these Islamic financial institutions, as well as the jurists and Shariah scholars who have been guiding Islamic banks since the last quarter of the twentieth century (Siddiqi, 21 April 2006)

Islamic banking on a large scale began in the last quarter of the twentieth century. A fundamental difference can be observed between the literature of that period and the earlier literature (when the concept of Islamic banking was still being developed). The latter was focused on ensuring that Islamic banks could offer financial services that were as similar as possible to those provided by interest-based banks. However, as the literature evolved, new financial products like *murabaha*, *ijarah muntahia bi tamleek* (lease ending in ownership), and *sukuk* became prominent, leading to a shift from the earlier theoretical frameworks developed in the 1950s and 1960s.

In the earlier period, economists who introduced the concept of Islamic banking had their focus on the Islamic way of life, of which they considered interest-free banking as a part, distinct from the capitalist banking system. Scholars like Dr. Anwar Iqbal Qureshi, Dr. Muhammad Uzair, Dr. Muhammad Abdullah al-Arabi, Professor Isa Abda, and Dr. Mahmoud Abu Saud were not specialized in Islamic jurisprudence (*fiqh*). However, as Muslims, they believed in the prohibition of interest and highlighted its destructive consequences in light of their knowledge of economics. Dr. Muhammad Uzair, for example, proposed a new banking system based on the Islamic principles of partnership and Mudarabah in his 1955 publication (Uzair, 1955). Their literature was echoed in the efforts made to establish Islamic banking and finance on a national level, especially in Pakistan, Iran, and Sudan.

However, the Islamic banks established in the Gulf countries were private ventures. These banks were set up by Muslim businessmen and wealthy individuals whose immediate goal was to make their investments profitable while avoiding forbidden (haram) practices. They also aimed to help the Muslims who avoided dealing with interest-based banks but were searching for legitimate ways to safeguard and profitably use their savings. In these Islamic banks, the role of Islamic jurists (or Shariah scholars) was to assist in their establishment and operation, as seen in the advisory roles played by scholars for Dubai Islamic Bank and Kuwait Finance House. Their focus was on specific issues, which they resolved using detailed Islamic jurisprudential rulings. The rulings of various Shariah boards can be found on the websites of these institutions such as Kuwait Finance House (www.kfh.com), Bank Faisal Sudani (www.fibsudan.com), Dubai Islamic Bank website does not contain fatwas but these could be found at www.harf.com.

However, the comprehensive issues that were the focus of the pioneers of Islamic banking and finance are absent from these fatwas (Islamic rulings). After Pakistan, Iran, and Sudan, countries such as Malaysia, Indonesia, Bahrain, and certain states of the UAE turned their attention to Islamic banking at a national level, opting for the Gulf model rather than those of Iran or Sudan. This model was also adopted by multinational banking corporations, like Citibank and Hong Kong Shanghai Banking Corporation, which entered the field in the last decade of the previous century and are now dominating it.

Formulating a system of interest-free banking that could meet all commercial needs and developing relatively secure and profitable methods for Muslim investors, while resolving the issues faced by these Islamic financial institutions in light of Islamic jurisprudence (*fiqh*) (especially in the Gulf countries, Egypt, and Sudan, from the late 1970s onward), was no small feat. The magnitude of this achievement becomes apparent upon reviewing the vast body of new jurisprudential literature and the thousands of fatwas issued in Arabic and other languages over the past 30 years. According to the author's limited knowledge, no other instance of such large-scale jurisprudential activity in the field of commercial and financial matters can be found in the last thousand years. This activity has sparked a new wave of intellectual movement throughout the Islamic world, benefiting other religious sciences and their teaching, as well as religious seminaries.

Despite acknowledging the unparalleled contributions of contemporary Muslim jurists and Shariah researchers in guiding Islamic financial institutions, it is a fact that their focus remained on the day-to-day issues of these institutions. They did not concentrate on the fundamental issues that distinguish the Islamic system from the capitalist system and their respective financial institutions from each other. Islamic banking and finance are intended to help achieve the objectives of Shariah, as discussed in Islamic literature before Islamic banks were established. However, this approach—issuing *fatwas* based on the objectives of Shariah or evaluating the overall framework against this criterion—did not become prevalent among these jurists and Shariah researchers.

It is not possible here to delve into the historical reasons for this approach. However, two facts demand a shift in this methodology:

1. The first fact is that the Imams of Islamic jurisprudence, such as Abu Hanifa and Malik bin Anas, would carefully consider the consequences of any method before endorsing it. Their decisions were based on public welfare. This is the nature of Abu Hanifa's principle of *Istihsan* (juridical preference) and Malik's principle of *masalih mursala* (public interest). The mere validity of a contract was not sufficient to endorse a method whose harm outweighed its benefit.
2. The second fact is that, over the past 30 years, the focus on micro issues and the fatwas focused on solving everyday problems have shaped Islamic banking and finance in such a way that, in terms of consequences, it is bringing us to the same place where interest-based banking and finance has brought humanity.

In the following pages, we will elaborate on this summary and present some suggestions for reform. In today's world, it is essential to have knowledge of modern sciences, particularly economics, to assess the outcomes and consequences of any investment method or financial practice. Generally, the law only ensures that the transactions between the parties are just. What impact do specific measures have on the welfare of society as a whole? What are the collective welfare requirements in the field of investment? These questions cannot be answered solely by the law.

Take, for example, the case of loans. The law will only examine whether the loan transaction is based on the free will of the parties, without fraud or coercion. However, whether the continuous increase in the total amount of loans in a society is good or bad, or whether the growing external debt of a country is harmful, are questions that cannot be answered by law or detailed jurisprudential principles alone. For this, economic analysis is essential. In fact, some political, social, and psychological aspects of the problem will also need to be considered, as the classical Islamic jurisprudence referred to these under the concept of public interest (*masalih aamah*). When it comes to financial matters, these public interests refer to the economic, political, social, and psychological effects that result from these transactions.

We argue that, following the footsteps of the Imams of Islamic jurisprudence, today's jurists and Shariah researchers must compare the benefits and harms associated with any financial matter before issuing a *fatwa* in its favor.

Our second point is that this comparison is not taught in traditional religious seminaries, nor are the related sciences included in their curriculum. It is also not possible for every jurist to gain expertise in these sciences. How to resolve this issue in an era of academic specialization is a separate question. But first, it must be established that expertise in religious sciences alone is not sufficient to weigh financial matters in terms of benefits and harms. Approving new financial instruments and methods as being in line with Islamic teachings and endorsing their legitimacy and widespread adoption is beyond the capacity of the current Shariah scholars or Shariah boards. A comprehensive method must be adopted to meet this need.

It might be asked, if it was possible for Imam Malik and Imam Abu Hanifa to weigh financial matters on the scales of benefits and harms, why is it being said that it is impossible for today's jurists? The answer lies in the differences between the world (especially the economic world) of a thousand years ago and the world of today, with its commercial and financial complexities. On the one hand, economic matters have become so complicated that understanding them requires knowledge of economics and other sciences. On the other hand, today's jurists do not have as broad a scope of knowledge and practice as the leading Imams of jurisprudence schools had.

Islamic finance has travelled a path from *murabaha to tawarruq* over the past few decades, and it is not possible to thoroughly evaluate every detail of this journey here. Fortunately, ample literature exists on the different stages of this journey. (Siddiqi, 2006).

Most of this literature reflects a jurisprudential perspective focusing on detailed matters. Keeping this in mind, we will not delve into the detailed jurisprudential aspects of these financial instruments and methods but will instead discuss their broader implications related to public benefits and harms.

Murabaha, Ijarah Muntahia Bittamleek (lease to own), parallel *Salam, Sukuk,* and *Tawarruq* all have one thing in common: they result in the creation of debt securities, although the nature of these securities may differ. In some cases, these debt securities are backed by real assets, such as land, property, raw materials, products, or agricultural goods, while in other cases, they are not. Our position is that the proliferation of debt securities not backed by real assets is harmful. *Qard Hasan*, or interest-free loans, are an exception because they are temporary and non-tradeable, and there is no prospect of profit in such transactions.) We believe that while debt securities may offer certain benefits on an individual level, their negative impact on society is far greater and more significant. Therefore, financial instruments and methods that lead to the proliferation of debt securities not backed by real assets should be prohibited. An example of this in contemporary Islamic finance is *Tawarruq* [see next], although some other methods can also lead to similar outcomes.

Tawarruq

As mentioned in the previous chapter, the addition of *tawarruq* (Obaidullah, 2005) in contemporary Islamic finance practice is relatively new. Some Islamic banks and financial institutions have started providing cash to borrowers through this method. Through *tawarruq*, account holders can also be promised a fixed percentage of profit. The *mutawarriq*, i.e., the cash-seeking customer, buys goods from the bank on credit and then sells those goods to a third party at a price lower than their purchase price to obtain cash. In the end, the customer receives cash, in exchange for which they must repay a larger sum of money after the predetermined credit period ends. Similarly, the bank buys something from the account holder on credit and then sells it to a third party at a price lower than its purchase price to get cash. The cash received by the account holder will be greater than the amount the bank received from the sale of the item, once the credit period is over. As a result of this, Islamic banks that follow the practice of Tawarruq open such accounts where deposited amounts are given a fixed profit after a specific period. At the same time, they also lend cash (as a loan) to those seeking cash, with a promise of repayment at a fixed increased amount after a specified period.

The Islamic Bank of Britain is at the forefront of practicing *tawarruq*. This practice was initially started by the National Commercial Bank in Saudi Arabia, along with some other Gulf-based Islamic financial institutions. Each *tawarruq* results in a new loan being created. Moreover, the amount of the loan generated through *tawarruq* is always greater than the cash received by the *mutawarriq*. Thus, in the above-mentioned first example, the customer, and in the second example, the bank, will receive less cash than the loan amount that will inevitably have to be repaid after the specified period (for the customer in the first example and for the bank in the second example).

In the following pages, we will analyses the effects of these two phenomena (the creation of new loans and the loan amount being greater than the cash received through it) on the level of economic contraction. But before going into details, as a point of reflection, we want to examine the potential outcomes and role of these loan certificates that will emerge and spread because of the implementation of *tawarruq*. Whether you look at the conventional financial market or the Islamic financial market, these certificates are repeatedly exchanged, and due to multiple speculative trades based on guesswork, they lose their connection to the real assets and trades they were initially linked to. The customer may have taken the loan to purchase something and invest it in a business, or the bank may have given the money received through the account holder to someone who would invest it in a productive business. But in the debt market, these considerations become a thing of the past. As a result of the transactions in this market, the issuance of certificates continues to expand until we have before us an inverted pyramid of financial instruments. The base of this pyramid is grounded in real assets, but the rest of the structure is paper based. It is important to note that the arena of *tawarruq* is now the money market, not the real market. The manners and methods of this market, the signals of the prices settled within it, and the economic significance of these signals are very different from those of the real market.

The Role of Loans in the Human Economy

The impact of an increase in debt on the economy depends on its use and outcome. Merely increasing debt is not synonymous with an increase in overall societal wealth. If the borrowed debt was used for wealth production, the result will be one of three possibilities: the newly created wealth (when measured in money) because of the loan and its use will either be equal to the debt amount, less than it, or more than it. Only in the last case can the increase in debt be considered a beneficial social process. In the first case, society has lost nothing, but in the second case, where the wealth created from the productive use of the loaned amount is less than the amount used, society's overall wealth will have decreased. As for the borrower, they will have to repay the loan by adding something from their previously existing wealth. In other words, only the lenders will benefit, as they will receive more of the already existing wealth.

The above outcome is unjust. The environment in which productive processes occur does not guarantee that the wealth invested in a productive process will necessarily and always result in a larger amount of wealth being produced. Since this is the case, there is no justification for guaranteeing the repayment of capital with an increase to those providing capital for productive processes. Additionally, debt-based financing causes inefficiency in organizing productive processes, meaning it results in poor performance. To achieve high performance, capital should be invested in the project expected to yield the highest returns, with the hope that the return on investment will be higher than that associated with other possible and available projects. However, the focus of the lender is on the financial creditworthiness and existing payment capacity of the borrower. If these are reliable, the repayment of the loan is certain. Loans are granted based on creditworthiness, while the project to be financed is given only secondary consideration, as the failure of the project does not affect the legal obligation of the loan repayment. In an economy dominated by debt financing, the use of productive capital will be inefficient. Excellent productive projects will remain unexecuted because their proponents lack high financial credit, while unworthy ones will easily get capital due to their high creditworthiness based on previously existing wealth. It is a common observation that nature has not based the distribution of intelligence and brilliance (on which high performance in business organization and the introduction of excellent projects depend) on the ownership of previous wealth and financial credit.

The two defects of debt financing (unjust and inefficient) have been well-explained by writers on Islamic finance, so there is no need to go into further detail here (Siddiqi, 2004). However, it is appropriate to emphasize one point. Giving a sum of money in the present with the promise of receiving a larger amount in the future is unjust because uncertainty is an inherent characteristic of the future. The borrower must convert the loaned amount into goods, services, raw materials, etc., to carry out a productive process in the time given. Upon completion of the productive process, the produced goods or products must be sold to obtain cash, which can then be used to repay the lender. However, there is no guarantee that this cash will exceed the amount originally borrowed.

In an economy dominated by debt-based financing, a debt market inevitably emerges. The life of a certificate created because of any loan lasts until the repayment of the loan. However, there is no reason why the lender should leave this certificate unused during this period. In addition to the traditional uses of debt certificates, in this era of financial innovation, new ways of utilizing these certificates are being discovered. (Iqbal, 2007). In summary, due to the potential uses of debt certificates, demand for them is created, and the interaction of supply and demand determines prices, thus fueling the debt market. As the economy grows, the debt market also expands, and demand for debt certificates increases further. Like any other market, speculation is common in the debt market, but the speculative nature of the debt market closely resembles gambling (Minskey, 1986). This is due to the specific nature of debt-based securities. Speculation is also possible in the market for goods and services, but there, speculation has some objective basis, such as stocks of goods, orders placed for imported goods, or enrolments in institutions preparing workers for related services. Moreover, goods and services often maintain a certain standard.

However, in debt certificates, such standardization is rare. Clearly, a debt certificate is only reliable if the repayment of the loan mentioned in it can be trusted. The value of a loan or its certificate is determined by numerous factors, such as the borrower's creditworthiness, the direction of the loan's use, the time of repayment, the place of repayment, and others. The information and estimates about these factors are not always consistent. Who is making the estimate, and when is it being made? This is of great significance (Stiglits, 2003). Since these estimates lack objective grounding, they are heavily influenced by news, rumors, and stories fabricated by the debt market players themselves. Cunning players manipulate the prices through these means and make profits by buying and selling the securities at the right time. Speculation in the debt market causes instability in the economy, which negatively affects its performance.

Disconnection Between the Market for Goods and Services and the Financial Market

As soon as the door to profit and trade in debt and debt-based securities opens, the map of human economics changes from one where trade is limited to actual goods and their ownership documents. The volume of trade it promises easily grows because the increase in goods and services is limited to the productive resources available at any given time, but the supply of new promises only requires some people to be willing to accept those promises. Moreover, like other traders, debt traders also begin to operate on credit. Further, loans are taken to trade loans. It is in the interest of debt traders that the credit market expands and flourishes, as they are not concerned with the fulfilment of promises or the repayment of loans, but with the profits that can be earned from manipulating debt-based securities. In a debt-based financial system, a significant number of shrewd individuals engage in this manipulation, which, like gambling, becomes a zero-sum game. In addition to business skills, other resources are also invested in the debt business. Not only does this result in the wastage of valuable productive capacities of human society, but it also exacerbates the inequality in the distribution of income and wealth.

Modern production processes take time, and organizing them requires pooling capital from many investors, so it is not surprising that during this financing process, documents consisting of promises and commitments are created. In normal circumstances, each document would be linked to real goods, services, or assets. In comparison to documents related to partnership, *mudarabah*, and sharecropping, there would be raw materials, goods for trade, or human labor, seeds, irrigation, etc., upon which the business depends. Similarly, in the case of leasing, *murabaha, salam*, and *istisna*, there would be buildings, machinery, grains, and products acquired through the contract. However, this does not necessarily apply to cash borrowed on loan. A debt certificate or debt-based securities are backed by nothing more than a promise to repay a sum of money. Even if real assets are acquired with the borrowed money, they have no direct connection to the debt document. If the lender has taken some collateral from the borrower, that's a different matter, but the debt certificate itself does not grant ownership rights over the goods or equipment purchased with the borrowed funds. Thus, when this debt document is transferred multiple times, it remains tied only to the promise. What was the money spent on? That record of origin fades away. Who initially took the loan? It becomes irrelevant. The credit market turns into one of anonymous borrowers and anonymous lenders. One of the defining features of the modern credit market is its anonymity and infinite nature.

Therefore, we can rightly say that in an economy based on debt financing, the financial structure becomes independent of the real economic structure, with its own distinct existence. It cannot be said that there is no connection between the financial structure and the real economy, but this connection is neither as direct nor as strong as it would be without debt financing. Experts argue that based on a low level of real assets, an artificial mountain of debt-based securities is erected. Instead of changes in the real economy (production, employment, supply, and demand) caused by factors like population, preferences, energy sources, and technology leading to changes in the financial structure, changes in the financial structure cause shifts in the real economy. As mentioned earlier, speculative gambling plays a major role in the changes within the debt-dominated financial structure. The shifts in the financial superstructure are driven not by actual or anticipated changes in the real economy but by the guesses financial players make about each other's estimates. As a result, the influence of these profit-maximizing financial players continues to grow.

A distinctive feature of the Islamic financial system is that it keeps the financial structure connected to and subordinate to the real economic sector. However, this quality is being undermined by the prevalence of *tawarruq* and the consequent spread of debt-based securities. Despite the differences in Islamic jurisprudence regarding the sale of debt (*bay' al-dayn*), the market for debt-based securities has flourished. Where the sale of debt has not been permitted, a workaround has been found: if a collection of securities is mostly comprised of ownership-based certificates (which are unanimously considered permissible) and only a minority are debt-based certificates (whose sale is deemed impermissible by most jurists), the entire collection is allowed to be traded. (Obaidullah, 2005 & Rafe, 2005)). As a result, it has become common practice to include a small portion of receivables-backed *Murabaha* certificates alongside ijara and Salam-based sukuk. Private Islamic financial institutions, as well as the Islamic Development Bank, have issued such sukuk containing these receivables. (Iqbal, 2007 & IDB, 2004). These Islamic bonds, like contemporary market bonds, on the one hand, promise the holder a fixed return at a specified time, and on the other, their prices fluctuate based on supply and demand.

Taking on debt is a significant responsibility. While personal needs are one thing, taking out a loan for a productive business should only be done when the borrower has a strong belief that the benefits from investing the loan in the business will be sufficient to repay the loan with something left over. The results of future-oriented businesses cannot be guaranteed, but there is hope that both the lender and borrower will exercise caution to avoid unbearable losses if expectations are not met. In the past, measures like demanding collateral, imposing fines for late payments, and socially ostracizing those who could repay but refused to do so were employed to improve the situation. The same approach was taken with governments and international institutions borrowing money. However, in the last few decades, the situation has changed. Consumers, businesses, national governments, and international institutions have been led to believe that by borrowing now, they can increase their productive capacity enough to repay the loan while still improving their standard of living, growing their businesses, running national development projects, or helping third-world countries advance.

When oil prices rose in the 1970s, there was an increase in liquidity in financial markets. To put this excess liquidity to work, a method of recycling was adopted. With the services of large global multinational banks and the mediation of new international financial and development institutions like the World Bank and IMF, a flood of loans was directed towards developing countries. National governments started spending beyond their tax revenues, leading them into debt. Consumers were offered credit card facilities, and traders were enticed to dream of expanding beyond their means. Eventually, the credit market became saturated with consumer debt, particularly mortgage loans, government bonds, domestic business and financial institution bonds, foreign government and private sector debt securities, and more.

In Islam, the prohibition of interest has greatly limited the role of debt in the economy. Since it is forbidden to demand more money in the future than was lent today, regardless of the loan's purpose or the identity of the parties involved, there is no possibility in an Islamic economy for debt transactions to become a profitable business, for a credit market to develop, for its volume to grow continuously, or for it to dominate the market for goods and services. However, the spread of *tawarruq* has broken this barrier. As a result, Islamic financial institutions, like other interest-based financial institutions, have turned to the credit market to find profitable uses for their excess liquidity, ensuring they remain competitive in profitability.

Monetary Policy in a Debt-Based Economy

In a debt-based economy, the creation of new money and the adjustment of the total amount of money, as needed, occurs through an increase or decrease in loans. Whether it is the high-powered money issued by the central bank of a country or the money created through commercial banks (derived deposits), or bank money, the basis of both is debt. For example, when the central bank of a country creates new money against the government's promise of repayment, the supply of high-powered money increases, and when a commercial bank grants a new loan to a borrower, the equivalent amount of new bank money comes into existence. (Siddiqi, 2002). As the supply of new money increases in the economy due to the growing population and the need for transactions in increasing production, the volume of debt in the economy also increases. As we mentioned earlier, with the rising amount of debt in the economy, the trend of speculation, akin to gambling, and as a result, instability and inequality in the distribution of wealth and income increase. All these things are against the principles and objectives of Islam. Therefore, Islamic economists agree on the need to bring an alternative to the debt-based monetary system that is free from the above-mentioned flaws.

In the Islamic monetary system, the expansion in the money supply should be linked to the real economy, that is, the needs of the market for goods and services. The best way to achieve this is to base the creation of money on investment rather than debt. (Mossin, 1973). As we have detailed elsewhere, new money is also created because of investment based on *mudarabah* (profit-sharing) (Siddiqi, 2002, Chapter Five) and the same applies to other financing methods besides loans. However, the promotion of *tawarruq* in contemporary Islamic finance has severely hindered the progress towards an Islamic monetary system. A new monetary system must be implemented and tested nationally, not within the private sector. As far as we know, this experiment has only been initiated in Sudan. (El Hiraika, 2004)

At the beginning of the discussion on *tawarruq*, we noted that the amount of debt in a transaction is always more than the cash provided in exchange. Regardless of how the transaction is completed, at the aggregate level, this mandatory increase has the effect of making economic expansion, or growth, a necessity. If the new wealth generated by the use of debt-based capital does not exceed the amount of capital borrowed, the system, i.e., the financing of the production process through debt, cannot last long because in this system, the profits of entrepreneurs who increase the wealth of society by making capital productive do not begin until after the payment of the capital and its interest. The survival and continuity of this system depend on continuous expansion and growth in the human economy.

The answer to the question of whether this can continue indefinitely cannot be given here. The current system of wealth production overlooks environmental limits and pollution tolerance to sustain mandatory growth. The pressure of competition and the necessity of growth keep businesses and their workers under constant stress. Moreover, the demand for added interest created by debt-based financing makes the commercialization of welfare services like education and healthcare inevitable, and its negative effects cannot spare even family relationships.

It is worth remembering that debt-based financing not only requires repayment with interest but also demands payment at the agreed time, and each extension of the term brings additional interest. It is also worth remembering that entrepreneurs need profit, which begins only after the payment of capital and its interest, so their main objective is to maximize this additional profit, as has been the case in recent decades. As the loan market grows, areas like education, healthcare, and family responsibilities increasingly depend on debt financing. At every step, the lender wants to receive more cash in return, and on time. Since human relationships and activities like education and healthcare, due to the lack of information and the massive information asymmetry between the parties, are not suitable for commercial organization, the results of debt-based financing in these areas cannot be positive.

Only that financial system can save humanity from the above-mentioned pressures and tensions and the endless race towards excessive growth, in which the profit of those providing capital and those increasing wealth through its productive use begins simultaneously, as in partnership (*musharakah*) and profit-sharing (*mudarabah*) or methods based on these. In this system, certain methods that result in the issuance of debt securities, such as *ijarah* (leasing), *murabahah* (cost-plus financing), etc., can be accommodated as needed. However, when profit-sharing methods dominate and the door to receiving more cash tomorrow for giving a little today is closed, only then can the heat of the loan market and the undesirable atmosphere created by the dominance of debt-based financing in the contemporary economy be avoided. This is why it is necessary not to adopt the method of *tawarruq*.

The Current Situation

It has not been long since *tawarruq* was implemented in contemporary Islamic finance, but its practice is increasing. The Shari'ah experts who have promoted it have focused on the contracts related to buying and selling but could not foresee its effects on the overall economy, whereas such matters must be evaluated in the light of benefits and harms, as we have explained in, "Shariah, Economics and the Progress of Islamic Finance: The Role of Shariah Experts," which can be found at www.siddiqi.com/mns. Modern *Shari'ah* scholars who consider *tawarruq* permissible point out that numerous earlier jurists also allowed it, raising the question of why it would now be deemed forbidden. However, the important point to consider is that the loan market that exists today did not exist in the past. There was no significant existence of debt securities or their trade, and the focus of business calculations was real goods and services, not securities. Economic instability in the goods and services market was due to natural disasters, famine, etc., not due to speculation in the securities market. Today's global interconnected loan market, made possible by advances in communication and reduced transport costs, did not exist in those times.

Moreover, the macroeconomic insights that have emerged

through the work of modern experts like Keynes were not available at that time. These insights highlight that actions that have one effect at the individual level can have a completely different effect when undertaken collectively. The fact is that neither was there a practice of collecting and analyzing data on large populations at that time, nor were the tools available for such analysis. Therefore, while the benefits of *tawarruq* for a few individuals were apparent, the harmful effects of its widespread practice on the entire economy could not have been understood.

How Should the Supply of Cash Be Handled?

There is no doubt that individuals and institutions may sometimes need cash that cannot be fulfilled through conventional means, for which there is no option other than *qard-e-hasan* (benevolent loan). In early Islamic history, this need was met through two means: loans given by individuals and the public treasury (*bayt al-mal*). In modern times, alongside the revival of the former method, it has been suggested that commercial banks should allocate a small proportion of the funds in their current accounts for short-term *qard-e-hasan* loans (Siddiqi, 2002, Chapter Eight). It should also be considered how *waqf* (endowments) and institutions for the collection and distribution of *zakat* (alms) and charity can be utilized to meet this need (Siddiqi, 2006, Pp. 22-23).).

In Iran, Islamic banks open *qard-e-hasan* savings accounts. To encourage deposits in these accounts, account holders are offered unspecified rewards and bonuses, which can be in the form of cash or goods. Additionally, as an incentive, those who deposit funds in these accounts are exempt from paying certain commissions and fees and are prioritized in the provision of services by the bank (Makiyan, 2005, pp 84-94). Through the funds deposited in these accounts, it has become possible for

Islamic banks in Iran to offer *qard-e-hasan* loans to those in need. Loans under the principle of *qard-e-hasan* are mostly given to small producers, farmers, and small-scale businesses. These loans are also available to individuals who, through no fault of their own, find themselves in situations where they cannot afford to meet personal needs, such as dealing with an illness (Makiyan, 2005 pp 87.).

Conclusion

Islamic finance is still in its early stages. If certain elements seem lacking in the nurturing and maintenance of this nascent plant, it should not be surprising. It is hoped that with time, people will pay attention to addressing these deficiencies and will strive to rectify them for the welfare of Muslims and humanity. This task cannot be left to the blind forces of the market. In this regard, efforts have been made to highlight the flaws that arise from relying solely on traditional legal methods without referring to the objectives of *Shari'ah*. Empowerment is from Allah ﷻ [alone]!

References

Ahmad, Imtiaz. 2010. *The Easy Qur'an* (English Translation) Farmington Hills, MI: Tawheed Center.

Abraham L. Udovitch, "Reflections on the Institutions of Credit and Banking in the Medieval Islamic Near East," in *Studia Islamica*. 1975, vol 41, pp.1-21, See page 9. Also see the same author's paper entitled: "Bankers without Banks: Commerce, Banking and Society in the Islamic Middle East", in the book: *The Dawn of Modern Banking*, edited by the same author, New Haven, Yale University Press, (1979), pp. 225-273, see page 257.

Abu Dawood, Sunan, Hadith # 3382, Book of Trade, Chapter 25.

Bukhari, Sahih, Hadith #1,

Chachi, Abdel Kader. 2005. "Origins and Development of Commercial and Islamic Banking Operations," *Journal of King Abdulaziz University Islamic Economics*, v 18, #2 (English).

Cizakca, Murat. 2000. A History of Philanthropic Foundations: The Islamic World from the Seventh Century to the Present, Bogazici University Press.

El Hiraika, Adam B. 2004. On the Design of Monetary Policy in an Islamic Framework: The Experience of Sudan. Jeddah, IRTI, Islamic Development Bank.

El-Gamal, Mahmoud A.1999. "An Economic Explication of the Prohibition of Riba in Classical Islamic Jurisprudence," *Proceedings of the Third Harvard University Forum on Islamic Finance*, Cambridge, Massachusetts, Harvard University Press.

El-Gamal Mahmoud. 2006. *Islamic Finance, Law, Economics and Practice*. Cambridge University Press, pp. 69-72 and 160.

Goiten, S.D. 1967. *A Mediterranean Society*, Vol. 1, Berkley, California

Goiten.1968. Studies in Islamic History and Institutions. Leiden, E.J. Brill.

Sunan Ibn-e-Ma'jah, Hadith # 2192. 2193, Chapter on Trade as well as Tirmidhi, Chapter on Business.

Iqbal, Munawar and Philip Molyneux. 2004. Thirty Years of Islamic Banking. History, Performance and Prospects, Palgrave.

Iqbal, Zamir and Abbas Mirakhor (2007). *An Introduction to Islamic Finance: Theory and Practice*. John Wiley and Sons (Asia), p. 341.

Iqbal, Zamir and Abbas Mirakhor (2007). *An Introduction to Islamic Finance: Theory and Practice*. John Wiley and Sons (Asia), pp. 190-192.

IDB. 2004. *IDB Sukuk Offering Circular.* Jeddah, Islamic Development Bank.

Makiyan, Nezamuddin. 2005, "The lending policies of Islamic Banks in Iran," in Munawar Iqbal & Rodney Wilson (eds.). *Islamic Perspectives on Wealth Creation.* Edinburgh, Edinburgh University Press.

Minskey, Hymen P. 1986. Stabilizing an Unstable Economy. New Heaven and London, Yale University Press, pp. 43, 117 and 177.

Mossin, Jan. 1973. Theory of Financial Markets. Englewood Cliff, N.J., Prentice Hall, Inc., p.162.

Obaidullah, Mohammad. 2005. *Islamic Financial services.* Jeddah: King Abdul Aziz University, pp. 109-112.

Obaidullah, Mohammad. 2005. *Islamic Financial services.* Jeddah: King Abdul Aziz University, pp. 160-162.

Rafe, Mohammad Md. Haneef. 2005. "Recent Trends in Innovations in Islamic Debt Securities: Prospects for Islamic Profit and Loss Structures," in S. Nazim Ali, *Islamic Finance Current Legal and Regulatory Issues.* Cambridge University Press, pp. 29-60.

Rispler-Chaim, Vardict, 1991. "Insurance and Semi Insurance Transactions in Islamic History Until 19th Century," *Journal of the Economic and Social History of the Orient*, v. 34.

Rushd, Ibn. 1985. *Badayatul Mujtahid* (in Arabic), vol. 2. Beirut; Darul Ma'arif.

Siddiqi, Muhammad Nejatullah. 1968. *Sirket aur Mudhrbet ke Sharie Usool*, New Delhi: Markazi, Maktaba Islami Publishers, pp. 83-84.

Siddiqi, Muhammad Nejatullah. 1988. *Muslim Economic Thinking*, Leicester, Islamic Foundation.

Siddiqi, Muhammad Nejatullah. 2002. *Interest Free Banking*. New Delhi, Markazi Maktaba Islami Publisher, Chapter five.

Siddiqi, Muhammad Nejatullah. 2004. *Riba, Bank Interest and the Rationale of its Prohibition*. Jeddah, Islamic Research and Training Institute and Islamic Development Bank, Chapter 4.

Siddiqi, Muhammad Nejatullah. 21 April 2006. "Shariah, Economics, and the Progress of Islamic Finance: The Role of Shariah Experts," Paper presented at a workshop at Harvard Law School Islamic Finance Project

Siddiqi, Muhammad Nejatullah.2006. "Islamic Banking and Finance in Theory and Practice. A Survey of State of the Art" *Islamic Economic Studies*, v 13, No 2, pp 1048, especially, pp. 8-11.

Stiglitz, Joseph E. and Bruce Greenwald. 2003. Towards a New Paradigm in Monetary Economics. Cambridge University Press, p. 271.

Uzair, Mohammad. 1955. *An outline of Interestless Banking*, Karachi, Dhaka, Raihan Publications.

Wizārat al-Awqāf wa-al-Shu'n al-Islāmīyah.1982. *al-Mawsu'ah al-fiqhiyyah* ; Contributor, Kuwait.; Publisher, Wizarat al-Awqaf wa al-Shu'un al-Islamiyah.

www.Elgari.com. See Mohammad Ali Elgari's article number 30 on Tawarruq.

APPENDIX TWO

The Future of Islamic Movements in the Context of the Objectives of *Sharia* and the Purpose of Creation[1]

It is clear to all of us that the purpose of God's creation of human beings is either to accept or reject the path of obedience of our Creator. Those who accept the path of obedience will be rewarded by God with eternal success; while those who reject it will be punished. We have been provided with Sharia—the path as mentioned in the Qur'an in order to make our life easier and so that we can manage life-affairs in a better way while enjoying the freedom accorded by the Almighty. In this essay we will reflect on what role Islamic movements should play in today's world in the contexts of the objectives of Sharia and the purpose of life.

The term Islamic movement refers to the organized efforts made during the last two centuries aimed at changing the decline

[1] Mohammad Nejatullah Siddiqi's, *Maqasid-e-Shariat* (revised edition, 2017) chapter no. 10 titled "*Islami Tehreek ka Musteqbil: Maqsid-e-Shariat aur Maqsid-e-Takhleeq ke Tanazur mein*," translated by Mohammad Ahmadullah Siddiqi

of the Muslims and making Islam a dominant worldview. The question of what methodology should be adopted by Islamic movements is related to what is on the horizon in the future. Therefore, it is necessary to understand the changes and developments that are forthcoming.

An Analysis of the Future Trends

It is generally understood that the future will be different from the past and the present. Let us think together in what ways and to what extent the future is going to be different so that we can adapt to the changes by developing new ways and means hoping that these will help Islamic movements in achieving the goal of inviting God's servants to His obedience and worship. First, let us discern in what ways the future world will be different from the present. The trends suggest that population will further increase, urbanization will progress means of transportation and communication and we will see unprecedented advancements. In most countries the demographics of the population will become more diverse; people of many faiths, cultures, colors, languages and ethnicities will live together.

The gap between rich and poor will increase. More people will participate in governance, but few will have real power. Role of local governments and international agencies will be more visible.

Family structure will be weakened; average age of people will increase; both men and woman will increasingly become self-centered and selfish; mutual cooperation among people and nations will decline; digital technology will take over many of the jobs previously carried out by humans; financial transactions will be more direct between the consumers and the financial agencies; quality of life will decline despite increasing wealth and resources; tensions and conflicts among powerful countries will be on the rise; environmental challenges will increase; social justice prevails only when people are willing to protect and care about each other's rights and governments are sincere in serving the people rather than being abusive and exploitative; these things depend on moral values and spirituality.

We have to develop a plan to deal with the impact of technological advancements on social life. We have to find out a way to convince people that social justice is necessary for a peaceful coexistence. Establishment of people-serving governments instead of abusive and exploitative governments is a challenge that we must pay special attention to and find out a solution.

Accomplishment of Objectives and the Future

Islam encourages maintenance of human freedom. People, in principle, are free despite technological advancements and its subsequent repercussions. People are free to do whatever they want as long as they remain within the bounds of Sharia and keep the Sharia objectives in perspectives because these are in the best interest of people themselves. Which sources shall we consult in order to learn about these boundaries and the objectives is an important question. Another important question is whether these boundaries and objectives are permanent or changeable. What are the criteria, if these are flexible? Another point to remember is that the role of boundaries is different from those of the objectives.

Objectives and Boundaries

Let us discuss the last question first. Indeed, the objectives are more important than the boundaries. Boundaries have been laid down to bring the objectives in harmony and to make them effective. Thus, the objectives are permanent while the boundaries have to be flexible. Objectives themselves do not change; any flexibility in the objectives relates only to the order in which they may be accomplished. Objectives are like standards and criteria. Fewer objectives may be accomplished if resources are fewer; more objectives may be achieved if more resources are available. However, the flexibility in boundaries may be both quantitative and qualitative so that attainment of objectives may be possible in changing circumstances. Let us try to understand this with an example. All human beings should get food, water, and a place to live. This is an objective. In order to achieve this, everyone who could get a job should work; those who could not work due to being a child or being of old-age, or due to any type of disability, their family members and close relatives must take care of them if they have the resources. However, if the families or relatives are not capable or if they do not take the responsibility, then the society as a whole is responsible; in many cases non-governmental bodies such as orphanages and other welfare organizations take the responsibility to look after such people. If even this does not happen, the State must take care of such people. The governments may impose taxes, in addition to collecting *Zakat*. In reality, however, in the fifteen centuries of Islam, there are numerous examples of misuse or abuse of this important responsibility in Muslim societies. Prophet Muḥammad's life is full of examples of fulfilling the needs of people. Even when most Meccans were not Muslims, he sent food when they needed it. The second Caliph. Omar, made arrangements to feed the general population of Medina when there was a famine. We have good examples of such activities in the developed countries when the concept of a welfare state became popular. In many such countries, every citizen gets free education, medical care, and other amenities. Muslim countries too have to decide about their role in fulfilling their obligations towards their citizens.

The above example was simple about which there is little room for disagreement. Let us take another example in which the possibility of disagreement is far and wide. Human dignity and respect are core principles of Sharia. That is why it is commanded by God to decide our collective issues with consultation (Shura'). Every human being deserves respect and honor which contradicts with the prevailing practices of tyranny and oppression. Islam does not accept that a few people dictate how everyone else should live, that rulership becomes hereditary, and that a certain segment of population is deprived of participation in the decision-making process. Examples of how everyone should be treated fairly and justly could be found in the practices of the Prophet and those of the rightly guided caliphs. When the Prophet, peace be upon him, came to Medina, he brought together all segments of the society and developed a document known as "The Constitution of Medina," under which the Prophet was the head of the newly established State, but non-Muslims were also part of this federation. The second caliph, Omar (r. 634-644) cancelled the protective tax "Jizya" for the Zoroastrians and imposed another tax. These examples of the past have to be understood in the context of that time. In our time this objective has to be achieved in the context of the generally accepted norms prevalent today. Even though there may be disagreement among the Muslim scholars, the equality of men and women, the participation of non-Muslims in governance, and respect for the international laws should be supported by the contemporary Islamic thought. Disagreements should be sorted out through discussion but the Sharia objective of human dignity and respect for all should not be compromised.

Our focus should be on the objectives, and we should not insist on how these were understood in the past if such understanding obscures our vision and hinders the attainment of any of the Sharia objectives. An important example of this would be to provide constitutional guarantees for equal protection and just treatment to both Muslims and non-Muslims.

Muslims should have the right to live their life according to their religion and values in every country they live regardless of their status as a minority or majority. Similarly, the non-Muslim citizens of a Muslim country should also be given the right to freely practice their religion.

Constitution should be developed through mutual consultation. These days no one enjoys absolute authority; judiciary, legislative branch and the executives share power and keep the checks and balances. It is not a logical argument that we cannot adopt such methods simply because there is no such precedence of power sharing in our past.

The Desirable Environment for the Attainment of the Sharia Objectives

A much better world will be the one in which all human beings have equal rights. They have the freedom to worship or not to worship a particular religion; they have the right to express their ideas and propagate their religion; they have the right to follow their own personal laws in their family affairs; they have the right to follow a civil law if they do not want to follow a particular religious law. In the remaining affairs, legislation should be bound by the promises and guarantees provided therein, and legislative process provides opportunities to all citizens to participate and there are provisions to amend the laws if the circumstances require a change. It would be better for all if no nation tries to dominate another nation. Attainment of peace, end of mutual discords, and freedom of expression are among the objectives of Sharia.

The world has become a global village in which people of different nationalities, races, colors and religions live together and have mutual relationships in business and other issues.

In the 19th century countries proclaim to have total authority to run their affairs and the majority population's wishes prevailed over the minorities. However, in this age every country has to abide by many international treaties, conventions and protocols; the majority cannot impose its wishes upon the minorities. Although in reality these trends are frequently violated by powerful nations but in the long run people and nations cannot afford to ignore diversity and international protocols. This is closer to the purpose of our creation. Everyone who enjoys freedom also realizes that this freedom is a test by the Creator about how diligently we exercise it.

Flexibility in the Objectives

An example of flexibility in the attainment of the Sharia objectives may be understood by the gradual process that Islam used to end slavery. In the seventh century, in particular among the Arabs, prisoners of war used to be made slaves, and the women prisoners were used as concubines. The entire economy was based on slavery. Islam took many measures to end these practices. It prohibited enslaving people during the time of peace. It encouraged slaves to buyout their enslavements and persuaded slave owners to free slaves in exchange of money. The concubines who bear a child from their masters have to be set free after the death of their owners. Islam encouraged Muslims to free slaves in exchange of money or something of monetary value (*fidya*), or even without any money just to please God. Despite these measures slavery was prevalent in the Muslim world until the West took action to end it. However, the Muslim rulers should have taken steps to end it, instead of promoting it to serve their vested interests. One should be reminded of the Prophet's last sermon in which he warned Muslims to be aware of the rights of slaves and to treat them well. Not only this, according to a hadith reported in Sunan ibn Majah, he repeatedly reminded Muslims to treat slaves well on his death bed. Now slavery is illegal according to the laws of most nations. No human being can be enslaved, and this is in line with the purpose of human creation (*maqsid-e-takhleeq*). Human beings are born free, and they should remain free so that they can fulfill their obligations towards God with their free will. The Prophet has closed this chapter with his clear instructions; so, human freedom should not be violated anymore. This was one example of flexibility in the attainment of Sharia objectives.

A gradual process was adopted to end slavery. Now there is no room to go back to the past when slavery was practiced. Some scholars have presented a different opinion on this issue; however, their opinions contradict with both the objectives of Sharia and the purpose of creation and therefore not acceptable.

Roots of the Objectives

The question was raised in the above lines about the sources from which these objectives should be derived. In principle, the answer to this question is that the sources are the Qur'an and the Sunnah (tradition of Prophet Muḥammad). At the same time the objectives have to be in line with human nature and can also be recognized through a rational approach. Human beings are born free and have been given by God the right to choose their own path for the journey of life. This approach supports the ideas of viceregency and the accountability in the hereafter. The argument that slavery has not been totally abolished by the Qur'an and the Sunnah is not acceptable simply because it contradicts the well-defined purpose of human creation and the Sharia objectives that human beings have been born free. This stance is closer to human nature and appeals to the human intellect. Purpose of creation is quite clear from various verses of Qur'an and the Sharia objectives are also clearly laid down in Qur'an and the Sunnah. Therefore, conclusions about various issues that contradict the purpose of creation, and the Sharia objectives are not acceptable.

A similar example is about the possession of land and immovable property and wealth after victory in war. Norms have been changing about this issue and so have been the Islamic directives. Now the Geneva Convention has provided detailed guidelines concerning these issues that most countries have accepted as binding. Such examples can be found in the past as well. Despite the insistence of several companions of the Prophet, the Second Caliph Umar did not allow the possession of land by the soldiers who won it after the battles in Iraq and Syria because they were against the higher purposes of the Sharia. So, now a ruling for the possession of land after victory in a war will not be acceptable, if anyone provides reference of certain verses because such a ruling will be against the established norms and conventions agreed upon by all the nations of the world.

Islamic Movements

Islamic movements emerged in the beginning of the 20th century. By the middle of the century, they were recognized by the characteristics that have now become their defining traits. At their formative stages they faced special circumstances as colonial rule was coming to an end. Islamic movements participated in the debate about the foundational principles of the emerging independent nations. They demanded that the sovereignty of God should be at the heart of the debate and the new constitution should be formulated based on the directives from the Qur'an and the Sunnah. However, that situation has changed now. The question of sovereignty is not a priority anymore. Nations are no more governed by foreign governments. The debate about sovereignty has gone on the back burners. Like other nations, Muslim majority countries are also searching for solutions to some practical problems.

Islamic movements have to work to find solutions as well. As far as non-Muslim majority countries are concerned, the real issue is to present the message of Islam in a way that the local population can find it useful for them; Islamic movements should now focus in presenting the life of Prophet Muḥammad as the benefactor of humanity. The issues that were at the top of the list until the middle of the last century are not at the top of the list anymore. Whether Muslim majority countries, or those where they are a minority, Islamic movements have changed their *modus-operandi*; they have learned to change their methodology in the changing circumstances. This also is an example of a better understanding of the Sharia objectives and flexible approach in using the sources and the means to attain the objectives. An example of this is the approach used by the Islamic movement in Tunisia during the elections prior to the suspension of the constitution.

It is, however, concerning that literature reflecting these new trends has not yet been prepared and published. On the one hand, the same old literature is in circulation as if these writings are above the changes in space and time, and on the other hand new strategies are implemented to deal with the changing circumstances. However, many old timers in the movements do not support such measures as they believe that the old literature should still guide the actions taken by the Islamic movements. This leads two problems. First, the conscience of the workers of Islamic movements feels guilty that they have left the path of steadfastness. People think that Islamic movements should have paved the way to adopt an Islamic constitution based on Islamic Sharia and the head of the state must be a Muslim, and so on. The question is what to do if the majority of the population is not willing to vote for an Islamic constitution, or the army is not willing to forcefully impose an Islamic constitution on people.

Then what should the Muslim conscience do?

The second problem is that some Muslim think that it is not necessary to gain support of general population for an Islamic state. However, Islamic movements consider the creation of a favorable opinion among people necessary. Generally, in most cases, Islamic law is restricted to the implementation of the laws related to punishment (*hudud*). Attainment of Sharia objectives—for example fair and just rule, welfare of citizens, appropriate distribution of wealth, bridging the income gap, making a country economically strong to reduce poverty, fighting to end corruption, and having an efficient administration and people friendly bureaucracy—receive little attention. Such Muslim groups target Muslims who differ with them and many times they use violent means. They just want to implement *hudud* (Islamic penal code) which frightens people from Islam and to think that the implementation of Islamic penal code is the top priority of the so-called Islamic state. Islam is being grossly misunderstood and the Prophet's image as mercy to the world is also damaged.

The problem is that even very sincere members of Islamic movements think that Islamic movements ought to follow the same methodology in all time and space. However, to achieve its goal of inviting people toward worshiping Allah ﷻ, Islamic movements can use different methods and should not be bound by a rigid and unchangeable methodology.

Examples from the life of Prophet, peace be upon him.

It is important that we look at the methods used by the Prophet in changing circumstances. Without going into the details, it should be noted that the Prophet was flexible in using different methods to attain various Sharia objectives. Following is a list of different circumstances and events that require our attention to understand the points made above.

1. Confinement in the valley of Abu Talib
2. The issue of living in Mecca after returning from the journey of the city of Taif
3. First and the second migration to Ethiopia
4. First and the second Pledges of Aqaba
5. The brotherhood scheme between the migrants of Mecca and the inhabitants of Medina
6. Construction of the Prophet's Mosque and establishment of a marketplace
7. The *Mithaq al-Madina* or the Convent of Medina and the development of a constitutional state of Medina
8. The Treaty of Hudaybiyyah
9. The general amnesty at the time of the conquest of Mecca
10. Preferred treatment of the Meccans in distribution of the "Al-Anfal" or the "Gains of War" after the *Ghazwat al-Khandaq*—the Battle of Trench
11. *Khutbatul-Wadā'*—The Farewell Sermon of Prophet Muḥammad delivered on 9th *Dhu al-Hijjah* 10 AH (632 CE) at Arafah.

The purpose of the above discussion on objectives, means, and flexibility in the boundaries was to initiate thinking and reflections that help make implementation of the Islamic teachings easier and popular among the general population and also remove the confusion about ways and means to attain Sharia objectives in changing circumstances. One problem is that many people selectively present only those examples from the tradition of the Prophet that support their points of view. They commit the same mistake in looking at the history of Islam. Such erroneous methods can be corrected only if we do not study the tradition and Islamic history to support our predisposed view on a particular issue. We should have an open mind and try to reach a consensus if different people arrive at different conclusions. Instead of passing judgement on others and throwing them out of Islam, we should be tolerant and respectful if we are unable to reach consensus. We can look at the Prophet's examples related to this issue in any authentic biography of the Prophet such as the Biography of the Prophet by Ibne Hisham. Instead of going into details, let us look at few examples from the life of the Prophet and reflect on the lessons we can learn.

At the height of their opposition to the Prophet, the people of Mecca started a boycott of the Prophet and other Muslims including the tribe to which the Prophet belonged. According to the tribal tradition, Prophet's uncle and the leader of the tribe of Banu Hashim, Abu Talib, moved to a valley along with the entire tribe that included Muslims and non-Muslims. The Prophet did not object to this tribal tradition; instead, he fully benefitted from it. He welcomed the support of his uncle and other non-Muslim members of his tribe.

In another instance, the Prophet left Mecca and went to the city of Taif in order to present to them the message of Islam. However, he has to return to Mecca when he faced even harsher opposition from the people of Taif. According to the custom, in order to come back to Mecca, the Prophet needed an influential leader of Mecca to declare his Protection to the Prophet. He accepted the offer of a non-Muslim who came forward and offered his protection. The lesson learned is that for the attainment of an Islamic objective, a prevailing custom of a non-Muslim culture or society can be accepted.

When the oppression of Meccans upon Muslims increased too much the Prophet instructed Muslims to migrate to Abyssinia—the Ethiopian Empire ruled by a Christian king famous for his kindness and generosity. The Muslims migrated to Abyssinia in groups, first, about a dozen and next about 100 Muslims migrated to Ethiopia. Despite many attempts by Meccans to persuade the King to expel Muslims, the king continued to provide refuge for Muslims according to the established norms of the time. The lesson from this migration is clear. Muslims can benefit from a good custom or norm regardless whether it is available in a Muslim or a non-Muslim country.

The Prophet, used to contact and present the message of Islam to people visiting Mecca during the time of Hajj. Once a group of people from Yathrib, later known as Medina, came to Mecca during the Hajj time. The Prophet met with them and presented the message of Islam. They invited the Prophet to migrate to Medina; they were fed-up with the ongoing tribal conflicts and hoped that the Prophet would be able to bring peace among the people of Medina.

Next year a larger group of people came to Mecca from Medina and again invited the Prophet to make Medina his new home. The Prophet accepted their offer but differed the implementation at God's Will. This is also an example of a bold decision in a difficult situation.

When the Prophet and his companions immigrated to Medina, they had to leave everything in Mecca, and they had no place to live. The Prophet established *Muakhaat* (pact of brotherhood) was a historic initiative in Medina, by pairing Muslim migrants (*Muhajirun*) from Mecca with local residents (*Ansar*) to foster unity, solidarity, and economic support. This arrangement continued for two years till the Meccan Muslims could sustain themselves. This was a unique arrangement in an extra ordinary situation. The normal rules of individual ownership etc., did not pose any challenge.

The main responsibility of the Prophet, peace be upon him,

was to guide, to spiritually train, and to morally uplift the people. People are able to do the chores themselves; however, certain issues deserve special attention. Jews dominated the marketplace in Medina, and they did not deal with Muslims fairly. The Prophet established a new marketplace for Muslims after the completion of the Prophet's mosque. He used to routinely supervise the management of the newly established marketplace.

In his book, the renowned scholar, Muhammad Hamidullah, has discussed in detail the Constitution of Medina.[2] The population in Medina included local Muslims, Meccan Muslims, Jews, Christians, and few other tribal groups. The prophet reached a historic agreement for the security and wellbeing of all the inhabitants of Medina. This has a great lesson for us. Government is formed by all the people and works for the wellbeing of all of its citizens.

Let us look at the Treaty of Hudaybiyyah. Its context is that the Meccan Pagan leaders did not allow Muslims of Medina to perform the Umrah (the lesser pilgrimage to Mecca). Instead of forcefully entering into Mecca, Prophet decided to return to Medina without performing Umrah. He entered into an agreement with the Pagan leaders of Mecca to come back next year for Umrah. He did not allow smaller differences to derail this treaty.

The Treaty of Hudaybiyyah teaches Muslims a great lesson: In order to achieve long-term goals, sometimes one has to compromise on shorter objectives so that the future of Muslim Ummah can be better.

Similar lessons can be drawn from the general amnesty

---

[2] Muhammad Hamidullah, *The First Written Constitution in the World: An Important Document of the Time of the Holy Prophet* (Lahore: Sh. Muhammad Ashraf, 1975).

announced after the historic victory of Mecca. Mecca was full of people who bitterly opposed the Prophet and his companions and tortured them in all possible ways. They tried to assassinate the Prophet himself. However, the Prophet overlooked all of the bitter moments of the past in order to develop a healthy and long-term relationship with the people of Mecca.

It was a general practice that the "Al-Anfal" or the "Gains of War" used to be distributed among all members of army after a victory. But after the Battle of Trench, Prophet Muḥammad distributed among the newly converted Meccan Muslims. This made some of the older companions of the Prophet from Medina not happy about it. The Prophet explained to them the wisdom behind his decision and they agreed. This shows that under certain circumstances one may be flexible in the actions taken for the larger common good of the society.

In his *Khutbatul-Wadā'*—The Farewell Sermon of Prophet Muḥammad delivered on 9th Dhu al-Hijjah 10 AH (632 CE) at Arafah, the Prophet emphasized that the priority objectives of Islamic Sharia include the unity of humankind, human dignity and respect, and establishment of social justice. Prophet underscored the following four issues:

1. Human equality;
2. the issue of slavery;
3. Fair and equitable treatment of women, and;
4. the abolishment of usury

All of them are long-term action plans, linked to our attitudes and our actions as well as to social institutions. These cannot be merely legislative actions. The social conditions at the beginning of the Prophet's life were miserable and bad. These improved over the 23 years of Prophet's lifetime. And the Prophet reminded for continued improvement and work in these areas.

As discussed above, these examples teach us that as situations keep on changing there is need for continuous strategizing our priorities. Every change presents a new challenge and demands a different solution. This means that Islamic movements are not bound by a rigid and unchangeable methodology. What is important is sincerity with Islamic objectives and a willingness to work within the framework of Islam. It is incumbent upon us to draw lessons from the life of the Prophet, from the history, from the observations of nature and from mutual consultations.

The future of Islamic movements in the contemporary world depends upon how successfully and promptly they are able to use the new means of communications. The issue is not of a particular organization. Old 0rganizations vanish and new organizations may be formed. What is concerning is that we do not make concerted effort to analyze the new and emerging situations, to draw appropriate lessons from the Qur'an and the Sunnah and history. For a better future, all of our institutions including the schools, seminaries, universities, the mosques and the pulpits, our homes and our marketplaces have to be proactive.

New Situations, New Possibilities

We are facing very disturbing and alarming situation in the world today. People will appreciate if the Muslim ummah and Islam can help alleviate the situation. I would like to present some details about it in the following lines. The list of problems is long; I will discuss only three important issues. These are, in order of priority, climate change, financial and economic system, and family and social relationships. I will explain how Islamic teachings can help solve these problems.

Climate change is a serious issue. The emission of life-threatening gases is damaging the Ozone layer that encircles the earth and protects it from the dangerous and hot gases emitted by the Sun. Earth's temperature is rising, ice is melting around the North Pole resulting in increased sea levels. Many of the coastal populations and islands may soon be under water. Many birds and other creatures are dying. Environmental balance is under threat. This is happening above the ground on Earth as well as in deep seas. Climate is changing. Frequency of hurricanes and flooding is increasing. Drinkable water reservoir beneath the earth is fast drying up. This issue alone requires major changes in our lifestyles and ways in which we use earth's resources.

The current financial crisis is troubling the world including those in the developed nations. The poor people who lost their means of income and savings are facing dire consequences. The inequities in income and distribution of wealth have peaked now. About one percent of the world population owns more than half of the world's wealth. Ninety percent of the people do not get to spend even 10 percent of the wealth. Five of the more than seven billion people are poor. About two billion of the poor people live on less than a dollar a dy. Just like rich people got richer and poor got poorer, the wealth inequities also increased among nations. Poor countries take loans from wealthier nations. When they fail to pay the burdensome interest on these loans, they are forced to increase taxes and prices of goods needed by common people. This leads to unrest among people which eventually threatens world peace as well.

We all know that the well-being of future generations depends upon stable families in which children are able to live with both parents. However, stable families are breaking due to ever-increasing divorce rates and children have to live with single-parents or sometimes with grandparents or even with foster parents. Larger family system is now reduced to smaller urban families where grandparents rarely live with their children. This affects the mental health of children who are deprived of wholesome growth. Societal relationships are established mainly on the basis of monetary benefits. Consequently, relationships lack stability and longevity. Greed and higher standards of life dominate human Rarely people sacrifice for others in the society. Most people value only those relationships that are materially beneficial for them. Whether politics, economics, government or the private sector majority people seek their own vested intrests.

Such a world can be saved from disaster only by those people who can sacrifice their own interests for the sake of stable human relationships, who prefer the welfare of the entire society over their self-interests, who can accept a little less comfort for themselves to save the humanity from catastrophic devastation, who are willing to share their profits with others to fight against the ensuing financial instability rather than using all their intelligence to let others suffer from economic instability and financial losses while they themselves prosper.

Islam reminds people of the accountability in the hereafter and encourages them to prefer the success of the eternal life even if that means incurring a little loss in this world. Humanity has witnessed such periods of civilization when political leaders chose to serve the people and business owners acted in the best interest of their customers and welfare of the labor class; mutual love and sincerity strengthened the foundation of family and social relationships were more important than profit making.

In the past we have seen that the world's religions, saints and sages, selfless elders, intellectuals and philosophers, poets and people from all walks of life have promoted the betterment of every segment of the society. Such efforts can replicated even today. Islam and Muslims, in cooperation with other like-minded people, can play a significant role in saving the world from the dangers posed by climate change, financial imbalances, and diminishing societal relationships.

The Present Muslim Society

It is unfortunate that Muslims have forgotten their role as being the "Khair ummah" or the best community for humanity at large. Instead of leading the humanity with their service and constructive engagement, they spend their time in fighting on issues of the historical nature; rather than uniting to serve the humanity, they are fighting on sectarian issues; instead of being a witness for God and His messenger, they are confused about their Islamic identity. We have to change our priorities to engage in cooperation with all people, resolve our internal differences, and make service of humanity as our main priority.

We need courage to forgive each other and forget our internal differences and focus on building a bright future for all humanity. With mutual cooperation and tolerance, we can play a constructive role for the betterment of humanity.

We need to empower ourselves financially to be free from dependence on others. Economic empowerment comes from business, trade and productive actions which will lead us to entrepreneurship and creative actions that are key to economic stability and strength. The Muslim community was raised like this. Its strength was both in spirituality and leadership in world affairs. Muslims have played a leadership role in strengthening human civilization in both worldly and spiritual affairs and they can still play that role by uplifting their moral consciousness by active participation in the wellbeing of all people as the renowned poet, Allama Iqbal said:

Keeping the vision at higher objectives, speaking with sweetness, and being kind-hearted

These are the qualities of a leader who intends to guide the human caravan to success.—Bal-e-Jibril-046

Contributors
in alphabetical order

Syamsul Idul Adha is currently the lecturer and a researcher at the Faculty of Islamic Economics and Business, State Islamic University of Ar-Raniry Banda Aceh. His interest is in the field of Islamic economics, Islamic Studies and the history of Islamic and pre-Islamic civilizations.

He is currently doing researches in many field including the legal-jurisprudence polemics in Ottoman Cash Waqf, the paradox of Arab-Islam Capitalism, Islamic Maritime Commercial Law and Muslim Maritime Trade during the pre-Colonial Indian Ocean Trade. He also conducted legal-policy study in the impact of mono-Banking system regulation, the strategic and implementation of Zakat policy, the survey of potential Zakat fundraising, etc.

Khurshid Ahmad (1932-2025) was a renowned scholar, academic, economist, prolific writer, policymaker and legislator. He was one of the prolific and pioneer writers in the contemporary Islamic economics ever since the 1970s. He was also the co-founder of the

Islamic Foundation in Leicester, UK established in 1973.

He was awarded Islamic Development Bank award in 1988. He was also recipient of King Faisal International Prize in 1990. He received Pakistan's highest civilian award Nishan-e-Imtiaz in 2011.

He served as Pakistan's Federal Minister for Planning, Development & Statistics in 1978. And was Deputy Chairman of Planning Commission in Pakistan looking after the Islamization of the economy during 1978-79. As Deputy Chairman of the Planning Commission, he worked to integrate Islamic principles into Pakistan's economic and policy frameworks. He also served as Chairman, Senate Standing Committee on Finance, Economic Affairs & Planning during his time as Senator in Pakistan.

Mohammad Manzoor Alam (1945-2026), did his Ph.D. in Economics from Aligarh Muslim University, Aligarh. He served as Associate Professor Deptt. of Islamic Economics, University of Imam Mohammad-bin-Saud, Riyadh, Saudi Arabia; Economic Advisor in the Ministry of Finance and National Economy, Riyadh, Saudi Arabia; and Chief Coordinator for the Translation of Meaning of the Holy Qur'an in different languages of the world at King Fahd Holy Qur'an Printing Complex, Madinah Munawwarah, Saudi Arabia.

He was the Board Member of the International Institute of Islamic Thought, USA; Founder Member of International Islamic Charitable Organization, Kuwait; and Member, Steering Committee, Istanbul Talks, Civil Solidarity Platform, Istanbul, Turkey.

He founded the Institute of Objective Studies, a renowned think-tank in the year 1986 and served as its chairman and chief patron. As the founder and guiding force of the Institute, he elevated it to remarkable heights, garnering international recognition for its research and academic excellence. Today, the Institute stands as a dynamic think tank dedicated to nation-building, upholding constitutional values, and advancing the interests of disadvantaged and marginalized communities. His life exemplified wisdom, compassion, and an unwavering commitment to societal advancement. He headed more than a dozen organizations in India working for the upliftment of marginalized communities particularly Muslims.

Syed Nazim Ali is a globally recognized scholar and institution-builder in Islamic economics and finance, with more than four decades of leadership in interdisciplinary research, academic platform development, and policy engagement. From 2014 to August 2025, he served as Research Professor and Director of the Research Division at the College of Islamic Studies, Hamad Bin Khalifa University (HBKU), Qatar Foundation, where he also led the Center for Islamic Economics and Finance and spearheaded major initiatives in Islamic finance, social finance, and faith-based approaches to community development.

He was the founding Director of the Islamic Finance Program/Project (1995-2014), affiliated with the Center for Middle Eastern Studies and Harvard Law School, and served as Acting Executive Director of the Islamic Legal Studies Program at Harvard Law School (2010-2013). He was also a Visiting Fellow at the Prince Alwaleed bin Talal Islamic Studies Program at Harvard University (2014-2017). During his Harvard tenure, he played a central role in organizing and leading major international conferences and forums, including the biennial Harvard University Forum on Islamic Finance (est. 1997), as well as Islamic finance workshops at the London School of Economics (2007-2017) and SOAS—University of London (2018-present), with conference proceedings published under his editorship.

Beyond academia, Prof. Ali has actively engaged with policymakers and regulatory institutions, including the U.S. Department of the Treasury, the Federal Reserve Bank of New York, and central banks in several countries, contributing to efforts to improve understanding of Islamic finance and address misconceptions about the industry. His research interests span Islamic finance, social financing, and Islamic information systems. He received his PhD from the University of Strathclyde, Glasgow, United Kingdom.

Salman Syed Ali is an economist. Educated at the University of Pennsylvania, USA, and the International Islamic University, Pakistan. He has over 36 years of professional and leadership experience divided between academia and the Islamic Development Bank in conducting research, training, teaching, and advisory in Islamic economics, finance, and financial sector development across many countries.

He has received training in economics and *fiqh* at the International Islamic University Islamabad, leadership training at the London Business School, UK, and finance training at the Swiss Finance Institute, Geneva, Switzerland.

He was the Lead Economist and Academic Coordinator at the Islamic Development Bank Institute (IsDBI), Islamic Development Bank (IsDB) and headed the Research Division at IRTI, IsDB. His work focuses on multiple areas of Islamic finance and Islamic economics. He has also developed expertise in the economics of blockchain, digital assets, Artificial Intelligence, and Poverty Measurement. Previously, he founded the cluster on Maqasid al-Shariah-based Socio-economic Development at IRTI, led the Research Division, and contributed to the Community of Practice in Islamic Finance. He had been the editor of the journal, *Islamic Economic Studies* from 2009 to 2024, and a Visiting Fellow in Islamic Finance at OCIS, Oxford University (2016-17).

His areas of interest are Islamic finance, capital markets, poverty evaluation, and game theory. He has several research articles and publications to his credit. He organized and moderated sessions at major international conferences. Represented IsDB in the Technical Committees and various Working Groups of the Islamic Financial Services Board. He led many research projects for IsDB and other international organizations and contributed to key development initiatives and policy reports for the progress of Islamic economics and finance.

Jasser Auda is a leading scholar in the contemporary Maqasid Studies (Objectives of Islamic Law). He has a multidisciplinary academic background, with a PhD in Islamic Jurisprudence and a PhD in Systems Analysis. He has been a member of several Islamic scholarly and Fatwa councils, and has contributed to the establishment of various educational and da'wah institutions in a number of countries. Throughout his academic career, he worked as a professor in a dozen universities around the world, and has lectured globally on Islam. He has authored 25 books in Arabic and English, some were translated into many languages. This year, 2026/1447, he publishes the first edition of his eight-volume Tafsir/Commentary of the Qur'an, titled: *Al-Tafsir Al-Maqasidi* (Objectives-Based Exegesis). Jasser Auda is a Senior Non-Resident Research Fellow at the Center for Islam in the Contemporary World at Shenandoah University (CICW), USA, and a Professor Fellow at the International Institute of Islamic Thought and Civilization (ISTAC-IIUM), Malaysia.

Mufti Barkatullah is Vice President and board member of World Council of Muslims for Interfaith Relations (WCMIR).

He is a senior lecturer of Islamic Finance at Ebrahim College in London, U. K. Mufti Barkatullah is a prominent Islamic Sharia law scholar with a strong background in economics and finance. Trained extensively both in traditional Islamic and modern Western educational traditions, he has served UK Muslims as a community worker, and Sharia judge at Islamic Sharia Council, London and head of Sharia at Halal Food Authority of the United Kingdom. Previously he has developed Islamic Sharia information databases on CD-ROM and recently hosted live phone-in shows on community TV channels.

Mufti Barkatullah is also a member of the Sharia supervisory boards for several Islamic financial institutions and banks, including the Islamic bank of Britain and several in India and other European countries. A graduate of the famous Darul Uloom Deoband with degrees of *Alim*, *Fadil*, and *Iftaa*, he is a world-renowned expert in Islamic finance, banking, and Islamic community affairs. He lives in London, U. K.

Mehmet Bulut is President of Istanbul Sabahattin Zaim University. He started his academic career as a Research Assistant in 1993, continued his career at Başkent University in Ankara. He has taken part at the university as the Head Department of Economics, Faculty Board Member and Member of Board of Directors. He became the founder Dean of Faculty of Political Sciences and Vice President at Yıldırım Beyazıt University in Ankara in 2011. He was chosen to serve at the Council of Higher Education (YÖK) as a Board Member by the Rectors and the representatives of the Universities and has been appointed by the President of Republic of Turkey in 2012.

He has been studying fields of long term (*longue durée*) economic development, reasons for intercountry economical differences, performance comparisons, international economy policy, Ottoman economics and civilization, Ottoman-European-

Atlantic Economic Relations, History of Economics, Economic Thinking, Financial History, Institutions, Islamic Economics and Finance.

Hafas Furqani is a Professor in Islamic Economics at the Faculty of Islamic Economics and Business, at the Universitas Islam Negeri (UIN) Ar-Raniry Banda Aceh, Indonesia.

He earned his Ph.D. (2012) and M.Ec. (2006) in Economics from the International Islamic University Malaysia (IIUM), and his B.A. in *Shari'ah Mu'amalah* from Universitas Islam Negeri (UIN) Syarif Hidayatullah Jakarta (2002). An accomplished scholar in Islamic economics, banking, and finance, Prof. Hafas has published widely in reputable journals.

Prof. Hafas has served as Visiting Fellow at Islamic Research and Training Institute (IRTI) IDB Jeddah (2012), Researcher at International Shariah Research Academy for Islamic Finance (ISRA) Malaysia (2012-2015),

His research and thought leadership continue to shape the discourse on Philosophy of Islamic economics, Islamic social finance, Islamic philanthropy of zakat and waqf, and the role of Islamic economics in addressing contemporary global challenges.

Mohamed Aslam Haneef is currently Deputy Rector (Research, Innovation and Development) and Professor at the Department of Economics, International Islamic University Malaysia. Current Research interests are in Social Economics and Finance as well as Islamic Futures. Co-Founder of an Islamic Microfinance programme, *I-Taajir*, implemented since April 2018. Has held various academic administrative positions including Head, Department of Economics and Founding Director, Centre for Islamic Economics where he led the development of its Strategic Plan.

PhD from the School of Development Studies, University of East Anglia, UK. Published extensively in Islamic economics and is joint editor of Islamic Economics: Principles and Analyses (2018) and joint author of Foundations of Islamic Economics (2023).

Was Fulbright visiting scholar at the Centre for Muslim-Christian Understanding, Georgetown University, US and Commonwealth Fellowship at the Oxford Centre for Islamic Studies. He sits on the Editorial/International Advisory Boards of a few journals on Islamic Economics/Islam, including, American Journal of Islam and Society (formerly AJISS). Appointed Executive Committee Member, International Association for Islamic Economics (IAIE), 2012 to date. Investment Committee member for PMB Investment Berhad, 2016 to date. Member of Management Board, IIIT East and Southeast Asia since May 2019 and Member, Board of Directors, Institute of Strategic and International Studies Malaysia since April 2023 to March 2026.

Anwar Ibrahim is the 10th prime minister of Malaysia since 2022. Anwar is the president of People's Justice Party (PKR), he has been Member of Parliament (MP) since 2022. Anwar Ibrahim is widely regarded as a reformer and an intellectual. He has advocated for Islamic democracy under the banner of "*Malaysia Madani*" and hopes Malaysia can serve as an example of democratic governance in the Muslim world. He supports the Islamic concept of *Ummah* as a framework for democracy in Muslim countries and emphasizes judicial independence, good governance, and rejection of authoritari-anism.

M. Zaki Kirmani an Indian scholar, holds a PhD in Chemistry and is recognized for his interest in the interrelations between science, society, and Islam. In the 1980s, he was instrumental in founding the Centre for Studies on Science as well as the Muslim

Association for the Advancement of Science in India. He has authored and translated several books in Urdu and English.

M. Yaqub Mirza (1946-2025) the inspiration behind the producing of this book was founder and President of the Center for Islam in the Contemporary World at Shenandoah University (CICW) and served as a beacon of light for those who knew him and worked with him throughout his lifetime. His goal was to serve God through CICW, by creating a vehicle for innovation and growth in the Muslim Community. CICW is in a long list of organizations that Dr. Yaqub founded, including Sterling Management Group, Inc., which negotiates mergers, acquisitions, and sales of various-sized companies located in different parts of the world.

In addition to being a leader in founding and developing CICW and SMG, Dr. Mirza had more than forty years of experience in stock investments and portfolio management. His work in finance led to the founding of Amana Mutual Funds. He also served on the Board of University Islamic Financial Corporation (UIF). Under Dr. Yaqub's leadership, CICW, together with UIF, AMANA and Sterling Charitable, began the Imams Generational Scholarship Fund in 2021 to serve the needs of the children of Imams.

He extended these efforts by serving on the boards of numerous academic institutions and education focused non-profits, including the International Advisory Council of the International Institute of Islamic Thought and Civilization (ISTAC) and International Islamic University of Malaysia. He was a member of the Board of Advisors, Byrd School of Business, and a member of the Board of Trustees of Shenandoah University in Winchester, VA. In addition, he was a member of the Finance Committee and Chairman of the Investment and Endowment

Committee of Shenandoah University. He was also a member of the Council of Advisors, Muslim Philanthropy Initiative at Lilly Family School of Philanthropy, Indiana University.

The Board of Trustees, Shenandoah University recognized Dr. Mirza's multiple contributions with a "Resolution of Appreciation" in October 2018. These awards reflect the generosity of Dr. Mirza in sharing his wealth of knowledge, resources and time to solutions-oriented thought leadership.

In addition to being an entrepreneur and leader in the world of Islamic non-profits and Islamic finance, Dr. Yaqub was a celebrated author, mentor and teacher. In 2014, he published his first book, *Five Pillars of Prosperity: Essentials of Faith-Based Wealth Building*, through White Cloud Press. In 2025, CICW published the 2nd revised edition with several updates. Dr. Yaqub's first book demonstrated his passion for education and interfaith work, which he developed in his next book, *Heavenly Returns: What the Abrahamic Faiths Teach us about Financial and Spiritual Well-Being*, co-authored with Gary Moore and first published in 2022 and reprinted in 2025.

Murniati Mukhlisin is an Indonesian Islamic finance practitioner and thought leader focused on financial literacy, fintech, and social finance. Through her Sakinah Finance initiative, she advances shariah-compliant ecosystems via education, consulting, and publications, reaching over 100,000 participants in 23 countries, including people with disabilities.

She is affiliated with Tazkia University and served as Rector (2017-2022). She co-founded the Indonesian Shariah Fintech Association (AFSI) and chairs its Supervisory Board, while holding positions in various Islamic economics-related organizations.

Her expertise includes zakat and waqf management, Islamic

political economy, and governance, bridging industry practice with global Islamic finance trends focused on sustainability and inclusion.

H. Abdur Raqeeb, a Chennai based entrepreneur and exporter of leather garments is presently General Secretary of Indian Centre for Islamic Finance, Convener, National Committee on Islamic Banking and has been promoting the concept of interest-free banking throughout India.

He is also the Editor of Tamil fortnightly '*Samarasam*' and has contributed several articles on technology & trade in the leather Industry and received awards from Council for Leather exports & Commerce Ministry for Exports. He has participated in the World Islamic Banking Conference at Bahrain, IDB—Islamic finance conference on Sukuk in London, UK., International Muslim Business Conference, Istanbul, Turkey.

Abdur Raqeeb has contributed several articles in media and journals, appeared in TV debates and was involved in social media to create "Financial Literacy in the Community" as well as creating awareness among the masses the need & relevance of Islamic Finance & Banking in the country.

Khurram Shahzad holds the position of Registrar at Minhaj University Lahore and Professor in the School of Economics and Finance, Minhaj University Lahore, Pakistan. He has a PhD in Economics from the Pakistan Institute of Development Economics, Islamabad, Pakistan. And has been teaching Advanced Microeconomics and Advanced Macroeconomics to postgraduate classes.

He is also the Chief Executive Officer of Minhaj Halal Certification, a certification body accredited by the PNAC and the Pakistan Halal Authority and Director of the Centre of Halal

Awareness, Research and Training.

His research primarily focuses on empirical economics, particularly the socioeconomic impacts of trade policies; Islamic Economics with special reference to the history of Economic Thoughts and Poverty Alleviation.

Mohammad Ahmadullah Siddiqi is Professor Emeritus of Journalism and Public Relations at Western Illinois University (WIU) where he has taught for 29 years. At WIU he served as the Journalism Program Director and later as Chair of the Department of English & Journalism. He has also served as the Dean of Academic and Student Affairs at Northwest Suburban College, Chicago. Dr. Siddiqi has authored several books and published more than two dozen articles in refereed publications. He serves on the editorial advisory boards of the Journal of Arab and Muslim Media Research (UK), Journal of Media Studies (Pakistan), and the Islamic Horizon magazine. He has conducted media workshops and seminars in more than 100 cities in North America as well as in about 40 countries in Europe, Asia, Africa and the Far East. Dr. Siddiqi is one of the founding members and current President of the World Council of Muslims for Interfaith Relations (WCMIR). He has served as a member of the Board of Trustees of the Parliament of the World's Religions from 2009 to 2015. In 2014, Dr. Siddiqi was inducted into the Collegium of Interfaith Scholars at Martin Luther King Chapel at Morehouse College, Atlanta, Georgia. He lives with his wife and two Children in the greater Chicago area.

Zulqernain Haider Subhani hails from India and currently serves as an Assistant Professor in the Department of Fiqh and Usul al-Fiqh, AbdulHamid AbuSulayman Kulliyyah of Islamic Revealed Knowledge and Human Sciences, International Islamic University Malaysia (IIUM). He specializes in Islamic Studies and Social

Sciences, with a strong academic focus on Islamic Fiqh and its engagement with the contemporary world. His scholarly interests extend across diverse areas such as *Fiqh* and *Usul al-Fiqh*, law, religion, civilization, politics, and contemporary social issues, reflecting an interdisciplinary approach that bridges classical Islamic thought with modern intellectual and societal challenges.

A distinctive feature of Dr. Zulqernain's research is his engagement with the intersection of women, Islam, and modernity, where he explores theoretical debates within Islamic thought and the social sciences.

Previously, he served as an Assistant Professor in Contemporary Islamic Fiqh at Al Jamia Al Islamiya, Santhapuram, India.

He has also edited a book on Professor Muhammad Nejatullah Siddiqi in Urdu with contributions from twenty scholars from India and abroad.

Imtiyaz Yusuf is Professor of Islam and Dialogical Studies at the International Institute of Islamic Thought and Civilization, International Islamic University Malaysia (ISTAC-IIUM), Malaysia and a non-Resident Research Fellow at the Center for Contemporary Islamic World (CICW), Shenandoah University, USA. He specializes in the study, teaching and research in the areas of Islam and Religion with a focus on Islam and Buddhism And also, Religion and Social Sciences.

Over last 30 years Dr. Yusuf has taught in multireligious settings at universities and research institutes in the United States, Thailand, Malaysia and Vietnam. Dr. Yusuf has published widely on Islamic Comparative theology, religion and practice in Southeast Asia, and is one of the rare scholars who specializes in Islam-Buddhism dialogue.

Muhammad Anas Zarqa holds a Bachelor's degree from Damascus University, and an MA and PhD (Economics) from the University of Pennsylvania, USA. Dr. Zarqa is also a Senior Advisor, Shura Sharia Consultancy, Kuwait. He also received extensive tutoring from his late father, Sheikh Mustafa Zarka, a renowned Sharia scholar & author.

He is one of the pioneers of contemporary Islamic Economics. He introduced the concept of the human being as being a *Homo-Islamicus* whose consumption behavior is deeply influenced by a consideration of the penalty or reward in the life after death and whose economic choices and behavior are regulated by Islamic ethics. He also distinguishes between lawful Shariah-based commercial loans and usurious loans.

Made in the USA
Monee, IL
04 November 2026

67385784R00246